Analysis and Critique:
How to Engage
and Write about Anything

Dorsey Armstrong, Ph.D.

D1469262

THE
GREAT
COURSES

PUBLISHED BY:

THE GREAT COURSES
Corporate Headquarters
4840 Westfields Boulevard, Suite 500
Chantilly, Virginia 20151-2299
Phone: 1-800-832-2412
Fax: 703-378-3819
www.thegreatcourses.com

Dorsey Armstrong, Ph.D.

Associate Professor of English
and Medieval Literature
Purdue University

Professor Dorsey Armstrong is Associate Professor of English and Medieval Literature at Purdue University. She received her A.B. in English and Creative Writing from Stanford University in 1993 and her Ph.D. in Medieval Literature from Duke University in 1999. She specializes in Middle English language and literature, Arthurian literature, Anglo-Saxon language and literature, and gender and feminist studies.

Professor Armstrong is the author of *Gender and the Chivalric Community in Malory's "Morte d'Arthur"* (University Press of Florida, 2003) and *Sir Thomas Malory's "Morte Darthur": A New Modern English Translation Based on the Winchester Manuscript* (Parlor Press, 2009). Professor Armstrong is currently editor in chief of the academic journal *Arthuriana* and is at work on a critical study of geography in the late medieval Arthurian legend. ■

Table of Contents

Table of Contents

Table of Contents

Analysis and Critique:
How to Engage and Write about Anything

Scope:

For thousands of years, writing has been a powerful way for us to share our thoughts and ideas. Even in the technologically saturated 21st century, we still express ourselves in writing almost every day. But all writing—whether it's an essay, a personal letter, or a detailed business report—is at its most effective and memorable when it's built on the fundamental critical and analytical skills that transform your words from good to great.

Regardless of your subject, your goal, or your occasion, this course will lead you on a path to more engaging and effective writing. One of the keys to effective writing is understanding literary genres and the ways their unique styles and characteristics can shape and inform your own voice. The first lectures of the course guide you through the five major literary genres: fiction, essay, poetry, drama, and autobiography.

From there, the focus shifts to the art of rhetoric and the ways it can help you adapt your writing to a variety of different situations. Some of the most applicable rhetorical concepts explored in this part of the course include deductive reasoning, commonplaces, and pathos. Your increased awareness of classical rhetoric will go a long way to helping you become a stronger writer by calling your attention to the basics of compelling analytical writing.

What about the act of writing itself, which can be daunting even to the most seasoned writer? The final section of the course is a step-by-step guide through the writing process that provides answers to frequently asked questions about each of writing's four major stages: researching, writing a first draft, editing, and rewriting. By the end of the course, you will know the feeling of having a masterful instructor standing right by your side as you learn to write about practically anything. ■

How to Write about Anything
Lecture 1

> Pretty soon, you'll begin to grasp that what makes it possible to really engage with a piece of writing, to really understand and get inside it, is not simply coming up with answers to questions about the piece, but it's actually understanding what kinds of questions need to be asked in the first place.

If you are taking this course, then you are someone who cares about good writing—both how to appreciate it and how to produce it. Over the next 24 lectures, we'll explore several different strategies that will help you learn to read and think critically by examining important works from several major genres of writing. You'll also learn to use the reading methods and critical-thinking skills developed through the study of these genres to write more effectively for any occasion, situation, or goal.

Great writers are always great readers, so in this course we're going to spend a lot of time learning how to be active, engaged readers. And you're going to find out that this will help you to become an effective and persuasive writer.

Let's jump right in and take an example of a piece of writing and consider how or why it doesn't really work:

> They had but one last remaining night together, so they embraced each other as tightly as that two-flavor entwined string cheese that is orange and yellowish-white, the orange probably being a bland Cheddar and the white ... Mozzarella, although it could possibly be Provolone or just plain American, as it really doesn't taste distinctly dissimilar from the orange, yet they would have you believe it does by coloring it differently.

On reading this, what are your first impressions? I hope that your first reaction is that it is terrible writing, even ridiculous. This is deliberately bad writing—the 2003 winning entry from the annual Bulwer-Lytton bad writing contest. Most of us can recognize bad writing, but apart from deliberately

Perfect, grammatically correct writing is not necessarily interesting or engaging.

bad pieces like the contest winner, we'd usually be slightly hard pressed to explain why the writing is bad, and what might be done to make it better. This course aims to help you both understand and recognize what makes writing good or bad, and then use that knowledge to produce strong and effective writing of your own.

The first unit of this course explores what the elements of successful writing are and how they depend on insightful reading, careful research, and rigorous analytical thinking. Successful writing requires us to develop active-analytical reading strategies (as opposed to passive-receptive reading habits). By examining excerpts from several novels and short stories, including the work of Jane Austen, Herman Melville, Edgar Allen Poe, and more contemporary writers, we'll learn how passive reading turns us into simple receivers of whatever a text has to offer (empirical information, emotional pleasure) while active, insightful reading empowers us to more effectively evaluate and interpret the meaning of what we read—making us better writers in the process.

Successful writing requires us to develop an effective and distinctive voice: a persona on paper that is both strong and flexible. We'll analyze the work of several well-known writers to learn how they create and develop their voices. We'll also study how these writers shift and modify their voices in response to changing circumstances or contexts, and how one writer often produces compelling writing in response to the work of another. We'll look at several examples of how authors anticipate, meet, and even shape readers' expectations.

Active, insightful reading empowers us to more effectively evaluate and interpret the meaning of what we read.

In addition, we'll examine the characteristics of powerful, persuasive prose to show you how to adapt and incorporate these strategies into your own writing. The essay is perhaps the richest and most varied genre for studying the characteristics of a good argument, and we'll study three classic essays from the English and American traditions to demonstrate effective strategies for starting, organizing, supporting, and concluding an argument. One of these essays is Jonathan Swift's "A Modest Proposal," which is subtitled: "For Preventing The Children of Poor People in Ireland From Being A Burden to Their Parents or Country, and For Making Them Beneficial to The Public," and which also includes the following lines:

> I have been assured by a very knowing American of my acquaintance in London, that a young healthy child well nursed is at a year old a most delicious, nourishing, and wholesome food, whether stewed, roasted, baked, or boiled; and I make no doubt that it will equally serve in a fricassee or a ragout.

What is the first thing that comes to mind, besides the horrific image of parents cannibalizing their children? Well, the sheer ludicrousness of the idea, presented in such a formal, rational tone, is meant to provoke an extreme reaction. Writing, when it's done well, is never just words on a page—good writing invites interaction. The reader engages with the words, interacts with the language and ideas of the author.

4

While the writing of autobiography requires only that one mine one's own past for information, very often persuasive writing will demand that you do a little outside research—and cite that research appropriately—in order to make your point more effectively and persuasively. We'll address research issues in two lectures later in the course. The lectures on research will include segments on the effective and ethical use of online research tools, and special attention will be devoted to the evaluation and application of material discovered through Internet-based searches.

The final portion of the course deals with the writing and revision process. By the time you finish this course, you'll possess a set of rewriting tools that will allow you to assess both minor and major editing comments and decide if and how you want to implement suggestions for revision. The course also includes a lecture that examines 10 common errors in grammar and usage. It explains the rationale for certain grammatical constructions and conventions so you'll know when something is incorrect, and why.

So even though this lecture is introductory in nature, you're already on your way to becoming a better reader and writer. As we continue on in this course, you will gain increased ability to recognize good writing and to produce powerful writing yourself. ∎

Suggested Reading

Barnet and Cain, *A Short Guide to Writing about Literature.*

Gardner, *Writing about Literature.*

Griffith, *Writing Essays about Literature.*

Guerin et al., *A Handbook of Critical Approaches to Literature.*

Harmon and Holman, *A Handbook to Literature.*

Kennedy and Gioia, *Literature.*

Lunsford and Ruszkiewicz, *Everything's an Argument.*

Roberts, *Writing about Literature.*

1. Consider the passages below, and try to determine what makes them good writing. Is it the style, a certain vocabulary, a particularly vivid image? Jot down a list of things that you find striking or engaging, and try to determine why.

The former tenant of our house, a priest, had died in the back drawing room. Air, musty from having been long enclosed, hung in all the rooms, and the waste room behind the kitchen was littered with old useless papers. Among these I found a few paper-covered books, the pages of which were curled and damp. ... The wild garden behind the house contained a central apple-tree and a few straggling bushes under one of which I found the late tenant's rusty bicycle-pump. He had been a very charitable priest; in his will he had left all his money to institutions and the furniture of his house to his sister. —James Joyce, *Araby*

The great pullman was whirling onward with such dignity of motion that a glance from the window seemed simply to prove that the plains of Texas were pouring eastward. Vast flats of green grass, dull-hued spaces of mesquit and cactus, little groups of frame houses, woods of light and tender trees, all were sweeping into the east, sweeping over the horizon, a precipice. —Stephen Crane, "The Bride Comes to Yellow Sky"

Although it was so brilliantly fine—the blue sky powdered with gold and great spots of light like white wine splashed over the Jardins Publiques—Miss Brill was glad that she had decided on her fur. The air was motionless, but when you opened your mouth there was a faint chill, like a chill from a glass of iced water before you sip, and now and again a leaf came drifting—from nowhere, from the sky. —Katherine Mansfield, "Miss Brill"

How to Write about Anything
Lecture 1—Transcript

Hello and welcome. I'm Dorsey Armstrong, and I teach English at Purdue University. I want to begin this course on how to become a better reader and writer with a story about my own experience with writing.

When I was applying to college—what seems like many, many years ago now—I was particularly worried about the essay part of the application. I slaved over this thing for weeks, and because this was before computers were really common, I had made several photocopies, believe it or not, of the page of the application that said "using the space below, write an essay on topic X."

I then wrote rough drafts, and I practiced trying to get them to "fit" in the space allotted for the essay. I checked spelling. I checked my paragraph structure. I made sure there was nothing offensive in my essay, and that it showed how great an asset I would be to my first-choice school.

Here's the thing—I did a ton of work on that essay, and today I cannot for the life of me tell you what it was about. In short, it was boring. It was perfect, but it was "safe," and I doubt that it would have made much of an impact on the admissions committee.

Two nights before I had to get the application in the mail, I realized that this was really bothering me. So, I sat down, and I wrote another essay, and this one I remember—it was about a life-changing experience I had as a junior in high school when I was selected to participate in this week-long creative writing program.

In that essay I wrote about how the week spent living in the barracks of a former military base on one of the San Juan Islands was the first time I really felt like a writer—and the first time I thought that this was something I could maybe do, maybe even for a career. I remember I talked about the other angst-ridden teenagers who were there with me—I think there were like 15 of us total—and I talked about how different we all were, and how much I really liked that because at the time I felt like everyone at my high school was so much the same.

So, I wrote a draft that night. I went to sleep, and the next day got up early, proofed it, and then I rolled one of the last copied sheets of that essay page into the typewriter—this tells you how old I am, typewriter not computer—and I typed it up. Then, very carefully, I taped it over the original essay, and I attached a note. In that note I explained what had happened—that I had had my essay done for a long time, but I just didn't really think it was me—so I had written another one that I liked better, and I hoped that it was okay that I was taping this sheet over the one below it—and, of course, I was really careful to tape all around the edges because I didn't want them to think that I was trying to sneak two essays in for the price of one.

I wouldn't be telling this story, of course, if it wasn't true that I got in. I don't know how much the essay mattered—and I don't know if the admissions officer thought I was trying to pull a fast one, or if he or she read both essays, but I am sure of one thing, and that is that the second essay I wrote and the one I wanted them to see was more engaging and more interesting than my first boringly perfect and perfectly boring attempt.

If you are taking this course, then you are someone who cares about good writing—both how to appreciate it and how to produce it.

Over the next 24 lectures, we'll explore several different strategies that will help you learn to read and think critically by examining important works from several major genres of writing, and we'll also give you the tools to learn to use the reading methods and critical thinking skills developed by studying these genres in order to be able to write more effectively for any occasion, any situation, any goal that you might have.

I say this a lot to my students: Great writers are always great readers, so in this course we're going to spend a lot of time learning how to be active, engaged readers—and you're going to find out that this will help you to become an effective and persuasive writer.

In this first lecture, we'll examine the layout and basic premises of the course, but let's jump right in and take an example of a piece of writing and consider how or why it doesn't really work.

This is something that's going to happen a lot during this course—my reading a quote and asking you to think about it—so I want you to start practicing what I call "active listening skills" right away. Really pay close attention to language, to the word choice, the tone of the piece, and try to determine what you find interesting or awkward from the very first words I read. So here's the first passage of writing I want you to consider:

> They had but one last remaining night together, so they embraced each other as tightly as that two-flavor entwined string cheese that is orange and yellowish-white, the orange probably being a bland Cheddar and the white … Mozzarella, although it could possibly be Provolone or just plain American, as it really doesn't taste distinctly dissimilar from the orange, yet they would have you believe it does by coloring it differently.

So on hearing this, what are your first impressions? I hope that your first reaction is something like "That is terrible writing!" or "That's ridiculous," or even "That is really funny!" because this is deliberately bad writing; it's the 2003 winning entry from the annual Bulwer-Lytton bad writing contest.

This is a contest—it's one that I particularly love—that draws thousands of entries every year from people who are trying to write the worst imaginary opening of a novel ever. The idea for the contest springs from the writings of Edward Bulwer-Lytton, who was this 19th-century British writer who was really popular in his day, but today most critics think his work is really overly dramatic and sensationalist. He is the writer who penned the clichéd lines you probably have heard even if you didn't know Bulwer-Lytton had written them. These are the lines:

> It was a dark and stormy night; the rain fell in torrents—except at occasional intervals, when it was checked by a violent gust of wind which swept up the streets (for it is in London that our scene lies), rattling along the housetops, and fiercely agitating the scanty flame of the lamps that struggled against the darkness.

You might be asking, what is wrong with this piece of writing? What indeed? Probably many of you had an instinctively negative reaction to both Bulwer-

Lytton's "dark and stormy night" opening and the winning entry in the Bulwer-Lytton contest, but you couldn't necessarily put your finger on why that was, besides perhaps thinking that a sentence that begins in describing a final embrace should not then move to a detailed discussion of different types of string cheese.

In other words, most of us could recognize bad writing, but apart from deliberately bad pieces like the contest winner, we'd usually be kind of hard pressed to always explain why the writing is bad—and what could be done to make it better. This course aims to help you both understand and recognize what makes writing good or bad, and then to use that knowledge to produce strong and effective writing of your own.

Let's consider a very different piece of writing—and this is a piece that is meant to persuade someone of something. So, consider this following piece, which is a short note written from a teenage girl to her mother.

> Mom—I need a raise in my allowance. I only get $10 a week, and everyone else in my class gets at least $12 a week; some get $15. I know we don't have a lot of money, but I am tired of being the only girl in my class with last year's jeans; it makes the whole family look bad. If you give me a higher allowance, I promise I'll never miss my curfew again. Jane.

So what's wrong with this example? I'm guessing that probably a lot of you are thinking: "Well, there's quite a lot wrong with it." First of all, there's the tone—the letter writer is asking for something, but her tone is really demanding. From the start, this obviously is going to make her chances of getting what she wants slim. She has already put her audience on the defensive and in a position that's going to be hostile to any request that she might be making. Second, there's her argument—she claims she needs more money so she can keep up with the style and economic status of her peers at school.

Her argument that "everyone" gets more for an allowance is weak because she doesn't support this statement with any evidence, and these statements also seem to suggest really a fundamental lack of understanding of her audience, who is unlikely to be swayed by the "but everyone else is doing it" approach.

Her statement at the end, that she'll never be late for her curfew again, is equally offensive to her intended audience in that it suggests that should she not get the allowance raise she's asking for, she's going to deliberately ignore or break the rules of the household.

Finally, although you can't necessarily tell just from hearing the note read aloud, her writing style is full of grammatical and mechanical errors, and this suggests sloppiness on her part—and thereby a lack of respect for her audience. If she doesn't even care enough to try to avoid a run-on sentence, why should her mother, who is her audience, believe that she'll behave with anything resembling responsibility or respect?

Now consider this revised version of the letter, which makes the same plea and uses the same pieces of evidence, but it does it a whole lot better:

> Dear Mom, I'm writing to ask if you would please consider raising my allowance from $10 to $12 a week. Although I recognize that finances are tight, I believe that the extra $2 a week is a manageable amount, and I believe I have proved over the last 6 months that I am a responsible saver and spender.
>
> I have asked Kayla, Emma, and Mary what they get for allowance: Kayla and Emma get $12 a week, and Mary gets $15. Thus, I feel that $12 is a reasonable request. As you know, I very often use my own money to pay for lunch at school, and I have proved myself to be very responsible, not having been late for curfew even one time in the last 6 months. Thus, I feel that I deserve the $2 per week increase. Thank you for considering my request.

What's different this time? First of all, the requester knows that this is exactly what she's doing—she's making a request of someone who can deny it or agree to it. The writer in the second example also has gathered together some compelling evidence that supports her position.

She offers evidence of her good behavior, her plan for the extra money (what she's going to do with it), and then she gives specific examples of people who receive the same or more for allowance. She acknowledges that funds are tight, but she gives an example of how she is responsible with money—and how she uses her allowance for more than what we might think of as mere frivolities. So, her letter is well-written with a humble and respectful tone. Her mother may still say no, and chances are this is what's going to happen, but she is much more likely to consider the request seriously than she would otherwise, or in the case of the first letter I read to you.

The first unit of this course explains, in greater depth, some of what we just did in comparing these two examples. We'll explore what the elements of successful writing are and how they depend on insightful reading or careful research and rigorous analytical thinking. Successful writing requires us to develop active analytical reading strategies (as opposed to passive-receptive reading habits). So, just think about those two terms side by side: active reading and passive reception; you're going to want to sort of file those terms away over the course of the rest of this lecture series.

By examining excerpts from several novels and short stories—including the work of Jane Austen (one of my personal favorites), Herman Melville, Edgar Allen Poe, and some other more contemporary writers—we'll learn how passive reading turns us into simple receivers of whatever a text has to offer (and that can be just raw data, empirical information, maybe emotional pleasure), but by contrast—active, insightful reading empowers us to more effectively evaluate and interpret the meaning of what we read, and I strongly believe this makes us better writers in the process.

For example, consider this passage from near the beginning of Geraldine Brooks's marvelous book *People of the Book*:

> When I put my hand on the glass, the cold seeped through. It was supposed to be spring; down in the small garden by the bank's entrance, crocuses were blooming. But it had snowed earlier that morning, and the bowl of each small flower brimmed with a foam of snowflakes, like tiny cups of cappuccino. At least the snow made

the light in the room even and bright. Perfect working light, if only I could get to work.

So, the image of flowers in the snow looking like tiny cups of cappuccino is what grabs our attention here—it's an image that's all the more powerful because obviously cappuccino has associations with warmth and heat, but the image is conveyed through the most unlikely—and if I can make a little joke here—literally polar opposite means, and this would be snow. Cappucino is hot. Snow is cold. It's the contrast that grabs our attention.

We'll examine several other examples of arresting images, word choices, etc., in the lectures to come, and we'll explore also how our recognition and understanding of their power can translate positively into our own writing.

Successful writing requires us to develop an effective and, I think most importantly, distinctive voice: You have to sound like yourself. A persona on paper that is both strong and flexible is really what you need to try and create. We'll analyze the work of several well-known writers such as Ernest Hemingway, Ralph Waldo Emerson, Henry David Thoreau, Nathaniel Hawthorne, Henry James—the list goes on and on; plus we'll also talk about some more recent essayists to learn how they create and develop their voices. We're also going to study how these writers shift and modify their voices in response to changing circumstances or contexts, and how one writer often produces compelling writing in response to the work of another.

So let's examine how one writer makes use of the words of another writer. Here's a passage from Virginia Woolf's *A Room of One's Own*, which many of you may already be familiar with, and the passage begins:

> Any woman born with a great gift in the sixteenth century would certainly have gone crazed, shot herself, or ended her days in some lonely cottage outside the village, half witch, half wizard, feared and mocked at. For it needs little skill and psychology to be sure that a highly gifted girl who had tried to use her gift for poetry would have been so thwarted and hindered by contrary instincts, that she must have lost her health and sanity to a certainty.

That is the quote from Woolf, and in this important work, Woolf makes the claim that there are so few great women writers because they have historically lacked the means and the time to produce great works of literature. Modern essayist and critic Alice Walker famously appropriated the words of Woolf to make a further point in her groundbreaking essay "In Search of Our Mothers' Gardens." In her piece, Walker expands on Woolf's argument to suggest that it's not just women who have lacked these resources, but women of color in particular. Here she takes Woolf's own words, and then she inserts her own as a kind of comment—so she's really cleverly using the power of Woolf's rhetoric both to make her own point as well as simultaneously criticizing Woolf's view to make a further point, which is that she believes Woolf omitted or ignored women of color in her really important seminal work. So, where Woolf describes a "woman born with a great gift in the sixteenth century"—Walker writes "insert 'eighteenth century,' insert 'black woman,' insert 'born or made a slave.' " Where Woolf argues that such a gifted woman surely would have been "thwarted and hindered by contrary instincts," Walker tells us to add the words: "chains, guns, the lash, the ownership of one's body by someone else, submission to an alien religion."

Here, Walker deliberately and explicitly takes Woolf's words, her voice, and transforms it to make a point of her own, to fill in a gap that she felt that Woolf had neglected in her work. So how do the words of a late 19th-/early 20th-century British woman change when they are appropriated and transformed by a 20th-century African American woman?

What does Walker's response reveal about the assumptions made by Woolf as well as the thinking of her intended audience given the context of the day? What does it mean for Walker to even engage in such an exercise in the first place?

Asking questions like these will be something we do throughout this course. Pretty soon you'll begin to grasp that what makes it possible to really engage with a piece of writing, to really understand and get inside it, is not simply coming up with answers to questions about the piece, but it's actually understanding what kinds of questions need to be asked in the first place.

Successful writing requires us to know our readers, and as the examples I just mentioned suggest, Walker felt that she needed to address a neglected potential element of Woolf's audience. Failing to accurately gauge the demands of an audience is one of the gravest mistakes a writer can make.

We'll look at several examples of how authors anticipate, meet, or even shape their readers' expectations—and in this instance, mysteries and detective stories are especially useful in figuring out this author-reader dynamic and how it does or doesn't work, so we'll spend some time studying classic examples of mystery and detective fiction. How many of us have reached the end of a mystery novel and been irritated because the solution seemed to come out of left field, or was too obvious from the beginning, or just didn't make any sense?

If you've ever felt disappointed at the end of a mystery novel—first of all, you're not alone; I'm right there with you—but second of all, you can learn a powerful lesson about not underestimating your audience and respecting their intelligence and their willingness to suspend their disbelief.

In addition to working on identifying the important aspects that we need to consider for thinking about our audience, we'll examine the characteristics of powerful, persuasive prose to show you how to adapt and incorporate these strategies into your own writing and make your arguments stronger.

Among the major literary genres, the essay is perhaps the richest and most varied resource for studying how you can go about making a good argument, and we're going to study three classic essays from the English and American traditions that demonstrate effective strategies for starting, organizing, supporting, and—finally—concluding an argument. One of these essays is Jonathan Swift's "A Modest Proposal," which is subtitled: "For Preventing The Children of Poor People in Ireland From Being A Burden to Their Parents or Country, and For Making Them Beneficial to The Public," and this essay also includes the following lines:

> I have been assured by a very knowing American of my acquaintance in London, that a young healthy child well nursed is at a year old a most delicious, nourishing, and wholesome food,

whether stewed, roasted, baked, or boiled; and I make no doubt that it will equally serve in a fricassee or a ragout.

What is the first thing that comes to mind besides the horrific image of parents cannibalizing their children? Certainly, it's the sheer ludicrousness of this idea, and it's the ludicrousness of the idea presented in such a formal, rationale tone—and this combination is meant to provoke an extreme reaction.

This is a kind of satirical writing that, by its exaggeration and the use of provocative statements and ideas, is really meant to provoke the reader into a state of outrage. In this case, Swift's essay is writing against many very offensive and elitist suggestions that circulated in his day for how to deal with the poor people in Ireland.

He's saying, essentially, if you're going to suggest ideas as offensive as X, or Y, or Z, well, let's just go all the way and cook the children up and serve them for dinner. In part, the argument is so persuasive because it carefully adheres to accepted standards of essay writing as it makes this totally ridiculous argument. In addition to strong arguments, successful writing may require the use of what we call "figurative language," and these could be metaphors, analogies, symbols, and also the skillful management of diction and syntax—and these are all key features of poetry.

So, what we're going to do to try and understand these terms and ideas is study the diverse examples that poetry can provide for making use of figurative language as well as multiple examples it offers of how attention to word choice and word order can dramatically increase the power and flexibility of your writing. Consider the contrast, for example, between the Greek poet Homer, who described the ocean as "the wine-dark sea"—and then several centuries later, the Irish poet James Joyce describes a large body of salt-water as the "snot-green sea."

So, obviously the two phrases have wildly different associations—a "wine-dark sea" might suggest civilization, calm, warmth, festivity, and a whole range of other positive associations. Joyce's word choice deliberately borrows from Homer only to then transform that phrase into something radically different and with radically different associations—"snot-green sea" gives us the associations of illness, cold, discomfort, bleakness—it's not happy, or positive, or festive. His image is all the stronger in that he conjures up the classic allusion and then replaces it with one that contrasts so strongly and so negatively.

Writing intended for oral presentation (like a speech, or a conference paper, or a wedding toast) provides a unique set of challenges—in particular these involve issues of tone and timing. Successful playwrights have a lot to teach us about these issues, and in this unit of the course we'll study several examples that can help us strengthen and sharpen writing that's meant to be read aloud to an audience.

One of the most famous lines ever spoken aloud: "To be or not to be; that is the question," the opening line from Hamlet's famous soliloquy in the Shakespeare play of the same name, derives much of its power from the fact that it is spoken—it's not written on the page to be read silently. Generations of Shakespearean actors have managed to convey to an audience their particular interpretation of the Prince of Denmark and many aspects of his personality simply in the way in which that line—and those that follow right after that line—are delivered. So, is he angry? Frustrated? Melancholy? It depends on how the actor delivers the line—and how we interpret it.

Writing, when it's done well, is never just words on a page—good writing invites interaction. The reader engages with the words—interacts with the language and the ideas of the author. Maybe it's a relationship that's not the kind we're used to when we think of the word "relationship," but it's no less personal or powerful simply because one of the parties is no longer there—or maybe even is long dead.

This is important to keep in mind whether you're crafting an online personal profile, writing a professional bio blurb or a job application letter—the challenges of creating a written self-portrait that will help you achieve your goals can be really daunting. You might be asking: "What details of my life should be included? What experiences and qualities should I highlight? What approaches would be most effective? What should I leave out?"

For example, which opening of an autobiographical account do you find more engaging?

Here's the first one: "I was born in mid-December in Long Beach, California, the eldest child of my parents." That opening is fine—it sets the stage; it gives basic information, but it's not particularly engaging. How about instead:

> On the night I was born, the hospital lost power in the middle of my mother's delivery. I came into the world by the glow of emergency backup generator lights while my father sat in the near-dark waiting room, without even a war movie to watch on TV.

The second (although autobiography) reads more like a story. It supplies details and even a little drama to get the reader interested.

While the writing of autobiography requires only that you mine your own past for information, very often persuasive writing will demand that you do a little outside research—and that you cite that research appropriately. I'm going to devote considerable time to how to conduct research and how to edit and revise your writing. The most important thing here is that practice is really the key—but not just practicing writing first drafts, but learning how to edit, and revise, and rewrite—in other words, using your first draft to help you get to a polished and engaging final draft.

To help you with this, I've crafted special writing exercises for each lecture, and you'll find these in your guidebook. I'll refer to these from time to time in the lectures themselves. If you don't have a chance to do the exercises, that's okay—you'll still be able to pick up the main points from listening to our discussion of them, but I encourage you to at least read them over and think about them if you can. In the exercises for this first lecture I'm going to give you three passages of writing, and I'm going to ask you to try and figure out what makes them "good writing." It can be as simple as identifying a word or image that's particularly interesting to you or something that just sounds really nice. As we continue on in this course, you will gain increased ability to recognize what makes good writing and how to produce powerful writing yourself. In our next lecture, we'll explore in greater depth what it means to be an insightful reader.

How to Be an Effective Reader
Lecture 2

Almost anything can be read or interpreted insightfully—from long-acclaimed works of literature to the most mundane set of directions from one place to another.

In analyzing a piece of writing, you may start with reactions such as "I like it" or "I don't like it," but you don't want to stop there. These initial reactions are what I call precritical responses. The difference between a reader who is simply interested and one who is deeply engaged can be found in if and how those readers move beyond those precritical responses to think about how and why a particular piece of writing affects them in certain ways. Moving beyond the precritical can allow you to appreciate even writing that you might not really like. It can help you recognize the writer's skill, appreciate the effort the writer made, and admire the emotions he or she is able to make you feel.

Let's talk about a precritical response and how you can move beyond it so that you can become a more engaged reader. Remember, the key to becoming a competent writer lies first in being an attentive reader. So, let's take a famous passage and see what we can make out of it. Here are the opening lines of Herman Melville's classic *Moby Dick*:

Call me Ishmael. Some years ago—never mind how long precisely—having little or no money in my purse, and nothing particular to interest me on shore, I thought I would sail about a little and see the watery part of the world. It is a way I have of driving off the spleen, and regulating the circulation.

Whenever I find myself growing grim about the mouth; whenever it is a damp, drizzly November in my soul; whenever I find myself involuntarily pausing before coffin warehouses, and bringing up the rear of every funeral I meet; and especially whenever my hypos get such an upper hand of me, that it requires a strong moral principle to prevent me from deliberately stepping into the street, and methodically knocking people's hats off—then, I account it high time to get to sea as soon as I can.

When I teach *Moby Dick*, I always ask students to give me an initial, precritical response to this passage. I want them to think about what feelings it gave them. Some students tell me, "I liked it" or "I didn't get what he was saying half the time." I'm always happy to get a student who says, "I'm excited to read the rest." Those are all precritical responses, so let's move past them and find out, using critical skills of engagement, why you might have any one of those reactions and how we can use those reactions as a starting point to achieve a deeper understanding of the text.

Let's start with those of you who responded with some version of "I liked it." Why did you like it? Well, for one thing, there's something powerful about the use of the first person and direct address, and the first three words of this text convey that this will be a work that does both. "Call me Ishmael"—the writer, or speaker, however we might imagine him, is talking directly to you, his audience, and telling you what to do. He goes on from there to tell you something about himself in the first person. This can be one of the easiest and most effective ways to grab your reader's attention—we all like to hear stories, and generally speaking, a first-person narrative gives us a deeply personal account that can be especially enthralling in that it allows us to see into the mind of another person.

> **A useful thing to remember when you're composing your own writing is that ... your audience can't immediately interact with you in the present moment, so above all you should strive for clarity.**

But what about a more negative precritical response, such as "I didn't get what he was saying half the time"? Those of us living in 21st-century America probably don't have any idea what hypos are—nor do we commonly come across coffin warehouses, or funeral processions into which you could easily join. And very few people wear hats these days, so the idea of expressing your discontent by stepping into the street and knocking them off of people's heads just seems bizarre.

But we can learn something important from this seeming disorientation. It tells us that we are in a world that is not 21st-century America, and the very strangeness of the narrator's attitude and behavior in relation to our modern sensibilities helps contribute to a sense of having escaped to a different time and place. Finally, the tone, style, and this wry comment on hypos (which likely refers to melancholy) and knocking people's hats off their heads also has a little bit of humor about it—at the very least, we know we're in for a story that's not going to be totally devoid of light moments. Through careful reading, what at first seems like a rather impenetrable passage can, in fact, allow us to get into the work and understand something about the setting of the story and the characters who inhabit it.

You've already learned a little something about insightful reading and how it can enhance our understanding and our enjoyment of the written word. If you recognize powerful, clever, nuanced moments in a variety of written texts as a reader, you'll soon start to be able to work these into your own writing. A useful thing to remember when you're composing your own writing is that

The Benefits of Rereading

A piece of writing has several lives—at least two and potentially many more—and this is something you should be thinking of as you are working on your own writing.

The first life of a piece of writing is when you read it the first time, when you experience it as a brand-new text that you've never encountered before. The second life of a piece of writing occurs when you consider and then reflect on what it is you've just read—you may think of words that struck you in particular; certain details; and whether the piece is written in the first or the third person, set in the past or the present, or any one of several other aspects.

The third—and to my mind, arguably the most interesting—life of the text is the last one. After you've read it once, reflected on the text, and then read it again, you read through it yet again, armed with your precritical response and perhaps a few insights that you've gleaned from your initial read-through. This third life of the text is when you can really start to apply the principles of insightful reading.

with the written word, your audience can't immediately interact with you in the present moment, so above all you should strive for clarity. You should anticipate questions or moments of confusion, and you should consider the self-image you're conveying to your audience. How are they going to interpret you and your personality based on what you've written? ■

Suggested Reading

Barnet and Cain, *A Short Guide to Writing about Literature*.

Carpenter, *Reading Lessons*.

Gardner, *Writing about Literature*.

Griffith, *Writing Essays about Literature*.

Guerin et al., *A Handbook of Critical Approaches to Literature*.

Harmon and Holman, *A Handbook to Literature*.

Kennedy and Gioia, *Literature*.

Lunsford and Ruszkiewicz, *Everything's an Argument*.

Lynn, *Literature*.

McLaughlin and Coleman, *Everyday Theory*.

Roberts, *Writing about Literature*.

Exercises

1. Consider the three excerpts below and practice some of the techniques of insightful reading we've explored in this lecture. For each, try to determine the setting (time and place) and mood of the story (is it humorous? gloomy?) and make a list of words and phrases that stand out and that careful attention to which can help you find a way of engaging with the text.

    With this excellent resolve for the future, Goodman Brown felt himself justified in making more haste on his present evil purpose. He had taken a dreary road, darkened by all the gloomiest trees of the forest, which barely stood aside to let the narrow path creep through, and closed immediately behind. It was all as lonely as could be; and there is this peculiarity in such a solitude, that the traveller knows not who may be concealed by the innumerable trunks and the thick boughs overhead; so that, with lonely footsteps he may yet be passing through an unseen multitude. —Nathaniel Hawthorne, "Young Goodman Brown"

Maman-Nainaine said that when the figs were ripe Babette might go to visit her cousins down on the Bayou-Lafourche where the sugar cane grows. Not that the ripening of figs had the least thing to do with it, but that is the way Maman-Nainaine was. It seemed to Babette a very long time to wait; for the leaves upon the trees were tender yet, and the figs were like little hard, green marbles. —Kate Chopin "Ripe Figs"

At the foot of these fairy mountains the voyager may have descried the light smoke curling up from a village whose shingle roofs gleam among the trees, just where the blue tints of the upland melt away into the fresh green of the nearer landscape. It is a little village of great antiquity, having been founded by some of the Dutch colonists, in the early times of the province, just about the beginning of the government of the good Peter Stuyvesant (may he rest in peace!), and there were some of the houses of the original settlers standing within a few years, with lattice windows, gable fronts surmounted with weathercocks, and built of small yellow bricks brought from Holland. —Washington Irving, "Rip Van Winkle"

2. Consider the list of words and phrases you made in exercise 1. Now, try your hand at rewriting each passage by substituting different words for those you've identified as key for engaging with the text. (What happens if you replace "Maman-Nainaine" with "Grandma" in the passage from "Ripe Figs"? How about if "fairy mountains" in "Rip Van Winkle" is replaced with "solid hills"?) What changes can be effected with just a few word substitutions?

How to Be an Effective Reader
Lecture 2—Transcripts

Welcome back. In our last lecture, we explored some powerful examples of persuasive or evocative writing—intriguing wordplay, the importance of tone and knowing your audience, and the strength that mastery of a particular form—such as the essay—can give your writing. In the exercises that I wrote to accompany Lecture 1, you were given three passages to try and analyze—not in any sort of in-depth way. What I was asking for there was a sort of first impression as to what makes the writing particularly good or engaging.

For example, in the first quote that I gave you in the exercises in the guide book—this was from James Joyce's "Araby"—you might have been struck by how the word choice and description gave an impression of gloominess or loneliness. There was the description of a room being full of "old useless papers," the garden was called "wild," a word in opposition to the careful order we usually associate with the idea of a garden. There was the "rusty bicycle pump" found underneath some "few straggling bushes"—all of this phrasing conveying a sense of neglect or abandonment. From Joyce's careful word choice and phrasing, the scene is set—his precision, which subtly conveys the tone of the scene, is what makes this, arguably, good writing.

Maybe you didn't even get as far as identifying key words and phrases. Maybe you only read each of the passages and jotted down or thought something like: "I like this because I get a strong sense of the place where it's happening" or "I don't like this passage—it makes me feel sad." If that's as far as you got, that is just fine—especially for your very first time attempting to analyze a piece of writing.

Reactions such as "I like it" or "I don't like it" are excellent places to start, but you don't want to stop there. These initial reactions are what I call "pre-critical responses." The difference between a reader who is simply interested and one who is deeply engaged can be found in if and how those readers move beyond those pre-critical responses to think about how and why a particular piece of writing affects you in certain ways.

Moving beyond the pre-critical can allow you to appreciate even writing that you might not really like; it can help you recognize the writer's skill; it can help you to appreciate the effort the writer made, and it can cause you to admire the emotions he or she is able to make you feel, even if you don't like the emotions—even if you find the process of reading that piece of text unpleasant.

For example, I greatly admire the writer Henry James, whose style is famously very dense; it's full of sub-clauses, and it requires deep concentration to fully understand the range of his artistic skill. But if you were to ask me if I like the writing of Henry James, the answer would be a resounding "no." At the other end of the spectrum, there are some modern writers of mysteries or thrillers whom I consider to be absolutely atrocious, clumsy writers, and they don't have really any sense of style, and they have what I think of as a tin ear when it comes to realistic dialogue—but at the same time, that might be exactly the kind of book I'd like to read if I'm lying on a beach somewhere.

Let's talk about a pre-critical response and then how you can move beyond it so that you can become a more engaged reader. Remember, as I've said before, the key to becoming a competent writer lies first in being an attentive reader. So, let's take a famous passage and see what we can make out of it. Here are the opening lines of Herman Melville's classic *Moby Dick*:

> Call me Ishmael. Some years ago—never mind how long precisely—having little or no money in my purse, and nothing particular to interest me on shore, I thought I would sail about a little and see the watery part of the world. It is a way I have of driving off the spleen, and regulating the circulation.
>
> Whenever I find myself growing grim about the mouth; whenever it is a damp, drizzly November in my soul; whenever I find myself involuntarily pausing before coffin warehouses, and bringing up the rear of every funeral I meet; and especially whenever my hypos get such an upper hand of me, that it requires a strong moral principle to prevent me from deliberately stepping into the street,

and methodically knocking people's hats off—then, I account it high time to get to sea as soon as I can.

Whenever I teach *Moby Dick*, I always ask students to give me an initial, pre-critical response to this passage. I want them to think about what feelings or emotions this passage gave them as I read it aloud. Some students tell me: "I liked it," or "I didn't get what he was saying half the time," or "I thought it was funny"—and sometimes I'm always happy to get a student who says: "I'm excited to read the rest." Those are all pre-critical responses—so let's move past them and find out, using critical skills of engagement, why you might have any one of those reactions and how we can use those reactions as a starting point to achieve a deeper understanding of the text.

Let's start with those of you who responded with some version of "I liked it." Why did you like it? Well, for one thing, if I was going to answer that question for you, I would say there's something powerful about the use of the first person and direct address, and the first three words of this text convey that this will be a work that does both. "Call me Ishmael"—the writer or speaker, however we might imagine him, is talking directly to you, his audience, and telling you what to do.

He goes on from there to tell you something about himself in the first person: When I do this, then I feel that. We're going to get up close and personal with the teller of this tale, and this writing in the first person can be one of the easiest and most effective ways to grab your reader's attention. We all like to hear stories—and generally speaking, a first-person narrative gives us a deeply personal account that can be especially enthralling in that it allows us to see into the mind of another person.

But what about a more negative pre-critical response—"I didn't get what he was saying half the time." Let's think about why that may be. Those of us living in 21st-century America probably don't have any idea what "hypos" are—nor do we commonly come across coffin warehouses or funeral processions into which you could easily join, and very few people wear hats these days—so the idea of expressing your unhappiness or discontent by stepping into the street and knocking them off of peoples' heads just seems bizarre.

26

But we can learn something important from this seeming disorientation. It tells us that we are in a world that is not 21st-century America, and the very strangeness of the narrator's attitude and behavior in relationship to our modern sensibilities helps contribute to a sense of having escaped to a different time and place. By the way, hypos is probably a contracted form of "hypochondria," and it means something like the narrator is in a bad mood— or he's depressed, or sad, or melancholy.

Finally, the tone, style, and this wry comment on hypos and knocking people's hats off their heads also has a little bit of something that is humorous about it—at the very least, we know we're in for a story that's not going to be totally devoid of a few light moments that might even provoke a laugh or two.

Let's take a different example, and this one from a time and place that's even further removed from our modern one. This passage is from Sir Thomas Malory's *Morte Darthur*—and it's one of the most important versions of the legend of King Arthur to be written before the modern period, and it also happens to be my particular scholarly area of specialty. This text comes from the end of the 15th century, and it's written in the Middle English of that period.

If I were to try and read it in the original Middle English, the spelling and syntax would look rather strange on the page, and the first lines would sound something like this:

> Than the kynge stablysshed all the knyghtes and gaff them rychesse and londys; and charged them never to do outerage nothir morthir, and allwayes to fle treson, and to gyff mercy unto hym that askith mercy, uppon payne of forfiture [of their] worship and lordship of kynge Arthure for evermore.

What's your first reaction upon hearing those lines? With the case of *Moby Dick*, likewise, you're at least certainly struck with a strong impression that we are in a time and place that's really different from the present. Even if you did not understand a word of what I said, you at least have been able to gather that one crucial piece of information—and from this one piece of information that we're far in the past, that we're not in the present—you can begin to build a deeper, more insightful understanding of the place, time, and values of the story.

These lines I just read to you begin what is known as the Pentecostal Oath—and it's called this because King Arthur's knights swear every year at the Feast of Pentecost to obey the rules of the Pentecostal Oath. The translation, which will be easier for you to understand, would sound something like this:

> Then the king established all his knights, and bestowed on them riches and lands. He charged them never to commit outrage or murder, always to flee treason, and to give mercy to those who asked for mercy, upon pain of the forfeiture of their honor and status as a knight of King Arthur's forever more. He charged them always to help ladies, damsels, gentlewomen, and widows, and never to commit rape, upon pain of death. Also, he commanded that no man should take up a battle in a wrongful quarrel—not for love, nor for any worldly goods.

As I noted a moment ago, this world may seem even more alien and strange to us than that described at the beginning of *Moby Dick*—and so it's even harder, maybe, to find a way past a pre-critical response. A lot of us might be inclined to say simply: "I am not really sure what is going on here, but I know this is not my world." But if we read carefully, we can learn something about the society depicted here.

First, money and land are important, and when a king wants to reward his loyal followers, this is what he gives them. If we read even more closely, we recognize that, in fact, he gives this as a reward in advance—so he gives these possessions to his followers as a sort of future promise of their loyalty. So already, even if we don't understand anything else, we can tell that this is a world where honoring those who have committed to follow you is a big deal.

Next, we can see that honor is an important element of this society—knights should not commit outrageous deeds or murder—and the suggestion here would be that there must be some kind of killing that's not murder, that's rightful killing—which is interesting. Also important, compassion and mercy—these are two more important character elements of a noble knight. The line about helping women suggests something similar; it's a very chivalric, noble attitude—one has to fight on behalf of women because presumably in this time and place, they cannot fight for themselves. On the other hand, this gallant sort of phrase or rule to always help ladies is kind of undone by the line about never committing rape.

Generally speaking, the only reason to instruct someone explicitly not to do something is because that very thing is, in fact, being done. In other words, you don't need to tell knights not to rape women unless some of them are, in fact, doing just that. In fact, the first printer of Malory's text, William Caxton, deleted that line from his 1485 edition. He wanted to sell copies of a book that people enjoyed because it told stories of noble knights doing fantastic deeds. A lot of people who bought his book were not nobles; they were members of classes below the nobility, like the merchants, who wanted to read books like Malory's in order to learn how to dress, how to talk, and how to act in a noble fashion. The line about never raping women would have totally marred the enjoyment of a lot of those people who had a particular idealized image of the court of King Arthur in their minds and who wanted to sort of be associated with, or like, the noble classes.

Finally, the last line of the Pentecostal Oath again emphasizes and clarifies the importance of wealth and property in this society, although obviously it's honorable to reward your followers with land and riches—and, of course, it's honorable to provide those things in advance. It's obviously dishonorable to engage in conflict solely for material gain, and it's also dishonorable to fight on behalf of one's lord or the woman you're in love with if the quarrel is not a just or a righteous quarrel—so, while personal loyalty is important, it's trumped by the nature of the dispute. In other words, while you certainly should protect your lady love and fight for her rights, you should not do this if she wants you to do something less than honorable.

Through careful reading, what at first seemed like a rather impenetrable passage can, in fact, provide us with several ways into the text—a kind of hook—so that we can get into the work and try and understand something about the setting of the story and the characters who inhabit it.

Let's try this exercise again, and this time let's try it with an excerpt from the beginning of James Joyce—as you can tell, he's one of my favorite writers you're probably starting to gather. We're going to talk about the opening of James Joyce's story, "The Boarding House." Here's how it begins:

> Breakfast was over in the boarding house and the table of the breakfast-room was covered with plates on which lay yellow streaks of eggs with morsels of bacon-fat and bacon-rind. Mrs. Mooney sat in the straw arm-chair and watched the servant Mary remove the breakfast things.
>
> She made Mary collect the crusts and pieces of broken bread to help make Tuesday's bread-pudding. When the table was cleared, the broken bread collected, the sugar and butter safe under lock and key, she began to reconstruct the interview which she had had the night before with Polly.

What immediately are the things that leap to mind when you consider this passage? Some of you probably right away noticed this huge emphasis on food and the way it's described. There are "streaks" of eggs ; there are "morsels" of bacon; there are crusts and leftover pieces of bread, and sugar, and butter. The mention of the food itself suggests plenty: Some people just ate a full breakfast with all the trimmings, but at the same time, you have these juicy nouns—morsels, streaks—and this reference also to the collecting crusts of bread instead of throwing them away and locking up the sugar and butter, and this indicates a really careful concern of resources.

So, is Mrs. Mooney, the question becomes, just a practical, efficient housekeeper—or is she in dire economic straits (and this necessitates that she's really careful with saving food and conserving as much as she can)? What clues help us answer this question? You probably noticed a few other details, and you're probably answering this question in your minds right now.

For one, she herself is not doing any of the actual work here—I'm sure you probably all picked up on the fact that she's sitting in an armchair while she watches her servant, Mary, performing these tasks. The fact that she

to the same location but given by a different person, you'll start to see a difference. Let's imagine if someone else were giving directions to the same place, they might say: "Turn left out the driveway, and then go right at the big, yellow house. After crossing over the train tracks, turn left at the street corner with the firestation on the corner."

What's the difference here? When we compare these two, we can immediately recognize a difference in the way each of the writers or speakers understands the world around him or her; one of them is thinking in terms of signs or distances: Go left at this street. Go this far—while the second writer has a different kind of mind; maybe he or she doesn't even know the names of the streets on which you're supposed to turn. The second writer or speaker looks not at road signs or the speedometer but at landmarks, recognizable buildings, train tracks, etc. If you really stop to think about it—in a way, each of these sets of directions tells a little story about the person who is giving them.

In fact, all writing can be a kind of storytelling, and it would be helpful for us to consider here the difference between the written and the spoken word. Because if you ask someone to tell you how to get someplace as opposed to writing it down, the response is really going to be different. For example, if you asked someone to tell you how to get to the post office, that response might be: "So, come out of the driveway and hang a left"—and here, as I'm doing right now, the speaker might make a hand gesture—"Go to the left. Then, you make a right"—another hand gesture—"You'll go for awhile, and you'll cross some train tracks"—then here, you might get a speaker doing a little overhand motion—"over the train tracks." You get the point.

Which set of directions would you rather get? If we try to think about the differences between these, many of us might say they'd prefer the spoken directions. Why is this? For one thing, the gestures I've just been making and describing can be helpful in figuring out exactly where it is you need to go. Also, some details are easier to convey when they're spoken rather than when they're written. In the spoken set of directions you are there to ask questions. You can get some clarification. You can request additional details—you, if you're confused, can ask someone to give you more information.

This is always a useful thing to remember when you're composing your own writing. With the written word, your audience can't immediately interact with you in the present moment—and so, you have to be very careful and clear—above all, you should always strive for clarity. You should anticipate questions or moments of confusion, and you should also always consider the self-image you're conveying to your audience. How are they going to interpret you and your personality based on what you've written? Because even in something as mundane as a set of directions from one place to another, you are creating a writerly or authorial persona.

Obviously, there are also elements that make the written directions more desirable than the spoken ones. For one, you can refer to the written directions repeatedly as you make your way from the house to the post office—so keeping all the details in your memory isn't essential. As you are driving, you can check the written directions in your hand: Look up; check the street signs; look down again. You have something to refer to, to help you along. I often think of the writer Lee Smith, who in an interview once described what it was like growing up in a town full of natural storytellers.

In her town, she said, if you asked someone how to get to the post office you might get a set of spoken instructions like: "Go down here; take a left, and you'll see it on your right"—or you could get something like: "I had a cousin who went to the post office once. Got bit by a mad dog." So, the second set of directions might be interesting if you have all the time in the world and would like to hear about the cousin who got bitten by the mad dog before you get your directions, but probably most of us would prefer something a little clearer, a little more succinct, a little more to the point.

But once again, just those two sentences—"I had a cousin who went to the post office once. Got bit by a mad dog"—whether they're spoken or written, they function as a kind of text, and if we read or interpret it insightfully, we can actually learn quite a bit that can deepen and enhance our understanding of this particular text or this particular statement and its speaker/writer.

If we stop and consider the work we've done in this lecture, whether it's in our discussion of literary texts or a set of directions, you may realize that a piece of writing has several lives—at least two and potentially many more, and this is something that people aren't always aware of, and it's really something you should be thinking of as you are working on your own writing.

The first life of a piece of writing is when you read it the first time, when you experience it as a brand new text that you've never encountered before. The second life of a piece of writing occurs when you consider and then reflect on what it is you've just read—you may think of words that struck you in particular, or certain details and whether the piece is written in the first or the third person, set in the past or the present, or any one of several other aspects. So, that would be the second life of a text.

The third—and to my mind, arguably the most interesting—life of the text is this last one. After you have read it once, reflected on the text, and then you read it again, when you read through it again you come to the text armed with your pre-critical response and perhaps a few insights that you have gleaned from your initial read-through. This third life of the text is when you can really start to apply what we've discussed today in terms of insightful reading.

What else can we take away from today's lecture? One thing that probably all of us have recognized or known instinctively but haven't quite consciously been aware of until today is that anything can be a text, and almost anything can be read or interpreted insightfully—from long-acclaimed works of literature to the most mundane set of directions from one place to another.

Spoken words also constitute a kind of text, and another thing that we've focused on consciously again today is the difference between the spoken and the written word. Certainly any number of societies had lively, complex, and fascinating traditions of historical memory and storytelling before they had writing, but the written word is in so many ways so very different from the spoken one—not least of all because the written word goes on to have a life of its own, and this life can be so many different things than would be the case with words that are spoken in the moment.

The major point that we explored over and over again today is how to find a way into a text that might seem initially impossible to find your way into.

How do you move beyond your pre-critical response and read insightfully so that you can deepen both your understanding and your enjoyment of the text? In turn, the practice of insightful reading can help make you a better writer—exploring the writer's craft from one perspective ultimately can help make you a better practitioner of that craft.

So in our next lecture, we're going to continue our exploration of what it means to be an engaged reader by deepening our understanding of literary forms and genres. One of the basics of engaging with writing is to understand the genre or type of writing it is. An awareness of how expectations of style and subject matter fit with a piece's perceived genre can help you become much more keenly attuned to your own writing—and help you to pay attention to considerations like the expectations of your audience.

In the next lecture, we'll learn to recognize different genres—focusing on five major types of writing that are common today: prose, poetry, drama, essay, and autobiography. We'll explore the dominant features of each and then learn how understanding, and recognizing, and using that knowledge can make us better readers—and thus, better writers.

How Literature Can Help
Lecture 3

It's always possible that your audience has only the time or inclination to read your piece of writing once, so you have to make that one time really count.

One of the basics of engaging with writing—as either an author or a reader—is to understand the genre, or type, of writing it is. An awareness of conventions of style, subject matter, and how other elements fit with a piece's perceived genre can help you become more keenly attuned to your own writing and help you to pay attention to considerations like the expectations of your audience. In this lecture, we focus on five major types of writing: poetry, drama, prose, essay, and autobiography. We'll explore the dominant features of each and then learn how understanding these features and their differences can make us better readers and thus better writers.

So if we have to briefly define each of these genres, what would we say? We might say that poetry is a form of writing that uses language in unexpected ways—by rhyming, by use of rhythm, or simply by patterning the language in unconventional forms.

The simplest way to define drama is to call it something that is performed in front of an audience. In a drama, we have to rely wholly on what we see and hear as an audience to make sense of the story: What the characters say and how they say it are what we use to determine state of mind, the relationships between them, and the plot of the drama that's unfolding. We have to also suspend our disbelief and imagine that somehow we are looking through what's often called the fourth wall—that which divides the audience from the actors on stage.

Prose fiction is perhaps the genre of writing most familiar to us. Types of writing that tell some kind of story—novels, short stories—are found everywhere. Within the genre of fiction we have all sorts of subgenres:

mystery, thriller, romance, historical fiction, science fiction, fantasy—the list goes on and on.

The essay is also quite easy to define in its broadest strokes—it is a piece of writing that seeks to persuade and inform, to support a particular position. Autobiography is quite simply the story of a life, told by the person who has lived it. As we've already seen, all of these genres might overlap with one another in interesting and provocative ways.

As a writer, you needn't limit yourself to the conventions of a single genre. You can use various conventions of writing in conjunction with one another to try and make a more powerful argument, or simply craft a more engaging piece of writing.

By reading from various genres, you can learn conventions that can help you produce more engaging writing.

As a writer, you needn't limit yourself to the conventions of a single genre.

But at the same time, just because you know how to employ the conventions of all of these genres doesn't mean that you should do that all at once.

Sometimes restraint can be the most effective strategy of all. You want to engage your audience, not completely overwhelm them, and while it may be impressive that you can work in a variety of genres, a display of this ability might not get you to your ultimate goal. The more you write, the more you will learn to walk this fine line between effective display and use of your writerly knowledge and simply showing off—something that is likely to turn off your audience and not help you in achieving your ultimate goal. ■

An Exercise in Using Multiple Genres

L et's consider how knowledge of the conventions of these various genres might be used to enhance something as mundane as a protest letter written to the local city council about something as commonplace as a leash law for dogs. Consider the following letter:

Dear City Council:

I am writing to ask that you consider establishing an off-leash area of the park for local dogs. Many other communities have designated off-leash areas for the pets of citizens, and these are usually carefully monitored and have strict rules about interaction between animals and cleaning up after them. This would be a positive thing for both the dogs and their owners. Thank you for considering this request.

Let's consider how we might punch this up a bit to make it more persuasive. First, let's think about how we might use conventions of poetry to grab the reader's attention. Perhaps we could find a more interesting choice of words to refer to the dogs, since they are the main focus of the letter. We could begin the letter with something like, "It is not for nothing that dogs are often referred to as 'man's best friend.' These furry, four-legged friends provide companionship and love to their owners." Here we have another poetic flourish in our use of alliteration in the second sentence.

From what other genres might we borrow? Autobiography seems to be obvious, as the writer of this letter would most likely not be in favor of doing something nice for dogs if she did not have some positive experience with dogs herself. Perhaps a line like, "As a dog owner for many years, and having lived in many different communities, I have seen first-hand how off-leash areas in parks are beneficial to dogs and provide members of the community—even those who are not dog owners themselves—a chance to enjoy watching these friendliest of animals romp, play, and interact with one another."

What about drama and fiction; could we bring those in? Well, we certainly could, but one thing we always need to consider as we work toward becoming engaging and effective writers is that you *can* have too much of a good thing. For example, you could add an imagined dialogue between the owner and his dog:

> Dog: "Oh please please please please could I run and play in this beautiful park?"

> Owner: "I would love to let you, but the law says I have to keep you on the leash."

> Dog: "But it makes me so happy to run free. And you have trained me not to jump on other people or dogs, and I know that you always pick up after me."

> Owner: "I know, buddy. I'm sorry that the city council members are such jerks."

This dramatic exchange is definitely attention grabbing. The argument is clear, succinct, and meant to play on our emotions. The emotional appeal can be a powerful one, but what's the drawback here? Some of the audience might find this approach a little odd and off-putting, and certainly no one likes to be told—even if it is in an imagined dramatic dialogue between a person and a dog—that your policy makes you a jerk.

Would employing conventions of fiction work better? Maybe. The above dramatic exchange could be rewritten to read more like a story, in which the owner of the dog looks at his pet and imagines him thinking the things he has him say in the dramatic monologue. Maybe he describes his "sad, wistful eyes" as he looks over the grassy field in the park; perhaps the author describes how he whines softly, how his ears twitch eagerly, how he looks hopefully up at his owner, wishing that he might be let off the leash just this once.

One thing that you will of necessity become quite skilled at as you work on your writing skills is knowing when to discriminate. Sometimes less is more, and the last thing you want to have happen is to have your main message become obscured by rhetorical flourishes that can overwhelm what it is you are trying to say.

Suggested Reading

Barnet and Cain, *A Short Guide to Writing about Literature*.

Carpenter, *Reading Lessons*.

DiYanni, *Literature*.

Gardner, *Writing about Literature*.

Griffith, *Writing Essays about Literature*.

Guerin et al., *A Handbook of Critical Approaches to Literature*.

Harmon and Holman, *A Handbook to Literature*.

Kennedy and Gioia, *Literature*.

Lunsford and Ruszkiewicz, *Everything's an Argument*.

McLaughlin and Coleman, *Everyday Theory*.

Roberts, *Writing about Literature*.

Exercises

1. Consider the following three passages and try to determine to what genre—poetry, prose, drama, autobiography, or essay—they belong. What are the elements of each that provide you with clues and help you make that determination?

I had made it to the shelter none too soon—the air was starting to feel damp, and I knew the rain was coming. I climbed the ladder and heaved myself onto the platform, and then almost lost my grip and fell backward; there was someone already there. "Careful!" he said and reached for my hand. It was Finn, my brother's friend. I let him help me up. "Sorry," he said. "I didn't mean to startle you."

"This is my place," I said. It came out meaner, more accusatory than I had intended. "I mean, I usually wait for the storm up here."

"Sorry," he said again. "I didn't realize."

We looked at each other awkwardly for a moment. "That's all right," I said, "you can stay if you want."

The flames came
Over the brim of the world
A terrible, hungry sunrise
That ate and ate the earth
Well into the sleeve of night
And out the other side

Laura: "It won't be long now. Here, give me that."
Edie: "What do you want that for?"
Laura: "It helps with the pain. Maybe. Can't make it any worse."
Edie: "Does it hurt now?"
Laura: "Just every five to seven minutes."
Edie: "What should I do?"
Laura: "Go and get your grandmother." *Cries out.*
Edie: "Are you sure I should go?"
Laura: "Better now than five minutes from now. I think this baby's coming sooner rather than later."

2. As you may have determined, the first example is prose, the second is poetry, and the third is drama. Now, try and revise each of those examples, moving them from one genre to another (for example, try to make a poem out of the prose selection; take the drama selection and rewrite it so that it reads like prose). What did you discover in trying to make these changes? Did you have to invent details? Add description? Change words to be more or less "poetic"?

How Literature Can Help
Lecture 3—Transcript

Welcome back. As we discussed in our last lecture, a piece of writing has essentially three lives: when we read it for the first time, knowing nothing about it; when we think about it, reflecting on the text and what we noticed the first time through; and the third life is when or if we reread it again, this time knowing what we already have read and considered. It's helpful to keep this in mind as you are considering your own writing—be it a short story, or a poem, or an essay for a class, or a job letter.

Your own writing might have several lives, and you should keep this in mind as you write—there will be a first impression of your writing, its first life, and what you hope for is that there will be at least a second life—that someone will stop to think and reflect on what it is that you have to say. Very likely, there may be a third life, when that person rereads your writing. But it's always possible that your audience has only the time or inclination to read your piece of writing once, so you have to make that one time really count.

One of the basics of engaging with writing—as either an author or a reader—is to understand the genre or type of writing it is, and in this lecture we're going to explore the basics of what I like to call "genre definition." An awareness of conventions of style, of subject matter, and how other elements fit with a piece's perceived genre can help you become more keenly attuned to your own writing—and help you to pay attention to considerations like the expectations of your audience.

I told you in the first lecture that great writers are great readers. In this lecture, we're going to see how you can pick up tools for good writing from poets, from dramatists, from writers of other kinds of texts—even if you yourself never intend to write a poem or a play. For example, if a reader thinks she's sitting down to read a mystery novel, turns to the first page, and encounters a series of sonnets, you can imagine that she's probably going to be very disappointed.

Even if they are the most beautifully poetic, exquisitely crafted, and cleverly executed sonnets ever to have been written, the reader is going to be unlikely to notice—and probably unwilling to expend any sort of effort in engaging with them—and this is because her expectations had been geared toward something very different, and when those expectations aren't met—when they're dashed—her frame of mind is not necessarily positively welcoming to this new and unexpected form of writing.

So, today we're going to focus on learning to recognize different genres and the elements that are most frequently associated with particular genres, and we're going to talk also about how you can make the most of utilizing a particular genre's conventions. We're going to focus on five major types of writing, and that is prose, poetry, drama, essay, and autobiography. We're going to explore the major and most prominent features of each and then learn how understanding and recognizing these features and their differences can make us better readers and then, of course, make us better writers.

Let's consider the two following examples of writing and see if you can tell me to what genre they belong. The first is short, but you can get enough from these few lines to make a guess I'm sure:

> The soul selects her own society
> and then, shuts the door
> to her divine majority
> present no more.

What have we got there? You can tell, probably right away, that this is a poem. What are your clues? First of all, there's the rhyme scheme, and there's the patterning there. So, this one is pretty obvious and pretty easy to figure out. Let's consider another example.

> Juliet: What man art thou that thus bescreen'd in night
> So stumblest on my counsel?
>
> Romeo: By a name
> I know not how to tell thee who I am:
> My name, dear saint, is hateful to myself,

Because it is an enemy to thee;
Had I it written, I would tear the word.

Even if you have never studied the work of William Shakespeare, most of us are familiar with the names Romeo and Juliet and know that they are characters in a famous play. It's true that many dramas contain long speeches by a single character, something that we call a "monologue." But another major clue that this is a piece of drama is the movement between the speakers with none of the indicators that we might normally find in, for example, a short story or a novel. If this dramatic exchange were part of a piece of prose writing, it would most likely be accompanied by cues like "said Juliet"; or "shaking his head sadly, Romeo said"; etc.; etc. So, those two examples are pretty easy to figure out for considering genre: One is poetry; one is drama. Let's consider three examples of prose writing, and see if you can identify which is fiction, which is essay, and which is autobiography.

Here's the first passage: "When Arabella awoke, she could see through the crack in the curtains that the sun was just starting to rise. Early as it was, she could hear sounds of stirring in other parts of the house, and knew she could not afford the luxury of falling back asleep."

This example is fairly easy to guess. It's fiction. Our clues here are the use of the third person, which is a common convention of fiction, and the use of a narratorial voice that is, to a certain degree, what we would call "omniscient"—the voice of the person describing the scene can see what the character Arabella is doing and can tell also what she is feeling—that she would like to fall back asleep, but she knows that she can't.

Here's the second passage I want you to consider:

> Most everyone you might ask would be willing to volunteer an hour or so a week to a worthy cause; very few people, however, have any idea how to turn their good intentions into action. As I outline below, the Helping Hands program can provide information on how to get involved with community activities and can easily be incorporated into the curriculum of most elementary and secondary schools.

This is quite clearly some form of essay. The formal tone, the argumentative approach—and here I mean "argumentative" in that the writer is making a claim and is purporting to support it with the sentences that follow—all of this suggests that this piece of writing is a persuasive essay of some type.

Here's the third passage I want you to consider: "I was born in a small town on the California coast. My earliest childhood memories are of the smell of salt air and the golden hues of the sand and the foothills which came down to meet it."

By process of elimination, this third passage would quite obviously seem to be autobiography. Other clues, of course, are the use of the first person speaker—the "I"—and also where this text begins—with the birthplace of the speaker/writer.

All of this signals autobiography, although many of you are probably thinking right now of pieces of prose fiction that you've read which begin with the birth of a character and make use of this first-person speaking voice.

These examples are fairly obvious, but now I'd like you to consider three more examples that are a little trickier and that also help to demonstrate the potential for overlap among these genres of prose writing.

Here's the first passage: "A long time ago, when all the grandfathers and grandmothers of today were little boys and little girls or very small babies, or perhaps not even born, Pa and Ma and Mary and Laura and Baby Carrie left their little house in the Big Woods of Wisconsin."

Unless you are already familiar with these writers or these pieces of writing that I'm going to be reading to you in just a moment in addition to this one, this task becomes a little more difficult. This first example comes from the beloved children's classic *Little House in the Big Woods* by Laura Ingalls Wilder.

Supposedly this book and those that follow it in the series are all an account of Wilder's childhood growing up as a pioneer girl—so your first answer might be this is autobiography, even though it's written as if it were a piece of fiction—a novel. However, those who have studied the life of Laura Ingalls Wilder have determined that she has changed a lot in the account of her life growing up on the frontier of the United States. Many episodes of her life have been left out; the names of many characters are changed; events that were separate get combined into one—or the timeline is shifted in the interest of the plot. This means that today her books are usually characterized as "historical fiction" rather than "autobiography."

A few of you might be thinking at this moment that to one degree or another, all autobiography is historical fiction—no one can accurately remember every conversation, every event, of his or her life. Probably plenty of people who write autobiographies alter the past—either on purpose or by accident because their memories are a little faulty.

It's a slippery slope, trying to decide where something crosses the line and ceases to become autobiography and becomes fiction instead. In the case of Laura Ingalls Wilder, she certainly used her autobiographical life experiences to write these books—and in its broadest strokes, most of what she describes most likely happened. For example, we know she did live through a very difficult winter with her family—that her sister Mary went blind, and she became a schoolteacher. None of these events is made up out of whole cloth, so to speak. At the same time, while her autobiography is the foundation of the fabric of these stories, she has fictionalized quite a bit—so we don't put her writing in the category of autobiography, but we classify it rather as a kind of fiction.

Let's consider another passage of writing: "When I wrote the following pages, or rather the bulk of them, I lived alone, in the woods, a mile from any neighbor, in a house which I had built myself, on the shore of Walden Pond, in Concord, Massachusetts, and earned my living by the labor of my hands only."

This passage is from Henry David Thoreau's essay "Walden" in which he used his own experiences during the time he lived at Walden Pond to argue for a return to a simpler, more self-reliant style of living than what he thought was the norm in America at the time. So obviously, although there are elements here of autobiography—the use of "I," the reference to personal experience, meaning the time he lived at Walden—this piece is more in the genre of the essay, and that's because his main purpose here is to make an argument about a particular kind of lifestyle—and his own autobiographical experience can be used to support his argument. The fact that this is so, one might say, is really incidental to that argument. At the same time, however, we should keep in mind that what Thoreau's essay proves is how powerful one's own experience can be when trying to make a particular claim or argument. So, both this piece and the passage from *Little House in the Big Woods* make use of autobiographical writing, but neither one really is, strictly speaking, autobiography.

Let's consider a third passage of prose writing:

> Dear Son: I have ever had pleasure in obtaining any little anecdotes of my ancestors. You may remember the inquiries I made among the remains of my relations when you were with me in England and the journey I undertook for that purpose. Imagining it may be equally agreeable to you to know the circumstances of my life, many of which you are yet unacquainted with ... I sit down to write them for you.

This passage—while couched as a letter from a father to a son—is, in fact, the opening of the autobiography of Benjamin Franklin. In this excerpt he says quite clearly that he means to relate the events of his life, but the conceit or what we might call the "premise" of his piece is that it's a personal letter. He has, therefore, constructed a specific audience—and in this case, it happens to be his son—to which he is supposedly writing. This premise or conceit allows him to speak a certain way, to make certain references and allusions that might otherwise be a little stilted or awkward. With the fiction of the letter in place, other people reading this piece are drawn in—in the sense that there is something exciting, thrilling, or maybe even a little illicit about reading what is characterized as personal correspondence.

So if we have to try and briefly define each of these genres, what would we say? We might say that poetry is a form of writing that uses language in unexpected or unconventional ways—by rhyming, by use of rhythm, or simply by patterning the language in non-conventional forms. We're going to talk a lot more about this in the lecture that's devoted entirely to poetry.

The simplest way to define drama is to call it something that's performed in front of an audience. Again, in the lecture on drama we'll discuss this genre's conventions in greater depth, but some things to keep in mind are that with drama you have to rely wholly on what you see and hear as a member of the audience to make sense of the story—what the characters say and how they say it are what we use to determine state of mind, the relationships between the characters acting on the stage, and the plot of the drama that's unfolding in front of us.

We also, in the case of drama, have to suspend our disbelief and imagine that somehow we're looking through what's often called the "fourth wall"—and probably a lot of you have heard this term before. This fourth wall is an imaginary, invisible divider that separates the audience from the actors on stage. Some edgier dramas purposefully "break" the fourth wall, and you might have characters step out of their role and directly address the audience, which is a clever move that at once acknowledges the particular convention of drama in the fourth wall while overturning that convention in rather delightful fashion at the same time.

Arguably, prose fiction is the genre of writing that's going to be most familiar to most of us. Novels, short stories, that kind of writing—other works that tell some sort of story—they're found everywhere. Within the genre of fiction alone we have all sorts of what we could call "subgenres"—mystery, thriller, romance, historical fiction, science fiction, fantasy—the list goes on and on. I could probably spend the rest of this lecture just listing the number of subgenres within the category of fiction. The essay is quite easy to define in terms of its broadest strokes; it's a piece of writing that seeks to persuade and inform—to support a particular position, for example. So, that's also easily defined—just like fiction, poetry, and drama.

Autobiography is quite simply the story of a life, told by the person who has lived it, and the essay—as I've said before—has as its aim the desire to prove a point, make a claim, persuade an audience of a point of view or particular argumentative position—and very often, autobiography and essay overlap to some degree. As we've seen, all of these genres can overlap with one another in interesting and provocative ways, and what I want you to understand in today's lecture is how recognizing where these dramas diverge from each other, how they can overlap, and how those overlaps can be productive or interesting can make you a more interesting and effective writer.

Let's consider how knowledge of the conventions of these various genres can be used to enhance something as mundane as a protest letter written to the local city council about something, let's say, as commonplace as a leash law for dogs. Let's consider the following example of a letter:

> Dear City Council: I am writing to ask that you consider establishing an off-leash area of the park for local dogs. Many other communities have designated off-leash areas for the pets of citizens, and these are usually carefully monitored and have strict rules about interaction between animals and cleaning up after them. This would be a positive thing for both the dogs and their owners. Thank you for considering this request.

That letter—it is fine as it is, but let's consider how we might punch it up a bit to make it a more persuasive request. First, let's think about the conventions of poetry and how we could maybe use them to grab your reader's attention. So, first of all, what's this letter about? It's about dogs and doing something nice for them—so perhaps we could find a more interesting choice of words to refer to these animals since they're the main focus of the letter.

What if we began the letter with something like: "It's not for nothing that dogs are often referred to as 'man's best friend.' These furry, four-legged friends provide companionship and love to their owners." Here we have a reference to the somewhat-clichéd but very, very familiar line about a dog being man's best friend, and then we have another little poetic flourish in the alliterative phrase "furry, four-legged friends."

What other genres could we borrow from in order to enhance this letter? Obviously certainly the essay is on call here—this letter is, indeed, a type of essay since it's trying to make an argumentative claim; it's trying to persuade someone to do something. In an essay, you want to use argumentation to persuade the audience to come around to your way of thinking. So, we've engaged with elements of essay from the beginning when we're talking about this letter, and we're using poetry in addition to try and advance the goal of this letter.

What else could we use? Autobiography, for one, seems to be obvious, as the writer of this letter would most likely not be in favor of doing something nice for dogs if he or she did not have some positive experience with dogs him or herself.

So, perhaps there could be a line that goes something like: "As a dog owner for many years and having lived in many different communities, I've seen firsthand how off-leash areas in parks are beneficial to dogs and provide members of the community—even those who are not dog owners themselves—a chance to enjoy watching these friendliest of animals romp, play, and interact with one another"—something like that.

This is a fairly effective use of autobiography that's directly relevant to the issue at hand, and so it works to engage and persuade the audience of this letter—and in this case, that audience is the city council.

So we've discussed how elements of the genres of essay, poetry, and autobiography can be used to make this a more engaging and effective piece of writing, but what about drama and fiction? Could we bring those in? We certainly could, but one thing we always need to consider as we work toward becoming engaging and effective writers is that you can have too much of a good thing. For example, you could add an imagined dialogue between the owner and his dog; it could be something like having the dog say:

> Dog: Oh please, please, please, please, please, could I run and play in this beautiful park?
>
> Owner: I would love to let you, but the law says I have to keep you on the leash.

Dog: But it makes me so happy to run free, and you have trained me not to jump on other people or dogs, and I know that you always pick up after me.

Owner: I know, buddy. I'm sorry that the city council members are such jerks.

What does the above last exchange have going for it? It's definitely attention-grabbing in that apparently this dog can talk—not only that, this dog can lay out in two sentences why he should be allowed to be off the leash, at least briefly. So, the argument is clear, succinct, and meant to play on our emotions.

The emotional appeal can be a powerful one, and this is what the writer is going for here. What's the drawback? Certainly some of the audience might find this approach a little odd and off-putting, and certainly no one likes to be told—even if it is in an imagined dramatic dialogue between a person and a dog—that your policy makes you a jerk. Nobody wants to hear that you've put something into place that makes people think of you so negatively.

Would employing conventions of fiction work better in this example? Maybe. The dramatic exchange could be rewritten to read more like a story in which the owner of the dog looks at his pet and imagines him thinking the things he has him say in that dramatic exchange. The writer could perhaps describe his sad, wistful eyes as he looks over the grassy field in the park, and maybe the author could describe how the dog whines softly, how his ears twitch eagerly, how he looks hopefully up at his master, wishing that he might be let off the leash just this once.

All of these examples demonstrate how you can use various conventions of writing in conjunction with one another to try and make a more powerful argument—or simply to produce a more engaging, interesting, readable piece of writing. At the same time, just because you know how to employ the conventions of all these genres of writing doesn't mean that you should do that all at once.

Sometimes restraint—knowing when to hold back—can be the most effective strategy of all. You want to engage your audience, not completely overwhelm them. While it may be impressive that you can work in a variety of genres—that you can show off that you know poetry, that you know drama, that you know fiction—that may not be what gets you to your ultimate goal; and in this case, your goal is to get an off-leash area of a dog park. The more you write, the more you will learn to walk this fine line between effective display and use of your writerly knowledge and simply showing off—something that's likely to turn your audience off and is not going to help you in getting what it is that you ultimately want.

As I've mentioned before, there are exercises that accompany each of these lectures, and it's a good idea if you can take a little time and at least read over them—or better yet, take a stab at writing them out. For example, in the exercises that accompany today's lecture, I give you short selections of poetry, prose, and drama, and I ask you to rewrite them—take the poem and write it so that it reads like a piece of fiction, or take the short fictional piece and turn it into a poem. These exercises aren't just good practice—they're fun, too, and you can learn a lot from taking a stab at them, which I encourage you to do. Each genre we've examined today offers tools for improving your own writing—no matter what genre you choose as your own. One thing that we've also touched upon several times in this lecture and the two preceding it is the issue of voice—or how you construct your writerly persona for your intended audience. In our next lecture, we will explore the issue of voice at considerable length, and we'll learn how you can shape your voice to best suit any number of specific circumstances, audiences, and goals.

Shaping Your Voice
Lecture 4

> The trick, as a writer, is to know for whom you're writing and what it is you're trying to convey.

In this lecture, we narrow our focus to prose fiction. In particular, we examine the issue of voice—this is sometimes called tone, style, or even diction. Voice is a critical component of any kind of writing, from the formal essay, to the letter to the editor, to the note you leave on your neighbor's windshield asking him please not to park in front of your driveway.

Let's consider the distinctive voice of a writer whose style is one of the most famous and most easily identifiable: Ernest Hemingway. His short story "Hills Like White Elephants" begins as follows:

> The hills across the valley of the Ebro were long and white. On this side there was no shade and no trees and the station was between two lines of rails in the sun. Close against the side of the station there was the warm shadow of the building and a curtain, made of strings of bamboo beads, hung across the open door into the bar, to keep out flies. The American and the girl with him sat at a table in the shade, outside the building.

What is the adjective that comes to mind if you try to describe Hemingway's style in a single word? One descriptor that comes up often when critics talk about Hemingway is "spare"; "simple" and "clean" are other words often used to describe

Voice is a critical component of any kind of writing.

Hemingway's style. Hemingway's voice engages the audience by what we might call writing by indirection. His style is deliberately simplistic—some might say maddeningly so—but is a distinctive choice that marks his writing out from so many others'.

In this story, he describes the scene, what the characters say to one another, and some other details—like the strings of bamboo beads. But the reader is forced to fill in gaps, to try and figure out what the real story is about, since Hemingway does not tell us what any of the characters are thinking or feeling or give much description of their nonverbal behavior. For example, this opening doesn't say anything about how the man and woman look—are they excited to be going somewhere? Are they slouched in their chairs? We've got to work it out for ourselves as we read.

One of the most famous literary voices from the last hundred years must be that of J. D. Salinger's Holden Caulfield. Consider the following two versions of an opening statement from the main character of *The Catcher in the Rye*:

> Most likely, you will want to know my history—the details of my birth and adolescence, what it was like to grow up with distant parents, and other similar matters—but I would actually rather not discuss that part of my life.

Now consider this version:

> If you really want to hear about it, the first thing you'll probably want to know is where I was born, and what my lousy childhood was like, and how my parents were occupied and all before they had me, and all that David Copperfield kind of crap, but I don't feel like going into it, if you want to know the truth.

Both of these passages have a particular voice, but one is arguably stronger, more arresting, more engaging than the other. Why is this the case? They both speak directly to the reader, as if Holden were having a conversation with him or her, and thus, they are arguably both very engaging from the start. And if you were to consider, on the basis of these sentences alone, which of these speakers you'd like to invite over to your house for dinner, most of us would pick the speaker of the first passage. Although he declines to tell the reader about himself, he does so rather politely.

The second speaker, on the other hand, comes across as somewhat emotional and angry. He uses coarse language, modifying the mention of his childhood with words like "lousy" and "crap," and the sarcastic mention of David Copperfield suggests a distaste for stories of the rags-to-riches variety. In other words, he seems unhappy, cynical, and maladjusted. Although you probably wouldn't want to have him as a houseguest, you probably are more interested in reading the story told by the second speaker than the first.

The second speaker has a realness and grittiness in his voice that makes his story compelling. There's a reason that polite, diligent, hard-working people rarely have unauthorized biographies written about them—it's just not as interesting to most readers as a life that is somewhat unconventional, in which the subject breaks rules or engages in bad behavior.

Choosing a certain kind of diction or sentence style contributes to the voice of a piece of writing, and by examining some famous writers and analyzing the voices they've constructed, you've gotten some idea of how important voice can be, and how just a few words or a certain arrangement can create certain expectations in your reader. ■

Suggested Reading

Barnet and Cain, *A Short Guide to Writing about Literature.*

Carpenter, *Reading Lessons.*

DiYanni, *Literature.*

Gardner, *Writing about Literature.*

Griffith, *Writing Essays about Literature.*

Guerin et al., *A Handbook of Critical Approaches to Literature.*

Kennedy and Gioia, *Literature.*

McLaughlin and Coleman, *Everyday Theory.*

Roberts, *Writing about Literature.*

Consider the following information: "On December 12, Aloyisia H. Society and Gerard Dashing were married at the Ourtown Country Club. The bride wore a pink wedding gown with green accents. The groom wore a white tuxedo and high-top sneakers. There were 400 people in attendance. The bride had 12 bridesmaids, and the groom had five groomsmen. Because of a catering accident, there was no food at the reception. The DJ did not show up, so the bride's younger brother provided music for dancing with his harmonica. After learning of the catering accident, the best man ordered 50 pizzas from A1 Pizza Delivery. When the pizzas arrived, the best man and the groom's father had a brief argument as to who would pay for them. The best man tried to punch the groom's father but accidentally hit the bride instead. The bride and groom left the reception early to retire to the honeymoon suite at their hotel."

1. Rewrite the passage so that it sounds as if the words are being spoken by a 14-year-old girl talking to her friends.

2. Rewrite the same information so that it reads as if it is being conveyed by that girl's mother to her father.

3. Now imagine that a member of Congress is stating these facts in front of a panel of high-ranking government officials, and rewrite the passage again.

4. Revise so that this same information reads as it would if a father was explaining this to his six-year-old son.

5. Now imagine how the six-year-old would tell his best friend.

Shaping Your Voice
Lecture 4—Transcript

Welcome back. In our last lecture, we explored five major genres of writing to begin to get an understanding of how different types of writing might be more or less appropriate for different goals.

We also explored how these categories of writing are never absolutely distinct from one another—fiction might contain lines that read as what we think of as poetry. Dramatic style might help make a piece of fiction more engaging. Autobiographical elements can help make an essay more persuasive, and as any great writer can tell you, a supposedly purely fictional piece of writing is rarely ever just that—the personal life of the writer usually informs the piece of writing in some way or another.

In the exercises that accompanied our last lecture, I asked you first to identify whether three selections were poetry, prose, or drama, and probably most of you had no trouble with that part of it, but then I asked you to try and rewrite each passage so that it was generically different—for example, to try and turn the prose into a piece of drama, or the drama into a poem. As you recall, this is the poem I asked you to revise:

> The flames came
> Over the brim of the world
> A terrible, hungry sunrise
> That ate and ate the earth
> Well into the sleeve of night
> And out the other side.

When you tried to put this into prose form, what happened? You might have had a few variations, ranging from those that kept a lot of the poetic language—so images like "the brim of the world" of flames that were eating rather than burning the earth—and you might only have changed the structure and punctuation a little. Another version might have gotten rid of almost all of the poetic elements in an attempt to give a straightforward account of what's happening here. You might have come up with something like: "The fire came over the horizon in the morning, burning the earth as far as the eye could see and lasting through the night and into the next morning." This conveys what the poetic lines are saying in a really straightforward fashion—so the audience understands the event that is being described, but at the same time they lose out on several of the poetic elements that might add a little extra something to this piece of writing.

At the same time that the prose version might be a little clearer and what we might call "accessible" to a wider range of people, what we also need to recognize is that this prose version, as simple as it is, still contains some poetic elements. For example, "as far as the eye could see"—this is more poetic than something like "burned a whole lot of the ground." So even though it's more straightforward, it still has elements of poetry in it.

Within the genre of fiction, there's a wide range of styles available—from the most prosaic, something like the language you'd get in an instruction manual on how to hook up your computer, and it can also be incredibly poetic. Indeed, some critics have argued that certain short stories read more like poems than stories at all. These short stories, many of them, are so carefully aware of language, and style, and nuance, and diction—instead of maybe being concerned with the plot—that really these stories are more like poems than short pieces of fiction. The trick, as a writer, is to know for whom you're writing and what it is you're trying to convey.

So, although we've begun to discuss several different styles of writing, today we're going to narrow our focus to prose, and this is the most common form of writing with which most of us engage on a regular basis, and we're going to narrow our focus even more so that we can really hone in on fiction. In particular, today we're going to talk about the issue of voice—and this is sometimes called tone, or style, or even diction, and it's a really important element of writing.

Voice is a critical component, I would say, of any kind of writing—from the formal essay, to a letter to the editor, to a note you might leave on your neighbor's windshield asking him: "Please don't park in my driveway." But let's consider an example of how voice can be used both as a means for a writer to establish his or her identity and then how the voice can be used to shape the expectations of your reader—in other words, make them have some idea about what's going to come next. Listen to this quote: "Most everybody seems to assume these days that if a guy is young and has money, he's looking for someone to marry."

What is that sentence trying to say? Think about that for a moment. You could probably sum it up pretty easily. Compare it to this version of the same kind of statement, but in a very different style: "It is a truth universally acknowledged, that a single man in possession of a good fortune must, be in want of a wife."

As I'm sure you've noticed, both of these sentences say essentially the same thing, but in very different voices. The first version is what we might imagine a modern person living in the 21st century might say casually while in conversation with friends. The second version, as many of you have no doubt recognized, is the famous opening line of Jane Austen's classic novel *Pride and Prejudice*. It most definitely does not sound like something someone today might say in casual conversation—rather, it signals and sets the tone for much of what is to follow in this book, and what follows is a story about upper-class 19th-century British people.

How can we tell that? First, there's the use of an objective third-person voice with an unusual and quite detached syntax: "It is a truth universally acknowledged"—who is doing the acknowledging? How is this "truth" determined to be such? The line itself also seems to be somewhat self-aware—there is a little, wry bit of humor here when it says "must be in want of a wife." If you consider that line—and the socio-historical context in which it was produced—we get an impression of mannered yet ambitious mothers making calculated moves to secure for their daughters the best marriage possible. If you consider the tone, style, and wit of the line, we as readers are now primed to expect certain things from the narrative that follows, and we might reasonably argue we'll be disappointed if we don't get what we're expecting.

Sometimes, however, what is interesting about voice in fiction is how you can set the reader up for certain expectations, and then—by playing with or twisting them—you can create a really memorable effect. For example, keeping with the Jane Austen theme, let's consider this quote from the recent sensation entitled *Pride and Prejudice and Zombies*. The opening line of this work shows how the imitation of the style of Austen when we transfer that to what is normally the cheap paperback world of zombie thrillers produces a new, comical effect. The writer demonstrates an understanding and ability with Austen's style while also humorously exploiting its limits. Here are the opening lines from this version: "It is a truth universally acknowledged that a zombie in possession of brains must be in want of more brains."

Part of what the adapter is relying on here is our familiarity with Austen's voice and our appreciation of the satire applied to it. In some sense, we as readers who know Austen are now in on an inside joke, and who doesn't like to be in on an inside joke—we all enjoy that. Part of the pleasure comes from recognizing that we get the joke because we are well-read. We've all read Austen. We're chuckling in part because we know some people maybe won't recognize or get the reference.

Now consider this original passage from *Pride and Prejudice*, in which the character of Mrs. Bennet wants to tell her husband the exciting news that a nearby estate has been rented by an eligible, wealthy, young bachelor:

> "My dear Mr. Bennet … have you heard that Netherfield Park is let at last?" Mr. Bennet replied that he had not. "But it is," returned she; "for Mrs. Long has just been here, and she told me all about it." Mr. Bennet made no answer. "Do you not want to know who has taken it?" cried his wife impatiently. "You want to tell me, and I have no objection to hearing it."

That's Mr. Bennet's reply. In this case you have a conversation between Mr. and Mrs. Bennet. It's rather straightforward. They're talking about this house being let or rented to an eligible, young bachelor, and Mr. Bennet seems sort of irritated with Mrs. Bennet's prattling on, and on, and on, and so the writer of *Pride and Prejudice and Zombies* then takes that idea, and he twists it:

> "My dear Mr. Bennet … have you heard that Netherfield Park is occupied again?" Mr. Bennet replied that he had not and went about his morning business of dagger sharpening and musket polishing— for attacks by the unmentionables had grown alarmingly frequent

in recent weeks. "But it is," returned she. Mr. Bennet made no answer. "Do you not want to know who has taken it?" cried his wife impatiently. 'Woman, I am attending to my musket. Prattle on if you must, but leave me to the defense of my estate!"

Obviously, what is really funny here is that Seth Grahame-Smith, the writer behind *Pride and Prejudice and Zombies*, imitates Austen's voice even when he changes the plot and the dialogue so that it's about zombies and not an upper-class British comedy of manners. It's the successful imitation of the voice—rather than the subject matter—that makes Grahame-Smith's book delightful in so many ways.

Let's consider another moment of distinctive voice, and this time from a writer whose style is one of the most famous and most easily identifiable, and this is Ernest Hemingway. His short story "Hills Like White Elephants" begins with the following quote:

> The hills across the valley of the Ebro were long and white. On this side there was no shade and no trees, and the station was between two lines of rails in the sun. Close against the side of the station there was the warm shadow of the building and a curtain, made of strings of bamboo beads, hung across the open door into the bar, to keep out flies. The American and the girl with him sat at a table in the shade, outside the building.

What's the adjective that comes to mind if you are trying to describe Hemingway's style in just a single word? One descriptor that comes up a lot and that you might have heard is the word "spare"; "simple" and "clean" are other words that are often used to describe Hemingway's style.

Hemingway's voice engages the audience by what we might call "writing by indirection." His style is deliberately simplistic—some people, myself included, would say occasionally it's maddeningly so—but a distinctive choice that marks his writing out from so many others.'

In this story, he describes the scene—what the characters say to one another and some other details, like the strings of bamboo beads, but the reader is forced to fill in gaps—to try and figure out what the real story is about since Hemingway doesn't tell us what any of the characters are thinking or feeling. He limits also descriptions of their non-verbal behavior. For example, this opening doesn't say anything about how the couple look—are they excited to be going somewhere? Are they slouched in their chairs? We've got to work it out for ourselves as we read.

A writer whose voice might be considered the polar opposite of Hemingway is Henry James. Some people might go so far to say that while Hemingway was a master of the simple sentence, James by contrast seems to have aspired to torturing the English language and writing the most complex sentences he could. You'll see this in a minute.

Here are just two sentences from his story "The Tree of Knowledge": "It was one of the secret opinions, such as we all have, of Peter Brench that his main success in life would have consisted in his never having committed himself about the work, as it was called, of his friend Morgan Mallow."

What's the difficulty here? For one thing, you might have noticed that this passage was a little difficult to follow if you were simply listening to it. Without question, James has established a voice that's meant for writing, not reading aloud really—although some people might want to argue with me about that, but I think it's much easier to read than to listen to James. One clue that tells us this is the piling on of subordinate clauses. Cues on the page in the form of punctuation help the reader make sense of what the author has to say—and even in this case, James has what we might call a "difficult voice," even in written form.

If you consider that opening sentence and we rewrite it and take out the subordinate clauses, it becomes something somewhat different: "It was one of the secret opinions of Peter Brench that his main success in life would have consisted in his never having committed himself about the work of his friend Morgan Mallow."

So, still a little tricky to follow, but it's much clearer than the first version we considered.

But then, of course, you might be asking: "Well, if we do that, what have we lost if we cut big chunks of the text out?" The subordinate clauses—what we might call "asides," and these were the phrases "such as we all have" and "as it was called"—do contribute to the voice of the work. These clauses convey immediately that the voice of this author is in some ways a critical one; he's making comments on the beliefs and actions of his characters.

Notice particularly that when he's describing the work of Morgan Mallow, James inserts "such as it was called," and in just those four words we immediately get the impression that this "work" is really not much to speak of—and perhaps it isn't even work at all. We don't even know exactly what the work is, but we do know that the attitude conveyed by the voice of the writer is a negative attitude, and that's the most important element here if we're considering the matter of voice.

Both Hemingway and James are considered by many—scholars and non-specialists alike—to be masters of the craft of writing, and their work suggests the really powerful effect that can be achieved when you willfully ignore some of what we consider to be rules of writing and you go off in your own direction.

I would be the first to say that they are, in fact, fabulous rule-breakers, but if I got a piece of writing like this from either one—or that was similar to either one—of these two examples, and I got a sample of writing from a student that was like either one of these, I'd be doing a whole lot of correcting and commenting. I might write something like: "This piece needs more detail and explanation" in the margin of something that sounded like a Hemingway piece. In a piece that was written in the style of Henry James, I'd probably write something like: "Your reader has no idea what the most important or key idea is if you start off this way." Also, I'd probably write in the margins of the Henry James piece: "Write clearly!" I might say something else like: "The main argument is obscured by your wordiness!"

As I always say to my students: Sometimes it is powerful to break the rules of writing, but before you do that, you need to show me that you know what the rules are—rules about writing in complete sentences; never beginning a sentence with "and," and etc., etc., and so on. These can produce really great, powerful effects when those rules are deliberately broken, but in order to understand just how powerful an effect you can create, it's a good idea if you have mastered the rule first—if you know how to execute it properly. Both Hemingway and James are quite conscious of the conventions they are choosing to disregard, and it makes their writing all the more powerful because of this.

One of the most famous literary voices from the last 100 years has to be that of JD Salinger's character, Holden Caulfield. Let's consider two versions of the opening statement from this main character of his novel *Catcher in the Rye*. Here's the first one I want you to think of: "Most likely, you will want to know my history—the details of my birth and adolescence, what it was like to grow up with distant parents, and other similar matters—but I would actually rather not discuss that part of my life."

Fair enough. Now consider this version: "If you really want to hear about it, the first thing you'll probably want to know is where I was born, and what my lousy childhood was like, and how my parents were occupied and all before they had me, and all that David Copperfield kind of crap, but I don't feel like going into it, if you want to know the truth."

Both of these passages have a particular voice obviously, but one is arguably stronger, and more interesting, and more engaging than the other. Why is this? They both speak directly to the reader, as if Holden was having a conversation with the reader—and so, arguably, they're both really engaging from the start. If you were going to consider these sentences alone, try to imagine which speaker you'd want to have over to dinner; probably most of us would pick the speaker of the first passage—because although he declines to tell the reader about himself, he says he doesn't want to talk about this rather politely.

The second speaker, on the other hand, comes across as somewhat emotional and angry. He uses coarse language, modifying the mention of his childhood with words like "lousy" and "crap," and the sarcastic mention of David Copperfield suggests a distaste for stories of the rags-to-riches variety. In other words, he seems unhappy, cynical, and maladjusted. Although you probably wouldn't want to have him as a houseguest, you probably are more interested in reading the story told by him, by the second speaker, than the first. Why is this?

The second speaker has a realness and grittiness in his voice that makes his story compelling. There is a reason that polite, diligent, hardworking people don't often have unauthorized biographies written about them—it's just not as interesting to most readers as a life that is somewhat unconventional, in which the main subject breaks rules or engages in bad behavior.

Truly masterful writers are those who are able to write in multiple voices depending on the needs of their fictional narratives. One of the best recent examples of this—and one of my favorites—comes from Barbara Kingsolver's novel *The Poisonwood Bible*. This book tells the story of a missionary family in Africa, and it tells the story from the various points of view of the mother and her four daughters.

I'll just give you a couple quick examples. Here is the mother's voice: "Once every few years, even now, I catch the scent of Africa. It makes me want to keen, sing, clap up thunder, lie down at the foot of a tree and let the worms take whatever of me they can still use. I find it impossible to bear."

Now consider the voice of the daughter, Rachel: "Well Hallelujah and pass the ammunition. Company for dinner! And an eligible bachelor at that, without three wives or even one as far as I know."

You can sense the difference immediately. The mother seems to be deeply introspective, sensitive, emotional, and coping with the aftermath of a life-changing experience. By contrast, the voice of Rachel suggests a character a little more shallow, more interested in the immediate present—a little flighty with a bit of judgmental attitude.

Then there's the voice of the youngest daughter, Ruth May, whose voice is compellingly that of a young child who reports what she sees as she sees it—from a perspective that's wildly different from that of her mother or of her older sister. At one point Ruth May says:

> Then we got in the plane and flew to Stanleyville … the back of the airplane was so full of bags I had to sit on them. … I looked inside: rocks. Sparkly things and dirty rocks … it was diamonds. I found that out and I can't tell how. … Mr. Axelroot said if I told, why then God would make Mama get sick and die. So I can't.

It sounds like a child's voice, one who would believe an adult who used a frightening threat in order to keep her from revealing a secret—and in this case, the secret is that Mr. Axelroot, the pilot of the plane, is in fact smuggling diamonds.

Kingsolver is a master at creating different voices for her characters, but if you think about it, we all do this to some extent every day—changing what we would call "the register" of our voices—depending on our audience or the goal behind whatever it is we're writing or saying. For example, the register or tone you use might change dramatically if you're talking to a friend in casual conversation versus if you were the president of the United States addressing congress. The president probably uses a different register or tone when he's addressing congress than he does when he's meeting with his chief of staff or talking to his wife.

Take a moment, and try and think of times when you've deliberately altered the tone of your voice—either because of your audience or because of a particular point of view or emotion you would like to convey. Surely, you probably can think of a few just off the top of your head.

Here's an example: Imagine your neighbor, a guy named Mr. Wafflebeard let's say, keeps parking his car so that it juts in front of the edge of your driveway. This is irritating, right? One day you decide to leave a note on his windshield. Consider two possible versions of this note. Here's the first I'd like you to think about: "Hi Mr. Wafflebeard—could you please possibly park your car a little further back from the edge of our driveway? I almost hit your bumper as I was leaving for work this morning, and I'd hate to ruin the paint job on your car. Thanks, Thaddeus."

How does that compare with this version—just four words and an exclamation point: "Do not block driveway!"

How important is voice in this exchange? In the first example, as you've probably already figured out, the tone or the voice seems intended to try and maintain neighborly relations. It suggests a concern for the well-being of Mr. Wafflebeard's property rather than simply irritation at the inconvenience that it has caused the note writer. Remember, he says I'm worried that I'll ruin the paint job on your car—and not, you're really bugging me by not parking your car where you should.

Also, the use of "Mr." instead of a first name for Mr. Wafflebeard shows respect—while the fact that the writer of the letter signs his first name indicates an effort at friendliness. All of these things together are clues that the writer is using to try and shape a response from his neighbor. In other words, if you get right down to it, he wants Mr. Wafflebeard to move his car, but he also wants to try and stay friends.

In the second example, where we have "Do not block driveway!" definitely what we could say about this is there is a hostile, unfriendly tone. Maybe this is, in fact, the voice that the writer wants to use. Maybe Mr. Wafflebeard has been blocking that driveway every day, no matter how many times the writer has nicely asked that he not do this—so the writer is fed up, and he wants Mr. Wafflebeard to get it. He wants Mr. Wafflebeard to understand that he is angry, and he is hoping that by maybe conveying his anger, he'll get a different result—or just some result. With a note like this, the lack of any form of address suggests also a lack of friendliness, a lack of respect—and the command-like nature of the note also suggests this as well.

What can we take away from today's discussion of prose fiction and the construction of voice? First of all, we gained a little clearer understanding of the difference between prose writing and other forms of writing, like poetry. You'll remember we worked through this when we talked about the first exercise from the last lecture. We also discussed how the one form of writing can use elements from the other to create a certain effect.

Choosing a certain kind of diction or sentence style contributes to the voice of a piece of writing. By examining some famous writers and analyzing the voices they've constructed, you've gotten some idea at least of how important voice can be, and how just a few words or a certain arrangement can create particular expectations on the part of your reader.

Austen's *Pride and Prejudice* leads us to expect a certain kind of a story set in a certain social and cultural milieu; *Pride and Prejudice and Zombies* takes those expectations and then takes great delight in turning them on their heads. From this we can see the power of understanding how a particular voice can work, and being able to adapt it for one's own ends can have powerful effects. We examined what we might call three extreme examples of unique voice—excerpts from Hemingway, from James, and from Salinger—and we saw that each breaks some traditional writing rules but does so to strong effect.

Hemingway forces us to read carefully and fill in the blanks. James is able to convey attitude and humor with just a subordinate clause here and there, and Salinger teaches us that sometimes an unfriendly or hostile voice can also be interesting and engaging if it's produced skillfully.

The example of the conflict between the neighbors over a parked car reminds us that we all use different voices on different occasions for different reasons. It reminds us also that audience is a crucial consideration whenever you are writing anything.

Because whenever you are writing, you are not only constructing a voice or an author's persona for yourself, but you are also constructing an audience. Even if you don't realize it, you are writing for someone specific—even if that someone is only yourself. Let's say if you're writing a diary or a journal, then you would certainly be the audience. In our next lecture, we'll talk about the other side of the coin of writing as an author, and we'll talk about engaging or constructing a reader—and the dangers of not adequately respecting your audience.

Knowing Your Reader
Lecture 5

Melville actually changed the ending in the American edition of _Moby Dick_ so that Ishmael survived. Although perhaps he didn't properly anticipate audience reaction with the first version, his decision to actually change the outcome of his story demonstrates the power of an audience and the need to be attentive to them and their demands.

In our last lecture, we started to talk about the genre of fiction, and how important voice is. A cleverly constructed voice can tell you something about the characters of a story or the author of a magazine article. In this lecture, we discuss the other side of that coin: the importance of knowing your reader, and how to identify and, indeed, construct an audience. One of the most important factors in good writing is the writer's understanding of the nature of his or her audience. Perhaps even more important is understanding what particular information you need or want to convey to your audience. In other words, you have to know what you want to say, how you want to say it, and why you want to say it.

We're going to start by analyzing some pieces of writing to deduce the intended audience. We'll try to determine how writers construct an audience and convey respect for the audience—or fail to do so— and what the consequences of that may be.

Let's consider a piece of writing that both establishes a strong narrator's voice and constructs an audience, the opening of the classic short story "The Yellow Wallpaper" by Charlotte Perkins Gilman. This is a

Charlotte Perkins Gilman constructs her audience and creates a strong voice through her character's diary in "The Yellow Wallpaper."

has a servant, that she sits and observes while not performing any actual work herself, in combination with the food references that are somewhat contradictory—there's a careful assessment of resources and a fanatical attention to crumbs and morsels—well, all of this together, I think, conveys a slightly more negative impression than we might have gotten if we'd just read it through once and hadn't really considered the passage.

If you get the sense by now that Mrs. Mooney is miserly and she's calculating and perhaps even a little mercenary, you would not be far wrong. For indeed, as the story progresses we learn that Mrs. Mooney has ruthlessly manipulated her daughter Polly and one of the boarders living in the boarding house in order to ensure a decent marriage for her daughter. This was something that was potentially difficult to secure for members of their particular social class—so what she has done is orchestrate a situation to make sure that Polly makes a good marriage, and in doing this she probably makes sure that her future financial situation is more secure than it would have been.

From these examples, brief as they are, you've already learned a little something about insightful reading and how it can enhance our understanding and our enjoyment of the written word. If you recognize powerful, clever, nuanced moments in a variety of written texts as a reader, you'll soon start to be able to work these into your own writing. Once you start reading texts insightfully, you'll start to notice the world around you can be read as a kind of text. You'll understand that pretty much anything can be a text—anything can be open to a wide variety of kinds of interpretation, and any text itself, even if it's not fiction—any text can be a kind of story.

So let's take what would be considered probably the most mundane of examples of writing—let's consider some directions from one place to another. Suppose you need to tell someone visiting you from out of town how to get to the post office from your house. Here's how the written directions might read; they might say something like: "Take a left out of the driveway, and then take a right on Jones Street. Go straight for about a quarter of a mile, and turn left on Smith. The post office will be about half a mile down on your right." After hearing that example, you're probably thinking: "Well, there's nothing that can be gained from reading insightfully here—so why should I bother?" But if we consider those directions given story of a woman going mad. She and her family have rented a home in the country to try and find some sort of "rest cure" for what is ailing her, and the premise is that we, the reader, are looking over her shoulder at her diary.

She chronicles the time spent in this house, and over time, we are able to watch her descent into insanity as we read her words. Here's the opening:

> It is very seldom that mere ordinary people like John and myself secure ancestral halls for the summer. A colonial mansion, a hereditary estate, I would say a haunted house and reach the height of romantic felicity—but that would be asking too much of fate! ... There comes John, and I must put this away—he hates to have me write a word.

So what do we make of this? We have a first person speaker who engages the audience by creating the sense of a conversation, and we are drawn in to the story by the fact that there's something fascinating about reading something meant to be private (her diary). The audience is even further drawn in by the fact of how we are witnessing a woman descending into madness while she herself seems unaware. The story gets weirder and weirder as it continues, with the main character describing how she sees a woman hiding in the pattern of the wallpaper of her room. In the narrator's words, this woman she sees "creeps" around the room at night.

At the climax of the story, she locks herself in the room with the dreadful wallpaper, and then we read the following words:

> Why there's John at the door! It is no use young man, you can't open it! How he does call and pound! Now he's crying to Jennie for an axe. It would be a shame to break down that beautiful door!

What are our reactions to those lines? Well the final line, about how it would be a shame to break down such a beautiful door, helps secure audience reaction in that it suggests how detached she is from reality if her husband is trying to break down the door and she doesn't consider why this might be. It really drives home how altered her mental state is.

But as good as this story is, it doesn't quite respect the audience as much as it should. Can you guess why? Is there anything that strikes you as wrong, or kind of a false note? Well, first of all, Gilman has hit upon a clever strategy to engage the audience—by creating the idea that we are reading the diary of a woman as she goes insane. But once we've got that premise established, it is a problem when we reach the climax of the story. Do we really think that the main character is pausing to write these sentences? What's happened here, clearly, is that we've gone from reading the main character's diary to reading her mind. We get the sense that the author was either hoping we just wouldn't notice or else that given the story's other strengths, we'd forgive her this one mistake. Either way, we as an audience might feel a little like the author wasn't offering us her full respect.

So we've talked about respecting your audience, but we should also be aware of how our writing constructs an audience—how our tone, our word choice, our style all signal whom the piece of writing is intended for. For example, let's consider two pieces of writing that convey the same pieces of information but are intended for vastly different audiences. These two quotes both describe the victory of William the Conqueror at the Battle of Hastings in 1066. Here's the first quote:

> The factors that led to William's victory are multiple and range from the mundane to the fantastic. Events quotidian and epic, natural and artificial, converged with extraordinary moments of luck, coincidence, poor planning and misfortune to produce a final conflict that seems as if it could have been lifted directly from the pages of Homer or Virgil.

Let's try to describe the intended audience for this passage. This piece of writing is a little bit long, with subclauses and more elevated diction. The syntax of the sentences—with their repetitive pairing of opposing ideas like "quotidian and epic, natural and artificial"—shows that the writer is consciously demonstrating his or her facility with language. The choice of words like "quotidian" indicates that this may be writing by and for those who are highly educated. Another clue about the intended audience is the final line, which references the works of the classical poets Homer and Virgil.

So who is the intended audience for this first passage? We can probably agree that the writer expects the readers to be highly educated, with knowledge of classical works. The seriousness of the tone also suggests that the readers are expected to be people who are at least dedicated amateur historians and possibly scholars conducting research on the topic of William the Conqueror and the Battle of Hastings. Here's a description of that same event in different form:

> William's conquest seemed unlikely at first, but a series of events—ranging from bad weather to bad luck—resulted in his surprising victory. The details of what happened make for a great story; it's one you'll never forget.

Obviously, this second passage is written a little more simply, and seems to be intended for a more general audience, one that maybe is only slightly interested in the topic or is new to this kind of historical reading. The author's approach here seems to be intended to draw people in, to intrigue them—the use of words like "luck," "surprising," and the final phrase "it's a story you'll never forget" all work to try and get the reader interested and to keep reading. The author seems to be saying here that historical information can be entertaining if it's presented in the right way. By contrast, the first passage seems to take as a given that the audience is already interested in the topic.

When you write, you construct not only an authorial persona, but you also construct an audience.

The second example is more simply written with more accessible language, but at the same time, it is not writing down to the potential audience. It writes *to* that audience, which seems to be imagined as a broad range of the population, anywhere from elementary school to adulthood. The second passage says, to almost anyone who starts reading it, "this could be written for me."

A chief lesson here is the idea that when you write, you construct not only an authorial persona, but you also construct an audience. No matter if you're writing the great American novel or a letter to the editor, on some level you have an idea of to whom you're writing. As the example of Charlotte

Perkins Gilman's "The Yellow Wallpaper" shows, you can create a fictional idea of audience within whatever piece you're creating, which can add to the interest and engagement of the actual audience. But perhaps the most important lesson here is to always respect your audience. ∎

Suggested Reading

Barnet and Cain, *A Short Guide to Writing about Literature.*

DiYanni, *Literature.*

Gardner, *Writing about Literature.*

Griffith, *Writing Essays about Literature.*

Guerin et al., *A Handbook of Critical Approaches to Literature.*

Kennedy and Gioia, *Literature.*

McLaughlin and Coleman, *Everyday Theory.*

Roberts, *Writing about Literature.*

Exercises

Your beloved Uncle Wilfred has died at the ripe age of 98. During his lifetime, he attended Youngblood Academy, served in the navy, married Aunt Sylvie, had three children—Ella, Peter, and David—and taught high school science. How and how much of this information would you convey to the following audiences.

1. An obituary in the local paper?

2. A letter to a good friend of yours who had met him on several occasions?

3. The Scholarship Committee, a body that you would like to see create a scholarship in his memory?

4. A former navy buddy of his who has not yet been informed of his death?

Try writing practice paragraphs to each of these audiences.

Knowing Your Reader
Lecture 5—Transcript

Welcome back. In our last lecture we started to talk about the genre of fiction and how important voice is. A cleverly constructed voice can tell you something about the characters of a story or the author of a magazine article.

Is the speaker male or female? A modern person or one living in 19th-century England? Educated? Angry? Genteel? All of these things can be conveyed by voice, and sometimes with just a very few words or the simple rearrangement of the order of words or clauses in a sentence, you can really give your readers a feeling for the voice.

In the exercises that accompanied Lecture 4, I gave you some pieces of information and asked you to try and rewrite the information as if it was being given by a variety of different people—children, parents, teenagers, a member of congress. If you didn't have a chance to get to the exercises, that's just fine. You still get my point that different people would use different voices to convey the same kind of information.

The goal, of course, was to get you to think about how you might construct the voice of the author to create the impression of a particular character who is doing the talking or describing.

Today we're going to discuss the other side of that coin, so to speak—and the other side of that coin is the importance of knowing your reader—and how to identify and, in fact, construct an audience. So, while the exercises for the last lecture focused on how to create an authorial or writerly persona, you'll see that the exercises for today will focus on how to identify, respect—and, in fact, create—a particular kind of audience.

I've stressed this point several times so far in this lecture series, but it bears repeating: One of the most important factors in terms of what makes a piece of writing good is the writer's understanding of the nature of his or her audience.

Perhaps even more important is understanding what particular information you need or want to convey to your audience. In other words, if we break it down into a nutshell, you have to know what you want to say, how you want to say it, and why you want to say it.

Writing without a clear idea of these factors is just fine for a first draft—and, in fact, drafting without a clear idea as to what it is you really want to say is an excellent way to figure out what it is that you want to say. This kind of drafting, writing your way to an argument or an argumentative position, is something we're going to talk about at length in a later lecture. But if you're writing anything—from a magazine article, to a short story, to a letter to the editor, to an essay for a class—you need to really have a focus to guide you, and this focus needs to include how you want to construct your voice, as we discussed last time, and also how you want to cater to and define your audience, and that's what we're going to address today.

We're going to start by analyzing some pieces of writing—working through them, as it were, to try and figure out the intended audience. We'll try to figure out how the writers construct an audience and how they convey respect for that audience—or, in some cases, fail to respect those audiences and what the consequences of that failure might be.

Let's consider the opening of Edgar Allan Poe's short story "The Black Cat." This story belongs to what we call a "subgenre" of fiction writing that's referred to as detective or gothic writing, and you can tell from the very first word the way in which the author is first of all creating a really clear specific voice for his narrator—and secondly, how he is constructing an imagined audience. Here's how the story opens:

> For the most wild, yet most homely narrative which I am about to pen, I neither expect nor solicit belief. Mad indeed would I be to expect it, in a case where my very senses reject their own evidence. Yet, mad am I not—and very surely do I not dream. But to-morrow I die, and to-day I would unburthen my soul.

After our last lecture, you've probably got lots of thoughts about construction of the voice of the speaker here. There's some sort of emphatic, kind of disjointed utterances. His admission with this wild tale is incredible, even to himself, and then he protests that he is not mad—and he does this at least twice. I imagine that all of this might make you think: "Okay, what we've got here is a crazy person."

So you probably had no problem nailing down this first issue of voice that we just identified—but now let's consider the other side of the equation and talk about how this, in fact, makes an audience. What's the first thing you think of when you try to imagine the audience that Poe creates for his work?

First off, we need to remember that just like a text can have multiple lives when we read, reread, and think about it, a text can have multiple audiences—one could be as much a fictional construction as the character himself, and that would seem to be the case here. Poe is writing the story so that it's about a madman describing something to an unknown individual—and the syntax and the structure here create the fiction that there's some sort of conversation happening, that one person is presumably telling a story to another person who we might imagine could ask questions, get some clarification, that kind of thing. So there's within the story a madman and his audience. Then, if we step back, there's another level of audience, and this would be the wider-reading audience that Poe wanted this story to reach, and so this is his original intended audience.

What Poe is trying to do is engage this audience, those people that he wanted to purchase or otherwise read his work, and he's drawing them in through the technique of the fictional audience of the story.

The idea here is that the readers will be so intrigued by what seems to be the chance to listen in on the conversation of a crazy person with some unknown character who appears to be asking questions or giving responses to the madman's story—the idea is that this audience will be so engaged they'll want to keep reading.

Then, of course, there are other levels of audience—for example, those of us who are reading the work of Edgar Allan Poe today, those of us who are studying him to try and understand his original intended audience, which could probably be defined as people living in 19th-century America who like stories that have something of the gothic or the horror about them. Someday, maybe a century from now, there will be another audience that not only studies Poe's writing, but also studies what we—people living in the 21st century—thought about Poe, how we discussed him, what we thought was important to his original audience.

Who knows—in a decade or so someone could be talking about how I am talking to you about how we understand Poe's audience. As you're probably starting to imagine, this audience thing, this issue of multiple levels of audiences, can go on and on forever. The best we can do as writers is try to clearly imagine our intended audience—and then respect that audience by offering them the best writing we possibly can.

Let's consider another piece of writing that both establishes a strong narrator's voice and constructs an audience. Here is the opening of the classic short story "The Yellow Wallpaper" by Charlotte Perkins Gilman. This is the story, as probably some of you know, of a woman who is going mad. She and her family have rented a home in the country to try and find some sort of "rest cure" for what is ailing her, and the idea is that we, the reader, are looking over her shoulder at her diary.

She writes about the time they spend in the house, and over time—as the diary progresses—we watch her descend into insanity as we're reading her words. Here's the opening of her story:

> It is very seldom that mere ordinary people like John and myself secure ancestral halls for the summer. A colonial mansion, a hereditary estate, I would say a haunted house and reach the height of romantic felicity—but that would be asking too much of fate! … There comes John, and I must put this away—he hates to have me write a word.

What do we make of this—particularly after our discussion of Poe's "Black Cat"? Again, we have a first-person speaker who engages the audience by creating the sense of a conversation. The main character is speaking in her own voice, talking directly to someone—in this case, it's her own diary—

and we're drawn into the story by the fact that there's something fascinating about reading something that's meant to be private.

In this case, the audience is drawn in further by the fact that we're witnessing a woman descending into madness while she herself seems completely unaware of this. The story gets weirder and weirder as it continues, with the main character describing how she sees a woman hiding in the pattern of the wallpaper of her room. In the narrator's words, this woman she sees "creeps" around the room at night. It's literally a creepy word that she chooses to convey this.

At the climax of the story, the narrator locks herself in the room with this dreadful yellow wallpaper on the walls, and then we read the following words: "Why there's John at the door! It is no use young man, you can't open it! How he does call and pound! Now he's crying to Jennie for an axe. It would be a shame to break down that beautiful door!"

How do you react to these lines? The final line, about how it's a shame to break down such a beautiful door, helps secure audience reaction in that clearly we can see that she is totally detached from reality, and she has completely lost it if her husband is trying to chop down the door and she's not considering why he might do this, but only, oh, it would be so sad to destroy such a beautiful door. It drives home how altered her mental state is.

But as good as this story is it doesn't quite respect the audience as much as it should. Can you guess why? I'm sure a few of you have already figured this out. Anything here that strikes you as wrong or kind of a false note? First of all, Charlotte Perkins Gilman has hit upon a clever strategy to engage the audience—and that, again, is creating a fiction or idea that we're reading the diary of a woman as she goes crazy. But once you have got that premise established, it's really a problem when we reach the climax of the story—the speaker is locked in her room, and her husband is calling for an axe.

Do we really think that the main character is pausing to write the sentences— "Why there's John at the door!" and "Now he's crying to Jennie for an axe!" What has happened here, clearly, is that we've gone from reading the main character's diary to reading her mind. Here, we get the sense that the author was either maybe hoping we just wouldn't notice, or else she hoped that given the story's other strengths—and it has many—that we'd forgive her this one mistake. Either way, we as an audience might feel a little like the author wasn't offering us her full respect.

There was something similar with the first version of Herman Melville's *Moby Dick*. In the first version of that text, which came out in England, the narrator, Ishmael, tells the story in the first person, but at the conclusion he drowns. Many contemporary critics wanted to know how was it possible for us to know this story if the person who is telling it doesn't survive.

This kind of suspension of disbelief—or what we might call a sort of "limited omniscient approach"—is more acceptable today among most critics, but at the time when Melville's work appeared, it was considered a major flaw. It was so major, in fact, that Melville actually changed the ending in the American edition of *Moby Dick* so that Ishmael survived. Although perhaps he didn't properly anticipate audience reaction with the first version, his decision to actually change the outcome of his story demonstrates the power of an audience and the need to be attentive to them and their demands.

We've talked about respecting your audience, but we should also be aware of how our writing constructs an audience—how our tone, our word choice, our style, all signal this piece of writing is intended for intellectuals, or for children, or for young adults, or specialists in archaeology, or people with a general interest in the Middle Ages.

So, by way of example, let's look at two more pieces of writing that convey the same pieces of information but are really intended for vastly different audiences. These two quotes both describe the victory of William the Conqueror at the Battle of Hastings in 1066.

"The factors that led to William's victory are multiple and range from the mundane to the fantastic. Events quotidian and epic, natural and artificial, converged with extraordinary moments of luck, coincidence, poor planning, and misfortune to produce a final conflict that seems as if it could have been lifted directly from the pages of Homer or Virgil."

Let's stop for a moment and try to come up with some words to describe the intended audience for this passage. This piece of writing is a little bit long. The sentences have some sub-clauses, and there's a kind of style or diction that we might describe as maybe elevated, perhaps, something like that. The syntax with their repetitive pairing of opposing ideas like "quotidian and epic, natural and artificial"—these sort of pairings demonstrate that the writer is really conscious about his or her ability to use language, and so the impression you get from this alone is that the writer is assuming that this is an audience that is accustomed to reading really stylized writing, and that maybe they even expect stylized writing.

Another big clue that probably set off clacks and alarms for you as you're trying to figure out for whom is this intended would be the choice of words like "quotidian," and this is what we used to call, in my day, an SAT word—so vocab that you would need to know in order to do well on the verbal portion of the SAT. "Quotidian," as most of you know, just means the same thing as "everyday" or "not unusual," something like that, but the writer here chose a synonym for that idea that you usually find used for and by people who are writing for those who are highly educated and who are highly educated themselves. It's a way of sort of signaling the author's status, at least in his or her own mind, and then sort of the nature of the audience that he expects to read this.

Another clue about the intended audience is the final line, which references the works of the classical poets Homer and Virgil. By making this reference and not bothering to explain who Homer is or who Virgil is, the writer signals that she or he expects the audience to be familiar with these poets and the epics they composed—so essentially no explanation is necessary. It's kind of a shorthand way of identifying the intended audience.

Now that we've worked through all that, how would you describe the intended audience for this passage? How does the tone, style, and word choice construct that audience or the audience that the writer desires? Again, we can probably agree that the writer expects his or her readers to be highly educated, to know classical works, and the seriousness of the tone also suggests that the readers the author is expecting are people who are, at the very least, really dedicated amateur historians—and more likely, they may be scholars who are conducting research on the topic of William the Conqueror and the Battle Hastings.

In other words, we can all be pretty sure that this is not meant for an audience of 6th graders, nor I don't think we'd expect to find it the beginning of an article that we might see in one of those magazines you see at the supermarket checkout stand. On the other hand, it could be something that would appear in what we might call a more serious publication like the New Yorker or Scientific American, but it might still be inaccessible or uninteresting to the general readership of those magazines. It reads more like the beginning of a scholarly chapter or article—you know, the kind with lots of footnotes, which is another way of signaling who you think you are as an author and who you think your audience is, and we'll talk more about that later.

That's the first example. Here's another example that conveys the same information in a really different way: "William's conquest seemed unlikely at first, but a series of events—ranging from bad weather to bad luck—resulted in his surprising victory. The details of what happened make for a great story; it's one you'll never forget."

Obviously, this second passage is written a little more simply, and it seems to be intended for a much more general audience, and this audience is maybe only slightly interested in the topic, or this audience is new to historical reading. The author's approach, in contrast with the first passage, seems to be to try and draw people in, to intrigue them—you have the use of words like "luck" and "surprising," and, of course, the final phrase—"it's a story you'll never forget"; all of this is working together to try and get the reader interested and to keep that reader reading.

Really, who doesn't like a good story? The author seems to be saying here that historical information can be entertaining if it's presented in the right way. By contrast, that first passage seems to take it as a given that the audience is already interested in the topic and doesn't need to be drawn in or encouraged to read further.

The second example is more simply written with more accessible language, but at the same time, you get the sense that the author is not doing what we might call "writing down" to the audience—in other words, making them feel less educated or informed than the writer is. This author is very skillfully writing to a clearly identified audience, and this seems to be imagined as the broad range of the population, anywhere from elementary school to adulthood. Clues that might exclude potential readers—like the references to Homer and Virgil—those are cut out so that no one who picks this up and starts to read is going to say: "Oh, this isn't for me." The second passage says to almost anyone who starts reading it: "Oh, this could be written for me."

Let's now consider some examples of student essay writing that either miss their targeted audience, misjudge their targeted audience, or in a couple of cases offend their targeted audience. While I'm focusing here for the moment on college-level essays, what I'm discussing applies to any type of writing—from letters to the editor, to magazine articles, to short stories.

Here's an actual passage from an actual student paper discussing a scene from Sir Thomas Malory's Morte Darthur—and as you may remember, this is a version of the story of King Arthur that was written in the Late Middle Ages. In this student paper, I came across the following passage: "Then comes the famous scene when Sir Lancelot gets shot in the butt by the lady huntress while he's sleeping. Now, I know even the best knight of the world needs to get some shuteye now and then, but he's got no business going around sleeping with his rear end exposed like that."

What's wrong with the way the writer imagines the audience of this essay? Probably most of you are thinking that the word "butt" for starters is rarely appropriate in any type of writing, for any audience—and you would be right, although there must be a few exceptions; I can't think of any of them at the moment, but there must be one or two.

In any event, remember, this is an essay for a college-level English class, so the use of slang like this is completely inappropriate. It might be appropriate in a conversation with your college roommate—but not in an essay that you're turning in to your professor. Also, the tone comes across as a little too conversational for a college-level writing class—there should be some degree of formality, as presumably you're writing this paper for a scholar who is something of an expert in this field.

The thing that gets me the most about this passage is that the student is basically right when he says Sir Lancelot has "no business going around sleeping with his rear end exposed." He doesn't. If you're familiar at all with the legend of King Arthur, then you know that Arthur's greatest knight is Lancelot, and the king depends upon him. If a knight is injured in the buttock, then that means he won't be able to ride a horse—and thus, he's really not a knight, and so the king is without the help of his greatest warrior. So, the student has absolutely the right idea, but the execution is all wrong.

The kind of chatty tone also suggests that the writer doesn't fully appreciate or respect the teacher-student relationship—he's writing to me as if we're friends who go out for pizza together, not as if I'm someone who is responsible for instructing him to prepare him for a career once he is out of school.

One thing you should always remember when you're writing a piece that you're going to submit for consideration to anyone is always err on the side of caution; use a more formal tone rather than one that suggests familiarity— and never, never assume that you're doing anyone a favor by giving them your brilliant writing for their consideration. You may hope that they feel that way after they read it, but don't assume that, because this may very well be the most brilliant argument ever made about Sir Lancelot, or the most scintillating magazine article, or the most amazing short story the world has ever seen, and you want the world to get a chance to see it, so don't blow it with inappropriate tone that makes your audience feel like the writer doesn't respect them.

How could we improve this student passage while essentially keeping the main point intact? First, obviously, we've got to change the tone a little— so let's change the first line, the one that says: "Then comes the famous scene when Sir Lancelot gets shot in the butt by the lady huntress while he's sleeping"; let's change that to something like: "The scene in which the sleeping Sir Lancelot is injured by the lady huntress—while humorous—is also very important." That works much better.

The second line, which memorably argued that Sir Lancelot had "no business" sleeping without his armor on, could be altered to say something like: "Although the character of Sir Lancelot has just been through an exhausting ordeal and needs to sleep, his decision to rest in the woods without his armor on is irresponsible. Any injury to his buttock means that he will no longer be able to act as a knight."

This revised version says the same thing as the original, but the tone, the word choice, and structure of the sentences constructs and defines the intended audience as someone with a serious interest in this topic, and not your college roommate who has casually asked you to explain what's so important about a scene in a book you're reading for class.

Let's think back and figure out what are the important things we learned in today's lecture. First off, and I think the most important thing, is the idea that when you write, you construct not only an authorial or a writerly persona, you also construct an audience.

It doesn't matter if you're writing the great American novel, or you're writing a letter to the editor or a non-fiction magazine article, or you're writing in your diary—on some level you have an idea of to whom you're writing. In the lecture before this one, we talked about finding your voice, and today you could say we talked about the other side of that situation, and we addressed the need to understand your listener.

Today we also learned about the different levels of audience. As the examples of Poe's "The Black Cat" and Charlotte Perkins Gilman's "The Yellow Wallpaper" show, you can create a fictional idea of audience within whatever piece you're creating, and this can add to the interest and engagement of the actual audience.

But I think if you only take one thing away from today's lecture, you really need to remember that we discussed how you always need to respect your audience. We talked about how Melville and Gilman, to some degree, didn't respect the intelligence of their audiences—or at least they seemed to hope that their audiences would give them a pass for inconsistencies in their writing.

More serious was the case of the student essay writer, whose tone, word choice, and style all suggested that he was not taking the assignment he had been given very seriously. As the two examples of the paragraph about William the Conqueror showed, it's entirely possible to convey the same information to two very different audiences—in this case, one that's made up of specialists and scholars, and another that's made up of the general population who might not be all that interested in the topic to start with.

In the exercises that accompany today's lecture, you'll be asked to convey the same basic pieces of information to some very different audiences, and this is a variation on the exercises from last time, when I asked you to convey the same pieces of information but as if they were being written or described by very different kinds of writers or speakers.

Now that we've spent two lectures talking about writerly identity and audience, we're going to turn our attention in the next lecture to mastering these skills as you construct an argument. In particular, we'll devote Lecture 6 to effective strategies for starting an argument, and we'll enhance our discussion with analysis of some of the greatest essays in the English and American literary traditions—namely Jonathan Swift's "A Modest Proposal" and Henry David Thoreau's "Civil Disobedience." We'll analyze the opening of these arguments to see what makes them so effective and then construct a tool kit to help you transfer these skills to your own writing.

The Art of the Essay—How to Start
Lecture 6

You want to make your opening as effective and engaging as possible so that people will keep reading.

In this lecture—and the three that follow it—we'll look more closely at methods for securing the kind of responses you want for your writing. We'll do this by shifting our focus to the ways successful arguments are constructed: how to open an argument as well as how to organize, support, and conclude it.

We'll start by evaluating and critiquing the opening of one of the most famous argumentative essays in the English literary tradition: Jonathan Swift's "A Modest Proposal," in which Swift sets up a satirical argument that the Irish should adopt a policy of eating their own children as a solution to the problems of widespread poverty and hunger. Here's his first sentence:

> It is a melancholy object to those who walk through this great town or travel in the country, when they see the streets, the roads, and cabin doors, crowded with beggars of the female sex, followed by three, four, or six children, all in rags and importuning every passenger for alms.

Jonathan Swift, whose satirical essay is a model of effective argumentation.

We haven't gotten to the satirical suggestion yet, but we do see in these opening lines a very successful blend of description and explanation that will subsequently serve as the foundation for his argument. You know from this single sentence what the problem is and why it's a topic worth making an argument about. So right away, Swift has our attention and probably our sympathy. He proceeds to add both specificity and substance to his opening:

> Whoever could find out a fair, cheap, and easy method of making these children sound, useful members of the commonwealth, would deserve so well of the public as to have his statue set up for a preserver of the nation.

Here we have a specific articulation of what's at stake—nothing less than the future of the commonwealth! So now we understand the problem, and we've been given some idea of how grateful the whole British Empire would be to the person who found a solution—you can imagine that in the minds of the reader, ideas for possibilities for becoming this savior are starting to churn. As we'll see, Swift's tongue is planted more-or-less firmly in cheek at this point, but he's clearly demonstrated an effective strategy for opening an argument: description of the topic at hand and explanation of its importance.

Right away, Swift has our attention and probably our sympathy.

I also want you to notice that Swift doesn't lard his opening with melodramatic, universal claims or unnecessary generalities. In other words, he doesn't waste time trying to make his subject seem important by giving us vague, empty statements such as "Hunger is a serious problem that needs to be solved." While these kinds of general claims may have some element of truth to them, they don't do anything to establish the importance of this particular argument about this particular instance of poverty and hunger. By firmly fixing his argument in a specific time and place and making a substantial claim about what's at stake, Swift gives his audience a compelling reason to keep reading.

I'd also like to point out the degree and type of details Swift includes in his opening. We get some indication of how bad the situation is (the children are dressed in rags), but he holds off on giving us a full-scale account of the horrors. He recognizes that an effective opening requires only a few, carefully chosen, details; they must add substance to the introduction but not become the main focus of the reader's attention. Here's what he says a few lines later:

> I have been assured by a very knowing American of my acquaintance in London, that a young healthy child well nursed is at a year old a most delicious, nourishing, and wholesome food, whether stewed, roasted, baked, or boiled; and I make no doubt that it will equally serve in a fricassee or a ragout.

So what, then, is the "modest proposal" of Swift's title? Why, to have the Irish eat their own children of course! Obviously, this is a satirical essay, and he's actually commenting on the other offensive proposals that have been put forth to deal with the desperate situation of the Irish at the time. But for all its satire, Swift's essay is a model of effective argumentation, and we can learn a lot from examining it more closely.

So let's see if we can use Swift's strategy to make our own openings more effective; in other words, let's see if we can craft an introduction to an argument that balances a specific description of a topic with a substantial explanation of its significance. And let's see if we can do it without falling back on generalizations or distracting details.

Imagine you've submitted a request to your health insurance provider for coverage of a particular medical procedure—only to have that claim denied as medically unnecessary. You need to craft an appeal letter to your insurer that offers a compelling argument. Let's focus on just the first four or five sentences. Your goal should be to balance a description of your situation with an explanation of its importance. Here's an example of what *not* to do when faced with this kind of writing task:

> I am suffering from a skin condition which started during an especially stressful project at work (I am currently on medical leave because of this condition). My primary-care physician, prescribed a corticosteroid, but it didn't work. I recently got in to see a dermatologist, and she prescribed a UV-light treatment. I submitted a claim for this treatment, but it was rejected as medically unnecessary. I am requesting an expedited review of the decision.

What are the drawbacks here? First, while the writer does provide specific details, they end up describing a personal medical history rather than the main problem at hand. A few personal medical details are useful in this situation, but too many distract from the writer's main goal. Also, while the writer does try to explain that the skin condition is a significant problem and that its cause may have something to do with stress, we come away with no clear idea of what's at stake in this particular instance. Let's try rewriting these first few lines:

> I'm writing to appeal your denial of coverage of a UV-light treatment for a diagnosed skin condition; this treatment was prescribed by my dermatologist. Your denial states that the procedure is medically unnecessary. I am requesting an expedited review of this case as I am currently on medical leave from my job due to the above-mentioned skin condition and will be unable to return until I receive treatment.

This version provides fewer personal medical details, but the ones that are included are specifically relevant to the problem of denial of coverage. They do not distract from the primary purpose of the letter. We also receive a clearer sense of what's at stake and thus have more persuasive evidence for an expedited review of the case. In a case like this, the opening can make or break you. Don't start out bland and vague and save the firepower for several paragraphs later—you've got to persuade your reader early on that at the very least, it is worth it to keep reading. ■

Suggested Reading

Griffith, *Writing Essays about Literature.*

Lunsford and Ruszkiewicz, *Everything's an Argument.*

Ramage, Bean, and Johnson, *Writing Arguments.*

Exercises

1. Imagine you've submitted a claim to your health insurance provider for a particular clinical procedure only to have that claim denied as "medically unnecessary." Draft the opening two paragraphs of an appeal letter meant to convince your insurer that the procedure must be covered. Try to balance a specific description of the situation with an explanation of its importance. Avoid general or universal claims. Gauge the effectiveness of your opening by using the "what?/so what?" litmus test discussed in the lecture.

2. Look at the introduction to an old e-mail you've written—one that attempts to make an argument about something—and measure its effectiveness using the "what?/so what?" litmus test. Then use the strategies and examples we've studied to help draft a more specific and substantial version of that introduction. Use the "what?/so what?" test to determine if your new version is more powerful and persuasive than the original.

The Art of the Essay—How to Start
Lecture 6—Transcript

Welcome back. In the previous lecture, we looked at some of the most crucial elements of effective writing. These included some themes that we're going to return to repeatedly in this course, and they begin with, first of all, understanding and respecting your audience. Other things that you need to pay attention to include identifying what information you need to convey to different readers, how you want to convey it—and finally, shaping the response of those readers to your work so that you can better achieve your writing goals.

Last time we studied the strategies that some successful fiction writers use to secure particular kinds of responses from readers, and in the exercises at the end of the lecture, you had the opportunity to hone your own ability to both identify and write for different audiences.

More specifically, in the exercises for last time I asked you to convey the news of your beloved Uncle Wilfred's death to four different audiences for four different purposes: First, I wanted you to try and write about your uncle as an obituary for the local newspaper; second, I wanted you to try and tell about his death in a letter to a good friend of yours who had met your uncle a few times; third, I wanted you to convey this news to a scholarship committee that you wanted to convince to create a scholarship in your uncle's memory; and finally, I asked you to try and imagine how you would write about this if you were getting in touch with an old navy buddy of your uncle's and this navy buddy had not yet been told of his death.

You may not have fully recognized it as you were completing these exercises, but each one required you to create a balance of description and explanation—description of the facts related to your uncle's death and explanation of that death's meaning.

Obviously, of course, both the descriptive and explanatory qualities of each of these four pieces of writing differed depending on the audience and the purpose—and this means how you understood and approached your readers and what responses you wanted to secure from them are going to differ based on your understanding of the situation.

For example, your Uncle Wilfred's old navy buddy certainly would have liked to hear about how much you loved to listen to your uncle tell the story of the time they both had too much to drink and got tattoos, but you can probably also imagine that when you were contacting the scholarship committee, this story was not high on the list of information you wanted them to know about your uncle. You would be much more inclined in a case like this to mention your uncle's wartime bravery rather than his antics between combat episodes.

In this lecture—and the three that follow it—we'll look more closely at methods for securing the kind of responses you want for your argument. We're going to do this by shifting our focus to the ways successful arguments are constructed. We're going to talk about how to open an argument as well as how to organize, support, and conclude it.

We're going to start by evaluating and critiquing the openings of two of the most famous argumentative essays in the English and American literary traditions—these are Jonathan Swift's "A Modest Proposal," which we have already spent a little time with, and Henry David Thoreau's classic "Resistance to Civil Government," and this is a text that you probably know by its more common title of "Civil Disobedience."

Just as a reminder, here's the first sentence from Jonathan Swift's "A Modest Proposal" in which Swift sets up the satirical argument that the Irish should adopt a policy of essentially eating their own children as a solution to the problems of widespread poverty and hunger. He says: "It is a melancholy object to those who walk through this great town or travel in the country, when they see the streets, the roads, and cabin doors, crowded with beggars of the female sex, followed by three, four, or six children, all in rags and importuning every passenger for an alms."

Obviously, we haven't gotten to the satirical part yet—there's absolutely nothing humorous about the picture Swift is painting here—but what we do see in these opening lines is a very successful blend of description and explanation that will subsequently serve as the foundation for his entire argument. In other words, this opening paragraph is really a model of how to combine explanation and description because you know from this single sentence what the problem is (Swift is describing mothers and children begging in the streets of Dublin), and also you know why it's a topic worth making an argument about (he explains, quite explicitly, every person is affected, whether you are a beggar or someone to be begged from—and moreover, this situation holds true he says whether you're in the city or the country). So, it's a universal problem—it's everyone's concern. So right away, Swift has our attention and probably our sympathy—this seems like an issue to which we should be paying attention, obviously.

Swift then proceeds to add both specificity and substance to this opening, and he says: "Whoever could find out a fair, cheap, and easy method of making these children sound, useful members of the commonwealth, would deserve so well of the public as to have his statue set up for a preserver of the nation."

Here, Swift has done a great job of articulating what's at stake here—it's nothing less than the future of the commonwealth! Oh, my goodness! So, definitely, we need to pay attention. We also get a reference to just how substantial the reward would be for anyone who could offer a solution to the problem—and seriously, who wouldn't want their own statue as the savior of the nation. I know I would. I would enjoy having a statue. But now we've understood the problem, and we've been given some idea of how grateful the whole British Empire would be to the person who found a solution—so, you can imagine that in the minds of the readers, ideas for possibilities for becoming this savior are starting to churn.

But as we'll see in a moment and as many of you already know, Swift's tongue is planted more-or-less firmly in his cheek at this point; nonetheless, even though this is satire, he's clearly demonstrated an effective strategy for opening an argument: He describes the subject or the topic at hand; he gives an explanation of its importance, and then he rounds it out with specificity and substance.

I often refer to this strategy as taking what I call an "expository" approach to an argument—and this means that your introduction is striking a productive balance between telling me what you're writing about and showing me why it matters. You can remember those two words: "telling" and "showing." I often tell my students that as they write they should be thinking about the "So what?" question. In other words, after you've done a beautiful job, say, imagining why or explaining why the character of Mr. Bennet in Jane Austen's *Pride and Prejudice* is really a cruel man and not a sympathetic figure, I might ask you "Okay, so what? Why is that important? Why should we care?" If you are always trying to keep that "So what?" question in mind as you write, your work is going to end up being all the stronger for it.

But going back to Swift for a moment—I also want you to notice that Swift does not lard his opening or stuff it with melodramatic, universal claims or really unnecessary generalities. In other words, he's not wasting time trying to make his subject seem important by giving us vague, empty statements, and we've all probably read these or written these. Sometime in the past we have come across statements like this or produced them ourselves— statements like: "Poverty has plagued human society since the days of cavemen" or "Hunger is a serious problem that needs to be solved."

Yes, true, this is correct, but these kinds of universal or general claims while they have an element of truth to them don't do anything to establish the importance of this particular argument about this particular instance of poverty and hunger. By firmly fixing his argument in a specific time and a specific place and then making a substantial claim about what's at stake, why it matters, the "So what?" question, Swift gives his audience a compelling reason to keep reading.

I also want to take a moment to point out the degree and the type of details Swift includes in his opening. We get some indication of how bad the situation is because obviously the children are dressed in rags, but Swift shows some restraint. He holds off on giving us a full-scale account of the horrors. He recognizes that an effective opening requires a few details, but these have to be chosen really, really carefully; they've got to add substance to the introduction, but not so much that they become the main focus of the reader's attention.

For example, if Swift had gone on and on about the lice in the children's hair, or the open sores on their shins, or he'd added any other number of really dramatic details, it might have been too much and caused the reader to stop reading. It's like those ads on TV that show you images of abused animals in order to try and get you to support a charity that helps pets who have been mistreated. I am an animal lover, and in theory I fully support charitable work designed to alleviate the suffering of abused animals; however, I do not actually know the name of the charity that produced these ads because I personally find them so distressing that I change the channel whenever the ads come on. Essentially, what Swift is doing here is he's calling our attention to the problem, but he doesn't give us so much information that we want to change the channel. He's given us just enough to make us care—and as we'll see, he's given us just enough to set us up for the joke that he's about to play on us without making us angry that we have invested too much of our sympathy or too much of our interest in this cause. Here's what he says a few lines later, and you may remember this from earlier in this lecture series: "I have been assured by a very knowing American of my acquaintance in London, that a young healthy child well nursed is at a year old a most delicious, nourishing, and wholesome food, whether stewed, roasted, baked, or boiled; and I make no doubt that it will equally serve in a fricassee or a ragout."

So what, then, is the modest proposal of Swift's title? As we've already discussed, it is to have the Irish eat their own children. Obviously, this is a satirical essay, and he is not really suggesting this—what he is doing is commenting on the other offensive proposals that have been put forth to deal with what was a really desperate situation of the Irish people at this time. But even though it's satire, Swift's essay is a model of really effective, good, compelling argumentation, and so we can learn a lot from it by examining it more closely.

Let's see if we can use Swift's strategy to make our own openings more effective—in other words, let's see if we can craft an introduction to an argument that balances a specific description of a topic with a substantial explanation of its significance, and let's see if we can do it without falling back on universal claims and generalizations or unnecessary and distracting details.

Let's take this for an example: Imagine you've submitted a request to your health insurance provider for coverage of a particular medical procedure, and let's imagine that the health insurance company has come back and said: "We're going to deny this claim; it's medically unnecessary." Now you're in the position where you need to craft an appeal letter to your insurer that offers a compelling argument in support of your case. Just take a moment, and don't try to compose the entire letter—just think in your head maybe what the first few sentences might say or what the major points are that you would want to convey as quickly as possible in this letter. Your goal here, again, should be to balance a description of your situation with an explanation of its importance. We have all been in a situation similar to this I imagine and had to craft a kind of appeal letter, and it can be really difficult to separate from your own emotions and what you think is important in a letter like this from what your audience is going to respond to in a positive way in terms of your making an argument.

Here's an example of what not to do when you're faced with this kind of writing task:

> I am suffering from a skin condition, which started during an especially stressful project at work (I am currently on medical leave because of this condition). My primary care physician prescribed a corticosteroid, but it didn't work. I recently got in to see a dermatologist, and she prescribed a UV-light treatment. I submitted a claim for this treatment, but it was rejected as medically unnecessary. I am requesting an expedited review of the decision.

What are the drawbacks here? Where does this writing sample fall a little bit short? First, while the writer does provide specific details, they end up describing a personal medical history rather than the main problem at hand. Remember, you have to try and separate out what is most important to you or most pressing to you when you're writing—and what is going to be the most effective thing in terms of making your argument persuasive. So, here the main focus should be conveying to the health insurance company the need for coverage of a particular procedure. A few personal or medical details are useful in this situation, but too many distract from the writer's main goal.

Also, what's happening here is that while the writer does try to explain that the skin condition is a significant problem and that its cause may have something to do with stress, we don't really come away with a clear idea of what's ultimately at stake in this particular instance. If this were the opening in a research paper on skin conditions, the reference to stress might be useful in establishing the argument's importance, but that's not the case here. The fact that the skin condition came about as a result of a stressful period in the writer's life isn't that important. What's important is that there is a condition, and it needs to be treated.

Let's try rewriting these first few lines, and I'll ask you to expand on this in the exercises at the end of today's lecture. You'll be doing something very similar. Here's a different version of this same letter:

> I'm writing to appeal your denial of coverage of a UV-light treatment for a diagnosed skin condition; this treatment was prescribed by my dermatologist. Your denial states that the procedure is medically unnecessary. I am requesting an expedited review of this case as I am currently on medical leave from my job due to the above-mentioned skin condition and will be unable to return to work until I receive treatment.

So, this version is a little better. What is better about it? First off, it provides fewer personal/medical details, but the ones that are included are specifically relevant to the problem of the denial of coverage. They don't distract at all from the primary purpose of the letter—and, in fact, they help make the argument; they make the case a little more clear, a little more important in terms of the eyes of the insurance company. They're going to see that this is a pressing matter.

So, we receive a clearer sense, too, of what is at stake—the writer is not going to be able to return to work until this treatment is received—and thus, you've got more persuasive evidence here for an expedited review of the case. This is why it has to be an expedited review—I've got to get back to my job, so it has to happen soon. In a case like this and several other situations, the opening can make or break you.

The person at the insurance company who is reading this does not have time to sort through details of your very stressful year—this may be really pertinent in your mind, but trust me it is not at all important in the mind of the person on the other end who is reading your letter. Likewise, I've heard from any number of magazine editors that they often can tell if an article is going to be worth considering after reading just the first paragraph—you want your reader to keep going, not toss your piece aside. In other words, don't start out bland and vague and save the firepower for several paragraphs later—you've got to persuade your reader early on that at the very least, it's worth it to keep reading.

Let's turn to another example of how to balance description and explanation in the opening of an argument. This time we're going to take a look at Thoreau's "Civil Disobedience." Here's one of the most famous passages from this text:

> I heartily accept the motto, "That government is best which governs least"; and I should like to see it acted up to more rapidly and systematically. Carried out, it finally amounts to this, which also I believe—"That government is best which governs not at all"; and when men are prepared for it, that will be the kind of government which they will have.

You can see in Thoreau's lines here a combination of description and explanation that adds up to a very specific and substantive argument about the role of government. In this case, what he's doing is making an argument against government's role in bringing about the war between Mexico and the United States (which lasted from 1846 to 1848), and this war also resulted in Mexico giving up a third of its territory, including most of what is now the Southwest of the U.S. and California.

There's absolutely no mistaking what Thoreau's topic is and what view he—and by extension we in his opinion—should have of it. Whatever happens next in this essay (and we're going to look at some of that, what happens next in the following three lectures), Thoreau has already established a foundation for a successful argument, and he's done this by describing a specific issue and making a substantive claim about it. We might not agree with his claim, but the clarity of his position probably makes us interested enough to continue reading—in other words, we're not going to be inclined to just throw the piece away and say: "Oh, I don't want to read this." There's enough here that is interesting and engaging that we're going to want to continue on.

Again, you've probably noticed I'm emphasizing the terms "specific" and "substantive" several times in this lecture. An introduction really needs both qualities in order to be successful. It has to be specific enough that we aren't left wondering what the scope of the argument will be. A good rule of thumb is if it takes more than one or two paragraphs to establish the subject and the range or the scope of your argument, you can be pretty sure that your introduction needs some revision.

Additionally, the opening has to offer enough substance—some indication of what's at stake for the audience—so that we won't be forced to ask ourselves why we should care about it. We may not have a complete sense of the claim's substance, and you want to save something admittedly for as your argument unfolds, and so more of the substance is going to come later— but the introduction shouldn't leave us wondering why the writer bothered picking up a pen in the first place or putting his or her fingers on keyboard. We need at least some idea of why we should care. We need a hint that's going to keep us going and continue reading.

To better illustrate what I mean when I talk about specificity and substance, let's look at some negative examples, and these would be ineffective openings that—unlike Thoreau's—suffer from excessive or really general descriptions of their topics, and they fail to provide a clear, substantive explanation as to why these topics matter. So what? Why should we care? Here's one of these negative examples:

> Human beings traditionally have relied on government to defend against outside enemies and protect individual rights. In recent years, people also have wanted government to provide them with economic support and financial security. The extent to which a government should address the economic advancement and financial security of its citizens can be a divisive issue.

What's your initial reaction to this opening? Do you want to keep reading? There is nothing inherently wrong with the statements—we might very well read them, and nod politely, and say: "Why yes, that's all true."

But there's also nothing particularly moving or striking about these statements either, and they're certainly not effective as an opening to an argument. In other words, after we finish nodding politely and saying: "Yes, yes, that's all true," we might then go on to ask: "But what's your point?" Again, we're back to the "So what?" question.

Or if we really want to get specific about it, we can call this way of evaluating the effectiveness of an introduction the "What?/So what?" test. This means, as I suggested earlier, that a successful introduction should tell me what the argument is and then why I should care enough to continue reading (the "So what?").

This example I just gave you offers a partial response to the "What?" question—so we know the writer is trying to say something about the traditional and contemporary roles of government—but the statements are really general, and the actual goal and the context of the writer's argument are really unclear. What government or governments is the writer concerned with? Is there a problem with the more-expansive nature of current government, or is it a good thing? You really can't tell from this passage alone.

If we want to get really picky, what does the writer mean by "recent"? In the last six months? In the last 20 years? "Recent" is a pretty open-ended adjective if we're talking about the whole sweep of human history. I'm a medievalist, so to me "recent" could mean the last couple of centuries or more. So, the fact that we're left with so many unanswered "What?/So what?" questions shows that what this introduction relies on too much is general description without offering a specific, substantial foundation for an argument.

Let's look at a more effective version of this intro that answers both the "What?" and the "So what?" questions, and here it is:

Government in the U.S. has been most successful when it has limited itself to national defense and protection of individual freedoms. While the U.S. government also can do much to provide economic benefits for its citizens ... any long-term attention it gives to the propagation and preservation of individual economic advancement ultimately undercuts its most important tasks: securing the country against outside enemies and guaranteeing the liberties of its citizens.

So, what's better about this opening? In this version, we receive both a more specific description of the context and the content of the argument as well as a clearer indication of the writer's position. We know the specific historical setting—the United States, which by definition really can't cover more than a couple hundred years or so and is also confined to a specific geographic location—moreover, we're given at least some indication as to why we should care about this piece of writing. We may totally disagree with the author's perspective on the role of the U.S. government, but we can't dismiss the argument out-of-hand due to a lack of substance; it has substance.

As we've seen, an effective introduction is one that uses a combination of description and explanation to make a clear, specific claim about a subject while also establishing the meaning or the significance of the argument. The timing and the placement of the claim is important as well. The sooner a writer articulates the claim—ideally within the first paragraph, although sometimes you can get away with moving that down into the second paragraph, within the first two paragraphs—the sooner this is articulated, the more likely the writer is to catch and hold our attention over the course of the entire argument.

Conversely, any delay or deferral of a main claim can significantly weaken the writer's chances of persuading us to continue reading along. No matter what it is that you're writing—if it's a short story, a magazine article, an essay for class, a letter to the editor—you want people to keep going past the first few sentences. If you didn't, why would you bother writing in the first place?

So, what do we take away from today's lecture? We've seen how a good opening is both specific and substantive, and it needs to pass the "What?/So what?" test—in other words, we need to understand what the piece is about and why we should care. I'm going to ask you to put this to the test in the exercises for today's lecture. In the two exercises I've given you I ask you to craft an imaginary or hypothetical claim to an insurance provider and also to consider an e-mail on how the "What?/So what?" test can work to make both those pieces of writing more effective.

A good opening is a wonderful thing, but it's not the only element you'll need to craft an effective argument. Yes, you want to make your opening as effective and engaging as possible so that people will keep reading. What you don't want is to lose your reader's attention just a few paragraphs later.

A written piece with a great opening and ho-hum support will come across, in many cases, as just plain lazy—"Well, I hooked 'em with this great opening" a writer might think, "and now I can just phone in the rest." Trust me—this will not engender good will on the part of your audience. As we'll see in the next three lectures, the strategies you use to organize, support, and conclude your argument are just as crucial in determining its overall success. Next time, we'll focus on the issue of organization.

How to Organize an Argument
Lecture 7

[A sequence or series], like all devices, has to be used with restraint. If you do too many sequences, you might as well be writing a grocery list.

Our last lecture dealt with introductions, but even the strongest introduction can't save a written argument that lacks coherence. By examining how arguments are structured and presented, you'll learn how to more effectively guide your readers from one point to the next and how to avoid structural flaws that may obscure your argument. In order to do this, we spend some more time with Jonathan Swift's "A Modest Proposal."

How do you organize a piece of writing? You might have lots of things you want to say and no clue how to get those things onto the page in coherent form. With some kinds of writing, a chronological structure works well—you start at the beginning and go on to the end. But sometimes, the most important parts of a text might be in the middle, and you don't want your readers to have to hunt for them. Another perfectly acceptable way to organize an argument is the basic five-paragraph model, expanded as necessary. In this model, your first paragraph states your main claim; paragraphs two, three, and four (or however many you need) each offer supporting points for that idea; and the final paragraph reiterates your main claim.

These approaches can work well as a basic argumentative structure, but I've found that the best way to guide your readers is to establish the key terms of your argument as early as possible and then return to and expand on those ideas throughout the piece. This kind of approach can easily work in concert with the basic five-paragraph or chronological approaches, but it adds a layer of sophistication to your argument that might otherwise be lacking.

Once the key terms and ideas of your argument are in place, the process of organization becomes a matter of consistently referring back to, linking, and developing those terms and ideas. What do I mean by key terms? Let's look at a classic example to get an idea. We recall from earlier lectures that Swift's "A Modest Proposal" makes a satirical argument that the Irish should adopt a policy of eating their children as a way to end poverty and hunger. Let's take a look at how Swift establishes the terms of his argument:

> I have been assured by a very knowing American of my acquaintance in London, that a young healthy child well nursed is at a year old a most delicious, nourishing, and wholesome food, whether stewed, roasted, baked, or boiled; and I make no doubt that it will equally serve in a fricassee or a ragout.

Obviously one of Swift's greatest challenges is to convince his audience to put aside the notion of children as children and replace it with the notion of children as food. And not just any old grub, but rather quite tasty food that can be served, Swift assures us, at least four different ways, maybe six if you're venturesome enough to try a fricassee or a ragout. To press this new association even further, Swift would have his audience know the following:

> A child will make two dishes at an entertainment for friends; and when the family dines alone, the fore or hind quarter will make a reasonable dish, and seasoned with a little pepper or salt will be very good boiled on the fourth day, especially in winter.

The lesson we can take from Swift is that there are innumerable ways to define a word and the concepts associated with it—even a word as seemingly straightforward as "child." In fact, the very absurdity of Swift's attempts to redefine a child as a food source is evidence of how good writers can—and must—convince audiences to see the topic on their terms. Of course, once you've committed yourself to redefining a word or concept, you must follow through by reiterating and developing the new connections you want your audience to make. That is to say, once you've introduced them to your language, you have to keep speaking it and expanding the vocabulary. Swift is an expert at using this strategy to organize his argument. He goes on to say:

> I have already computed the charge of nursing a beggar's child ... to be about two shillings per annum, rags included; and I believe no gentleman would repine to give ten shillings for the carcass of a good fat child, which, as I have said, will make four dishes of excellent nutritive meat.

Swift continues to affirm the child-as-food connection, but now he adds an extra twist. He takes an entirely logical next step by addressing the issue of economics and commodification—and he does this by running his own cost-benefit analysis of child as livestock. By this point, we're so far onto Swift's turf and so deeply immersed in his language, terms, and meanings that we cannot help but follow along. We've already accepted his notion of child as food and made it our normative definition (or at least suspended our disbelief). In order to keep going and follow his logic, we have to recognize that this is a deliberate exercise in absurdity—but we keep going because through this satire, an important point is being made.

You should approach the organizing process as though you are trying to teach your readers a new language with its own particular vocabulary and grammar.

So, organizing an argument requires you to establish some sense of continuity as you move from one point to the next—that's a basic premise of any writing guide. But establishing that continuity involves more than making sure you have effective transitions between paragraphs and points. Rather, you should approach the organizing process as though you are trying to teach your readers a new language with its own particular vocabulary and grammar—one for which you've set and developed the terms.

In addition to establishing the key terms and ideas of an argument, the process of organization should involve careful attention to transitions. If the links from one point to the next aren't there—or aren't strong enough—the argument won't be as effective as it could be. The easiest, and most successful, strategy for crafting transitions is the repetition-variation approach. By that I mean taking a word or phrase from the end of one paragraph or section of an argument and using it, preferably with some slight variation, as the beginning of the next paragraph or section. Another form of transition—somewhat less elegant but certainly effective when used judiciously—is the sequence or series. A sequence or series can be a dynamic form of transition, but you need to be careful about boring your readers with too many lists.

By this point, you've learned how to begin an argument, and you've acquired some strategies for organizing your writing. But even the most engaging opening and the cleverest structure will be useless if you don't adequately support your argument—if you don't tell your reader, as clearly as possible, "so what?" In our next lecture, we'll look at strategies for supporting your claims and making your argument as persuasive as possible. ■

Suggested Reading

Griffith, *Writing Essays about Literature.*

Lunsford and Ruszkiewicz, *Everything's an Argument.*

Ramage, Bean, and Johnson, *Writing Arguments.*

Exercises

1. Look back at the last written argument you crafted—whether a grant proposal, a business presentation, or a letter to your boss requesting a raise. Did you include a paragraph or section early in the piece that helped establish and define the terms and ideas of the argument in a way that was favorable to you or that supported your main claim? Did you refer back to and develop those terms and ideas as your argument unfolded? If not, draft such a paragraph and include it in the piece. If so, try revising the paragraph or section and making it even stronger.

2. Go back to the paragraphs I asked you to draft during the lecture about your idea of "government"—how you think it should be defined and what ideas you believe should be associated with it. Study the transitions you made from one paragraph or section to the next. How did you link your points and ideas? Try revising one of those transitions using either or both of the two strategies we've studied (repetition-variation and sequence/series).

How to Organize an Argument
Lecture 7—Transcript

Welcome back. In the previous lecture, we discussed strategies for crafting more effective introductions to written arguments. We learned how to balance description and explanation or how to successfully convey a topic to our audiences even as we show them why it matters.

We also learned how to add specificity and substance to our claims. You may remember I used those words "specificity" and "substance" quite a bit last time. We learned how to do this through careful use of details and by avoiding generalizations and universalizing statements—statements like: "Since the beginning of time, humans have written poetry." Right? That's a statement that may be true—but way too general. Finally, we practiced using the "What?/So what?" test to gauge the strength of our introductions and identify ways to make them even more powerful. In other words, you want your readers to know what your topic is and why they should care—and that is the "So what?" part.

But as I suggested at the end of our last lecture, even the strongest introduction can't save a written argument that is disjointed or lacks coherence. If you're wandering all over the place in your writing—just sort of writing your thoughts down as they come to you without any sort of plan or organizational model to guide you—you're going to lose your readers' attention pretty quickly—and, of course, that's the last thing you want to have happen.

By examining how arguments are structured and presented, you'll learn how to more effectively guide your readers from one point to the next and how to avoid structural flaws and inconsistencies that may distort or obscure the main purpose or goal of your argument. You want to make sure that your reader understands what it is you're trying to say and they're not trying to work so hard to figure it out. In order to do this, we're going to spend some time with our old friend Jonathan Swift, whom we've talked about quite a bit up till this point and his essay "A Modest Proposal." We're also going to talk some more about Thoreau's classic essay "Civil Disobedience," and we focused on Thoreau a little more last time. Today, we're also going to spend some time with Thomas Paine's "Common Sense," and this will help with understanding the issue of organization of an essay.

How do you organize a piece of writing? You might have lots of things you want to say and no clue how to get those things onto the page in some kind of coherent form. With some kinds of writing, a chronological structure can work really well—you start at the beginning; you write through the middle, and you go on to the end. But sometimes, the most important parts of a text might be in the middle, and you don't want your readers to have to hunt for the best bits—in other words, you don't want them to be buried and hard to find.

So, chronology is one way to organize a piece of writing. Another perfectly acceptable and workable way is to follow some version of the basic 5-paragraph model—and you can expand it if you need to do more than 5. You could use the same model in 7 or 8 paragraphs or even 10. A lot of you are probably already familiar with this model. In this situation, the idea is that your first paragraph states your main claim. Paragraphs 2, 3, and 4 (or however many you need) each offer supporting points for that main claim or idea that you stated in the first paragraph, and then the final paragraph reiterates your main point. Or, if you want to boil this down even more, as one colleague of mine says, the basic form of this model is just three steps: Number one: Tell your reader what you're going to tell them. Number two: Tell them. Number three: Tell them what you just told them.

These approaches can work well as a basic argumentative structure, but I've found that the best way to guide your readers from one point to the next is really to establish what I call the "key terms" of your argument (and you should do this as early as possible)—and then you can return to, and expand on, these key terms, on these main ideas throughout the piece. As one of my own instructors used to say: "Get them on your turf; make them speak your language." This approach can really work very nicely and easily with the basic five-paragraph or a chronological approach, but using key terms adds a layer of sophistication to your argument that might otherwise be lacking.

Once the key terms and ideas of your argument are in place (so, in other words, once you've got the audience on your turf), then the process of organization becomes a matter of consistently referring back to, linking, and developing those terms and ideas—in other words, as you write, you are helping the audience learn to speak your language. Right about now you're probably wondering: "Okay, what does she mean by key terms? She said it at least seven times up to this point." Let's look at some classic examples to get an idea of what this means, and I think this is the easiest way to understand what I mean when I say "key terms" or "key ideas."

First, let's go back to Swift, and let's look at how Swift establishes the terms of his argument in "A Modest Proposal." By now, you probably can recall quite easily that this essay is a satirical argument about how the Irish should adopt a policy of eating their own children as a way to end poverty and hunger. You might remember that we've discussed this one passage in a few lectures, but just in case you're not thinking of it right now or the details have escaped you, here is the passage that I really want you to pay attention to today. It begins:

> I have been assured by a very knowing American of my acquaintance in London, that a young healthy child well nursed is at a year old a most delicious, nourishing, and wholesome food, whether stewed, roasted, baked, or boiled; and I make no doubt that it will serve equally in a fricassee or a ragout.

Obviously one of Swift's greatest challenges—and again, we're approaching this with tongue firmly planted in cheek—is to convince his audience to put aside the notion of children-as-children and replace that notion with children-as-food—and they're not just any old grub, but rather quite tasty food that can be served, Swift assures us, at least four different ways: stewed, roasted, baked, or boiled (and maybe six different ways if you're venturesome enough to try a fricassee or a ragout). To press this new association even further, Swift wants his audience to know a little bit more, so he continues on, and he says: "A child will make two dishes at an entertainment for friends; and when the family dines alone, the fore or hind quarter will make a reasonable dish, and seasoned with a little pepper or salt will be very good boiled on the fourth day, especially in winter."

The lesson we can take from Swift is that there are innumerable ways to define a word and the concepts associated with it—even a word as seemingly straightforward as "child." In fact, the very absurdity of Swift's attempts to redefine a child as a food source is evidence of how good writers can—and I would argue must—convince audiences to see the topic on their terms. Unlinking a word from one set of meanings and associating it with an entirely different set of ideas can be an extremely effective way to catch and hold your reader's attention—and it can also be a way that you convince them to see the world in a different light. So Swift's key term or idea here is child or children, but the language he uses to discuss children—all of these terms are drawn from the world of cuisine and cooking. So his key terms— the world of cooking—and child is detached from what we might think of as its typical key terms.

Once you've committed yourself to redefining a word or concept, you have to follow through by reiterating and developing the new connections you want your audience to make—that is to say, once you've introduced them to your language, you have to keep speaking it and expanding the vocabulary. Swift is an expert at using this strategy to organize his argument, and he continues on, and he says:

> I have already computed the charge of nursing a beggar's child …
> to be about two shillings per annum, rags included; and I believe
> no gentleman would repine to give ten shillings for the carcass of
> a good fat child, which, as I have said, will make four dishes of
> excellent nutritive meat. Those who are more thrifty (as I must
> confess the times require) may flay the carcass; the skin of which
> artificially dressed will make admirable gloves for ladies, and
> summer boots for fine gentlemen.

Swift continues to affirm the child-as-food connection, but now he adds an extra twist. Those of you who are familiar with the essay no doubt recognize the move that he's making. For the rest of you, think for a moment. What new set of terms and ideas is Swift bringing into the mix? What new language does he seem to be using?

That's right. After establishing this new definition of the child as food, Swift takes what is now an entirely logical next step, one could argue, by addressing the issue of economics and commodification—and he does this by running his own cost-benefit analysis of the child as livestock. His argument is quite compelling: What could be better than a food source that is not just tasty and nutritional, but a good buy as well? What businessman worth his salt (ha ha) could pass up such a bargain?

Swift then rounds out the new set of associations by pressing the notion of child-as-food-as-commodity to the final logical step, which I read to you at the end there, where he notes that: "Those who are more thrifty (as I must confess the times require) may flay the carcass; the skin of which artificially dressed will make admirable gloves for ladies, and summer boots for fine gentlemen."

Let's pause for a moment to recap the organizational pattern Swift has established for us. First, we're introduced to the radical idea of children as potential food source; next, we're led to consider them in more detail as a culinary dish (or rather a series of dishes) that would be welcome at the family dining table; next, we're made to understand the value of this new food source in both nutritional and economic terms; and finally, we're prompted to consider the idea that children, having served their purpose at the dinner table, could also provide some rather useful material for gloves and boots—and that, having fed us, they could clothe us (or at least accessorize us), too.

By this point, we're so far onto Swift's turf and so deeply immersed in his language, terms, and meanings that we can't help but follow along. Like Swift, we may not venture so far as to flay the carcass for gloves and boots, but that's only because we've already accepted his notion of child-as-food and made it our normative definition as well. Or at least for the purposes of getting through this essay, we've completely suspended our disbelief—we've put what would be our natural reaction—which I'm guessing here would be horror—we've put that natural reaction off to the side. If we're going to be able to keep reading, we would have to do that out of necessity. In order to keep going and follow his logic, we have to recognize that this is a deliberate exercise in absurdity—but we keep going because in or through this satire, an important point is being made.

Once again, I would urge you to pay close attention not just to the pattern of organization that Swift lays out for us, but to the underlying principle of redefinition and redevelopment of familiar terms and concepts that makes this pattern possible. He pushes us along, treating children like animals, and then we move to food sources, to commodities to be bought and sold. We follow him from one point to the next because he guides us with careful organization.

So, clearly organizing an argument requires you to establish some sense of continuity as you move from one point to the next—that's a basic premise of any writing guide; Swift demonstrates both that continuity and progression between points. But establishing that continuity involves a whole lot more than just making sure you have effective transitions between paragraphs and points; rather, you really need to approach the organizing process as though you are trying to teach your readers a new language with its own particular vocabulary and grammar—and this is a vocabulary and grammar for which you have set and developed the terms.

I don't at all mean to suggest that you ignore standard advice about organizing arguments—identify your main point and then marshal or arrange your other subordinate points in support of that main point—but I do hope that you can see that this sort of advice I'm giving you about key terms sort of floats over a deeper set of strategies that require us first to control the language that we use to present our ideas—and then to build on and expand that language as our argument unfolds.

Let's take a moment to try out this strategy in our own writing. Start by choosing a word that most people would easily recognize and connect to a conventional set of meanings—say, for example, "government." Probably pretty much everyone has a general idea of what government is and a general sense of what it does. Try drafting three or four paragraphs in which you take control of the term "government" and define it for yourself.

If you can, right now you can stop the tape and do this, or if you're driving in the car—don't have the means by which you could stop the tape and draft a few paragraphs—all you have to do is sort of think: "Okay, if I had to write three paragraphs on government, what are some of the terms I would use in each of those paragraphs?" So just take a moment and try and come up with some key terms. You would start by associating it with the idea or meaning you think is most important—and then build on and develop that meaning in subsequent paragraphs. What you want to do is try to reiterate and expand on your initial definition and then use that process—reiteration and expansion—to organize your writing.

Again, if you're not in a place or a space where you can easily stop the recording and do this, that's just fine—just take a couple seconds to think of ideas you associate with government and how they might progress from one to another. We're going to revisit this exercise at the end of the lecture, and you can get some sense then I think of what I'm looking for. For those of you who right now have the chance to try this exercise, I'll ask you to revise those paragraphs and make them even stronger a little bit later on.

Let's take a look at how Thoreau establishes the terms of his argument in the second paragraph of "Civil Disobedience"—this is a paragraph that will serve as kind of a what we might say "microcosmic guide" for the organization of the essay as a whole, and Thoreau says:

> This American government—what is it but a tradition, though a recent one, endeavoring to transmit itself unimpaired to posterity, but each instant losing some of its integrity? It has not the vitality and force of a single living man; for a single man can bend it to his will. It is a sort of wooden gun to the people themselves.

While their styles are different, Thoreau and Swift do share a common investment in redefining commonly held ideas about their topics, and both of them are seeking to establish their own set of terms that they can then use to present their arguments—and to present those arguments more effectively and compellingly.

Thoreau's goal is to acknowledge government as a necessary tool for satisfying a public need, but he also wants to argue that through constant misuse in application, this tool has become more apt to control citizens than to be controlled by them. Here, one more time, think of that—he's arguing the tool of government is more likely to control citizens than the citizens are likely to control the government. So that's the important distinction he's making. He goes on in a later passage to say: "The people must have some complicated machinery or other, and hear its din, to satisfy that idea of government which they have. Governments show thus how successfully men can be imposed on, even impose on themselves, for their own advantage. It is excellent, we must all allow."

Thoreau then proceeds to refashion the notion that government does things for people and replaces it with the idea that people themselves are the key source of agency—he's saying that government has actually limited the potential of Americans to achieve liberty, property, and education. In a paragraph full of emphasis, and the emphasis that you'll hear me use here is in the original, Thoreau goes on to say:

> Yet this government never of itself furthered any enterprise, but by the alacrity with which it got out of its way. *It* does not keep the country free. *It* does not settle the West. *It* does not educate. The character inherent in the American people has done all that has been accomplished; and it would have done somewhat more, if the government had not sometimes got in its way.

As readers familiar with "Civil Disobedience" will recognize, Thoreau uses the key ideas in the selections we've looked at as the organizational structure for the entire essay. He returns to, and elaborates on, them in subsequent paragraphs—always building on them and never moving off to another idea or term that isn't somehow connected to what we find in these initial paragraphs.

Again, if you want to create your new own terms and ideas—your own key set of main points—you want to make sure that you don't give your audience too many that they get lost and they can't follow you. So, Thoreau is a great example of how he limits himself, and all his key terms flow naturally from his main idea about government. Again, Thoreau is not exactly Swiftian in style (he uses satire in other pieces, but never to the extent that Swift does when he proposes that the Irish should eat their babies). At the same time, the underlying approaches to organization on the part of these two authors are very much the same in that each one recognizes the power of getting an audience on his turf and compelling them to accept new perceptions of what seem to be familiar ideas.

Let's take a look at another example—and this one comes from Thomas Paine's famous essay pamphlet "Common Sense." In that essay Paine says:

> Society in every state is a blessing, but government even in its best state is a necessary evil; in its worst state an intolerable one; for when we suffer, or are exposed to the same miseries by a government, which we might expect in a country without a government, our calamity is heightened, reflecting that we furnish the means by which we suffer.

What key terms and ideas does Paine define for himself? It shouldn't be too difficult to see in this case that he wants to both redefine and reclaim two notions—society and government—and he feels that people have mistakenly and unfortunately confused these two notions with each other. Society and government are not the same thing. He's not going so far (at least not yet) as to offer entirely new definitions of these terms; at this point, his goal is to realign two sets of meanings that he thinks have been incorrectly assigned.

Like Thoreau, he also wants to underscore the extent to which government has limited and restricted the potential of people rather than supported or enhanced it. As those of you who've studied "Common Sense" already know, Paine uses this paragraph as the organizational basis for the whole rest of the essay, and he consistently refers back to, and expands on, the terms and ideas that he introduces here.

In addition to establishing and defining the key terms and ideas of an argument, the process of organization should involve really careful attention to transitions. If the links from one point to the next aren't there—or if they aren't strong enough—then the argument won't be as effective as it could be.

The easiest and most successful strategy for crafting transitions is what I call the "repetition variation approach"—again, one more time: the "repetition variation approach." By repetition variation I mean taking a word or phrase from the end of one paragraph or section of an argument and using it, preferably with a small change or a slight variation, as the beginning of the next paragraph or section.

To illustrate this strategy, let's look at Paine's "Common Sense" one more time. Here's the end of one paragraph in the piece. Paine writes: "However prejudice may warp our wills, or interest darken our understanding, the simple voice of nature and of reason will say, it is right."

Notice that Paine uses the words "nature" and "simple," and he's going to build on those words and their associations as he transitions into the next paragraph. So be listening for the words "nature" and "simple" as he goes on: "I draw my idea of the form of government from a principle in nature, which no art can overturn, that the more simple any thing is, the less liable it is to be disordered, and the easier repaired when disordered."

There is nothing especially complicated or difficult about this transition strategy, but I'm always surprised by how often my students either completely ignore or underuse it in their writing, because it's really a way that they can form connections quite easily from one point to the next and one paragraph to the next.

Another form of transition—somewhat less elegant but certainly effective when used carefully and judiciously—is the sequence or series, and sometimes I call this "first, next, then" or "first, secondly, thirdly," but "sequence series" works just as well as a sort of catch-all phrase to hold that idea in your mind. You probably have tried this yourself, and it's a really useful means of organizing information, but you have to be really careful about boring your readers with too many lists. In Paine's examination of the

English Constitution, he goes ahead, and he lists the following issues, and he does it this way:

> First. The remains of monarchical tyranny in the person of the king.
>
> Secondly. The remains of aristocratical tyranny in the persons of the peers.
>
> Thirdly. The new republican materials, in which the persons of the commons, on whose virtue depends the freedom of England.

As you can see from this example, a sequence or a series can be a really dynamic form of transition. Not only has Paine managed to convey a lot of information clearly and succinctly, but he has also set his reader up to move from one point to the next.

But, and I bet a lot of you out there are anticipating what I'm about to say here, this device like all devices has to be used with restraint. If you do too many sequences, you might as well be writing a grocery list, because by the time you get to the 20th element in your list, your readers' eyes will have glazed over—and they're not going to remember what points 1, or 5, or 7 were. Five points or elements in a series is really about the limit of what your average reader's mind can keep track of. Three points is much easier, and that's really my limit—three points and a list. So, first, next, then; firstly, secondly, thirdly—three points; that is manageable.

As I mentioned earlier, a sequence or series can be an effective form of transition if it's used carefully and judiciously. Not only should you limit the number of elements or ideas in a sequence or series, but you should limit the number of times you use this device. In practical terms, I'd recommend no more than one sequential or series-based transition in a written argument of less than 10 pages. In a longer piece, say if you're writing something that's 10 to 20 pages, you could effectively make use of two or perhaps three sequence series transitions, but you really don't want to do more than that because pretty soon your reader is going to be bored; they're going to say: "Aha, he's doing the same thing again"—sequence series, sequence series, and you don't want them to stop paying attention to what you're writing because they're distracted by the stylistic moves you're making over and over again.

What do we take away from this lecture? I hope you'll continue to keep in mind—and that you'll practice—the strategy of identifying and defining for yourself the key terms of your argument. Other more basic forms of organization can work with this approach, but organizing your writing in terms of a few key ideas that you define can greatly enhance basic structural strategies, like the chronological model or the five-paragraph model.

Obviously, you certainly don't need to follow Swift's radical example when it comes to expressing the content of your argument—you don't have to redefine children as food; that has already been done. But you should certainly follow the basic model he offers for organizing the points of his argument: Begin with your own definition of a key word or idea, and then expand and build on its meanings in ways that invite (or, in fact, compel) your readers to accept your terms and language.

I also hope you'll pay attention to the mechanics of transitions—the practical strategies for moving from one paragraph or point to another that we saw in Paine's work. Repetition variation and sequence series are time-tested and effective ways of topping off and complementing the organizational foundation you have established by taking control of the language and terms of your argument. In the exercises for today's lecture, I'm going to ask you to practice the repetition variation and sequence series strategies in a paragraph or two about government and by looking back at a recent e-mail you have written in which you tried to persuade someone of something.

By this point, you have learned how to begin an argument, and you have acquired some strategies for organizing your writing. But even the most engaging opening and the cleverest structure will be completely useless if you don't adequately support your argument—if you don't really try to tell your reader, as clearly as possible, "So what?". In our next lecture, we'll look at strategies for supporting your claims and making your argument as persuasive as possible.

Supporting Your Argument
Lecture 8

It's true that association, speculation, and the appearance of correlation can actually have a really persuasive effect on an audience. ... Nearly all forms of advertising and marketing rely in some way on the willingness of people to be persuaded by claims and arguments based on speculation and association.

In this lecture, we'll build on our discussion of how arguments can be organized by examining a closely related quality of persuasive writing: the selection and presentation of evidence. More specifically, we will study key strategies you can use to more effectively support a written argument.

Our first key strategy: Evidence does not explain itself. It's never sufficient simply to refer to a piece of evidence in your writing and expect readers to make a link between it and the claim you're trying to support. To write persuasively, you have to show your readers how and why your proof is relevant to your argument.

If it works for you, try thinking of yourself as the prosecuting attorney on "Law and Order." It's not sufficient for you to walk over to the evidence table, point out the murder weapon, and proclaim, "Ladies and gentlemen, this is the actual weapon used in the homicide. Thank you very much for your time. I know you will find the accused party guilty of murder." A good prosecutor would need to offer a detailed and comprehensive explanation that connects the gun and the alleged killer. She or he would want to cite forensic reports, crime-scene photos, testimony from eye witnesses, and any other sources that would help convince the judge and jury that the murder weapon is a valid piece of evidence and supports a guilty verdict.

Our second key strategy is to provide a direct link between your evidence and your conclusion. Very likely you've encountered arguments in which proof was offered up without any concrete reason why the evidence should be interpreted a certain way. Arguments that rely on statistics or the findings of scientific studies are especially prone to this particular failing. My favorite example is the raft of arguments out there for and against the health benefits of drinking coffee. I like coffee—a lot—and I'm always hoping to read a solid argument in favor of drinking more of it.

While it's easy to find articles that tout the benefits of coffee drinking, it's not so easy to find articles that use evidence convincingly and responsibly to make that argument. It's not a lack of evidence that causes this problem. In fact, there is quite a substantial cottage industry among researchers who devote their time and energy to examining the effects of caffeine consumption on rats. I have no doubt that these studies are, on the whole, well conceived, carefully conducted, and scientifically valid. The problem comes in where articles and blog entries draw on such research to support arguments about whether coffee is good or bad for humans, and in what quantities we should or should not consume it.

Admitting that alternative viewpoints exist can have the seemingly paradoxical effect of strengthening one's own argument.

To be specific, the subjects of the scientific studies are rats, not humans, and caffeine is not the same thing as coffee. Of course it's easy to conflate caffeine and coffee, but any argument that relies on evidence taken from a caffeine-rat study must include some explanation of how those effects, positive or negative, can support a conclusion about the effects of coffee drinking on human beings. Without careful explanation of how this evidence needs to be considered and attention to the context and differences between rats and humans, the argument is nothing more than speculation based on possible association. The claims you make based on evidence must be direct and definitive and show a clear cause-effect relationship.

Our third key strategy for supporting an argument is the use of concessions. Admitting that alternative viewpoints exist can have the seemingly paradoxical effect of strengthening one's own argument. This may seem counterintuitive to some writers: Why acknowledge the validity of some idea that may compete with your own? Wouldn't that undermine the argument you want to make?

As we'll see from the following examples, just the opposite is true. Rather than undermining an argument, concessions can actually strengthen it. By acknowledging and dealing with counterevidence, you establish yourself as a trustworthy commentator on a particular subject.

Here's an example of a concession from Thomas Paine's "Common Sense":

> Some writers have explained the English constitution thus; the king, say they, is one, the people another; the peers are an house in behalf of the king; the commons in behalf of the people; but this hath all the distinctions of an house divided against itself; and though the expressions be pleasantly arranged, yet when examined they appear idle and ambiguous.

What exactly is Paine conceding here? Well, he's acknowledging that other writers have offered an explanation of Great Britain's government that sounds well-balanced and rational—yet, as Paine argues, this appearance of balance and rationality belies a hierarchy of power that favors elites while granting little authority to commoners.

Paine uses this concession to highlight, by contrast, the possibilities for government in America that he will sketch out later in the essay. It's important to recognize here that Paine uses a concession to highlight and support his own position. In other words, he's not necessarily giving ground to his opponents; rather, he's sketching out their argument as a way of bringing his own views into sharper relief—underscoring the best parts of his case even as he shines some light on the weakest parts of theirs.

It's also important to recognize that Paine is using this concession to bolster his own credibility—mainly by demonstrating his thorough understanding of other points of view. His concession shows that he's done his homework and can offer a detailed assessment of the pros and cons of other possible positions on this topic.

When it comes to supporting an argument, we've identified three crucial points: first, the need to explain how a particular piece of evidence helps you make your case to an audience; second, the need to provide a connection between evidence and conclusion that is direct, definitive, and based on cause-effect; and third, how acknowledging the arguments of others can serve to strengthen your own argument. ∎

Suggested Reading

Griffith, *Writing Essays about Literature*.

Lunsford and Ruszkiewicz, *Everything's an Argument*.

Ramage, Bean, and Johnson, *Writing Arguments*.

Exercises

1. Choose an editorial column from your favorite newspaper and examine the way the author uses evidence to support her or his argument—what kinds of explanations (if any) does she or he include to connect that evidence to the editorial's main claim? Try rewriting the column—see if you can offer more convincing connections between the evidence and the claim.

2. Find a letter to the editor that you disagree with and draft a response that challenges the letter-writer's position; include at least one concession that helps highlight, by contrast, your own position on the issue.

Supporting Your Argument
Lecture 8—Transcript

Welcome back. In the last lecture, we looked at several strategies that effective writers use to organize their arguments. Drawing on examples from Jonathan Swift's "A Modest Proposal," Henry David Thoreau's "Civil Disobedience," and Thomas Paine's "Common Sense," we learned how arguments can be structured and presented in order to successfully guide readers from one point to the next.

We also looked at methods for avoiding structural flaws and inconsistencies that could distort or obscure the main purpose or goal of an argument. Remember, when you are writing anything, you want to carry your reader along on the current of your words and ideas—you don't want them to get stuck, to have to go back, to reread, to try and figure out what the heck your main idea is and where you're going with it.

In this lecture, we'll build on our discussion of how arguments can be organized by examining a closely related and equally important quality of persuasive writing, and this important quality is the selection and the presentation of evidence.

More specifically, we'll study key strategies you can use to effectively support a written argument. In later lectures, especially 15 through 18, we're going to look at some rhetorical concepts that you can use to supplement and complement these strategies I'm going to talk about right now—and with those supplemental strategies you can make your arguments even more powerful—but for now, we're really going to examine the basics of how you use evidence to make a claim.

I think we need to start by establishing a crucial but often overlooked aspect of supporting an argument, and I can't stress this point enough: Evidence does not explain itself. In fact, I think this point is so important, let me repeat it: Evidence does not explain itself. To write persuasively, you have to show your readers how and why your proof is relevant to your argument—and what I mean by this is that it is never sufficient simply to refer to a piece of evidence in your writing and then expect your readers to make a link between it and the claim you're trying to support. That's asking them to do the kind of work that you should be doing in your writing. Your audience certainly may be smart or intuitive enough to form this kind of connection without your help, but they might not interpret the evidence in precisely the way you would like—or even worse, they might interpret it in precisely the way you would not like.

So by way of example, let's think of a courtroom TV drama like *Law & Order*—and we're all familiar with this. Have you ever seen one of the lawyers on the show simply introduce the murder weapon into evidence and then say nothing about it? "Your Honor, I'd like to submit this bloody kitchen knife as people's exhibit A. The prosecution rests."

What's wrong with this approach? First of all, you've got about 22 minutes of TV time that you have to fill in the order or the courtroom portion of the show, and just presenting the murder weapon and having the prosecution rest is not going to cut it. As you can obviously see, the bloody kitchen knife alone does nothing to prove the prosecution's case. If the prosecution can establish that the prime suspect bought the knife, was seen with it chopping tomatoes 10 minutes before the murder, and then throwing it—covered in blood—into the garbage can 10 minutes later, well then you've got something—and it's the same thing, the same idea, when we're dealing with evidence in writing.

A crucial step in supporting an argument is to provide a convincing explanation of how the proof you're using adds weight to—and validates—the claims that you're making. In order to marshal your evidence to provide the most persuasive argument possible, you should try thinking of yourself as a prosecuting attorney in a first-degree murder case—and you should also think of yourself as a prosecutor who is fortunate enough to have the actual gun, or knife, or lead pipe, or candlestick, or whatever it was that the accused party used to commit the crime.

Or, if it works for you, think of yourself as one of the actors on *Law & Order*. In such a scenario, it's important to recognize that even with the murder weapon on display, it's not sufficient—it's not enough—for you, as the prosecutor, to walk over to the evidence table, point out the murder weapon, and proclaim: "Ladies and Gentlemen: This is the actual weapon used in the homicide; here it is, sitting right on this very evidence table. Now, thank you very much for your time. I know you will find the accused party guilty of murder in the first degree." That's just not going to work.

Similarly, if you're trying to get people to care about, say, saving endangered sea turtles, you can't simply write: "Studies show that sea turtle habitats are half the size they were 20 years ago." Okay, now we're back to that "So what?" question. You need to explain how and why the decline in habitat size is important to the survival of the sea turtle. For all your readers know, sea turtles may have found it tiring to swim so far and are delighted to have less territory to cover.

Obviously, I'm being kind of facetious here—we can all probably figure out that decline of living area—it's not a good thing for any animal—but when you're writing and you're trying to convince someone using pieces of evidence, you need to really spell out the significance of that piece of evidence to your argument. In fact, failing to adequately explain how a piece of evidence is tied to your argument could have the unintended—and I'm pretty sure certainly unwanted—effect of actually undercutting and diminishing the power of your proof.

So, what's at stake is not just the possibility that you might miss a chance to make your argument stronger—it's also the possibility that you might end up making it far weaker, and certainly that is not something that you want.

A good prosecutor would* need to offer a detailed and comprehensive explanation that connects the gun and the alleged killer. She or he would want to cite forensic reports—and if it's a knife, it would be a forensic report on the blade; if it's a gun, ballistics reports. The prosecutor would need to talk about the wound, the angle of the attack, fingerprints, crime scene photos, testimony from eye witnesses, and any other sources that would help convince the judge and jury that the murder weapon is a valid piece of evidence and persuade them to view it in a way that supports the argument for a guilty verdict.

So, how do we determine whether or not we're providing a relevant and substantial explanation of how our evidence supports our argument?

Again, we need to think back to the "What?/So what?" test we used in Lecture 6 to gauge the effectiveness of an opening to an argument. The same logic applies when we shift our attention to supporting that argument: We need to tell our readers what the evidence is, but we also have to show them why that evidence matters in a particular way.

Let's look at an example from Thomas Paine's "Common Sense." In this segment of his argument, Paine is addressing the status of monarchy—or hereditary succession—as a form of government. More specifically, he's debunking the notion that monarchies are especially good forms of government for preventing civil wars. Here, what he's doing is specifically addressing a claim that was made in favor of monarchy, and he's addressing that claim head on. He says:

> The most plausible plea, which hath ever been offered in favour of hereditary succession, is, that it preserves a nation from civil wars; and were this true, it would be weighty; whereas, it is the most barefaced falsity ever imposed on mankind. The whole history of England disowns the fact. Thirty kings and two minors have reigned in that distracted kingdom since the conquest, in which time there have been (including the Revolution) no less than eight civil wars and nineteen rebellions.

You can see that Paine answers the "What?" question by invoking a set of concrete, historical facts as evidence to support his claims, and then he frames them with some really highly charged emotional language to try and play on his reader's sympathy.

What part of the passage demonstrates Paine's use of objective, historical evidence? Take a moment. Think back. What's the objective evidentiary part of the claim of the passage?

That's right: He points out that under a long-running monarchy there have been "thirty kings," "two minors," and there have been "no less than eight civil wars and nineteen rebellions." Pointing out the ratio of kings to civil wars and rebellions is really a crucial step in his argument. Eye-popping statistics like these have the potential to be tremendously persuasive.

Statistics alone, however, are not enough. As in the hypothetical murder case scenario I described earlier, you can't just point out the evidence and then leave your audience to connect the dots and come up with the conclusion you want them to reach. Paine recognizes this, and he includes two phrases that give an emotional, subjective spin on his presentation of the statistics.

Think back and see if you can identify what those phrases are. They might have jumped out at you as you were listening when he says: "The most plausible plea, which hath ever been offered in favour of hereditary succession, is, that it preserves a nation from civil wars" and then he goes on to say "were this true, it would be weighty; whereas, it is the most barefaced falsity ever imposed on mankind." He continues: "The whole history of England disowns the fact. Thirty kings and two minors have reigned in that distracted kingdom since the conquest, in which time there have been (including the Revolution) no less than eight civil wars and nineteen rebellions."

Listening to that passage again, what words jumped out at you? They are really not that difficult to catch. It is "barefaced falsity" and "distracted kingdom"—those two phrases, when taken together, suggest both a deliberate attempt to deceive and a willingness to be distracted or diverted. So how does Paine want his readers to interpret the evidence he cites? It's not just a matter of throwing numbers out there and expecting them to identify the disconnect between what people say the monarchy does and what actually happens under monarchical rule. Paine also wants them to recognize that there is a complex process going on that gives rise to this disconnect. It's a process in which everyone seems complicit—at least they are to some degree. He says the aristocratic elite—the members of the ruling class—are to blame because they perpetuate the "barefaced falsity" of the claim that monarchy prevents civil wars, yet he says the mass of people who do not hold power—the "distracted kingdom"—must bear some of the blame as well for continuing to believe in the capacity of the monarchy to prevent civil war when there is so much evidence that this, in fact, is not the case.

So what we have in this brief argument by Paine is a very effective example of how to cite evidence and how to explain the way it should be perceived and interpreted.

Probably, it's very likely that you've encountered arguments in which proof was offered up without any specific or concrete reason why the evidence should be interpreted a certain way or lead us to one particular conclusion rather than another. Arguments that rely on statistics or the findings of scientific studies are especially prone to this kind of mistake.

My favorite example (and pet peeve actually) is the raft of arguments out there for and against the health benefits of coffee drinking. I have to confess I like coffee. I like it a lot, and I'm always hoping to read a solid argument in favor of drinking more of it. I'm originally from Seattle, and as some of you may know, it's practically a law there that every citizen in the city has to consume several cups a day.

Honestly, you really can't go more than 200 feet in Seattle without finding a source of coffee—and it's one of my favorite things about that city. Obviously, I may be biased in this regard, but as you can imagine, I am nonetheless extremely pleased when I come across a piece of writing that assures me that I am doing good things for my body and my mind when I drink my favorite latte—of course, always in moderation, right?

While it's easy to find articles that tout the benefits of coffee drinking, it's not so easy to find articles that use evidence convincingly and responsibly to make that argument.

Here, it's not a lack of evidence that causes this problem. In fact, there's a quite substantial, amazingly large cottage industry among researchers who devote their time and energy to examining the effects of caffeine consumption on rats. It really is quite amazing. You can find study upon study dedicated to measuring and evaluating the effects of caffeine on the cognitive abilities of rats, on the immune systems of rats, the kidney functions of rats, on the neurological health of rats. I could go on, and on, and on, but I think you get the idea here.

Let me just be clear: I don't have any quarrel with these studies. I have no doubt that they are, on the whole, well-conceived. I'm sure they're carefully conducted, and I'm sure they're scientifically valid—and, of course, I always hope the rats are enjoying their caffeine as much as I enjoy my coffee.

But there's another cottage industry that has sprung up alongside the scientific studies, and there are literally hundreds, if not thousands, of articles and blog entries that draw on this research for evidence to support arguments about whether coffee is bad or good for you, and in what quantities human beings should or should not consume it, and things like whether when you drink your coffee is as significant as how much you drink. I think you get the idea that I'm trying to get across here.

This is where the problem is when it comes to supporting this argument: The subjects of the scientific studies are rats, not humans, and the caffeine that the rats are getting is not the same thing as coffee. Of course, it's really easy to conflate caffeine and coffee—we often do that ourselves. We think of those two things as being almost interchangeable, but they're really not one and the same. It's not precisely true that caffeine equals coffee—or coffee equals caffeine. Any argument that relies on evidence taken from a caffeine/rat study has to include some explanation of how those effects, positive or negative, can support a conclusion about the effects of coffee drinking on human beings—and perhaps, more importantly, whether I should feel smug or guilty about my third cup of the day. I tend to feel smug and delighted, full disclosure.

Without careful explanation of how this evidence needs to be considered and attention to the context and differences between rats and humans, this argument is really nothing more than speculation based on possible association. The scientific evidence about rats and caffeine might suggest some correlations, but without a solid explanation as to how such evidence supports an argument about coffee drinking and humans, we have absolutely no basis for believing the proof that these writers cite that it's valid one way or another.

On the plus side (for me and my caffeine-addicted self), the lack of an explanation of the evidence's relevance allows me to dismiss any arguments that would get between me and my Grande Skinny Vanilla Latte. See, I've got the terminology down. On the negative side, this same lack might allow me to dismiss out-of-hand some proof that there may be downsides to downing another cup, or two, or three, or seven every day.

So, what can we learn from these interesting but ultimately flawed attempts to link evidence from studies of highly caffeinated rats to conclusions about heavy-coffee-drinking people? If the first key point we learned from the murder trial scenario and the excerpt from Thomas Paine was that you—the writer—have to provide an explanation of how your proof supports your claims (because evidence does not explain itself), then the second key point we have to keep in mind, courtesy of those highly caffeinated rats, is that the connection you make between your evidence and your conclusions has to be strong.

The claims you make based on evidence have to be direct; they have to be definitive, and they have to really work to show a clear cause and effect relationship. If your connection is not direct; if in order to get from point A to point B, we have to wander around for a while; if it's not definitive; if it's not clear and easy to see, and if it's not based on a clear cause and effect relation—and if instead you're relying on association or speculation, or what we'd call "correlation"—you run the risk of undercutting your argument rather than supporting it.

There's one sort of warning or caveat here, and it's true that association, speculation, and the appearance of correlation can actually have a really persuasive effect on an audience. There is absolutely no denying that these strategies for presenting evidence can convince people to do or believe certain things they might not otherwise do or believe. I think if you just think about it for a moment, you'll realize that nearly all forms of advertising and marketing rely in some way on the willingness of people to be persuaded by claims and arguments based solely on speculation and association.

For example, ads for shampoo, we've all seen them, and they tend to show people with beautiful, shiny, lustrous hair. The association here is clear— we're meant to draw a conclusion that is really quite simple: Use our product and your hair will look like this. This association is pretty basic. But ads for things like cars and laundry detergent take it a little further: Buy our car, an ad seems to suggest, and by association, beautiful women will want to go out to dinner with you! We've all seen those kinds of car ads.

Another ad might suggest: Use our detergent and your home will be a place of order and sunlight with beautiful, obedient children. "Look," the advertisers want you to think, "that woman's home looks like it has been in *Architectural Digest*! She uses Wonder Clean! If I use Wonder Clean, maybe I can be the kind of woman with a house like that." We all instinctively know this. It's really just Marketing 101.

Still, although the association thing can work, the most effective and lasting arguments don't rely on these kinds of approaches. They certainly do and they can make use of emotional, non-objective language—just like Paine does in his argument against the supposed virtues of monarchy—right when he says "barefaced falsity" and "distracted kingdom"—those are terms that are laden with emotion, with associations. They're non-objective, but they don't combine empirical proof and emotional explanation to make speculative or specious claims. In other words, someone like Paine, even though he's using non-objective language, he's not trying to use it to support a claim that can't be supportive. Someone like Paine is not misrepresenting (either knowingly or out of ignorance) the relevance of his evidence to his conclusions; instead, a good writer, like Paine, will give you a strong piece of evidence and then explain how and why that evidence is important.

Just a moment ago, when I warned you against relying on speculation, association, and correlation as strategies for framing evidence or proof, I also acknowledged and admitted that these methods do, in fact, hold significant persuasive power. That act of acknowledgment—my admission that such approaches do work in many cases—is a classic example of our third key strategy for supporting an argument, and this third strategy is the use of concessions.

So when I noted that the advertising and marketing campaigns often persuade people by presenting evidence in less-than-forthright ways, I was, in fact, conceding that their approaches must have some efficacy. They must work. They must have some chance for success—even if the methods themselves are faulty.

My willingness to concede this point is an example of how admitting that alternative viewpoints and methods exist can have I think it's like a seemingly paradoxical effect, but it's a real effect nonetheless. It has the seemingly paradoxical effect of strengthening your own position or argument. This may seem at first totally counterintuitive to some writers. Why acknowledge the validity of some idea or approach that could compete with your own? Wouldn't that undermine the argument you want to make?

As we'll see from some examples, just the opposite is true. Rather than undermining an argument, concessions can actually strengthen it. By acknowledging and dealing with counter-evidence, you establish yourself as a reliable and trustworthy commentator on a particular subject.

Here's an example of a concession from Paine's essay. He says:

> Some writers have explained the English constitution thus; the king, say they, is one, the people another; the peers are a house in behalf of the king; the commons in behalf of the people; but this hath all the distinctions of an house divided against itself; and though the expressions be pleasantly arranged, yet when examined they appear idle and ambiguous.

What is Paine conceding here exactly? He's acknowledging that other writers have offered an explanation of Great Britain's government that sounds well-balanced and rational—yet, as he continues to argue, this appearance of balance and rationality really belies a hierarchy of power that favors elites while granting little authority to commoners. So, in other words, this model, while it might seem workable on the surface, if you look beneath it, you find it's really not satisfactory.

Paine uses this concession to highlight, by contrast, the possibilities for government in America that he sketches out later in his essay—and specifically here, he talks about the possibility for a balanced, rational legislative system that does not favor one particular group, a group of elites. In the American system, Paine argues, appearances will actually match up with reality, and this is not like the British system, in which appearances of equal representation really mask long-standing structural inequalities of economics and political power. So, he's saying the British model may look like it's giving everybody power, but it's not at all.

It's important to recognize here that Paine uses a concession to highlight and support, by way of contrast, his own position. In other words, he is not necessarily giving ground to his opponents; rather, he's sketching out their argument as a way of bringing his own views into sharper relief—he's underscoring the best parts of his case even as he shines some light on the weakest parts of the opposite case.

It's also important to recognize that Paine is using this concession to bolster his own credibility—mainly he's doing this by demonstrating that he thoroughly understands and has a full command of other points of view related to this argument. His concession shows that he has done his homework, so to speak, and he can offer a detailed assessment of the pros and the cons of other possible positions on the topic. Again, we're more likely ultimately to be persuaded because he has anticipated and addressed a piece of evidence or claim that runs against his own position. He hasn't tried to ignore it or obscure the other point—in fact, he's done just the opposite.

So, when it comes to supporting an argument, we've identified three crucial points: First, the need to explain how a particular piece of evidence or proof works in your favor and helps you make your case to an audience; second, we discussed the need to provide a clear connection between the evidence and the conclusion that you want your audience to reach. This needs to be a direct connection rather than an association; it's got to be definitive rather than mere speculation, and it has to be based on cause and effect. So, we have to be able to see the clear connection. Third—and finally—we learned how concessions, acknowledging the arguments of others, can actually serve to amplify and strengthen your argument—in part by highlighting the features of your point of view as opposed to somebody else's, and also by showing how credible you are as a writer, how thoroughly you've studied the strengths and weaknesses of other positions while establishing and consolidating your own. In the exercises that accompany today's lecture, I want you to work on this—in particular, I want you to work on writing, say, an editorial column or a letter to the editor, and when you're doing this, to try and work in a concession as you're making a claim or a point.

In our next lecture, we'll move on to a discussion of how you can conclude the essay in the most effective way possible. You want your audience to recall as easily as possible the main points of your essay, to understand how they work together to support your main claim, and you want them to remember your evidence as being clearly relevant to the matter under discussion. In other words, you want to take them out with a bang, and in our next lecture, we'll discuss just how you can best do that.

Finishing Strong
Lecture 9

We can glean from Swift's closing lines an important reminder and a striking example of how conclusions can be used to anticipate and refute, in advance, charges that an argument for some broader goal or cause is actually self-serving. You don't have to follow Swift's over-the-top style, but we shouldn't hesitate to emulate the spirit of his conclusion when we perceive that some similar possibility of a personal attack will follow in the wake of us making our own arguments.

In the previous three lectures, we've studied strategies for starting, organizing, and supporting arguments. Now we focus on methods for crafting more effective conclusions—how to wrap up and finish off your presentation of an argument in ways that solidify your claims, make your case, and perhaps even leave your readers wanting to hear more about the issue.

You've probably been told at some point by an English teacher that conclusions must include a summary of the highlights of an argument. This is certainly true: An effective conclusion should include some sort of recapping of the main ideas that structure your argument. But you should not simply repeat verbatim what you say in your introduction. A little variation shows that you've really thought about wrapping this argument up in a compelling and engaging way.

What else should you do with a conclusion? How can you effectively finish an argument by doing something other than—or more than—summarizing for your readers the key points you've made? Here again, our famous essayists, Thomas Paine and Jonathan Swift, can provide some answers. Let's look first at Paine's final two paragraphs in "Common

Thomas Paine's strong conclusions influenced the American Revolution.

Sense," keeping in mind that just prior to these paragraphs, Paine does provide his readers with the kind of summary we are discussing.

> Under our present denomination of British subjects we can neither be received nor heard abroad: The custom of all courts is against us, and will be so, until, by an independence, we take rank with other nations.

> These proceedings may at first appear strange and difficult; but, like all other steps which we have already passed over, will in a little time become familiar and agreeable; and, until an independence is declared, the Continent will feel itself like a man who continues putting off some unpleasant business from day to day, yet knows it must be done, hates to set about it, wishes it over, and is continually haunted by the thoughts of its necessity.

The strategy Paine uses is one you certainly can and should follow in crafting your own conclusions. This is a negative consequences conclusion—meaning he uses these last few lines to underscore the negative things that could happen if readers are not persuaded by his argument and fail to support his vision of governmental reform.

I want to emphasize here that Paine is not using the negative consequences approach as a scare tactic—he knows that few readers, especially those who are still uncertain as to the validity of his argument, are likely to be persuaded by apocalyptic claims. But he also knows that his readers are likely to respond if presented with a clear statement of what the ultimate consequences may be if they choose not to accept his argument.

What we learn from Paine is that effective conclusions can underscore ultimate consequences without resorting to ultimatums.

In other words, what we learn from Paine is that effective conclusions can underscore ultimate consequences without resorting to ultimatums. Stating ultimate consequences is like saying, "if we do not do x, then y will happen," whereas stating an ultimatum is like saying, "you'd better do *x*, or else *y* is your fault." Ultimatums put a tremendous (and needless) strain on the writer-reader relationship and are likely to alienate undecided readers. Stating something as an explanation of ultimate consequences doesn't put your reader in as defensive a position.

Let's take a look at another example of an effective conclusion—this one from Jonathan Swift's "A Modest Proposal." Swift offers a version of Paine's negative consequences approach, but he provides an extra twist—a variation that I call the no viable alternatives strategy. Recall that Swift's satire— following the structure of classical Latin satires by Horace and Juvenal— proposes an outlandish solution to a seemingly intractable problem. In this case, the problem is the pervasive poverty in Ireland, and the solution is to allow poor parents to sell their children to the rich so the rich can devour them as tasty and satisfying meals.

Swift is mocking both the British imperialist treatment of Ireland and a prevailing impulse among politicians and reformers of his day to suggest simple, cure-all solutions to complex social and economic problems. In his conclusion, Swift offers a direct challenge to those who would support such naive attempts at social engineering:

> I desire those politicians who dislike my overture, and may perhaps be so bold as to attempt an answer, that they will first ask the parents of these mortals, whether they would not at this day think it a great happiness to have been sold for food, at a year old in the manner I prescribe, and thereby have avoided such a perpetual scene of misfortune as they have since gone through by the oppression of landlords, the impossibility of paying rent without money or trade, the want of common sustenance, with neither house nor clothes to cover them from inclemencies of the weather, and the most inevitable prospect of entailing the like or greater miseries upon their breed forever.

Swift's conclusion suggests that alternatives to his proposal for changing the status quo aren't likely to be viable. Notice that he doesn't launch a direct attack on any particular plans that other writers have offered; rather, he points out that such plans are not likely to work unless and until their authors consider the causes and implications of the problem as fully and as carefully as Swift has. He also offers a kind of litmus test to determine whether alternative proposals would be as viable as his: asking the parents of impoverished children if a particular proposed solution would be something they would choose. Including your own version of Swift's litmus test—a criterion against which alternatives to your claim must be measured—is a powerful strategy for persuading readers that you offer the best solution to the problem at hand.

A third tone you can take in your conclusion is the positive consequences strategy. Here your goal is not to point out the negative things that may occur if readers do not accept your claims but rather to underscore the fact that some potentially positive things will not be manifested. An argument that stresses the negative potential outcomes in its conclusion can be powerful, but one that manages to end on a hopeful note could be more persuasive.

So what lessons should we take away from this final lecture in our four-part series on crafting successful arguments? I cannot stress enough the importance of using the conclusion to recap the main thesis and key points of your arguments. I would also strongly encourage you to go beyond a basic summary and explore the three strategies we've covered here: negative consequences, no viable alternatives, and positive consequences. I'd also urge you to think about ways of using conclusions to pique your readers' curiosity as Paine did. Finally, I hope you'll be mindful that you may need to use a conclusion to preemptively defend yourself against challenges that would seek to undermine your claims. If you can anticipate how someone might argue against you, you'd better address it head-on rather than ignore it. ∎

Suggested Reading

Griffith, *Writing Essays about Literature.*

Lunsford and Ruszkiewicz, *Everything's an Argument.*

Ramage, Bean, and Johnson, *Writing Arguments.*

1. Rewrite the final two paragraphs of Thomas Paine's "Common Sense" (see above) by following a positive consequences strategy (perhaps not as difficult a task as it sounds, given that we have the benefit of 200-plus years of hindsight and examples of the good things that could happen if the colonies achieved independence from Britain and formed themselves into a new nation).

2. Draft a negative consequences conclusion to Henry David Thoreau's "Civil Disobedience" (discussed in the lecture)—not a gloom-and-doom scenario but a thoughtful and persuasive discussion of what the consequences would be if democracy devolved rather than evolved in the ways Thoreau imagines.

Finishing Strong
Lecture 9—Transcript

Welcome back. In the previous lecture, we discussed three important concepts for supporting an argument. The first was the necessity of explaining the meaning of your evidence to your readers—of providing a clear link or connection between your proof and your claims.

As I mentioned last time, evidence does not explain itself. You'll remember the example of the prosecuting attorney presenting the murder weapon in a court case but not bothering to explain its relevance. It's not enough to show us evidence in support of your argument—you have to show us, and then you have to tell us in no uncertain terms how that evidence is relevant.

The second key point in our last lecture was to make sure that the links or the connections you forge between your evidence and your argument are not based on association, or speculation, or just simple correlation. This is especially crucial when your argument is relying on statistics or what we might call "empirical evidence."

You probably remember my pet peeve about the tendency of many writers to draw on scientific studies of caffeinated lab rats to speculate on the effects of coffee drinking on human beings. While it's true that such connections—based as they are on association or correlation—can often carry some real persuasive force, their ability to sway someone's opinion is usually short lived and not sustainable. To support a lasting, substantial, convincing argument, you need to draw clear connections between your proof and your claims, and these connections have to be direct; you can easily see how you got from A to B; they have to be definitive; they have to clearly explain how this works, and they have to be based on a cause-effect relationship.

Finally, we discussed the importance of using concessions—recognizing that other people may hold different points of view than your own and conceding that those opinions have to be acknowledged. We studied how an effective and successful writer, like Thomas Paine, uses concessions to actually strengthen his own argument. He presents an opposing viewpoint as a means of highlighting, or calling attention to, the differences between that argument and his own—and it's these differences that he then uses to underscore the strengths of his claims and the weaknesses of his opponents. So while concession might at first seem like a strategy that would undermine your argument, it really can end up strengthening it.

We saw how his use of concessions bolsters his own credibility as a writer by demonstrating how thoroughly he's studied alternative arguments—and so the fact that he has done his homework, so to speak, makes his own claims that much more convincing. We're much more likely to trust the person who acknowledges counter-arguments to his own than we are the person who tries to ignore or hide counter-evidence, and I'm sure that you found yourself in a position sometimes when you're making an argument or you think: "Oh, if I could just ignore this counter-evidence, then it will make my argument stronger," and that's not the case; it will actually weaken it.

So, in the previous three lectures, we've studied strategies for starting, organizing, and supporting arguments—and these are strategies that will make your writing more powerful and persuasive. Today, we're going to focus on methods for effective conclusions—in other words, how to wrap up and finish off your presentation of an argument in ways that really solidify your claims, establish your viewpoint, make your case—and perhaps, we can hope, even leave your readers wanting to hear more of what you have to say about the issue, topic, question, or problem you've been addressing and discussing.

I know very well—because I have been there myself—that by the time you reach the end of a piece of writing, you're tired, and you just want it to be done—so maybe you dash off a conclusion that isn't really that well thought out, and you have got to fight this impulse. If you need to go do something else and then come back to your writing in order to really focus on writing a good conclusion, then do that—just don't neglect the end of your argument. It's the final impression; it's your final chance to make an impact on your reader.

You've probably been told at some point by an English teacher or a writing instructor that conclusions have to include a summary of the highlights of your argument—so you have to reiterate points that you have already made, and those teachers and writing instructors would be correct. This is certainly true. An effective conclusion should include some sort of recap of your main ideas that have structured your argument all along.

I always encourage students to touch again, briefly, on the main points of their arguments when they come to the conclusion. They may think that it's redundant and boring (after all, they have been writing about this thing for days, and so the conclusions seem really obvious to them, but readers, who haven't been working on this thing for days, are generally grateful for a short summary of what the argument is about and why it matters. Of course, the key component of this short summary needs to be a restatement or a reiteration of the main thesis of the argument—or the primary position or viewpoint you've chosen to argue for or defend in this piece of writing.

If you have followed the strategies we've covered in the previous three lectures, the basic elements of your conclusion should already be established—meaning you really shouldn't have to work too hard to formulate this summary that goes in your concluding paragraph—but at the same time, you need to take the writing of this conclusion as seriously as possible and as seriously as any other dimension or element of the writing process.

Most importantly, and I can't stress this enough, you should not simply repeat, verbatim, word for word, what you say in your introduction. A little variation shows that you have really thought about wrapping this argument up in a compelling and engaging way. But what else should you do with a conclusion? How can you effectively finish an argument by doing something other than—or more than—just summarizing for your readers the thesis and key points that you have already articulated for them throughout the rest of the piece of writing?

Here again, the famous essayists we have been talking about—Paine, Thoreau, and Swift—can provide us with some concrete examples and some answers. Let's look first at Paine's final two paragraphs in "Common Sense." I should note here that just prior to these final paragraphs, Paine provides his readers with precisely the kind of summary or recap of his argument's key points to which I referred just a few moments ago.

He actually begins his summary with the phrase: "To conclude:"—as a general rule, I recommend not using the "to conclude" phrase if at all possible; it's a little boring and unoriginal, but at the same time, it does make clear for your readers that they are going to get a summary of your argument— so it can be useful in terms of signposting and directing your reader to the particular portion of your writing. After his "To conclude," Paine goes on to list and restate four points ("First …, Secondly…, Thirdly…, Fourthly …), and these four points constitute the heart of his argument.

But the most important thing to keep in mind, for our purposes at least, is that Paine does not stop after he has presented his four-point summary. He goes on to include these final two paragraphs—and in doing so, he raises the quality level of his conclusion from good to outstanding. Here is the first of the two paragraphs I want you to consider: "Under our present denomination of British subjects we can neither be received nor heard abroad: The custom of all courts is against us, and will be so, until, by an independence, we take rank with other nations."

As you're no doubt well aware, the main point of Paine's pamphlet is to call for the independence of the 13 colonies from Great Britain. He has been making this point in a variety of ways throughout the essay, but just in case we missed something, he states it here in no uncertain terms—and with a succinct eloquence that is truly memorable. After this, he then moves on to his final paragraph, where he says:

> These proceedings may at first appear strange and difficult; but, like all other steps which we have already passed over, will in a little time become familiar and agreeable; and, until an independence is declared, the Continent will feel itself like a man who continues putting off some unpleasant business from day to day, yet knows it must be done, hates to set about it, wishes it over, and is continually haunted by the thoughts of its necessity.

So, the strategy Paine uses is one you certainly can and should follow in crafting your own conclusions, especially as a supplement to your summary or recap of your larger argument's thesis and main points. Paine's approach in these final paragraphs is what I like to call a "negative consequences conclusion"—everyone store that phrase away: negative consequences conclusion, and this means that he uses these last few lines to underscore the negative things that could happen if readers are not persuaded by his argument and fail to support his vision of governmental reform.

I want to emphasize here that Paine is not using the negative consequences approach as a scare tactic. He knows that few readers, especially those who are still uncertain as to the validity of a particular argument, are likely to be persuaded by overly dramatic or apocalyptic claims—but he also knows that his audience is likely to respond if they are presented with a clear statement of what the ultimate consequences may be if they choose not to accept his argument.

In other words, what we learn from Paine is that effective conclusions can underscore ultimate consequences without resorting to ultimatums. Stating ultimate consequences is more like saying: "If we do not do x, then y will happen"—whereas stating an ultimatum is like saying: "You'd better do x, or else y is your fault."

I offer this advice to my students whenever we discuss the tone and content of conclusions: Do not confuse ultimate consequences with ultimatums. I want them to understand, as Paine does, that ultimatums put a tremendous (and needless) strain on the writer-reader relationship, and such a move is likely to alienate undecided readers and close off the possibility of future discussion of an issue, problem, or question. Stating something as an explanation of ultimate consequences doesn't put your reader in as defensive a position as an ultimatum does.

There is one final element of Paine's conclusion I want to touch on before we look at another example—that element is the curiosity factor. Notice that Paine does not go into extensive detail about what the ultimate consequences will be if people are not persuaded by his argument against maintaining the status quo of British rule.

He makes it clear that the consequences will be negative, but he doesn't elaborate on the degree or the type of negativity—except maybe he suggests that it will resemble the feelings of a man who has some unpleasant task to do but keeps putting it off—only to find himself dogged by the sense that he's doing himself a disservice by procrastinating. This is not a nice state of mind to find yourself in, to be sure, but it's certainly not an emotionally devastating one either.

This is, I think, a calculated move on Paine's part, and it serves as a strategy for both downplaying the difficulty of rebellion against British rule while simultaneously arousing his readers' curiosity about the matter.

Following this restrained and relatively low-key approach, Paine crafts a conclusion that is meant to pique his readers' interests in other potential consequences of staying under British rule—consequences that Paine indirectly suggests that he would be willing to elaborate on in subsequent written arguments (and, in fact, this is what he goes ahead and does). Even if Paine's readers are not yet ready to fully accept his claims, they should be sufficiently intrigued to read whatever else he might have to say about this topic—and what writer doesn't hope that readers will want to read more of her or his work?

Let's take a look at another example of an effective conclusion—this one is from Jonathan Swift's "A Modest Proposal," which we've discussed at length in some of our earlier lectures. Swift is offering a version of Paine's negative consequences approach, but he provides an extra twist—and this is a variation that I like to call the "no viable alternatives"—there is no other option here. Recall that Swift's satire—following the structure of classical Latin satires by writers like Horace and Juvenal—proposes this outlandish solution to a seemingly impossible problem. In this case, the problem is pervasive poverty in Ireland, and the solution is to allow poor parents to sell their children to the rich so that the rich can eat them so that they can provide tasty and nutritious meals.

I should add that Swift is mocking both the British imperialist treatment of Ireland and this impulse among politicians and reformers of his day to suggest really simple, cure-all solutions to what were complex social and economic problems—so he is criticizing that as well as a general attitude towards the Irish.

In his conclusion to "A Modest Proposal," Swift offers a direct challenge to those who would support these naïve attempts at social engineering. Again, he does this in satiric mode, and his tongue is planted firmly in his cheek. Since he, himself, has just finished outlining this simple—and simply ridiculous—plan for fixing the problem, he then has us primed to be ready to listen to what he says next, and here it is:

> I desire those politicians who dislike my overture, and may perhaps be so bold as to attempt an answer, that they will first ask the parents of these mortals, whether they would not at this day think it a great happiness to have been sold for food, at a year old in the manner I prescribe, and thereby have avoided such a perpetual scene of misfortune as they have since gone through by the oppression of landlords, the impossibility of paying rent without money or trade, the want of common sustenance, with neither house nor clothes to cover them from inclemencies of the weather, and the most inevitable prospect of entailing the like or greater miseries upon their breed forever.

So, when I say no viable alternatives what I mean is that this strategy gives you a way in which the conclusion focuses not so much on ultimate consequences of accepting or not accepting the argument—but instead suggests that alternatives to this proposal for changing the status quo aren't workable; they aren't viable at all.

Notice that he doesn't launch a direct attack on any particular plans that other writers have offered; rather, he just points out that any such plans are not likely to work unless and until their authors consider the causes and implications of the problem as fully and as carefully as Swift himself has.

He also offers a kind of litmus test to determine whether any alternative proposals would be as viable as his. He asks the parents of impoverished children if a particular proposed solution would be something they would choose. Swift implies that if the answer is no, then the proposal cannot be considered a worthwhile alternative to his—since his has already passed the test.

Including your own version of Swift's litmus test—some criterion or standard against which alternatives to your claim or proposal have to be measured—is a powerful strategy for persuading readers that you—and not someone else—will offer the best solution or answer to the problem at hand.

In essence, what you're doing is using your conclusion to establish the rules of the game—the terms for assessing the strengths and the weaknesses of any arguments other than yours that deal with the same or similar issues. If other arguments can't measure up to yours—using the standards you've set—then they can't be viewed as viable alternatives—and thus, your argument is the winner!

There is one other element of Swift's brilliant conclusion that we can apply to our own work, but I want to save that for the last item of the lecture. Before we get there, I want us to look at an example from a conclusion that takes a different tone than Paine's or Swift's—because as powerful and as entertaining as their arguments can be, both Paine and Swift finish up on something of a negative note—and I don't at all want to leave you with the impression that a strong conclusion necessarily has to carry a negative tone.

Let me be clear: I'm not suggesting that either Paine or Swift is overly pessimistic—it's clear from the larger arguments they're making that they believe their claims and proposals have the potential to really make some positive, productive change.

Because really, why bother to write an essay like this unless you're actually hoping some change will occur as a result. Neither of these writers offers an especially upbeat ending to his work, and I think it's in our best interest to examine a writer who does. An argument that stresses the negative potential outcomes in its conclusion can be powerful, certainly, but one that manages to end on a hopeful note is really arguably going to be much more persuasive. I think most of us like to think in terms of: "If I follow the suggestion of writer A, good things can happen" rather than: "If I don't do what writer B says, then bad things will happen."

For this example I want to turn to Thoreau's "Civil Disobedience" and examine his final thoughts and the ways he presents them. You'll recall that Thoreau's main thesis involves a dual claim, a two-part claim. First, he argues for the merits of limited government—and this is like when he insists in the opening of the essay: "That government is best which governs least"—and the second part of this claim is that he insists on the primacy of the individual over and against any governing body—so the individual is more important than the collective or the group. He makes this point even to the point of arguing that resistance to an unjust government is not simply an option but is actually a kind of civic duty or an obligation on the part of the individual.

Given the strength of Thoreau's critique of government intervention into the lives of individuals and his strident, strong opposition to the tyranny of the State (and this is whether it's in the form of wars against other nations or raising taxes against its own citizens), what's really intriguing to see here is how he softens his tone in the final lines of "Civil Disobedience," and he allows himself to imagine what an ideal government might be like, and he says:

> I please myself with imagining a State at least which can afford to be just to all men, and to treat the individual with respect as a neighbor; which even would not think it inconsistent with its own repose if a few were to live aloof from it, not meddling with it, nor embraced by it, who fulfilled all the duties of neighbors and fellow-men. A State which bore this kind of fruit, and suffered it to drop off as fast as it ripened, would prepare the way for a still more perfect and glorious State, which also I have imagined, but not yet anywhere seen.

The reflective tone Thoreau takes in this conclusion in no way contradicts the main content of the argument that he has been making throughout "Civil Disobedience." In fact, it provides a large measure of support for his claims by relying on what I like to call the "positive consequences strategy"— meaning he uses his conclusion to emphasize potential new possibilities for a less-intrusive government, and these possibilities will go unrealized if readers fail to heed his arguments. In other words, his goal is not to point out the negative things that may occur if readers do not accept his claims, but rather he wants to underscore the fact that some potentially positive things won't happen.

Thoreau also includes a dimension to his conclusion that mirrors something like what we saw in Paine's final lines. Try and think back if you can to Paine's final lines, and see if you can recall a similarity between the two. That's right: It's the curiosity factor. Like Paine, Thoreau does not go into extensive detail about what the "more perfect and glorious State" he imagines is really like. He makes it clear that the consequences will be positive, but he doesn't elaborate on what those positive consequences will look like— just as Paine makes clear that the consequences he is alluding to would be negative; he doesn't elaborate on the type or the degree of that negativity. So what we said of Paine holds true for Thoreau as well. Even if his readers are not yet ready to fully accept his vision, they will be sufficiently intrigued to read whatever else he might have to say about this topic—and in Thoreau's case, maybe they will be excited to read these writings as well.

Earlier I promised to end this lecture with one last piece from Swift's satirical argument in favor of transforming the impoverished children of Ireland into a culinary staple for the richest members of that society, and I'm sure you'll find that it was worth waiting for—not only because it's entertaining, which it is, but also because it exemplifies yet another method you can employ to make your own conclusions more effective. Here are the final lines of "A Modest Proposal":

> I profess, in the sincerity of my heart, that I have not the least personal interest in endeavoring to promote this necessary work, having no other motive than the public good of my country, by advancing our trade, providing for infants, relieving the poor, and giving some pleasure to the rich. I have no children by which I can propose to get a single penny; the youngest being nine years old, and my wife past child-bearing.

Here Swift sends his readers off with the assurance that he has got nothing to gain, in a financial sense, from his proposal. He maintains an intellectual investment in the argument, of course, and he notes his satisfaction in doing something for the broader public good, but he takes really special care to point out that no economic benefits will be forthcoming for him personally if his argument is accepted and his proposal is implemented.

Swift's razor-sharp wit and the satirical edge he uses are still readily apparent—there is no question about that—but this is also a deliberate attempt to thwart any what we might call *ad hominem* challenges to his writing—these would be attacks on him, on his personality. These attacks against his character or charges that his arguments are biased due to a personal stake in the outcome aren't going to work because of what he has done here at the end.

Obviously, Swift's preemptive strike is, like the rest of his argument, carried out in ironic terms. There is no chance he'd be accused of crafting such an argument in the hopes that it would be implemented and lead to a financial windfall. In other words, there's no way we could imagine that he would write such a piece and then he'd go say: "I'll go first and sell my child to show you how profitable it can be!" Still, he was correct, and his preemptive strike indicates this. He's correct in a more general sense to anticipate there's going to be some form of backlash from his readers.

They may not have suspected him of plotting to pad his pocketbook, but many certainly were offended by the graphic nature of his argument—even though it's presented as a satire. So, it would be safe to say that Swift was, in fact, responding to the possibility of ad hominem attacks, just not from anyone who might seek to advance his own children-as-hors d'oeuvres social welfare scheme.

We can glean from Swift's closing lines an important reminder and a striking example of how conclusions can be used to anticipate and refute, in advance, charges that an argument for some broader goal or cause is actually self-serving. You don't have to follow Swift's over-the-top style, but we shouldn't hesitate to emulate the spirit of his conclusion when we perceive that some similar possibility of a personal attack will follow in the wake of us making our own arguments.

So, what things should we take away from this final lecture in our four-part series on crafting successful arguments? I can't stress enough the importance of using the conclusion to recap the main thesis and key points of your argument. But I would also strongly encourage you to go beyond a basic summary and explore the three strategies we have covered here today. Those are, as you remember, the negative consequences approach used by Paine, the no viable alternatives model that Swift gave us, and the positive consequences model that Thoreau used. I'd also urge you to think about ways of using conclusions to pique your readers' curiosity, to get them interested, as Paine and Thoreau do—how they touch on consequences without going into extensive detail as a means of enticing readers to consider other arguments they might have to offer.

Finally, I hope you'll always be mindful of the possibility that you may need to use a conclusion to preemptively defend yourself against critiques and challenges that would seek to undermine your claims by labeling them as selfish or self-serving. If you can anticipate how someone might argue against you and what they might say, then you'd better address it head-on rather than ignore it. As Swift makes clear, conclusions are a powerful place to dilute or defuse such attempts and turn the tide of readerly opinion in your favor.

Now that you have all become experts on how to produce effective arguments, I'd like you to turn your newly critical eyes to some literary works and consider how they can help you become more engaging writers. In our next three lectures, we're going to focus on poetry and drama and what we can get out of having an understanding and appreciation of writing in these genres.

The Uses of Poetry
Lecture 10

> You would not be alone if you were thinking that the definition of poetry is probably something like the U.S. Supreme Court's infamous definition of pornography, which is "I can't define it, but I know it when I see it."

In this lecture, we explore how understanding poetry can help us become better readers and writers. First, what do you think poetry is? You may think of definitions like "a poem rhymes," "it has a particular rhythm or pattern," or "it uses words in unusual ways." Consider the following piece of text:

I have eaten
the plums
that were in
the icebox

and which
you were probably
saving
for breakfast

Forgive me
they were delicious
so sweet
and so cold

If you hear this read aloud, you might think it's not a poem but instead a note of apology. In fact, it is a very famous poem by William Carlos Williams. Part of what makes it a poem is not the words themselves but how the words are laid out on the page. You'll also notice that phrases and sentences are cut in unusual places—places you would not expect to find a pause in everyday writing.

This poem has no punctuation—the only guide to how to read the piece is where the line breaks occur. By popping up in unexpected places, they call our attention to certain words or combinations of words that we might not otherwise notice. For example, the word "saving" has its own line; this makes us ponder, maybe, if it is not just the saving of the plums that is being referenced, but some larger, deeper idea of saving. Similarly, "forgive me" stands alone, also raising in the minds of the readers possible larger ideas about forgiveness in general.

The final two lines of the poem also seem to mark it as something not typical of a note left on the kitchen table. Apologizing for eating the plums doesn't require the writer to tell the reader how the plums tasted—that's a little extra poetic flourish. And that final word, "cold," is interesting in that it really doesn't describe what the plums tasted like but instead the fact that they had been in the icebox, and it thus calls us back to that word, "icebox," early in the poem. That's another word that may have caught our attention, in that it's archaic. So the choice of that word tells us something perhaps about the age of the poet or gives us an idea that the speaker of the poem lives sometime in the past.

Let's take a look at John Donne's elegy "On His Mistress Going to Bed." Donne was one of the most revered poets of the English Renaissance, and his work today remains some of the most studied and enjoyed in English literature. Read these lines from the middle of the poem:

> Licence my roving hands, and let them go
> Before, behind, between, above, below.
> O, my America, my Newfoundland,
> My kingdom, safest when with one man mann'd,
> My mine of precious stones, my empery;
> How am I blest in thus discovering thee!
> To enter in these bonds, is to be free;
> Then, where my hand is set, my soul shall be.

We could spend days unpacking this poem—it is a delightfully clever play on the idea of exploration, referencing the discovery of what Europeans thought of as the New World. There is also a double entendre or two. How would you describe the tone of the poem; what are some words that spring to mind? "Joy" might be one, "delight," or even "ecstasy." If the words weren't enough to convey the speaker's happiness, then the exclamation point in "How am I blest in thus discovering thee!" certainly does.

What else makes Donne's poem so compelling? One of the most important elements of this poem is metaphor, which is similar to another poetic device, simile. A simile makes a comparison between two things by using the words "like" or "as." An example of a simile would be "her eyes were like the ocean" or "her eyes were as blue as the ocean"; a metaphor would be if you simply said "her eyes were oceans." In the case of Donne's poem, the metaphor is that his lover's body is an undiscovered country ripe for exploration.

Metaphor and simile can be effective devices for engaging a reader's attention.

Metaphor and simile can be effective devices for engaging a reader's attention, as can devices like synecdoche: when you use a word describing a part to mean the whole. For example, in the classic line "all hands on deck," the word "hands" stands in for "people." A close relative of this device is metonymy: when a word that describes something associated with an idea is used in place of the logical word. The classic example is "The White House said today." Obviously, the words "White House" are standing in for the president and his or her representatives.

But how can reading and understanding poetry help us with our own writing? We can learn to recognize skillful treatments of language that help the words on the page add up to more than the sum of their parts. We can also be conscious of making more dramatic choices in our style and diction. What I think is most important is that poetry can intrigue us, can get us to think intensely about a certain subject in new or unexpected ways, and can also simply delight us with its use of wordplay. ∎

Suggested Reading

Barnet and Cain, *A Short Guide to Writing about Literature.*

DiYanni, *Literature.*

Gardner, *Writing about Literature.*

Griffith, *Writing Essays about Literature.*

Guerin et al., *A Handbook of Critical Approaches to Literature.*

Kennedy and Gioia, *Literature.*

Roberts, *Writing about Literature.*

Exercises

Each of the sentences below is written in fairly straightforward, plain prose. Rewrite each so that you make use of figurative or poetic language to punch up the sentence. Example: "She had blonde hair." Rewrite: "She had hair the color of ripe wheat."

1. It was a cold and rainy day.

2. She was a tall, thin woman with brown eyes and short, dark hair.

3. The countryside had lots of green hills and trees.

4. He was excited to learn that his sister was coming home soon.

The Uses of Poetry
Lecture 10—Transcript

Welcome back. In our last four lectures, we discussed the basics of argumentative writing—how to start an argument, support it, and conclude it. Today, we're going to turn our attention back to issues of genre and explore how understanding specific styles of writing—like poetry—can help us be better readers and writers no matter what we're trying to say or to whom we're trying to say it.

Let's stop for a moment and consider the question: "What is poetry?" Probably as you consider that question, many of you are thinking something like: "A poem rhymes," or "It's got a particular rhythm or pattern," or maybe even something a little broader than that like "Poetry is using words in unusual ways." You would not be alone if you were thinking that the definition of poetry is probably something like the U.S. Supreme Court's infamous definition of pornography, which is: "I can't define it, but I know it when I see it."

When I ask students if they can define poetry, I often get a series of responses kind of along what you were probably just thinking when I posed the same question to you. They'll tell me: "It sometimes rhymes" or "It's written in a different style than 'normal' writing." Think for a moment about how you would define poetry. What makes a poem a poem and not something else?

Consider the following short piece of text:

> Mary, Mary, quite contrary
> How does your garden grow?
> With silver bells and cockleshells
> and pretty maids all in a row.

Is that a poem? Most of us would say: "Yes, it follows a pattern; it rhymes," and most of you may recognize it as a nursery rhyme from your childhood. So we could probably all agree that's a poem.

Now consider this:

> I have eaten
> the plums
> that were in
> the icebox
>
> and which
> you were probably
> saving
> for breakfast
>
> Forgive me
> they were delicious
> so sweet
> and so cold

Now many of you are probably thinking: "Well, that's not a poem; that's a note of apology that someone has written to someone else." But, in fact, what I just read to you is a poem, and it's a very famous poem by the poet William Carlos Williams. Part of what makes it a poem is not the words themselves or the content—but how the words are laid out on the page, and I know you can't see it right now, but I want you to listen to it again, and this time notice where I pause—those are breaks between lines, and what you'll most likely notice when you're paying attention to the pauses is that phrases and sentences are cut off in unusual places—places where you wouldn't expect to find a pause. It would be unexpected to have a break there in what we might call "normal" or "everyday" writing. Here's the poem again, and this time I'm reading it to really emphasize the line breaks on the page:

> I have eaten
> the plums
> that were in
> the icebox

and which
you were probably
saving
for breakfast

Forgive me
they were delicious
so sweet
and so cold

This poem has no punctuation—there are no commas, periods, exclamation points, nothing—so the only guide as to how to read the piece is to use the line breaks, to see where they occur—and in this case, what the breaks do by popping up in kind of unexpected places is call our attention to certain words or combination of words that we might not otherwise recognize as sort of standing apart or being outside of the realm of kind of normal writing.

For example, in this poem, the word "saving" has its own line—there aren't any other words on that line—so, obviously, our attention is called to the word "saving," and it makes us ponder, maybe, if it is not just the saving of the plums that is being referenced here, but maybe there is some larger, deeper idea of saving that is at work. Similarly, "Forgive me" stands alone—again, suggesting not only forgiveness for the eating of the plums, but also, I would say, raising in the minds of the readers possible larger ideas about forgiveness in general.

The final two lines of the poem—"so sweet/and so cold"—also seem to mark this piece as something that is not typical of a note left on the kitchen table. It's one thing to apologize for eating plums, but apologizing for eating the plums doesn't require the writer to tell the reader how the plums tasted—it's a little extra flourish that signals that something poetic is happening here.

That final word, "cold," is interesting in that it really doesn't describe what the plums tasted like—but, instead, the fact that they had been in the icebox, and that in turn calls us back to that word "icebox," which occurs early in the poem. Probably as you were listening to it, that was a word that caught your attention, and it probably caught your attention because it's what we would call "archaic"—it's old. It would be really unusual to hear anyone use that word nowadays—we'd be more likely to say "refrigerator."

So, the choice of that word tells us something perhaps about the age of the poet—or gives us an idea that the speaker of the poem at least lives sometime in the past. In any event, it tells us that we're not dealing with what we might call straightforward modern-day normal or average writing.

"Great," you may be thinking, "but how can this help us with our own writing?" At the very least it calls attention to how important the arrangement or the structure of words on a page can be. For example, consider this sentence, something like: "It seemed like a good idea, but the end result proved otherwise." All right, that's pretty straightforward. There's not a lot that seems out of place or unusual there, but if we altered the structure—if we put in what we could call "poetic stops"—then the impact is heightened. So, let's play with the sentence. Let's put a period after the word "idea" and another after the word "but" so that this one sentence now becomes three, and it reads: "It seemed like a good idea. But. The end result proved otherwise." Many of you are probably thinking right about now: "But according to the rules, you can't have this single word 'But' followed by a period!" and you would be right; technically speaking, you can't, but that's the other thing that poetry can teach us—how breaking the rules can create a dramatic and memorable effect.

Here's another poem by William Carlos Williams:

> so much depends
> upon
> a red wheel
> barrow
> glazed with rain
> water
> beside the white
> chickens

Is this a poem? Most of you probably said "yes." How do we know? After the practice run we did with the first poem, you were probably listening fairly attentively for the line breaks and noticed that they appeared in odd or unexpected places. Also, this piece, although you can't necessarily hear it, it does have a pattern—a three-word line, a single-word line, and then a break, and that pattern repeats throughout.

For example, line one has three words—"so much depends"; line two has one word—"upon," and then there is a two-line break before the next line picks up. That conscious structure also declares that this is a poem. Another thing about it is that it has a strong pictorial quality; in other words, it calls up to our minds a pretty vivid picture, at least in the contrast between the colors red and white.

Even more than the first example, this poem seems to be conveying or suggesting something that's not readily obvious—"Why," I'm sure many of you are asking, "does so much depend on a red wheelbarrow, rainwater, and some white chickens?" If you could answer that question convincingly, you would become the darling of the academic world.

Literally thousands of pages of analysis and interpretation have been written about this poem since it first appeared in 1923, but I want to stress that trying to figure out what Williams is trying to say is not what's most important here—nor I would argue is trying to figure out what a poem means, the most important thing about poetry in general. Instead, what I think is most important is that poetry can intrigue us, can get us to think intensely about a certain subject in new or unexpected ways, and can also simply delight or stun us with its use of word play or images.

So we're back to that initial question: What is poetry? Poetry has occasionally been defined as something like "beautiful violence done to language," and I tend to think that that definition comes pretty close, but we might want to refine it a little bit. Scholar Terry Eagleton—in trying to describe what literature is—famously has said, and I quote:

"Literature transforms and intensifies ordinary language, deviates systematically from everyday speech. If you approach me at a bus stop and murmur: 'Thou still unravished bride of quietness,' then I am instantly aware that I am in the presence of the literary." So, if someone comes up to you at the bus stop, for example, and says: "Is this the number 10?" well, then, that's not really poetic nor does it seem to be literary.

But if someone comes up to you at a bus stop and says: "Thou still unravished bride of quietness," you can think: (1) This is a poet, or (2) This person is crazy, or (3) All of the above. I would argue that history has suggested that number 3 is more often than not the correct choice here.

Eagleton's definition of literature also helps to get us closer to a definition of what poetry is—and we've gotten a little closer to having some idea of what a poem is or can be even if we can't come up with a totally satisfactory definition. By now at least you surely understand that poetry plays with words and images in unexpected ways, no matter what else it does. So now that we have a working definition—and it's general and vague admittedly, but we have a working definition—you then might want to ask a question: "Why bother to study poetry at all?"

The mature and academic argument would be that by examining works by some of the greatest poets in the past and recent times, we can learn to recognize particularly clever or skillful treatments of language that help the words on the page add up to more than the sum of their parts, and that's sort of a poetic image in and of itself—the words on the page add up to more than the sum of their parts. While you might not want to write your job letter in rhyme, or structure your next essay along the lines of the free verse of William Carlos Williams, the study of poetry can teach us how both following the rules and breaking them can produce really dramatic and engaging effects.

The other answer to the question: "Why study poetry?" is quite simple, and that's because it's fun. Engaging a poem can be a wonderful exercise in analysis—and we can get even more pleasure from doing this once we understand some of the basic conventions of this style of writing. So in this lecture and the next one, we're going to examine poetic devices like "metaphor" and "simile," words you have probably heard before but maybe aren't quite clear on the definition of. We're also going to look particularly at how poetry's contradictory reverence for, and love of, playing with language make writing in this genre some of the most powerful and persuasive you are ever likely to encounter.

As you probably recall from some of our previous discussions, voice is a big deal no matter what kind of writing you're doing. For example, if you consider the following excerpts from famous poems, and you try to define what kind of voice they each have, you probably will come pretty close to hitting on the right answer. Is the voice or tone happy or sad? Arrogant? Angry or excited? By practicing this, you can get a feel for how powerful voice can be. Let's start by considering just the first stanza, just the first four lines, of John Keats's "Ode on a Grecian Urn." This is, when you get right down to it, a poem about an old vase, but it has become one of the most famous literary works in the English language. Here are the opening lines:

> Thou still unravished bride of quietness,
> Thou fosterchild of silence and slow time,
> Sylvan historian, who canst thus express
> A flowery tale more sweetly than our rhyme.

What are some of the first things you notice here? There is rhythm and rhyme, obviously—that's going to be probably the first thing that catches our attention and maybe announces to us: This is a poem—but what about the tone or the voice?

From the very first word, we're given a strong suggestion that we are dealing with subject matter of what we might call "a higher order." "Thou" is the first word, and this is a form of address you really don't hear any more and that many of us associate with an earlier time period or with extremely formal forms of address—although, originally, I will tell you that "thou" was the informal form of addressing someone in English, but that fact is neither here nor there and really not important for our purposes today, but as a medievalist I couldn't help but point that fact out. For most of us today, as an audience, the word "thou" is most likely to conjure up associations with something like the King James Bible.

Other words that kind of signpost to us that the tone of this piece is rather formal or elevated are words like "canst" and "sylvan"—the first you can probably figure out no problem; it's an older, archaic form of "can"; the other word, "sylvan," is absolutely bursting with associations with the classical world, the world in which the great epic poets Homer and Virgil wrote.

Technically speaking, "sylvan" just means having something to do with the woods, but if you were an educated person in John Keats's day, that word alone should immediately conjure up images of Greek and Roman gods and some minor deities and mythical woodland creatures frolicking through the forest. A moment ago, when I said Keats's poem is about an old vase—well, it is, but it's about a vase that belongs to the great works of art of the ancient world. Any museum worth its salt will have a Grecian urn or two, and these are some of the most spectacular pieces of art to be preserved from antiquity.

So knowing all of this, what is the tone of the poem? What is its voice? Probably many of you are thinking of adjectives like "reverent," or "full of awe," or "admiring," and these would all be right. There is also a kind of delicacy, humility, and respect that Keats is conveying through his word choice.

After that example, it should be fairly easy for you to determine the tone of the next sample. This comes from Edwin Arlington Robinson's poem "Luke Havergal." I'm just going to read you the third stanza:

> Out of a grave I come to tell you this,
> Out of a grave I come to quench the kiss
> That flames upon your forehead with a glow
> That blinds you to the way that you must go.
> Yes, there is yet one way to where she is,
> Bitter, but one that faith may never miss.
> Out of a grave I come to tell you this—
> To tell you this.

You may have no idea what is going on in this poem—and, in fact, you would not be alone. Many scholars, in fact, have had long debates about what is going on here—but even without knowing the subject matter of the poem, can you at least tell what the tone is? Is it happy? Definitely not. Somber? Most definitely. "Gloomy," "frightening," and "threatening" are some other words that come to mind when I try and think of what the tone of this poem is. Your first clue here is probably the phrase "Out of a grave." We can all probably agree that not much good has ever really come out of a grave. Other words that contribute to the mood are words like "quench," "blinds," "bitter," and some others. The images that these words and phrases conjure up are definitely not sunshine and springtime. So we can nail down the tone pretty easily, and let's compare that to our last example of poetry for today, John Donne's elegy "To His Mistress Going to Bed." Donne was one of the most revered poets of the English Renaissance, and his work today remains some of the most studied and enjoyed in all English literature. Let's listen to these lines from the middle of the poem:

> Licence my roving hands, and let them go
> Before, behind, between, above, below.
> O, my America, my Newfoundland,
> My kingdom, safest when with one man mann'd,
> My mine of precious stones, my empery;
> How am I blest in thus discovering thee!
> To enter in these bonds, is to be free;
> Then, where my hand is set, my soul shall be.

We could spend days "unpacking" this poem—it's a delightfully clever play on the idea of exploration; it references the discovery of what Europeans at that time thought of as the New World. You'll recall that line: "O, my America" that probably leaped out at you. At the time when Donne was writing, English society was all abuzz with this fever of discovery and exploration. Fortunes were being made as people rushed off to exploit the natural resources of the Americas.

You may have picked up as I was reading this that there are maybe a double entendre or sometimes it's so obvious it's essentially a single entendre, but a double entendre or two. If we're thinking about the issue of voice, though, how would you describe the tone of the poem? What are some of the words that spring to mind when you're trying to describe how this poem sounds, the kind of feeling it's trying to convey? I think certainly "joy" might be one, "delight," or even "ecstasy." Remember, he says: "O, my America"—that O, that emphasis is all in one letter, a sense of happiness, of discovery.

O, my America, my Newfoundland
My kingdom safest when with one man mann'd
My mine of precious stones, my empery
How am I blest in thus discovering thee!

If the words themselves weren't enough to convey the speaker's happiness, then if you're reading it you notice the exclamation point after "How am I blest in thus discovering thee!"—and it certainly creates emphasis and makes clear that the speaker here is in a state of extreme happiness.

What else makes Donne's poem so compelling? One of the most important elements of this poem is his use of what we call a "poetic device." Donne uses several, but the dominant one that's being used here is something called "metaphor." Probably most of you are familiar with metaphor, and it's similar to another poetic device called "simile." Quite often, people get metaphor and simile confused, and that's very understandable because they're alike in many ways, but here's a quick way, a quick definition, so you can distinguish between the two: A simile makes a comparison between two things by using the words "like" or "as." An example of a sentence that uses a simile would be: "Her eyes were like the ocean" or "Her eyes were as blue as the ocean." A metaphor would be if you got rid of the "like" or the "as," and you simply said: "Her eyes were oceans." In the case of Donne's poem, the metaphor is that his lover's body is an undiscovered country ripe for exploration, and he makes brilliant use of it.

There are numerous other poetic devices, and our ability to recognize them and know when they're being skillfully employed by a poet can really enhance our pleasure when we read a poem. There are devices like alliteration, assonance, consonance—all of these things have to do with the way words sound, and these are often used in poems that have a rhyme scheme.

Metaphor and simile can be effective devices for engaging a reader's attention—as can devices like "synecdoche," when you use a word describing a part to mean the whole; for example, the classic line: "All hands on deck." It does not mean what it literally says: Everyone put their hands on the deck. It means all people on board the ship get up on deck now. The word "hands" stands in for "people." A close relative of this device is "metonymy," when a word that describes something associated with an idea is used in place of the usual, logical, practical word.

Here, the classic example is: "The White House said today." Obviously, the White House is not speaking, but the words "White House" here are standing in for the president and his representatives. Similar examples would be things like: "The Vatican announced today" or "Wall Street reacted strongly." So, as you can see, there are poetic devices that we use every day in our normal everyday lives.

"That is all well and good" you might be thinking, and we could spend several hours discussing numerous poetic devices that exist, and we could come up with examples of each. "But how," you are probably wondering, "can this make me a better writer?" The ways in which understanding poetic devices can make you a better writer are a little obvious, but how do we take that and then apply it to our own writing? I mean you could probably identify it in other writing: "Oh, here's how a poetic device made this piece stronger." But then taking what you have learned and then applying it to your own writing, that's a little trickier. At its most basic, we can take that working definition of poetry—that it's language used in unusual or non-typical ways—and by taking that working definition, we can at least be conscious of how we might make more dramatic or effective choices in our style and diction when we write.

Let's consider something quite simple, like the description of a house, and here is a quote: "The exterior was dark green, and the huge lawn that surrounded it was just a shade or two lighter. There was a brick walkway leading up to the front door." That's pretty straightforward, and you might think there's no reason to change anything here, but if you were trying to intrigue your reader and draw her in, you might try and punch things up a bit.

For example, what if you wrote: "The exterior was dark green, like the forest at twilight, and the lawn that surrounded it was an ocean of emerald—the walkway to the front door, a streak of blood that marred its perfection."

Okay, so that's a little over the top, but this version is definitely more interesting. How many poetic devices did you notice? There's at least three at work here—one simile and two metaphors—and by adding some devices and some key words—"twilight," "emerald," "blood"—you suddenly have a much more interesting piece of writing, especially if your intention is to set the scene for a murder mystery full of rich, glamorous characters.

If your goal, however, is to place an ad in a real estate magazine to persuade someone to buy your house, then perhaps you've gone in the wrong direction here. In the exercises for today's lecture, I've given you some really straightforward sentences, and I've asked you to make them more interesting by rewriting them with some of the poetic devices we've talked about today in mind.

When you're doing these exercises, I really want you to push the envelope and go a little bit overboard just so you start to get the hang of this poetic language thing, but as I've said before, sometimes less really is more, and showing some restraint is always a good idea. A paragraph that has simile, metaphor, synecdoche, and other devices all used together might be a technical tour de force, but you don't want your readers to be so dazzled by your writing that they miss the major point of what it is you're trying to say.

So, what have we learned from today's discussion of poetry? At the very least, we have some idea of what poetry is—even if we can't exactly define it in so many words. We saw how sometimes the arrangement of words can make a poem—even if the words themselves don't say anything that unusual.

This was the case with the William Carlos Williams poem about the plums. It could be read as if it was just a note left on the breakfast table, but what we can take away from this lesson is, again, the importance of the arrangement of words on the page. Even if you're not writing a poem, but rather an essay, a magazine article, a short story, or a letter to the editor, how you arrange your words can have almost as much of an impact as what your words say.

We also talked about recognizing voice or tone in poetry, and we looked at three famous examples:—the "Ode on a Grecian Urn," "Luke Havergal," and "To His Mistress Going to Bed" to better understand how voice or tone

167

can be created. We discussed some of the most common poetic devices, like metaphor and simile, and we saw how they can be used in non-poetic works to create greater impact.

As you might be thinking, we've just scratched the surface when it comes to poetry, and there's a whole lot more to be said about how to engage a poem and how to use what you know about poetry to improve your own writing. In our next lecture, we're going to continue our exploration of poetry, and we're going to spend some more time talking about diction, syntax, and the benefits and drawbacks of working in English—one of the more delightfully idiosyncratic languages. I hope you'll join us for more.

Poetic Diction and Syntax

Lecture 11

English has an unusually large vocabulary drawn from a number of different languages that come from different branches on the family tree of languages. A lot of other languages have no need of books like a thesaurus. This huge smorgasbord of words in English is one of the great things about our language—but we have so many options that it can also be problematic.

In this lecture, we deepen our discussion of poetry by focusing on issues of diction and syntax. As we do this, we'll address the need to pay attention to matters of connotation, association, and the particular difficulties caused by the nature of the English language—which is one of the few languages that has so many synonyms that it's necessary for every schoolchild to learn to use a thesaurus.

Consider the following sentence: "We have to come up with some kind of scheme to deal with this." Upon hearing this, what are your immediate reactions? Is the person who said this honest and trustworthy? Why? What you're probably focusing on is the word "scheme." What if the sentence had read "We have to come up with some kind of plan to deal with this"? How do you feel about the speaker now? Honest? Trustworthy? Or maybe you can't tell one way or another.

> **It's not just word choice that can have an impact—word order also is important.**

If you look up "scheme" and "plan" in a dictionary or thesaurus, you'll find that they are usually given as simple equivalents of one another. But in addition to a word's definition, there is also a word's connotation to consider. In American English, as well as some other versions, the word "scheme" has negative associations—it connotes something illegal, underhanded, deceptive.

So we've established that word choice is an important consideration when you're writing and that learning about this from poetry can help make your writing more engaging. But it's not just word choice that can have an impact—word order also is important. What I'm talking about here is syntax, or the grammatical ordering of a sentence so that it makes sense.

For example, the sentence "The king married the queen" makes perfect sense; if we were to mess with the syntax so that the words read "Queen king the the married," this makes no sense at all. The sentence "The king married the queen" is a perfect example of the most common sentence structure in English: subject-verb-object. But listen to just three sentences in a row using that structure: "The king married the queen. They lived in a castle. They were good rulers." Do you want to keep reading if the whole paper or article follows this structure? Probably not. Why? Because it's boring! Now what if we changed the syntax a bit? What if we said "The king and queen—they got married. In a castle they lived, and ruled well." That might seem a little stilted, but hands down it's more interesting than the first version.

Poetry can be a good teacher when it comes to understanding syntax as well as word choice, and perhaps the poet to most famously play with matters of syntax is E. E. Cummings. Here is the opening of Cummings's "anyone lived in a pretty how town":

> anyone lived in a pretty how town
> (with up so floating many bells down)
> spring summer autumn winter
> he sang his didn't he danced his did.

What do you think of these lines? Even though we can't do a really accurate "translation" by simply correcting the syntax or changing the word choice, we get some images and some idea of what the poet is trying to convey. Let's start with the basics—there's someone who lives in a town, and it seems as if there are church bells that ring in this town, throughout the year, and this person maybe sings and dances or maybe doesn't.

Now, you could make all sorts of interpretations that are very different from what I've just suggested, but you get the point that even though the syntax is confusing, some images can be discerned if we think hard about it. And it's that mystery—it is what is hard (or initially confusing) about this poem—that makes it so good and so interesting. I wouldn't suggest you just throw the words of your story up on the page in random order and leave it to your reader to sort out, but you could try to vary your word order as a means of engaging your reader.

The more you read—of all kinds of writing—the better you will be as a writer. Of course, the other piece of advice is simply to write, and to have as many eyes as possible look at what you are writing. This is a case where you certainly *can* learn by doing, and the more you do, the better you get. Practice what you've learned from these lectures over and over and over again. ∎

Suggested Reading

Barnet and Cain, *A Short Guide to Writing about Literature.*

DiYanni, *Literature.*

Gardner, *Writing about Literature.*

Griffith, *Writing Essays about Literature.*

Guerin et al., *A Handbook of Critical Approaches to Literature.*

Kennedy and Gioia, *Literature.*

Roberts, *Writing about Literature.*

Exercises

Consider the following sentences. Rewrite each so that the syntax is different, and consider what effect this has. In some cases, you may need to combine two sentences into one. Example: "She was tired after a long day at work." Rewrite: "After working a long day, she was tired."

1. I was driving along the road. I saw my favorite coffee shop and decided to stop.

2. There is nothing better than hot coffee with cream and sugar on a cold morning.

3. I balanced my coffee, scone, and wallet as I went back to my car.

4. I drove around for a while before I was able to find the on-ramp.

Poetic Diction and Syntax
Lecture 11—Transcript

Welcome back. In our previous lecture, we began our discussion of poetry and made attempts to define it, understand what makes it different from normal language, and identify some poetic devices that might be useful in our own writing. Today, we're going to continue and deepen our discussion by focusing in particular on issues of diction and syntax, which we touched on just a bit last time.

As we do this, we'll need to address the need to pay attention to matters of connotation, association, and the particular difficulties caused by the nature of the English language itself because it is one of the few languages that has so many potential synonyms for certain words. It's interesting that English is one of those languages in which it's necessary for every school child to learn how to use a thesaurus.

As you certainly remember from your elementary school days, a thesaurus is a book that lists synonyms for various words, and it's a useful thing to have if you want to avoid repeating the same word over and over in a piece of writing—for example, you can describe something as "fast," or "quick," or "speedy," or even "moving with alacrity," and they all mean roughly the same thing.

English has an unusually large vocabulary drawn from a number of different languages that come from different branches on the family tree of languages. A lot of other languages have no need of books like a thesaurus. This huge smorgasbord of words in English is one of the great things about our language—but we have so many options that it can also be problematic, as you'll see in a moment.

Consider the following sentence: "We have to come up with some kind of scheme to deal with this." Upon hearing this, what are your immediate reactions? Is the person who said this honest, trustworthy? Why or why not? What you're probably focusing on is the word "scheme." What if the sentence had read instead something like: "We have to come up with some kind of plan to deal with this"? How do you feel about the speaker now? Is the speaker honest, trustworthy? Or maybe you just can't tell one way or another.

If you look up the word "scheme" and "plan" in a dictionary or a thesaurus, they're usually given as simple equivalents of one another. But in addition to a word's definition, there is also a word's connotation or association to consider. In American English as well as some other versions, the word "scheme" has negative associations—it connotes something illegal, underhanded, or deceptive.

It's a plan, sure, but not any plan in which a law-abiding citizen wants to be involved. You might hear any number of villains described as scheming or otherwise planning dastardly deeds. A word closer to "scheme" than "plan" might be "plot," as many bad guys in books and movies hatch nefarious plots to enrich themselves, or else they plot their revenge. Again, these three words—scheme, plot, and plan—have essentially the same definition, but the nuances of connotation mean that they can indicate positive or negative qualities of the person or thing with which they're associated.

When I teach history of the English language, I try to get my students to appreciate how huge the vocabulary of English is by giving them an assignment in which they have to take a famous speech, or poem, or song, and then they have to rewrite it using only words that are native to the English language.

When they're doing this exercise, I also make them note the origin or what we call the "etymology" of the non-native words. Do those words come from Latin? Do they come from Greek? Do they come from French?—etc., etc., and let me tell you, I have gotten some pretty interesting versions of Abraham Lincoln's "Gettysburg Address" out of this assignment.

For example, the word "perish" in the famous lines "government of the people, by the people, for the people shall not perish from the earth"—not a native English word—it comes into middle English around the year 1200 via French, but it's not found in Old English—and that's where I have my students start, with the language spoken by the Anglo-Saxon peoples who invaded Britain starting in the 5th century—that's where English ultimately has its roots, and since "perish" isn't found in Old English, students have to change that word.

In trying to find a native English workaround, they often find they have to change the whole structure of that line, and everyone is pretty dissatisfied with what they come up with—"shall not die out on earth" is the most common rewrite I get, but it lacks the power, and the punch, and the rhythm that using the word "perish" gives that line.

When I give this assignment, my students are explicitly forbidden from using the poetry of Gerard Manley Hopkins, who was famous for trying as hard as he could to use only native English words in his writing—so, obviously, if you're a student in my class, and you pick a Hopkins poem for this project, you'd have the assignment completed in about five minutes, and you really wouldn't have learned much of anything.

So you can understand the point I'm making here. To make it even clearer, I've slightly rewritten one of Hopkins's best-known poems, and what I've done here is I've replaced several of his more colorful, interesting words with what I think at least are less-exciting ones. This poem is called "Pied Beauty," and for it to make sense, you need to know that "pied"—spelled p-i-e-d—means having patches or spots of two or more colors. So here's my version, with most of what seem the most interesting words replaced. I haven't changed everything, but I think I've changed enough so that when you compare the two versions, you'll hear and understand a real difference. So again, here's my version:

> Glory be to God for multi-colored things—
> For skies of more than one color as a spotted cow
> For reddish spots all spotted upon trout that swim;
> Fresh roasted chestnuts as the shell falls off; finches' wings;
> Landscape arranged and divided—dip, unplanted land, and
>   plowed land
> And all professions, their equipment and tools and apparatus.
> All things in opposition, original, unadorned, unusual;
> Whatever is inconstant, spotted (who knows how?)

With quick, slow; sweet, sour; shining, dim;
He gives birth whose beauty is past change:
Praise him.

What's your reaction to this poem? Does it describe multi-colored or spotted things? Yes, indeed it does. Do you understand what the poet is trying to say? Probably—essentially, Hopkins is saying that things that are multi-colored or dappled have a unique beauty—from animals, to nuts, to the land, to those who work at a trade or a craft.

In several places, I used words that mean the same things as what Hopkins was trying to say in essence, but I used a word that's very common today—like the word "profession," which I use to take the place of a simpler word—but one that has an older connotation. In that position, Hopkins uses "trades" where I said "profession." What else could I have said? How about "career"? That would work, too, but neither "profession" or "career" has the same connotation as "trade," and I think that's a word that suggests not just what one does for a living, but that one works with one's hands to earn one's living.

That's enough of me. Let's go back to Hopkins's original poem in all its glory. This is it:

Glory be to God for dappled things—
For skies of couple-color as a brinded cow
For rose-moles all in stipple upon trout that swim;
Fresh-fire coal chestnut-falls; finches' wings;
Landscape plotted and pieced—fold, fallow, and plow
And áll trádes, their gear and tackle and trim.

All things counter, original, spare, strange;
Whatever is fickle, freckled (who knows how?)
With swift, slow; sweet, sour; adazzle, dim;
He fathers-forth whose beauty is past change:
Praise him.

What do you think of that version? Do you understand what he's trying to say? The answer is, probably not so much if you're just hearing it for the first time. In many ways, this poem overwhelms the senses with its sound and rhythm—the first time listening to it, a lot of the words probably don't even make any sense—"brinded," "stipple," and "adazzle" are all words that no one I know uses on a regular basis, and even words we do know—like "plotted," "fallow," and even "plow"—are used here in arrangements that we don't normally encounter.

They're put together here in combinations that make greatest use of their sounds—of alliteration or words that begin with the same sound, of assonance or repetition of the same vowel sounds within words, and of consonance or the use of a similar consonant sound in a series of words. To be sure, Hopkins uses many more poetic devices than just these, but for our purposes today, these are the major ones that stand out—especially in a line like "Landscape plotted and pieced—fold, fallow, and plow." There's even some good old-fashioned rhyme in there, but it's not in a pattern that's easy to follow or typical of more simplistic poetry. Let's listen to that first stanza one more time, and I really think you can't listen to Hopkins too much. There's always room for one more listen:

> Glory be to God for dappled things—
> For skies of couple-color as a brinded cow
> For rose-moles all in stipple upon trout that swim;
> Fresh-fire coal chestnut-falls; finches' wings;
> Landscape plotted and pieced—fold, fallow, and plow
> And áll trádes, their gear and tackle and trim.

The second time through what new things did you pick up on? For one, you might have noticed the rhyming pattern a little bit more—it's much more complex than a simple rhyming couplet, but there is rhyme there, and it's a really compelling kind of rhyme. If you can remember back that far—it has been a few minutes now—how do you think that compares with my rather simplified version, in which I replaced some of the more interesting words with different ones?

To be sure, in my version, I'm betting that getting the meaning and getting a clear idea of all the images that are being evoked—it's still more difficult than in the first, altered version I gave you. My version is probably a little clearer. Hopkins is probably a little less clear, but which would you say is more beautiful or more compelling? I'm betting and I'm hoping that at least 90 percent of you prefer Hopkins's original version, even if it makes you work harder to try and understand it—because frankly sometimes, it's the hard that makes it good. As readers or listeners your full attention is demanded, is claimed, as you try to work out what's going on here. There certainly is delight to be had in savoring the sound, even if you're not at all getting the meaning right away. In fact, there are some poems famously that are all about sound. For example, Lewis Carroll, who wrote *Alice in Wonderland*, composed the poem called "Jabberwocky," which is full of words that almost sound like real words or maybe a combination of real words, but it's not quite there. Here are a few lines from "Jabberwocky":

> Twas brillig, and the slithy toves
> Did gyre and gimble in the wabe:
> All mimsy were the borogoves,
> And the mome raths outgrabe

What did you get out of that? Anything? If we start to break it down, you'll see that at the very least, even if the words are nonsense, you have an idea of what function the nonsense words are serving in this poem. Let's think about the first line again: "Twas brillig, and the slithy toves."

What have you got with that? The poem begins by telling us that it "Twas brillig." What the heck is brillig? This is spelled b-r-i-l-l-i-g. I have no idea, but I could guess that it's meant to be an adjective or a word describing when all these events are happening—so just substitute something like "It was evening" or "It was beautiful," and you'll see what I mean.

The second half of that line, "and the slithy toves" were doing something. What is slithy? What are toves? "Slithy" is probably an adjective that modifies "toves," which I'm guessing—and I bet you are, too—is some kind of noun—so "slithy toves" could be something like "slimy frogs" for example.

And what are these slithy toves doing? We can tell from the syntax that they're performing actions, and that these actions include "gyring" and "gimbling"—"Did gyre and gimble in the wabe." You get the picture. Even though it's nonsense, if we engage the poem—if we really start to think about it—our brains start to fill in at least some of the blanks, and we can start to make some kind of sense of it.

Now would I suggest that you use nonsense words in your own writing to try and get your readers to pay really close attention as they figure out what it was you were trying to say? No, I wouldn't—you don't want to make your readers work too hard because some of them may just give up and stop reading, and we definitely don't want that, but at the same time the examples of Hopkins and Carroll show the power that words can have—not just in their meaning but in their sound as well, and that's something to which we should all be paying attention as both readers and writers.

So, we've established that word choice is an important consideration when you're writing—no matter what it is that you're writing—and that learning some lessons about this from poetry can help make your own writing more interesting and engaging. But it's not just word choice that can have an impact—word order is also important. What I'm talking about here is syntax or the grammatical ordering of a sentence so that it makes sense.

For example, let's take the sentence: "The king married the queen." This makes perfect sense, but if we mess with the syntax so that the same words read this way: "Queen king the the married"—this makes no sense at all. The sentence: "The king married the queen" is a perfect example of the most common sentence structure in English—what we would call "subject-verb-object."

When I'm grading student essays, I frequently find myself writing: "Try to vary your sentence structure," and I write this in the margins of any number of papers, as very often people only write subject-verb-object sentences because that's what they know how to do, and they know how to do it correctly so they'd rather use the same form over and over and get it right than attempt something more complex, which might be more interesting but which has greater opportunity for them to screw up. So let's take three sentences in a row that use subject-verb-object and think about how they sound and whether or not they're interesting or engaging: "The king married the queen. They lived in a castle. They were good rulers." Do you want to keep reading if the whole paper or article follows this structure? Most of us would say: "Probably not." Why? Because it's boring!

What if we changed the syntax a bit? What if we said: "The king and queen—they got married. In a castle they lived and ruled well." That might seem a little stilted, but hands down it is way more interesting than: "The king married the queen. They lived in a castle. They were good rulers."

Poetry can be a good teacher when it comes to understanding syntax as well as word choice, and perhaps the poet to most famously play with matters of syntax is E. E. Cummings. I'll show you what I mean. Here's the opening of Cummings's poem "anyone lived in a pretty how town":

> anyone lived in a pretty how town
> (with up so floating many bells down)
> spring summer autumn winter
> he sang his didn't he danced his did.

What do you make of those lines? Even though we can't do a really accurate translation by simply correcting the syntax or changing the word choice, we get some images—and we get some idea about what the poet is trying to convey. If you had to paraphrase this or guess what's happening, what would you say?

We can start with the basics—there's someone who lives in a town apparently, and it seems as if maybe there are church bells that ring in this town, perhaps throughout the year, and this person maybe sings and dances, or maybe he doesn't:

> anyone lived in a pretty how town
> (with up so floating many bells down)
> spring summer autumn winter
> he sang his didn't he danced his did.

You could make all sorts of interpretations that are very different from the one I've just suggested, but you get the point that even though the syntax is confusing, some images—a town, bells, the seasons—can still be discerned if we think hard about it. Again, it's that mystery—it is what is hard or initially confusing about this poem—that makes it so good and so interesting. But also, again, I would not suggest that you just throw the words of your article or story up on the page in random order and leave it to your reader to sort it out—but you could try to vary your word order as a means of engaging your reader.

Now, by way of example, let's consider three versions of the opening of a short story, and you try to determine which version you think is the most effective. Here's the first one, and the story begins: "It was the week after the big rain. I was with my mother in the market. We each had baskets over our arms. My feet were getting muddy. I was tired and wanted to go home. Then I heard shouting on the other side of the square."

What do we think of this? We certainly understand what's happening—there's a speaker; the speaker describes when and where she is, what the weather is like, and the fact that she wants to go home. Then, something potentially very interesting starts to happen when the shouting is mentioned. It's certainly clear, this passage, but is it really compelling? Maybe it's interesting enough, but let's consider a revised version that plays a little bit with word choice and sentence structure. Here's the second version:

> For a week, the big rains had been over, and finally it was dry enough for us to venture out to the market—my mother and I each with a basket slung over an arm. Mud was creeping up through the soles of my shoes, and the weary ache in my shoulders was beginning to make me long for home when suddenly the cheery calm of the market was shattered by shouting on the other side of the square.

What's different here? The basic information is the same, but the language is more interesting—the rains are over, but now we know not just that the rain is over, but that it was so wet the mother and daughter didn't even want to try to go to the market. The first few sentences of the original version are now combined into one that flows a little more engagingly and smoothly, and the speaker's tiredness is conveyed much more compellingly—she's not just tired, but she feels weary in her bones.

The shouting that draws her attention is described more excitingly—it shatters the "cheery calm of the market," and that's a phrase that suggests much more about this market scene than what we got in the first version. We could imagine that there's a lot of activity, but that everyone is in a pretty good mood—and so it makes a much stronger contrast when we get to the part about the shouting.

So, arguably, the second version is more compelling than the first—or at least we could say it's more interesting in terms of its descriptive terms and sentence structure. Could you ever go too far? Indeed, yes, you could. Let's consider another version of the opening of this story:

> A week after the tears from heaven ended, my mother and I were in the bustling, happy chaos of the market, where food and gossip alike were bought and sold. We each had an empty cornucopia waiting to be filled on our arms. A slurry of dirt and water was gradually breaching the barrier of leather that encased my feet, and a great weariness far beyond my years was kindling a yearning in my heart for the warm comforts of my own hearth when a fusillade of shouting ripped the tranquility of market day at the seams.

Do you find this passage interesting? Probably a lot of us would say: "Well, yes." If you were going to go on and ask yourself: "Do you think this writer is trying too hard?" most of us would probably also answer "yes" to that question.

If you can, in some sense, see the sweat of the writer's labor, recognize where he or she turned to the thesaurus for a more complicated word when a simple one would do, then you know that you're in the presence of a writer who is perhaps not a master of the craft—but is trying to seem as if he or she is. The trick for any good writer is to write compelling, beautiful prose—and make no mistake, that takes a lot of hard work—but you also don't want too much of your labor to show.

The writer of the third version of that opening passage has read a little too much poetry and is a little too excited to employ poetic devices and complicated phrases where the simple would do just fine. On the other hand, the writer of the first passage is a little too cautious, a little too afraid to move beyond the borders of what's comfortable and what he or she knows he or she can do right.

As I said in one of our earliest lectures, one of the keys to being a good writer is knowing how to give your reader enough information while also exercising sufficient restraint. You want to engage and enthrall your reader—you don't want to overwhelm your audience with flowery phrases that totally obscure the main message of your writing.

So, how do you get from version one to version two of this story opening I read you without risking descent into what is arguably a kind of poetic madness that will get you version three? As with any type of writing, it's practice that makes perfect—or at least readable—and practice certainly involves lots and lots of reading.

The more you read—of all kinds of writing—the better you will be as a writer. If you talk to great practitioners of their craft—be it writers, or artists, or musicians—one thing you usually discover is that they're all sort of omnivorous consumers of works within their trades. Great musicians tend to appreciate all kinds of music. I myself have known an alternative rocker or two who profess undying love for Patsy Cline or Tchaikovsky—and I've heard of famous abstract artists who find inspiration in the very carefully faithful-to-life portraits of artists such as Rembrandt or Vermeer. I've also heard writers of science fiction describe their fondness for a well-written autobiography. In other words, read—and you will start to learn how to write.

Of course, the other piece of advice is simply to write and to have as many eyes as possible look at what you are writing. This is a case where you certainly can learn by doing, and the more you do, the better you get. Practice what you have learned from today's and the other lectures so far—over, and over, and over again—and you'll really start to get the hang of it.

The exercises for today's lecture will help you get started with this. I've given you a few sentences that I want you to try and rewrite so that the structure is different and a little more interesting. But you don't have to stop at the examples I've given you—you can play this kind of game every day, all day long, in real life.

Billboards, ads on TV, flyers posted on telephone poles—these and other pieces of text we look at every day by the thousands can be your practice space. I do this all the time in elevators that have ads in them. "Our breakfast buffet is the best in town" one might say, and in my head I rewrite it so that it says: "The Best in town is how people describe our breakfast buffet." Another ad might say: "The lowest prices on widgets!" and in my head I rewrite it so it's more interesting and it says something like: "Lower prices on widgets? You can't find 'em anywhere!"

So today we learned how word choice and word order are important as you think about your own writing, and we looked at several examples from the genre of poetry that help to make this important point really clear. In our next lecture we're going to move from poetry to the genre of drama, and we're going to discuss how understanding the conventions of performance onstage can help us be better readers and writers—and more specifically, help us prepare for moments when we might be expected to speak in public. How is the spoken word different from the written one, and why does it matter? We're going to try and answer that question in our next lecture.

Drama—Writing Out Loud
Lecture 12

The award-winning writer Sherman Alexie ... when asked what advice he has for young writers ... often tells them to take a drama class or some acting lessons. And this is because good writers are very often asked to read their work aloud, and sometimes they have to take questions. If they aren't at least halfway decent performers, then the audience is going to be somewhat bored, no matter how much they might actually love the written works of the author.

D rama is performance. All the information we get about characters, situations, and plot points in a dramatic production has to come out of the mouths of the actors on a stage. Understanding the generic conventions of drama can help make us better readers and better writers— especially if we are writing something that is meant to be read aloud. Writing intended only or primarily to be read on the page can get away with things that writing meant to be performed out loud cannot. This lecture will focus on understanding how drama can help you become a better "out loud" writer.

Let's start by considering the following wedding toast:

John and Jane: You guys are the best! I hope you have many long happy years together. Congratulations!

Nothing wrong with that, you might be saying—it's clear and to the point. But now consider this second toast:

John and Jane: May the best day of your past be the worst day of your future, may your home always be too small to hold all of your friends, and may you live as long as you love and love as long as you live.

Which toast would you prefer to receive at your wedding? The second toast does a beautiful job of wordplay, parallel sentence structure and symmetry, creative use of images, and words appropriate to the occasion. But even the most beautiful words are going to suffer if they are delivered awkwardly, and that first, simple toast can seem superior when read clearly and sincerely. It's all about the delivery.

You may be thinking, I really don't need to express myself with the spoken word all that often, so this is not something I need to think about. But at some point in your life, you are going to have to do something dramatic in this sense—whether it's giving a presentation at work, defending yourself in traffic court, or proposing to your significant other. Each of those situations will go far more smoothly if you keep some basic rules of dramatic performance in mind.

Even the most beautiful words are going to suffer if they are delivered awkwardly.

Let's take an example of a famous speech. The St. Crispin's Day speech from Shakespeare's *Henry V* is one of the best-known speeches in Shakespeare and serves as a good example for our purposes today because it is making an argument. First, some quick background information: In 1415, King Henry V of England crossed the English Channel to press his claim to the French throne. For reasons that are too complex to go into here, he had with him only a small band of warriors—some estimates place the size of the English contingent at around 6,000, while the French army numbered around 36,000. Just before the battle, King Henry V gave his men a speech of encouragement to try and compensate for the overwhelming odds against them.

Whatever it was that Henry really said, Shakespeare undoubtedly vastly improved it in his version. Just before the speech begins, the king's cousin Westmoreland laments that there are so few of them on the battlefield and expresses a desire for some of the men who chose to stay in England to join them in battle. Here's the king's response:

What's he that wishes so?
My cousin Westmoreland? No, my fair cousin;
If we are mark'd to die, we are enow
To do our country loss; and if to live,

The fewer men, the greater share of honour.
God's will! I pray thee, wish not one man more.

So how does he begin? The king acknowledges the situation but chides his cousin for expressing concern about their numbers. He acknowledges that there are relatively few of them, but he characterizes this as a bonus: There will be more honor to go around. He then turns his attention to those members of the host who may still be having doubts about the battle they are about to fight, announcing:

> Rather proclaim it, Westmoreland, through my host,
> That he which hath no stomach to this fight,
> Let him depart; his passport shall be made,
> And crowns for convoy put into his purse;
> We would not die in that man's company
> That fears his fellowship to die with us.

In other words, if you don't want to fight, we'd rather have you leave, for it means more honor for us. In one move, Henry has made sure that everyone who fights with him is there willingly. Henry then uses a series of emotionally laden images to further persuade his listeners. He paints a picture of life after the battle, when the men are safely home and greeted as heroes; he characterizes the upcoming battle as a glorious struggle that will confer honor upon those who participate; and he says that even in their old age, when they've forgotten everything else, the men will remember the feats they did on St. Crispin's Day.

Corel Stock Photo Library.

King Henry V of England, whose St. Crispin's Day speech inspired his army to fight against extreme odds.

According to Henry, not only will those who fight beside him earn honor and nobility, but their names will be on everyone's lips. This speech is a brilliant example of knowing your audience, turning a bad situation to your advantage, and persuading people of the rightness of your cause so that they back you eagerly. And then Henry concludes with some of the most famous lines in all of literature, words that are majestic and powerful and poetic, that in one fell swoop ennoble all those who fight beside him, as he goes so far as to emphatically include himself as their equal:

> We few, we happy few, we band of brothers;
> For he to-day that sheds his blood with me
> Shall be my brother; be he ne'er so vile,
> This day shall gentle his condition;
> And gentlemen in England now-a-bed
> Shall think themselves accurs'd they were not here,
> And hold their manhoods cheap whiles any speaks
> That fought with us upon Saint Crispin's day.

So what do we take away from this dramatic example? When it comes to words meant to be read aloud, presentation style is key—words read aloud need inflection, emphasis, and a certain degree of enthusiasm for them to be effective. And perhaps more than with any other kind of writing, you need to really prepare. In other words, practice what you are going to say before you get in front of a microphone and try to say it. Whether it's an office presentation or a political speech, walking through it at least once out loud will help you do a better job.

What else? Well, as always, know your audience! King Henry V certainly knew his and was able to appeal to all their ideals and values. Make sure you're not talking down to or over your audience, and try to be appropriate. But perhaps most important is the need to really be sincere. ∎

Suggested Reading

Barnet and Cain, *A Short Guide to Writing about Literature.*

DiYanni, *Literature.*

Gardner, *Writing about Literature.*

Griffith, *Writing Essays about Literature.*

Guerin et al., *A Handbook of Critical Approaches to Literature.*

Kennedy and Gioia, *Literature.*

Roberts, *Writing about Literature.*

Exercise

1. The following exchange between two characters can be understood in a variety of different ways depending upon how the director and actors decide to play the lines. Rewrite the scene as a piece of prose fiction, rendering the mood of the scene as (1) angry, (2) excited, (3) sad, and (4) indifferent. What cues or clues do you have to give your reader that a playwright may choose to leave ambiguous?

    Mother: "You're late again."
    Son: "I'm not late. Your clock is wrong."
    Mother: "No, your watch is wrong."
    Son: "In any event, I'm home now."
    Mother: "Where were you tonight?"
    Son: "Out with friends"
    Mother: "Which friends?"
    Son: "You don't know them."

Drama—Writing Out Loud
Lecture 12—Transcript

Welcome back. In our last two lectures we explored how an understanding and appreciation of poetic forms can help enhance our experience as both readers and writers. We discussed the powerful impact that the deliberate breaking of the rules of writing can have and also the need to demonstrate an understanding of the rules before breaking them.

An unusual turn of phrase, a deliberately provocative word choice, descriptive terms that take the reader by surprise—all of these can be powerful tools that give your writing more punch and draw your reader in.

At the same time, we also discussed how too much of a good thing can be, well, too much. Piling on poetic devices—crafting sentence, after sentence, after sentence that tweaks the conventions of what we might call "straightforward" writing—all of this can signal to your audience that you're simply trying too hard, and it's more likely to turn your audience off rather than draw them in.

Today, we're going to explore a genre that has great potential for this "too much" syndrome and the "trying too hard" situation, and this type of writing is dramatic writing. Drama, arguably, has the most potential for being an overdone genre simply by its nature. Drama, of course, is performance, and all the information we get in a dramatic production about characters, about situations or plot points—all of this—it has to come out of the mouths of the actors on a stage, There's no description like: " 'I don't know,' Mr. Jones said, feeling quite perturbed."

In a dramatic production, the character of Mr. Jones would simply have to say the line: "I don't know," and then he'd have to convey his perturbedness—if I can make up a word here—he'd have to convey that perturbedness in the way he delivers the line or the way he acts as he delivers it.

Understanding the generic conventions of drama can help make us better readers and better writers—especially if we are writing something that's meant to be read aloud. Writing that is intended only—or maybe only primarily—to be read on the page can get away with some things that writing meant to be performed out loud cannot. A simple example will suffice here, and it's one that I think we're all familiar with—just think of a tongue twister like "she sells sea shells down by the sea shore."

There's really no problem if we read a line like this silently to ourselves in a book or a magazine, but if you ask an actor to perform this nightly on stage, then you're likely to get a screw up here and there. I'm sure all of us can think back to any number of newscasts you have seen on TV where the newscaster stumbles over a word or two—and sometimes this is just because the juxtaposition of certain words side by side don't look to be problematic when they're on the teleprompter, but these same combinations of words can end up being a real challenge when they're spoken aloud.

I'm sure we've all heard newscasters say things like "earthcake" instead of "earthquake," or maybe they pronounce the name of a foreign city that they have only ever seen on the page and never had to say aloud. I heard once the city of Prague (which is spelled P-r-a-g-u-e)—I heard it called "Prah-goo "on the air. In a lecture series like this, I'm bound to make a few mistakes along these same lines.

In my Teaching Company course on the medieval world, for example, I once tried to explain the medieval controversy over the dating of Easter. It's a really complex situation, and I was trying to make it clear, but as I was trying to be clear, I got confused. I got tripped up. I tried to explain what I had in my notes. I did a second take; I screwed that up. Finally, I had to stop filming completely and write out, word for word, exactly what I was trying to say in three simple sentences and then read it off the paper in my hand. Otherwise, everyone would have been just totally lost and confused. It was perfectly clear to me when I had jotted it down in my notes and I thought about it, but when it came time to say it out loud, I just messed the whole thing up. So, there's a difference between the spoken and the written word that we need to be conscious of.

So, today we're going to talk about some of the points of dramatic convention, and we're going to focus less on an explanation of what drama is and more on understanding how drama can make you be a better "out loud" writer.

Let's start by considering wedding toasts. Many of us at one point or another get called on to make wedding toasts, and let's look at two wedding toasts side by side. Here's the first one: "John and Jane: You guys are the best! I hope you have many long, happy years together. Congratulations!"

You might be saying: "There's nothing wrong with that; it's clear; it's to the point." We understand that the bride and groom are being congratulated, and people think they're wonderful.

But now consider this toast: "John and Jane: May the best day of your past be the worst day of your future; may your home always be too small to hold all of your friends, and may you live as long as you love, and love as long as you live."

Which toast would you prefer to receive at your wedding?

I'm guessing that most of us would probably say the second toast. Why? Given everything we've discussed so far in this course about poetic devices, engaging writing, getting your reader or listener's attention—the second toast does a really beautiful job of making use of word play, parallel sentence structure, symmetry, creative use of images, and words appropriate to the occasion.

With the phrases like "the best day of your past be the worst day of your future" and "live as long as you love, and love as long as you live" you have got some alliteration; you have got some rhythmic sentence patterning; you have got a beautiful juxtaposition of ideas—and then the line about "may your home always be too small to hold all of your friends," this creates an image of a house bursting with happy people. It's a really nice toast.

Now I want you to consider would there ever be a situation when you might prefer that first, very simple, very unoriginal toast to the second, very clever, very poetic one? Sure, and I will give you an example of what that situation might be. Listen to these two toasts again: "John and Jane: You guys are the best! I hope you have many long, happy years together. Congratulations!" That's toast one. Now listen to the second toast again: "John and Jane: May the best day of your past be the worst day of your future; may your home always be too small to hold all of your friends, and may you live as long as you love, and love as long as you live."

What is different here? The toasts still have the same words. There's the same simple sentiment in the first one, and the second has a more elegant, thoughtful, poetic sentiment. But I think all of us would probably want to pick the first toast as our choice in this situation. Why? There is one word: delivery. Even the most beautiful words ever written are going to suffer if they're delivered awkwardly, if they're mumbled, if they're read in a rush, if they're mispronounced—you get the picture. A beautiful piece of text is made ugly when the person who is speaking does not take the care to read the piece well.

In fact, the award-winning writer Sherman Alexie—and some of you may have read his work; he has won lots of prizes; he has become very famous lately, and he is from my hometown of Seattle, so we're very proud to claim him—when asked what advice he has for young writers, Sherman Alexie often tells them to take a drama class or some acting lessons, and this is because good writers are very often asked to read their work aloud, and sometimes they have to take questions. If they aren't at least halfway decent performers, then the audience is going to be somewhat bored—no matter how much they might actually love the written works of the author.

I can tell you, having seen Alexie in person, it definitely paid off in his case. In person, that man, he can tell a story. He can make you laugh. He can bring you to tears almost more effectively than his written works do. He is much more entertaining than any standup comedian I've ever seen, and the way he presents himself makes me want to come up with all sorts of reasons to have dinner parties to which I could invite him because he would be the life of the party, and everyone would have a terrific time.

So, a consideration of drama can help us better understand a couple of aspects of words written to be performed aloud—what the words say, and how those words are said. These two things work together, and you really cannot separate them. The most wonderful performance by an actor is not going to save clumsy writing, and the most moving monologue loses all of its force if it's not spoken convincingly.

A lot of you may be thinking right now: "Well, I really don't need to express myself with the spoken word all that often, so it's not a big deal whether or not I practice or I think about this," but at some point in your life you're going to have to do something that counts as dramatic in the sense that we're talking about here. It could be a presentation at work. It could be defending yourself in traffic court, or it could be proposing to your significant other.

Each of these situations will go far more smoothly if you keep some basic rules of dramatic performance in mind. Keeping these issues in mind will also help if you are trying to engage with a dramatic performance, analyze and understand it, and then write about it. But unless you're analyzing an actual performance of a play, writing about drama can be a little tricky. Very often in a case like this, you might be asked to form an argument based on a reading of the text version of a play, and there could be multiple possible interpretations as to how you should play a particular scene or deliver a particular line.

There are, as you might imagine, advantages to reading drama in text form, on the page—the advantages here are: you can go back; you can reread; you can rethink; you can move at your own pace. The disadvantages of engaging with a play only on the page are that you lose nuances that get conveyed by the staging—by the tone, delivery, the facial expressions, and the gestures of the actors.

Let's take an example of a famous speech from Shakespeare and talk about things that we should consider if we're trying to engage with this moment—and then lessons we can learn from trying to understand the important aspects of this scene.

I've picked a pretty famous speech—it's what is known as the St. Crispin's Day speech, and it's from Shakespeare's play *Henry V*. It's one of the more famous speeches in Shakespeare, and it serves as a good example for our purposes today because this is a speech in which the king, Henry V, is trying to persuade. He's trying to encourage; he's trying to make an argument. Most likely, if you are ever called on to do any public speaking, you also will be trying to persuade someone of something—to get them to agree that your analysis of sales figures from last quarter is really astute, that you should have a traffic ticket stricken from your record, that the woman you're asking to marry you should say "yes."

First, some very quick background for those of you whose Shakespeare or whose history is just a little bit rusty. In the year 1415, King Henry V of England crossed the English Channel to press his claim to the French throne. For reasons that are far too complex to go into here but which I find fascinating and would be delighted to speak about at great length at a later time, he had with him only a small band of warriors. Some estimates place the size of the French army at around 36,000; some people say it was as high as 50,000, and the English are somewhere around 6,000, maybe 8,000.

Whatever the exact numbers, the English were vastly outnumbered, and that's the important thing here. Just before the battle, King Henry V gave his men a speech of encouragement to try and compensate for the overwhelming odds against them.

Whatever it was that the real King Henry actually said, Shakespeare—I'm sure—vastly improved it when he wrote the St. Crispin's Day speech, and then he put it into the character Henry's mouth. The speech is called this because the Battle of Agincourt at which this supposedly occurred was fought on the feast day of St. Crispin—and if anyone really cares that's October 25—and again, the year is 1415. Just before the speech begins, the king's cousin, Westmoreland, laments that there are so few of them here on the battlefield, and he expresses a desire for some of those men who chose to stay in England to join them in battle. Here is the king's response:

> What's he that wishes so?
> My cousin Westmoreland? No, my fair cousin;
> If we are mark'd to die, we are enow
> To do our country loss; and if to live,
> The fewer men, the greater share of honour.
> God's will! I pray thee, wish not one man more.

How does he begin? First off, he acknowledges the situation. He makes a concession as we've talked about in earlier lectures. He acknowledges the situation, but then he chides his cousin—gently—for expressing concern about their numbers. Then, he goes on to tell those who are assembled that they are a large company—large enough that if they were to die, their loss would be felt throughout England. But then the king makes a slight shift, and he also acknowledges that there are relatively few of them, but he then characterizes this as a bonus. He says: "The fewer men, the greater share of honour"—in other words, there's going to be more honor to go around.

He then continues his speech by appealing to the desire for honor that all his men presumably share. In the next lines, he expresses a lack of concern with the treasures and the spoils of war, and he indicates also that should he die and be stripped of clothes, and arms, and goods, it will not matter as long as he has his honor. He says:

> By Jove, I am not covetous for gold,
> Nor care I who doth feed upon my cost;
> It yearns me not if men my garments wear;
> Such outward things dwell not in my desires.
> But if it be a sin to covet honour,
> I am the most offending soul alive.
> No, faith, my coz, wish not a man from England.
> God's peace! I would not lose so great an honour
> As one man more methinks would share from me
> For the best hope I have. O, do not wish one more!

Here, the king has cleverly taken the idea of covetousness—and this is usually a bad thing—and he has totally turned it on its head. It's noble to covet honor, and so greatly does he covet honor that he's pleased with the small regiment who have accompanied him, as he's not going to have to share this honor with too many other people.

So far the king has done a good job of characterizing a disadvantage as a great advantage. He then turns his attentions to those members of the host who may still be having doubts about the battle that they're about to fight, and he announces:

> Rather proclaim it, Westmoreland, through my host,
> That he which hath no stomach to this fight,
> Let him depart; his passport shall be made,
> And crowns for convoy put into his purse;
> We would not die in that man's company
> That fears his fellowship to die with us.

In other words, if you don't want to fight, we don't want you with us. We'd rather have you leave, for it means more honor for us—and heck, we'll pay your way. We'll give you some cash so you can get out of here. So in one move, Henry—or Shakespeare speaking through Henry's mouth—has essentially made sure that everyone who fights with him is there willingly and not under duress. He then uses a series of emotionally laden images to further persuade his listeners—I mean, talk about knowing your audience! He absolutely understands the values of men in this time, this place, this specific moment, and he appeals to all the values of men of his day and time. He tells his men:

> This day is call'd the feast of Crispian.
> He that outlives this day, and comes safe home,
> Will stand a tip-toe when this day is nam'd,
> And rouse him at the name of Crispian.
> He that shall live this day, and see old age,
> Will yearly on the vigil feast his neighbours,
> And say 'To-morrow is Saint Crispian.'
> Then will he strip his sleeve and show his scars,
> And say 'These wounds I had on Crispian's day.'
>
> Old men forget; yet all shall be forgot,
> But he'll remember, with advantages,
> What feats he did that day.

Here, the king paints a picture of life after the battle, when the men are safely home and greeted as heroes. He characterizes the battle they're about to take part in as a glorious struggle that's going to confer honor upon those who participate—and says that even in their old age, when they've forgotten everything else, the men will remember the feats they did on St. Crispin's

Day. He then takes this to the next level, suggesting that those who fought there will become household names throughout the realm—noble as the cause may be, there's an understanding here of the basic human desire to be known, to be valued and recognized. He says:

> Then shall our names,
> Familiar in his mouth as household words-
> Harry the King, Bedford and Exeter,
> Warwick and Talbot, Salisbury and Gloucester-
> Be in their flowing cups freshly rememb'red.
> This story shall the good man teach his son;
> And Crispin Crispian shall ne'er go by,
> From this day to the ending of the world,
> But we in it shall be remembered.

According to him, not only will those who fight beside him earn honor and nobility, but they will become something like the medieval version of superheroes or major celebrities, with their names on everyone's lips. This speech is a brilliant example of knowing your audience, turning a bad situation to your advantage, and persuading people of the rightness of your cause so that they back you eagerly and not reluctantly. Then, Henry concludes with some of the most famous lines in all of literature—words that are majestic, and powerful, and poetic—and in one fell swoop he ennobles all those who fight beside him. In other words, he says they are just as noble as he is. He goes so far as to call the men fighting with him his "brothers," and he emphatically includes himself or names himself as their equal by using the words "we" and "us" repeatedly. He says:

> We few, we happy few, we band of brothers;
> For he to-day that sheds his blood with me
> Shall be my brother; be he ne'er so vile,
> This day shall gentle his condition;
> And gentlemen in England now-a-bed
> Shall think themselves accurs'd they were not here,
> And hold their manhoods cheap whiles any speaks
> That fought with us upon Saint Crispin's day.

It is a truly great, moving speech, and it brings the men to whom the king speaks in the play—the characters who are going to fight beside him—it brings them to their feet in a fervor of allegiance and willingness to fight for their lord; likewise, it instills in the audience watching the play a sympathy and an admiration for Henry V. I mean, man, do you want him to beat those French after this speech! The touching line in which he calls their company "we happy few" causes a lump to rise in the throat if it's spoken correctly. They are the underdog, loyal to one another, fighting against the big, bad enemy for a noble cause.

You probably have noticed that I'm obviously not at all a trained actor, but I think I did some justice to those lines. But what if the actor playing Henry V finished his speech?

> We few, we happy few, we band of brothers;
> For he to-day that sheds his blood with me
> Shall be my brother; be he ne'er so vile,
> This day shall gentle his condition;
> And gentlemen in England now-a-bed
> Shall think themselves accurs'd they were not here,
> And hold their manhoods cheap whiles any speaks
> That fought with us upon Saint Crispin's day.

It does not matter how glorious Shakespeare's words are if they are spoken as if they are being read off the back of a gardening catalog. No one is rushing off to fight the French if the king is trying to persuade them like this.

So what do we take away from this and the other dramatic examples we've discussed today? It seems clear that when it comes to words meant to be read aloud, presentation style is key—remember, I used that word earlier in this lecture: delivery. Words read aloud need inflection; they need emphasis and a certain degree of enthusiasm for them to be effective at all. Here, perhaps more than with any other kind of writing, I think you really need to prepare in advance if you're going to be speaking or reading aloud.

In other words, it's a really good idea to practice what you're going to say before you get in front of a microphone and try to say it. I know any number of people who think: "Oh, I'm not going to worry about it, and I'm sure something will come to me when I get up there and I have to talk," and you can always tell who those people are because they are completely unprepared for whatever it is they're about to try to say. Whether it's an office presentation or a political speech, walking through it at least once out loud will help you do a much better job than you would otherwise. At that same time you're reading it aloud, practicing aloud, this can also alert you to any moments where the phrasing is really awkward or if a sentence is really long and you're going to run out of breath if you try and read it aloud, or if a sentence looks fine on paper and it just doesn't come across clearly when you speak it; reading it might be fine—spoken, it might be a complete mess.

On a related matter, whether we're engaging a dramatic piece that's already written or we're getting ready to read some writing of our own aloud, it's also a good idea to remember that the words themselves are only half the story. How the actor saying the lines smiles, frowns, gestures, or walks—all of these contribute to our understanding and interpretation of the words that are being spoken. My colleague Charlie Ross, who works on drama, says that—for example—the representation of the relationship between the characters of Iago and Othello in Shakespeare's play also called *Othello*, the relationship between these characters can be dramatically different—not from just staging to staging, run to run, but performance to performance, so from one night to the next—just on the basis of how the character of Iago looks at Othello at just one key moment.

The look itself is nowhere in the script—it's completely a choice of the actor and director, and how they decide to play that scene can change the whole play. The same goes for you if you're saying something in public. If you are wishing the happy couple every happiness in the world but frowning as you do so, people are going to wonder what you're unhappy about, and they're not going to believe that your feelings and your statements match up.

What else? As always, know your audience! King Henry V certainly knew his, and he was able to appeal to all their ideals and values. Make sure you're not talking down to or over your audience, and try to be appropriate. I have seen more than one groomsman at a wedding try to be witty by making some kind of dirty joke with his toast, and let me tell you, this does not usually go over very well in a room that's filled with elderly relatives of the bride and groom. Trust me on this.

So, in the exercises attached to today's lecture, I really want you to be focusing on how you could do the same kind of dialogue in different moods— how you could have a scene and how it might be written or performed so that the mood that comes across is happy, or angry, or bored. So I want you to play with that a little bit so you can get the idea of how the same words can convey very different feelings depending on how it's performed. But perhaps the most important thing from today's lecture is to understand the need to really be sincere, to be convincing—and in order to do this you're going to need to draw on personal experiences and feelings that you have had in the past to try and capture the attention and good will of your audience. In our next lecture, we're going to talk more about autobiography, which is a special category of writing filled with its own unique pleasures and pitfalls.

What You Can Learn from Autobiography
Lecture 13

> TMI—too much information—is one of the most common and devastating mistakes you can make in a situation that calls for written self-presentation.

This lecture begins our examination of the value of autobiographical writing, and we'll be studying several extremely powerful tools that autobiographers use to achieve their writing goals. Our ultimate aim is to learn how those tools work and how we can incorporate them into our own work.

Whether you're crafting an online personal profile, a professional bio blurb, or a job application letter, the challenges of creating a written self-portrait can be daunting. What experiences and qualities should you highlight, and what approaches are most effective? When should you give lots of detail, and when should you hold back? Through careful analysis of excerpts from the autobiography of one of America's most famous and successful individuals—Benjamin Franklin—this lecture reveals several strategies you can use when faced with a writing task that calls for self-presentation.

When it comes to autobiographical writing, the best way to be effective is to be selective.

Successful autobiographical writing is kind of like being the favorite guest at a dinner party—you have great stories to tell, but they don't go on too long, and your stories make the other people at the dinner table feel included. Personal anecdotes from successful autobiographers can be wonderfully instructive because they show us how to describe our best qualities without coming across as arrogant. As we'll see, when it comes to autobiographical writing, the best way to be effective is to be selective.

Let's start with an anecdote from Benjamin Franklin's autobiography:

> I disliked the trade, and had a strong inclination for the sea, but my father declared against it; however, living near the water, I was much in and about it, learnt early to swim well, and to manage boats; and when in a boat or canoe with other boys, I was commonly allowed to govern, especially in any case of difficulty; and upon other occasions I was generally a leader among the boys, and sometimes led them into scrapes, of which I will mention one instance, as it shows an early projecting public spirit, tho' not then justly conducted.

The strategy Franklin follows in this anecdote from his early childhood is one I call IAA—which stands for interests, abilities, and achievements. Most occasions that call for autobiographical writing require us to describe at least one—and sometimes all three—of these areas. Franklin begins by telling us something about his general affinity for water- and boat-related activities—and also, by way of contrast, that he's not terribly interested in being bound into a formal apprenticeship for a conventional trade. Franklin is also presenting himself as someone whose interests blend fairly well with

Benjamin Franklin as a boy. Franklin skillfully wrote about the early abilities that would eventually serve him as a leader.

his abilities. Although he has a facility for things aquatic and nautical, the straightforward way in which he presents this information doesn't come across as bragging or boasting.

What really stands out, even in this very short piece of autobiographical writing, is a sense of overall unity of interests and activities at a very young age. And the skills he seems to be gently pointing to have to do with being a leader—so he's setting the stage for future events that will undoubtedly be an important part of his autobiography. From the beginning, he has a focus that is guiding him as he selects stories and events to relate to his readership.

When faced with the often daunting prospect of writing about your life in order to achieve a specific goal, it's all too easy to respond by pushing as much information as you can at your readers. Give your readers only the most important, pertinent details up front. If they want to know more, they know how to find you! I recently had the opportunity to attend a lecture by an amazing scholar, and while the talk itself turned out to be spectacular, the experience was marred by the fact that the person who gave the introduction took 25 minutes to recount the speaker's activities and accomplishments—while the speaker herself only ended up lecturing for about 35 minutes.

For most of us, in most writing situations, how we present our achievements and accomplishments is the thing that will matter most. For an example of how to approach this dimension of autobiography, let's look at another excerpt from Franklin:

> There was a salt-marsh that bounded part of the mill-pond, on the edge of which, at high water, we used to stand to fish for minnows. By much trampling, we had made it a mere quagmire. My proposal was to build a wharff there fit for us to stand upon, and I showed my comrades a large heap of stones, which were intended for a new house near the marsh, and which would very well suit our purpose. Accordingly, in the evening, when the workmen were gone, I assembled a number of my play-fellows, and working with them diligently like so many emmets, sometimes two or three to a stone, we brought them all away and built our little wharff.

This anecdote is instructive: Note the way Franklin presents his achievements. In particular, note the balance he strikes between individual accomplishment and collaborative effort. It may seem to be a minor point, but it matters a great deal when your writing goal is to convey your accomplishments without seeming arrogant or overblown. One of the most powerful—and relatively easy—tactics a writer can employ in autobiographical situations is to alternate the use of personal pronouns so as to provide a mix of "I" and "we" statements and descriptions.

So what have we gained from studying Benjamin Franklin's approach to autobiographical writing? First, we learned the value of confining personal information to the three key areas of interests, abilities, and achievements. Remember also that your autobiographical writing will be that much more powerful and persuasive if you can find a way to connect your individual accomplishments to a broader collaborative effort. Finally, try presenting your faults or failures as part of a larger process of self-development—indications of talents that were not fully realized. Put another way, make sure your vices appear more like virtues in the making. ∎

Suggested Reading

Freedman and Frey, *Autobiographical Writing across the Disciplines.*

Smith and Watson, *Getting a Life.*

Exercises

1. Choose an event from your personal or professional life that you believe exemplifies some of your best qualities or skills. Use Franklin's strategy of presenting at least some of these qualities or skills as not-yet-fully-realized.

2. Choose an event from your personal or professional life that allows you to define yourself through your relations with other people. Describe this event in such a way that your individual talents and skills are made apparent through your interactions with others.

What You Can Learn from Autobiography
Lecture 13—Transcript

Welcome back. As you probably remember in some of our earlier lectures, we studied the basic elements of effective written arguments, and we learned how we could incorporate those elements into our own work to become more successful at persuading readers to see things from our point of view.

We began, appropriately enough, by studying introductions. We examined various strategies for crafting a powerful opening to an argument, and we learned how to establish a primary thesis and then lay the groundwork for later development of key terms and concepts. We shifted our attention then from crafting introductions to organizing an argument as a whole, and we examined methods that you can use to guide your readers from point to point while never losing sight of your primary claim.

After our survey of organizational methods and strategies, we moved on to a discussion of the ways good writers support their arguments—specifically, how they could establish the relevance and the validity of their evidence and explain how the proof they have chosen adds weight or power to their claims. Finally, in the last lecture of that argumentative series, we turned our attention to conclusions.

We discussed the importance of providing a brief summary of an argument's main thesis and its key points, and we also looked at several other ways conclusions can help strengthen an argument, whether by outlining the positive or the negative consequences of accepting or rejecting a particular set of claims—or maybe by demonstrating a lack of viable alternatives to one's own point of view.

After we finished our argumentative series, we went back a little bit and spent some time with poetry and with drama and talked about how using elements of those types of writing could help make your arguments more powerful. So now, with this lecture, we begin a two-part examination of the value of autobiographical writing, and we'll be studying several extremely powerful tools that autobiographers use to achieve their writing goals. Our ultimate aim today is to learn how those tools work and how we can incorporate them into our own writing

Whether you're crafting an online personal profile, a professional bio blurb, or a job application letter, the challenges of creating a written self-portrait that are going to help you achieve your goals can be really daunting. What details of your life should be included? What experiences and qualities should you highlight, and what approaches are most effective? When should you give a whole lot of detail, and when should you hold something back?

For example, if you're writing something about your own life, a mention of the fact that you climbed Mount Rainier might be worthy of inclusion in a whole lot of different writing scenarios. You could argue that the fact that you are a mountain climber gives us a little clue about your personality, and in most situations this information is going to work to your advantage. It's like a shorthand way of saying: "I'm tough. I'm up for a challenge. I have determination."

At the same time, with a few possible exceptions, we don't want to hear a long narrative about how long and hard you trained for that climb, or how tired you felt during it, or how exhilarated you were after completing it. So today we're going to talk about knowing when, what, and how much to say when you're engaged in writing about yourself.

Through careful analysis of excerpts from the autobiography of one of America's most famous and highly successful individuals—and this is Benjamin Franklin—this lecture is going to show you several strategies that you can use when you're faced with a writing task or an occasion that demands that you give us some form of self-presentation or representation. We're going to look at ways to apply these strategies in any situation that requires you to construct a personal narrative or to convey some kind of information about yourself to a reader or readers.

In particular, you're going to learn how to use that really valuable tool—the personal anecdote. The personal anecdote is really an essential building block for all great autobiographies. We're going to talk about how you can catch and hold the attention of readers while simultaneously enhancing your credibility through the use of anecdotes. You're also going to learn how to avoid the pitfalls caused by what I like to refer to as "TMI"—Too Much Information. Giving someone too much information can alienate your audience and end up preventing you from reaching whatever the objective is that you were going for with this piece of writing.

Successful autobiographical writing is kind of like being the favorite guest at a dinner party—you have great stories to tell, but they don't go on too long, and your stories make the other people at the dinner table feel included. They're able to relate to something you say, or they feel that your sharing of a story from your past is a way of trying to connect with them, and it's not just an attempt on your part to shine a spotlight on yourself and say: "Hey everyone, listen to how fantastic I am."

Personal anecdotes from successful autobiographers can be wonderfully instructive because they show us exactly how to self-promote without sounding shallow—and how you can describe your best qualities without coming across as arrogant. Arrogant and shallow are two things that you never want to convey when you're writing about yourself. As we'll see when it comes to autobiographical writing, the best way to be effective is to be selective. Let me say that one more time: The best way to be effective is to be selective. Let me show you what I mean by taking an anecdote from Benjamin Franklin's *Autobiography*, and here's what he says:

> I disliked the trade, and had a strong inclination for the sea, but my father declared against it; however, living near the water, I was much in and about it, learnt early to swim well, and to manage boats; and when in a boat or canoe with other boys, I was commonly allowed to govern, especially in any case of difficulty; and upon other occasions I was generally a leader among the boys, and sometimes led them into scrapes, of which I will mention one instance, as it shows an early projecting public spirit, tho' not then justly conducted.

The strategy Franklin is using here in this anecdote is one that I like to call IAA—so I use an acronym to sort of remember it, and this stands for Interests, Activities, and Achievements—IAA. It's a shorthand way of reminding yourself—and it's how I remind myself and my students—that most occasions that call for autobiographical writing require us to describe or to address at least one—and sometimes all three—of these areas: what our interests are—so there's the I, what abilities we have that may be related to those interests—there's the first A, and what goals we may have achieved that are relative to these interests and abilities—there's the second A; IAA.

I want to point out how Franklin begins by telling us something about his general affinity for water- and boat-related activities—and also, by way of contrast, he's not terribly interested in becoming a formal apprentice for a conventional trade. In this case, this would have been something like candle-making or soap-making, and that's initially what his father wanted him to do. As Franklin tells us, this was not something he was at all interested in. I mean, really, can you blame young Benjamin Franklin for preferring not to take up an occupation like this?

We can also glean from this really brief anecdote that Franklin is presenting himself as someone whose interests blend pretty well with his abilities. He has an affinity for the ocean—which leads him, as he says, to learn to swim well when he's young—and he has an "inclination for the sea," which results in his ability to "manage boats." Although he has got a facility for things aquatic and nautical, the straightforward way in which he presents this information doesn't come across as bragging or boasting—but rather, it's a simple statement of fact.

What really stands out, even in this very short piece of autobiographical writing, is a sense of overall unity of interests and activities. We get the idea that Franklin's natural inclinations and affinities both lead to and mesh with the skill set he's developing, even at a very young age. The skills he's developing, they seem to be pointing towards something that has to do with being a leader—so what he's doing with this anecdote is setting the stage for future events that are undoubtedly going to be a really important part of his *Autobiography*. So from the beginning, he has a focus that's guiding him as he selects which stories and which events to tell that will relate or be interesting to his readership.

So as we can see, this anecdote includes just enough detail to give us a sense that Franklin is pretty good at what he does, and that he's managed to parlay the connection between his interests and his abilities into some concrete and relatively impressive achievements. As he tells us, when he found himself in a boat with other boys, he was "commonly allowed to govern, especially in any case of difficulty" and, naturally enough, his achievements as a sort of proto-ship-captain are what set him up for a broader and more general position of leadership among his peers, especially later in his life.

Another thing that makes us really like the Benjamin Franklin of this anecdote is that he's also kind of self-deprecating; he acknowledges that he was somewhat of a mischief maker when he says: "I was generally a leader among the boys, and sometimes led them into scrapes, of which I will mention one instance, as it shows [and this is important] an early projecting public spirit, tho' not then justly conducted." In other words, Franklin is saying: "I was no angel, and let me tell you about one of the stunts I pulled," acknowledging his own shortcomings, but at the same time what he's doing is pointing out that when marshaled or directed in the right way or direction, his early mischievous inclinations and actions could actually be used to eventually get some positive outcomes.

If you were a corporate headhunter or a hiring coordinator looking for someone to fill a management position, Franklin—even at 10 years old— would present himself as a pretty good-looking candidate for the job. In fact, that's really not too far from what Franklin himself was aiming for when he crafted this autobiographical anecdote.

I mean, he's not precisely going after a management position, but he was trying to explain, after the fact, how his early interests and skills eventually led him to achieve the kind of power and influence that most of us associate with Franklin and his legacy today. Because most of us today tend really only to think of Franklin as one of the Founding Fathers, as a kind of "elder statesman" figure, this passage about some of his youthful escapades provides us with a deeper and more interesting picture of him than what most history books record—and it probably also makes us like him a little bit more than we did before we knew this story.

As I mentioned earlier, most occasions that call for autobiographical writing—whether they're job application letters, or requests to your boss for a raise or a promotion, a personal-information profile for a company newsletter, or it could be a blurb for an online career or social networking site—each of these situations requires you to provide a description of yourself that deals with the three areas of Interest, Ability, and Achievement—again, IAA, and I like to call this when we're thinking of it generally the IAA umbrella because a lot of stuff comes under that heading, the IAA.

The autobiographical narrative you present will be most effective if, like Franklin, you choose information that can be categorized as belonging to either the I, the A, or the other A—so it's under this umbrella. In other words, if you happen to be a doctor, the simple fact that you had a pet dog does not really count as an ability or an achievement, and it's not an interest that's particularly noteworthy—so it might not have a place in a piece of autobiographical writing that you're producing. But things change if when you were seven you found an injured dog lying by the side of the road, and you nursed it back to health, and this is what set you on the road to working in the medical profession—well, then, yes, that would fit nicely, very nicely, into our IAA classification.

As long as we're having fun with acronyms, let me point out another benefit of restricting the range of your autobiographical writing to specific interests, activities, and achievements. Focusing on IAA—or more specifically, what types of interest, ability, or accomplishment—this information trying to figure out what's most relevant to a particular autobiographical writing task—this is going to help you avoid that TMI problem—Too Much Information. TMI—Too Much Information—is one of the most common and devastating mistakes you can make in a situation that calls for written self-presentation. Too much information, offering more to your readers than what they need or they want, this is going to make the rest of your writing seem irrelevant or uninteresting and detract from whatever your main goal was in writing the piece to start with.

Again, let's think about that hypothetical dinner party. Isn't there always someone at those parties who tells you way too much about him or herself? In my case, I always seem to get into a conversation with someone who thinks that his or her latest medical issue is a fascinating topic for dinner table conversation. Your reader or your dinner party guest might be interested to know that you just had gall bladder surgery, but they really don't need a blow-by-blow of the diagnosis, the treatment, and the recovery—unless, of course, the anecdote about the diagnosis, the treatment, and the recovery is hysterically funny, which somehow I doubt would ever be the case in a situation like this one—but I hold out the possibility that perhaps it could be good dinner table conversation if the right person is telling the story, but that's not 99 percent of us, so don't go there.

When faced with the often-daunting prospect of writing about your life in order to achieve a specific goal, it's all too easy to respond by just pushing as much information as you can at your readers. Job application letters that should be a page and a half end up running four or five pages long. Resumes that should be two pages at most somehow end up looking like the Oxford English Dictionary.

Biographical profiles on a website that are meant to be no more than a paragraph or two, well sometimes you can see these balloon to twice or even three times that size. You need to give your readers only the most important, pertinent details up front. If they want to know more, they know how to find you. Trying to make yourself look more competent or qualified by padding your resume or job application letter with a lot of extra information is really only going to make you look like you're padding your resume or job letter.

I recently had the opportunity to attend a lecture by an amazing scholar in one of my areas of intellectual interest, and the talk itself turned out to be great—it was really actually spectacular and a very rewarding presentation. But the overall experience was really almost ruined by the fact that the person who gave the introduction took 25 minutes to recount the speaker's activities and accomplishments—while the speaker herself actually ended up talking only for about 35 minutes.

Again, it was a fantastic lecture, but the person who wrote and presented the introduction was obviously suffering from a seriously acute case of TMI— an inability to recognize the difference between a useful amount of personal description and a flood of biographical details that really didn't do anything but distract the members of the audience, who got more and more irritated that they were sitting here and being prevented from hearing the speaker they actually had come to hear.

So, in addition to always keeping in mind the need to confine your autobiographical writing to the realm of IAA—and keep that material as specific and as relevant as possible—what else can you do to avoid the problems associated with TMI—or a more general problem of unfocused or kind of random, haphazard self-presentation?

Your autobiographical self-presentation is going to be much more powerful if—again, like Franklin—you offer a narrative that is both progressive and unified. So, what do I mean by progressive and unified? By that I mean you start with a description of your interests; you then show how those interests are tied to your individual skills and talents—and then, finally, how those skills and talents have resulted in particular achievements and accomplishments that make you very well-suited for whatever larger goal it is you're trying to achieve—whether that means getting a job, getting a raise or promotion, or simply getting yourself noticed by the right people, either socially or professionally, or both.

All too often, when faced with the task of writing something autobiographical, people tend to try and begin at the beginning and then move in chronological fashion until they get to the end. If you're actually writing a proper autobiography—and here what I mean is something like a book-length treatment of your life—this is probably the best way to structure the thing, generally speaking. The reader can follow your chronology if you start at the beginning and go to the end.

But even in a longer work like this, an anecdote drawn from any point in your life can work as a really interesting and engaging starting point—it can give us a preview; it can shed light on who you are—who you became— before we go on and read about the process of that becoming. If the anecdote is compelling enough, then we might be totally willing to wade through some relatively uninteresting stuff about your childhood just so we can get to the main matter of your life that produced the you that did something so interesting.

While none of the three areas I've been discussing—Interests, Abilities, and Achievements (IAA)—is inherently more important than another when it comes to writing about who you are and what you have done, it's also crucial to recognize that for most of us, in most writing situations, how we present our achievements and accomplishments is the thing that's going to matter most. For an example of how to approach this aspect of autobiographical writing, let's take a look at another excerpt from Franklin. He tells another story in which he says:

> There was a salt-marsh that bounded part of the mill-pond, on the edge of which, at high water, we used to stand to fish for minnows. By much trampling, we had made it a mere quagmire. My proposal was to build a wharff there fit for us to stand upon, and I showed my comrades a large heap of stones, which were intended for a new house near the marsh, and which would very well suit our purpose. Accordingly, in the evening, when the workmen were gone, I assembled a number of my play-fellows, and working with them diligently like so many emmets, sometimes two or three to a stone, we brought them all away and built our little wharff.

So this anecdote is entertaining just as it is instructive, but I think for our purposes it's better for us to try and focus, at the moment, on the instructive elements—specifically, the way that Franklin is presenting his achievements. In particular, I want to point out the balance he strikes between individual accomplishments and a collaborative, group effort. This may seem to be a totally minor point, but it matters a great deal when your writing goal is to convey your accomplishments without seeming arrogant or overblown.

I have had the opportunity to look at hundreds of job application letters and resumes—those of my students, those of people who are applying for jobs at the institutions where I've worked—and it never fails to amaze me how often an applicant will overemphasize her or his individual achievements and totally fail to properly or effectively describe collaborative or group-based accomplishments. This is especially puzzling and distressing to me because if you take a moment to reflect on the process of autobiographical writing, you'll see that it's not such a terribly difficult balance to maintain.

As we see in that passage from Franklin, one of the most powerful—and relatively easy—tactics a writer can employ in autobiographical situations is to alternate the use of personal pronouns so as to provide a mix of "I" and "we" statements or "I" and "we" descriptions. If you look and listen closely to Franklin, you'll notice that even in this brief anecdote, he strikes a nearly even balance between the use of "we" or "our" and "I" and "my" pronouns. For example, consider that last line again. He says: "in the evening, when the workmen were gone, I assembled a number of my play-fellows, and working with them diligently like so many emmets, sometimes two or three to a stone, we brought them all away and built our little wharff."

In fact, if you go so far as to tally up the numbers in the passage as a whole, you'll find that Franklin uses approximately five, I think it is, "we" or "our" pronouns for every three "I" or "me" pronouns. In other words, his larger strategy is to foreground his individual achievements, but he does this always in relationship to the larger group of which he's a member.

It would be overly simplistic to say that Franklin's approach is a version of that classic sports cliché: There is no "I" in team. We've all heard that plenty of times, and anyone who studies Franklin's life learns quickly that he's not a person who ever lacked self-confidence—indeed, you could say that he had one of the most, shall we say, robust egos of any man of his age. But, when it comes to autobiographical writing, he recognized and he took seriously the need to place his individual accomplishments within a larger, collective framework.

Another benefit of associating or embedding your individual activities and achievements within a larger group context is the opportunity to more effectively represent yourself by selectively describing your faults and your virtues—or, to be more accurate, choosing to include faults that could be interpreted as virtues in the making.

Let's look back one more time at Franklin's description of his effort to organize his friends to help "borrow" stones that are supposed to be building a new house, and he gets his friends to help him move the stones meant for the house and turn it into a wharf so that they can have an easier place for minnow fishing. Of course, the boys are caught, and this is not least of all because the workmen could probably see exactly where the stones had gone: "Oh, they were here, and now they're over here making a wharf." Franklin goes on to tell us that all the boys are punished by their fathers, and Franklin's own father reportedly told him "that nothing was useful which was not honest."

We can see how Franklin presents himself as having an abundance of natural talent, and all he needs—all that's required—is some guidance and some maturing on his part so that the potential he has can be properly realized. Note also that the number of positive qualities he manages to associate himself with include things like initiative, creativity, ambition, management skills, the ability to work hard and to collaborate with others.

Essentially, he has presented himself as a kind of "diamond in the rough." I'm not suggesting that your next job letter should include a story such as this from your own childhood, but I do want you to understand how powerful this strategy can be, especially if you're following Franklin's example of presenting faults that could easily be interpreted as maybe sometime down the road becoming strengths.

If you do this, you manage to avoid coming across as arrogant while still showing yourself in a really positive light. Part of what's so appealing about Franklin's account of his youthful activities is that he is cheerfully acknowledging his early mischief-making, and he is not attempting to excuse it—he is not trying to explain it away. He's letting you know what he did when he was a kid, and while you probably don't want to spend too much time on the things you did that were wrong, or the pranks that you pulled, or anything else that could be considered a weakness or a failing, being able to laugh at yourself is a really attractive quality—and that's part of what Franklin is doing here and part of what makes his anecdotes so appealing.

So what have we gained from studying Benjamin Franklin's approach to autobiographical writing? First, we learned the value of confining your personal information to just three key areas, and these are Interest, Abilities, and Achievements—IAA. Remember also that your autobiographical writing will be that much more powerful and persuasive if you can find a way to connect your individual accomplishments to a broader collaborative effort.

Practice using the "I/we" and "my/our" pronoun configurations to strike a balance between self-promotion and associating yourself with a group or groups.

Finally, try presenting your faults or your failures as part of a larger process of self-development—in other words, cast them as indications of talent you had that was initially simply misdirected or not fully realized—put it another way, follow Franklin's lead and make sure your vices appear more like virtues in the making.

In our next lecture, we'll continue to talk about autobiography and explore how this kind of writing can be used to establish yourself as a leader or authority figure. We'll talk some more about Benjamin Franklin and also about Frederick Douglass, the former slave who wrote his way to an incredibly important position of authority. His writing is some of the finest you will ever encounter in the specific subcategory of autobiography.

Writing and Leadership
Lecture 14

> **Autobiography is perhaps the richest and most underused source of practical knowledge for anyone seeking to present herself or himself as qualified to take on a leadership role and make effective use of it.**

In this lecture, we're going to expand on the important link between autobiographical writing and leadership. The subject of leadership—its different qualities, its various styles, its capacity for success or failure—has garnered massive amounts of attention in the fields of business, education, government, and athletics. Actually, there is hardly a field where leadership is *not* the center of attention. Many of the books, seminars, and workshops offered on leadership are based on sound research in the fields of management and organizational studies. Some are based on less substantial evidence or offer little more than pep talks, without any clear way to actually apply this stuff to your own life. But none of them that I've encountered focuses on the crucial and generative link between writing and leadership—or, to be more specific, how the study and practice of autobiographical writing can help you better understand how leadership skills are developed.

The study of autobiography can also help you see how different approaches to leadership are defined. It can also give you concrete examples of how you can put these strategies into practice to achieve your professional and personal goals.

To help us better apprehend the link between autobiography and leadership, we continue our study of Benjamin Franklin's life story, and we add some examples from the autobiographical work of another figure: Frederick Douglass. In this excerpt from an account of Douglass's boyhood in the 1820s, he describes how he learned to read—something slaves were expressly forbidden to do:

> The plan which I adopted, and the one by which I was most successful, was that of making friends of all the little white boys whom I met in the street. As many of these as I could, I converted

into teachers. With their kindly aid, obtained at different times and in different places, I finally succeeded in learning to read. When I was sent of errands, I always took my book with me, and by going one part of my errand quickly, I found time to get a lesson before my return. I used also to carry bread with me, enough of which was always in the house, and to which I was always welcome; for I was much better off in this regard than many of the poor white children in our neighborhood. This bread I used to bestow upon the hungry little urchins, who, in return, would give me that more valuable bread of knowledge.

Every time I read this passage, I'm astonished by how insightful Douglass is when it comes to forging an emotional connection with his readers—soliciting their sympathy while never putting himself in a position to be pitied.

What similarities do you see between Douglass's and Franklin's childhood anecdotes? Certainly both excerpts evince a general sense of resourcefulness and ingenuity—specifically an ability to get others to help them achieve their goals. And both show how determined and dedicated their authors are to their respective tasks. But it's important for us to see how both writers also use their autobiographical anecdotes to implicitly suggest that good leaders need to exist in

The abolitionist Frederick Douglass wrote three effective autobiographies.

a kind of reciprocal relationship with those around them. Reciprocal, in this case, does not mean a relationship of equals; by any measure, both Franklin and Douglass benefit far more from these interactions than their peers do. Still, the autobiographical descriptions underscore what you can gain by writing about yourself not simply as a representative of or for a group—but as someone for whom reciprocity is a crucial function of leadership.

The take-away point here is that whatever events or achievements you choose as the centerpiece for the autobiographical writing you've been called upon to do, take the time to imagine and then describe them through some connection with other people: people with whom you've worked, people you've supervised, people who are part of whatever network you've served as a leader.

Another thread that runs through nearly every great autobiographical text is a judicious and effective use of emotional expression.

Another thread that runs through nearly every great autobiographical text is a judicious and effective use of emotional expression. By judicious, I mean an expression of feeling that is not made for an overt dramatic effect. In fact, in most cases, the more intense and emphatic an autobiographical representation of emotion is, the less effective it is. By contrast, an understated approach carries with it a much greater chance of establishing an intimate connection with readers. To illustrate the effectiveness of emotion expressed in a minor rather than a major key, let's take a look at an especially poignant event from Franklin's *Autobiography*—the death of his son from smallpox and his guilt for not having the child inoculated:

> In 1736 I lost one of my sons, a fine boy of four years old, by the small-pox, taken in the common way. I long regretted bitterly, and still regret that I had not given it to him by inoculation. This I mention for the sake of parents who omit that operation, on the supposition that they should never forgive themselves if a child died under it; my example showing that the regret may be the same either way, and that, therefore, the safer should be chosen.

I want to emphasize that there is no requirement for Franklin to include these brief remarks on his loss or the feelings he experiences as a result. He could have left them out with no consequences, personal or professional. Yet he makes a deliberate decision to include this event—and to take care to describe it in a way that directly connects his individual loss to something much larger than himself. It's easy enough to recognize the selflessness Franklin evinces—his willingness to share this information for the sake of his readers—and there's no reason to suspect that he has some ulterior motive or agenda.

At the same time, however, we would be remiss as students of Franklin's work if we didn't note that his decision does, when taken within the broader context of the *Autobiography* as a whole, add considerable credibility to his role as a leader and garner him significant sympathetic support. It's not a self-serving move in a direct sense, but it does have the ultimate effect of enhancing his status as a representative figure who speaks for and to a larger group. Franklin's strategy for establishing leadership is what we might call the use of soft power—the ability to achieve one's goals by establishing intimacy and cultivating personal connections with a larger public body.

So what have we learned from Franklin and Douglass—and how can we apply it to our own autobiographical writing? Keep in mind that autobiography is a rich source of knowledge for understanding how leadership skills can be developed and how different styles of leadership can be employed to help you achieve your goals. You would be well served to follow the models of Franklin and Douglass and present yourself as a leader who establishes productive reciprocal relations with those around you and never allows an individual accomplishment to be represented without some connection to those with whom you serve.

Keep in mind also the potential benefits of judicious emotional expression when the occasion requires you to write about your interests, abilities, and achievements. When the circumstances of a writing situation are such that an expression of emotion could work in your favor, remember that less really is more, and a low-key pitch and understated tone will draw your readers closer, inviting them—as an effective leader does—to listen longer and hear more of what you have to say. ■

Suggested Reading

Freedman and Frey, *Autobiographical Writing across the Disciplines*.

Smith and Watson, *Getting a Life*.

1. Choose an event from your personal life and write a short autobiographical description, patterned after Franklin's brief treatment of his son's death, that puts your private experience in service to a broader public problem or issue.

2. Imagine you've just received a promotion that puts you in charge of a group of people who previously were fellow employees at the same level. Now draft an e-mail—using some of the autobiographical strategies we've studied in the excerpts from Franklin and Douglass—to help establish your position as a leader while maintaining a productive relationship with your former peers.

Writing and Leadership
Lecture 14—Transcript

Welcome back. In the last lecture, we studied several key elements and features of autobiographical writing that you can use to make your own written self-presentations more successful—whether you're describing your skills and accomplishments in a college admissions essay, crafting an argument to convince your boss you deserve a promotion, or putting together your biographical profile for an online professional or social networking site.

We studied the work of one of America's most famous and successful autobiographers—Benjamin Franklin—and we learned how to more effectively organize and focus your presentation of personal information into three basic areas: interests, abilities, and achievements. We also discussed the importance of creating a progressive, unified narrative of these three areas that illustrates how your interests helped you develop a skill set—and how that skill set, in turn, led to your specific accomplishments and achievements.

Following Franklin's examples, we also learned how to highlight our individual accomplishments while also framing them within the context of a group-based effort or team-building situation—and this is what I like to call the "I/we strategy." We saw how Franklin made excellent use of this, coming off as both a natural leader and a popular member of a group.

Finally, we looked at his strategy for presenting faults and weaknesses in a positive light; in other words, we saw how Franklin was able to present his mistakes as evidence of talents that had simply been misdirected or skills that had not yet been fully realized—his virtues in the making essentially as part of a life that was still a work in progress. The boy who played clever pranks in his youth became a man who used that cleverness to help create a nation.

One of the most striking and intriguing elements of the anecdotes we discussed in Franklin's autobiographical writing was his presentation of himself as a kind of leader figure. Even at 10 years old, he already demonstrated leadership capabilities among his peers. When he's venturing out on the water in a boat with his friends, he says they look to him as their captain, especially if the situation was difficult or dangerous.

Back on land, he showed himself to be a miniature version of a project manager as he organized a team of his friends to take stones that were supposed to build a new house for someone, and instead he and his friends used them to construct a wharf so they'd have a better location for their fishing. It sounds as if growing up with Ben Franklin—it would have been a lot of fun to have him as a friend.

In this lecture, we're going to expand on this important link between autobiographical writing and leadership. The reason we're going to be examining this topic in greater depth is because the subject of leadership— its different qualities, its various styles, its capacity for success or for failure—has garnered massive amounts of attention in all kinds of fields: in business, in education, in government, in athletics; the list goes on and on. There's hardly a field or area where the topic of leadership is not the center of attention. The shelves of bookstores and libraries literally groan under the weight of all these leadership guides and management studies. If you browse a professional website in your field, more often than not you'll find some notice, or ad, or link that describes a leadership seminar or a workshop that promises to transform you into the ideal CEO—or at the very least it makes you a better manager or administrator.

Even late-night TV infomercials tout these 10-step programs that are guaranteed to increase your self-motivation or help you discover hidden talents and strengths and will transform you into a more effective leader—or your money back. Given the choice, most of us would want to be leaders rather than followers, wouldn't we?

Many of these books, seminars, and workshops are based on sound research by experts in the fields of management and organizational studies. Some are based on rather less substantial evidence—sometimes they borrow their general information from other sources, and all they're doing is kind of repackaging this as a new discovery. Some of these really offer not much more than pep talks or sort of really generalized power of positive thinking suggestions, and there's no clear way to actually apply this stuff to your own life.

But none of them—at least none that I've come across in my research—focuses on the crucial link between writing and leadership—or if we want to get more specific, how the study and practice of autobiographical writing can help you better understand how leadership skills are developed.

The study of autobiography can also help you see how different approaches to leadership can be defined—and here I'm talking about things like a top-down management style, where one person makes most of the decisions, as opposed to something like a more inclusive, collaborative approach, where a group of people might vote or discuss various actions or decisions. What I think is most interesting and important about autobiographical writing is that it really can give you concrete examples about how you can put these strategies into practice to advance your career or achieve your professional and personal goals.

Let me put this another way: Have you ever considered how many highly successful leaders have written autobiographies? I'm sure that if you took just a minute or two, you could jot down a list of 10, 20, or even more famous figures whose writings exemplify this connection between writing about your interests, abilities, and accomplishments and becoming a more effective leader of a group, a company, a movement, or even a nation.

Here's my own list—starting, of course, with Benjamin Franklin. Who else would be on this list? There's Mahatma Gandhi—leader of India's struggle to become an independent nation? Or how about Helen Keller, who became one of the most successful leading activists and advocates for reforming treatment and education methods for those who have disabilities? If we continue on, there's Booker T. Washington, whose autobiography *Up from Slavery* remains a classic study of the development of a leader in the face of overwhelming adversity. Or there's Ronald Regan's *An American Life*, which is one of the top-selling autobiographies of 1990. Even the famously self-effacing Abraham Lincoln wrote three brief autobiographical sketches that described some of the circumstances that eventually led him to the presidency.

Then there are a couple of my favorites. There's the brilliant Hildegard of Bingen, one of my personal all-time favorite autobiographical writers. She's born into a noble family in or around the year 1098, and Hildegard became a founder of monasteries, a religious visionary, a gifted composer and artist, and a leading theologian whose wisdom and insights were sought by everyone—from the common folk up to popes and emperors. She's a fascinating woman and a really unique example from her period.

Then there's also Margery Kempe, a late medieval English woman who was illiterate but who was so convinced of the importance of her religious experiences that she essentially browbeat a scribe and a couple of priests into taking dictation from her and writing down the experiences of her life. Her book is often called the first autobiography in English, and it was actually lost for a few hundred years. When it was discovered in the 20th century, it sent medieval scholars into a frenzy.

Many of us now believe that one of Kempe's goals in writing her autobiography—whether or not she consciously realized this—was to try and set herself up for sainthood. Talk about the link between autobiography and leadership—sainthood is about the top of the heap when it comes to leadership and influence.

One could argue that highly successful leaders pen autobiographies because there is usually a substantial audience of people who want to read their stories, and they want to read them in order to be entertained or inspired—or because they want a behind-the-scenes look at someone they find fascinating or controversial. True enough.

But if we look more closely at some examples from the works of these figures, we find something else holds true far more often than not, and this is their autobiographical texts offer valuable tools and strategies that show how individuals can establish themselves as leaders or representative figures who are speaking not just for themselves—but also to and for a larger group.

Autobiography is perhaps the richest and most underused source of practical knowledge for anyone seeking to present herself or himself as qualified to take on a leadership role and make effective use of it. Whether you're running as a candidate for president of your local school board, or you want to be someone in an upper-level management position, or you're struggling with a college admissions essay, the following examples I think will help you represent yourself and your capacity for leadership in the best possible way.

To help us better get at this link between autobiography and leadership, we're going to continue our discussion of Benjamin Franklin's life, and we're going to add some examples from the autobiographical work of another figure as well: Frederick Douglass. As most of you probably know, Douglass was a former slave who made his way north and to freedom in the 1830s, and then he subsequently became one of the most famous and influential abolitionists of the 19th century.

After the Civil War, he became a leading figure not only within the African American community—but also in the nation as a whole. He served as a statesman and a diplomat, and eventually he was named the U.S. ambassador to Haiti. He wrote three separate autobiographical accounts of his life, each one extremely successful in both commercial and critical terms.

Here's an excerpt from an account of his boyhood in the 1820s—and this occurs not long after he'd been moved from the backcountry of Maryland's Eastern Shore to Baltimore, and there he was "bound out," as it was called, by his master to work in the local shipyards.

In this selection, Douglass describes how he learned to read—something slaves were expressly forbidden to do—and I should add that slavery and education were generally deemed totally incompatible by southern slaveholders; this is something that Douglass recognized really early in his life, and it made him even more determined to become literate. He tells us that:

> The plan which I adopted, and the one by which I was most successful, was that of making friends of all the little white boys whom I met in the street. As many of these as I could, I converted into teachers. With their kindly aid, obtained at different times and in different places, I finally succeeded in learning to read. When I

was sent of errands, I always took my book with me, and by going one part of my errand quickly, I found time to get a lesson before my return. I used also to carry bread with me, enough of which was always in the house, and to which I was always welcome; for I was much better off in this regard than many of the poor white children in our neighborhood. This bread I used to bestow upon the hungry little urchins, who, in return, would give me that more valuable bread of knowledge.

Every time I read this passage, I'm astonished by how insightful Douglass is when it comes to forging an emotional connection with his readers—he solicits their sympathy, but he never puts himself in a position to be pitied.

I'll come back to this point about the relationship between emotional expression and leadership later in the lecture, but right now I want you to think about the similarities you see between Douglass's description of getting young white boys to help him learn to read and the description Franklin gives us—that we discussed in the previous lecture—of getting his friends to help him build a fishing wharf out of stones that were supposed to be building a neighbor's house.

Certainly both of these excerpts give a general sense of the resourcefulness and ingenuity of Douglass and Franklin, and specifically what we see here is an ability to get others to help you achieve your goals. Both passages show how determined and dedicated their authors are in terms of their respective tasks that they have set themselves.

But it's important for us to see how both writers also use their autobiographical anecdotes to suggest that good leaders need to exist in a kind of, what we might say, reciprocal relationship with those around them. Reciprocal in this case does not mean a relationship of equals; by any measure, both Franklin and Douglass benefit a whole lot more from these interactions than the people with whom they're interacting do.

Still, the autobiographical descriptions underscore what you can gain by writing about yourself not simply as a representative of a group—but as someone for whom reciprocity is a crucial function of leadership. Douglass clearly understands that what the poor, literate white boys need is something to eat, and if he could supply this, he would get what he felt he most needed—and that is knowledge.

Here's another example from Douglass's autobiography, and in this episode, he describes how he taught himself to write—again, something slaves were expressly forbidden to do. First, he learned individual letters and two-letter combinations by watching carpenters in the shipyards mark pieces of lumber with letters that identified which side of the ship those pieces were designated for: "S" for starboard; "SF" for starboard forward; "SA" for starboard aft, etc. With this knowledge, Douglass then moved on to try and establish a set of reciprocal relations with people who could help him. He says:

> When I met any boy who I knew could write, I would tell him I could write as well as he. The next word would be, "I don't believe you. Let me see you try it." I would then make the letters which I had been so fortunate as to learn, and ask him to beat that. In this way, I got a good many lessons in writing, which it is quite possible I should never have gotten in any other way.

If you were to read or reread the various autobiographies I mentioned earlier—those by Gandhi, Helen Keller, Booker T. Washington, or Ronald Reagan—you'd notice a similar thread running through every text: It's this theme of reciprocal relations—and again, reciprocal doesn't necessarily mean relations that help both parties to benefit equally, but both parties do get something.

In addition, the reciprocity model applies even if the leadership style of the author seems more top-down than collaborative. In fact, Douglass suggests implicitly in the anecdote that we just looked at—and Franklin also argues this explicitly throughout his *Autobiography*—that it's even more crucial for top-down leaders to always present themselves and their accomplishments in some sort of reciprocal relationship to those around them.

You can weave this same thread through your own autobiographical writing, especially if your goal is to describe or define your leadership qualities and style for a potential employer, or a new boss, or a college admissions committee. Come to think of it, if I were in the position of advising prospective college students—or the parents of prospective college students—about writing one of those autobiographical admissions essays, the first thing I'd recommend would be to have their child read Franklin's *Autobiography*—or any one of Douglass's three narratives—before they start writing.

The take-away point here is that whatever events or achievements you choose as the centerpiece for the autobiographical writing you have to do, take the time to imagine and then describe those events or achievements in or through some connection with other people: people that you work with, supervise, who are part of whatever group or network you're a member of, and people who have served you in return.

Earlier in this lecture, when we were discussing the first excerpt from Douglass's autobiography, I mentioned that every time I read that particular passage, I'm amazed by Douglass's gift for establishing a particular kind of emotional connection with his readers—he solicits their sympathy but never puts himself in a position to be pitied.

I want to come back to that point now and expand on it a bit. The use of emotional expression is one of the most complex dimensions of autobiographical writing; if you handle it well, you will generate all sorts of powerful persuasive feelings that will compel your audience to follow wherever you want to lead them. It's also, then, going to help you achieve your goals. If you don't do a good job with this emotional aspect, you're pretty quickly going to alienate your readers, and you may find that it's impossible to convince them to support you, accept you, or help you with any requests you might make.

Another thread that runs through almost every great autobiographical text is a careful use of emotional expression. By careful I mean an expression of feeling that's not made for an overly dramatic effect. In fact, I think that in most cases, the more intense and emphatic the representation of an emotion is—so the more insistent you are that you felt sad or you felt angry—the less effective it ends up being. In contrast, I think a low-key or understated approach has a much better chance of making a productive connection with your readers.

To illustrate the effectiveness of emotion when it's expressed in what I like to call a minor rather than a major key, let's take a look at an especially moving event from Franklin's *Autobiography*—and this is the account of the death of his son from small-pox and the guilt that Franklin feels because he didn't have the child inoculated. He says:

> In 1736 I lost one of my sons, a fine boy of four years old, by the small-pox, taken in the common way. I long regretted bitterly, and still regret that I had not given it to him by inoculation. This I mention for the sake of parents who omit that operation, on the supposition that they should never forgive themselves if a child died under it; my example showing that the regret may be the same either way, and that, therefore, the safer should be chosen.

I want to emphasize that there's no requirement, or reason, or rule dictating that Franklin needs to include some comment on the loss of his son or the feelings that he had as a result of that. He could have left this out with no consequences at all, but he makes a deliberate decision to include this event—and he takes care to describe it in a way that directly connects this individual loss that he experiences to something much larger than himself—and in this case, you could say that's sort of like the health of the general public. It's easy enough to recognize the kind of selfless attitude that Franklin has here—his willingness to share this information not for his own sake but for the good of his readers—and there's no reason to suspect that he has any ulterior motives here.

At the same time, we would be remiss as students of Franklin's work if we didn't note that when he decides to include this, when taken within the broader context of the *Autobiography* as a whole, what this scene does is add considerable credibility to his role as a leader, and then it helps him to get really significant sympathetic support for anything else he might want to say or do. It's not a self-serving move in a direct sense, but it ultimately has the effect of enhancing his status as a kind of representative figure who speaks for and to a larger group.

I want to reiterate my warning here about incorporating emotional expression into your own autobiographical writing, because for many people it is just too tempting to try and provide a really intense description of a really intense situation—and obviously, when people do this the hope is that by dramatizing a set of emotions they can then trigger a sympathetic response in their readers—and whether that sympathy manifests itself as shared anger and outrage at some injustice, or it's commiseration over some sort of trauma that they have all experienced, or if it's a collective sense of accomplishment or well-being. Please don't mistake my meaning here: I am not trying to tell you to avoid the use of emotional moments or language, but I am recommending that you study Franklin's model carefully and thoroughly before you make use of emotional appeals in autobiographical writing.

So, think back to the tone of that passage and note the overall tone of it—again, it's intimate, but the intimacy is low key. It's understated—and what's even more crucial here is that there's a clear effort to try and define the meaning of this experience not at just an individual level—it's not just about his personal grief and guilt—but he's trying to talk about it in a broader, collective sense that connects the experience to something larger than himself. Franklin's strategy for establishing leadership is what we might call the use of "soft power"—or the ability to achieve one's goals by establishing intimacy and cultivating personal connections with a larger public body or group.

Now let's take a look at our final excerpt—and this one is from the last paragraph of Frederick Douglass's *Narrative*. At this point in the autobiography, Douglass has reached the North and is just starting to become involved with the abolitionist movement. He has been invited as a guest to a lot of antislavery meetings and lectures, and other people have told his story for him to sometimes very skeptical audiences. They're holding him up as proof that slaves are worthy of freedom, and if you gave them freedom they would make good use of it. Although Douglass had been encouraged to speak on his own behalf, at this point in the *Narrative* he has only done so for black audiences. But in the moment I'm going to read to you he finally decides to speak to a white audience, and when he does this, he takes the first step in what is going to become a hugely successful career as an activist and reformer. He starts off by saying that he's reluctant to speak, but finally, at an antislavery convention in 1841, he feels compelled to tell his story, and another person attending urges him to go ahead and do this. Then Douglass says:

> It was a severe cross, and I took it up reluctantly. The truth was, I felt myself a slave, and the idea of speaking to white people weighed me down. I spoke but a few moments, when I felt a degree of freedom, and said what I desired with considerable ease. From that time until now, I have been engaged in pleading the cause of my brethren—with what success, and with what devotion, I leave those acquainted with my labors to decide.

Douglass's goal in these final lines of the *Narrative* is to make himself accessible to a broader audience, and he does this in part by revealing a personal and highly emotional experience—and in this case, it's public speaking, and it's accompanied by fear and anxiety.

What he's also doing is addressing a tension or a paradox that we see a lot when we're dealing with leader figures, and this is: How do you maintain connection to a group that you represent when the very process of becoming that group's leader sort of separates you from it in some way? In other words, by taking up the "severe cross" of speaking to a white audience, Douglass is acknowledging not simply a fear of public speaking—but also the burden of representing a group that he no longer has a direct connection to since he has managed to successfully escape from slaveholding territory.

So in this sense, Douglass faced far more of an imperative than Franklin to include emotional experiences in his autobiography. Failing to describe his first speech to a white audience would have undermined his goal of taking on the role of a representative leader for the reform of black-white relations. At the same time, Douglass recognizes the need to articulate his emotions in an understated fashion.

There is certainly evidence of the strength and intensity of his feelings, but we receive that message sort of obliquely rather than directly—and this is a strategy that allows Douglass to create just enough of a sense of intimacy to solicit sympathy from his readers—but not so much that they feel overwhelmed by the sentiments he's expressing.

So what have we learned from our extended looks at Franklin and Douglass, and how can we apply it to our own autobiographical writing? Keep in mind that autobiography is a rich source of knowledge for understanding how leadership skills can be developed and how different styles of leadership can work—winning that seat on your local school board, getting promoted to project manager, or convincing people on the admissions committee that you are an ideal student for your dream college.

In each case, you would be well-served to follow the models of Franklin and Douglass and present yourself as a leader who establishes reciprocal relations with those around you—with your fellow board members, your team, your student peers—and it would be good to try and present yourself as someone who never allows an individual effort or accomplishment to be represented without some connection to those people that you're serving.

You have got to keep in mind as well the benefits of careful understatement when you're dealing with emotional expression. Don't rely on the intensity of an emotional experience to try and form an intimate connection with your readers—all you're going to do is push them away. Instead, you should try to create a sense of intimacy like Douglass and Franklin do—you selectively reveal a set of feelings that readers can identify with, but they won't feel overwhelmed by them.

When the conditions or circumstances of a writing situation are such that if you expressed emotion it could work in your favor, remember that really, once again, less is more. Low-key pitch, understated tone—that's going to draw your readers closer and invite them in.

In our next three lectures, we're going to continue to focus on how to create a compelling and engaging identity as a writer by making use of some key ideas from the area of classical rhetoric. These are ideas and traditions that go back to ancient Greece and Rome, both places where the ability to present yourself compellingly through speech or writing was raised really to something of an art form. By studying what the Greeks and Romans studied, you'll gain greater awareness of how to present yourself in your writing and be better able to recognize and appreciate how and when other writers do this effectively.

The Rules of Rhetoric
Lecture 15

The art and practice of posing rhetorical questions in order to communicate more effectively was one of the concepts that ancient and classical thinkers like Quintilian, Aristotle, and Cicero first studied and articulated. In other words, it's not as if classical rhetoric somehow evaporated or disappeared once we moved into the Modern Period, although a lot of people actually seem to think that this is the case.

In this lecture, we take a broader look at some of the concepts that serve as the foundation for successful arguments and autobiography. These ideas really serve as the foundation for almost all forms of effective writing.

Four of the most readily applicable rhetorical concepts that you can use to strengthen your writing are commonplaces, stasis, deductive reasoning, and inductive reasoning. A commonplace is a piece of truth that is wrapped up in easily recognizable language. The notion of truth I mean here is not some empirical fact—rather, it's some thought that's familiar enough to a certain group of people that they're going to respond positively to it, even if they can't always precisely identify why. An example of a commonplace for most Americans is the notion that we have a right to the pursuit of happiness. It's one of the most widely recognized and accepted ideas from the Declaration of Independence, and I think it's safe to say that the majority of U.S. citizens, no matter what their politics, would respond positively if a writer were to invoke this idea. The use of commonplaces can give the reader a feeling of solidarity, and then the writer can move on to address other points that might generate disagreement. In other words, it's a way of getting everyone into a similar, comfortable intellectual space before you start to present a case that may not be so familiar to them.

The next concept is stasis. In classical rhetoric, stasis refers to the general agreement between opposing parties about what the terms of the argument are. Parties that are in conflict often won't agree on a common definition of the argument's terms and therefore can't move beyond that initial disagreement. You can see how the concept of stasis is related to the notion of the commonplace—both hinge on the need for agreement.

So why should stasis matter when it comes to writing? Just as effective writers must make an effort to identify commonplaces that are relevant to their readers, they also have to make an effort to identify the terms of an argument and recognize when those terms have been agreed upon and when they have not. I'm not suggesting that writers must always strive for stasis or that they must change their terms or viewpoints in order to do this. But it's possible to craft a powerful piece of writing simply by showing readers how and why stasis has not been achieved with regard to a particular issue: to identify the terms that are problematic and to clarify the overall scope and the content of the debate, even if it seems that the debate itself can't be resolved.

Deductive reasoning is the kind that many people are familiar with from detective stories and murder mysteries.

In addition to a lack of stasis, one of the reasons that certain debates are not easily resolved is because the writers who address the issue don't make effective use of different forms of reasoning to appeal to their audience. This brings us to our next two rhetorical concepts: deductive and inductive reasoning. Deductive reasoning is the kind that many people are familiar with from detective stories and murder mysteries. Deductive reasoning begins with a generally accepted declaration or premise—something that most people take to be true most of the time. The writer then uses that premise to make sense of a specific event, occurrence, or phenomenon.

The opening lines of Jane Austen's famous novel *Pride and Prejudice* set up just such an occasion for deductive reasoning by establishing a general premise about the circumstances of wealthy, unmarried men, and as you may recall that opening line is:

> It is a truth universally acknowledged that a single man in possession of a good fortune must be in want of a wife.

Indeed, a lot of the characters in that novel are young men with fortunes and young women with the potential to be wives. So we might, then, read the whole rest of the book in light of that opening claim, and so long as the characters act or speak in ways that seem to affirm Austen's foundational premise, everything that happens within the fictional world of the novel makes sense.

As you might guess, not all instances of reasoning follow the deductive pattern. Sometimes a process is inductive—meaning a writer will examine particular events or subsets of phenomena and use them as the basis for then constructing a premise that would apply to any events or incidents that are similar to that one. In other words, to reason inductively is to move from particulars to generalizations. If we were to rewrite *Pride and Prejudice* following an inductive pattern, we would begin not with those famous first lines, but we'd begin by describing the words and actions of each single male character, assessing any differences and oddities of behavior, weighing them against similarities—and, ultimately, identifying the most common traits linking them to each other. Our descriptions would probably take into account how each single male interacted with female characters who could be potential wives, and we'd want to make it apparent to our readers that the men with more money generally seemed to be operating under the assumption that getting yourself a spouse would be a necessary thing to do. Inductive reasoning opens up lots of potential theories, but it's up to the writer to decide which ones are most important to identify for the reader.

Inductive reasoning can be put to effective use in your writing, and you should always keep it in mind as an alternative to the deductive process—especially when you're faced with a writing task that compels you to describe a wide range of evidence and try and make sense of it for your audience. As the ancient and classical rhetorical scholars would remind you, as the writer, you are in charge of determining what commonalities in your evidence are most worthy of being presented as truths that should be universally acknowledged. ■

Crowley and Hawhee, *Ancient Rhetoric for Contemporary Students*.

Exercises

1. Use the process of induction (in relation to whatever content/subject you like), and craft a thesis or main claim for an argument.

2. Use the process of deduction (in relation to whatever content/subject you like), and craft a thesis or main claim for an argument.

The Rules of Rhetoric
Lecture 15—Transcript

Welcome back. In our last two lectures, we examined some of the key elements of successful autobiography, and we studied strategies and tools you can use to make your own writing more effective on those occasions when you are called upon to provide a personal narrative—to offer some written account of who you are—in order to prove to, or convince, someone that you are worth noticing. This can be whether you're trying to wow a college admissions officer, impress a potential new boss, or establish valuable contacts through a professional or social networking site.

We saw how autobiographers such as Benjamin Franklin and Frederick Douglass crafted progressive, unified accounts of their lives; how they described their interests in relation to a set of skills and talents; and how they then parlayed those skills and talents into successful careers.

Franklin and Douglass also provided us with important insights into the fundamental and crucial link between autobiography and leadership—how framing your individual accomplishments within the efforts of a larger group can actually enhance your status as a potential leader—as somebody with the ability to initiate and maintain productive, reciprocal relationships with those around you. In particular, we talked about how Franklin and Douglass rely on careful and understated use of emotionally charged moments, personal experiences, in order to establish a sympathetic connection with their audiences.

We discussed how you can develop and employ this kind of connection in your own autobiographical writing, whatever your goal or your purpose might be, and this can help you persuade readers to take a favorable view of your interests, your skills, and your record of achievements. In other words, you can use this to make them like you.

In this lecture, we're going to build on our study of the key elements of autobiographical writing—and we're also going to further develop the key points we covered in that four-part examination of arguments in Lectures 6 through 9. To do this, we're going to take a broader look at some of the concepts and ideas that serve as the foundation for successful arguments and autobiography—and these concepts really serve as the foundation, I would say, for almost all forms of effective writing.

These concepts and ideas that I want to talk about starting today fall under the broad categorization or umbrella of what scholars call "classical" or "ancient" rhetoric, and they're inspired by the writings of famous figures like Plato, Aristotle, Cicero, and Longinus. These are thinkers whose work was first formulated and articulated during what we call the Classical and Helenistic Greek eras and the Roman period—and that's about roughly 500 BC through about the 1st century AD.

Such rhetoric focuses on situations and circumstances rather than conventions or rules. It's the situational focus that's really valuable for us as writers because it helps us to not be overly bound by certain conventions and formulas for our work. If we use rhetorical concepts as a guide, you can remain aware of certain expectations and rules, but you're aware also of possibilities and opportunities that can open up when you break those rules or ignore those conventions. So, in other words, this approach can help you adapt your writing to a variety of different situations and make the most of them.

This kind of rhetoric also focuses on ethics—meaning it acknowledges that while we don't have to be bound by convention, we nevertheless have certain obligations to different communities within which our writing circulates; it's not just a free-for-all. Rhetoric reminds us that we can shape our writing to take advantage of shifting situations, but at the same time we can't ignore connections to, and dependence on, ideas and beliefs that our communities hold dear.

Still, at this moment, you might find yourself asking: "Why on earth should we concern ourselves with classical rhetoric? It's something that people who died a long time ago were really interested in, not us. What kind of practical use could these ideas have in today's world?" It's a fair question, and I'd like to point out it's also a rhetorical question. If you were asking it, you'll realize that in the very act of doing so, you're already providing an answer for yourself.

After all, the art and practice of posing rhetorical questions in order to communicate more effectively was one of the concepts that ancient and classical thinkers like Quintilian, Aristotle, and Cicero first studied and articulated. In other words, it's not as if classical rhetoric somehow evaporated or disappeared once we moved into the Modern period, although a lot of people actually seem to think that this is the case.

In fact, what happened was that these notions and ideas that came from classical rhetoric became so tightly woven into the fabric of Western culture's various forms of expression that we can't even see them anymore. Put another way, classical rhetoric has always been with us—it's just that it's hiding in plain sight. It's everywhere, so because of that it actually seems like it's nowhere.

By the way, the phrase "hiding in plain sight" is also something that has its roots in the work of ancient and classical rhetoric. It's a variation of what Aristotle would have called a "commonplace," and this is one of our key terms for today—a commonplace. A commonplace is a theme or topic that can be easily communicated to an audience using a well-known word or phrase, and the phrase itself can be brief, and the idea or topic associated with it is usually something that's a little more complicated and abstract. In this case, "hiding in plain sight" refers to the tendency of human beings to overlook or miss things that would otherwise be obvious to us. It's also a way of suggesting that things that seem deeply mysterious or inaccessible are often actually more familiar or more understandable than we might think at first.

Most important, it's a reminder that the things in our world that can be most beneficial—or most dangerous—are generally found in close proximity to us and not somewhere on the distant horizon. We can put this another way—whatever the problem, issue, or question may be, the answer, the solution, is probably a whole lot closer to home and a lot easier to spot than you might think.

I want to be clear here: You don't need to know where the term "commonplace" comes from or actually where any of the rhetorical terms in this lecture (or the next two) come from. It's not my goal today to have you learn these terms and memorize them. My goal is to help you become more familiar with the ideas behind the terms—or perhaps, really, it would be more accurate to say that what I want to happen today is for you to re-familiarize yourself with these ideas, so that you can apply them to your own writing in ways that are deliberate and effective.

After all, if you think about it, most of us already make use of things like rhetorical questions and commonplaces when we write. As I said, it's actually difficult not to use them since they're so deeply woven into the fabric of Western culture. But most people miss out on opportunities to maximize the benefits of these ideas because they're not always mindful or aware of them—and they don't tend to use them regularly or systematically to make their writing more powerful.

So our aim, then, is to identify, to define, and then provide some examples of rhetorical concepts that you probably already have some familiarity with, but that you probably aren't using deliberately or systematically in your own writing. That's our goal for today.

Some people have a real gift for this sort of thing; consciously or unconsciously, they manage to incorporate the most fundamentally powerful elements of rhetoric into whatever it is they're writing. But for most of us, the process of effectively applying these ideas requires a whole lot more deliberate effort and a really heightened awareness of what rhetorical elements are going to help us most in a given writing situation.

So in today's lecture we're going to look at what I think are four of the most readily and widely applicable rhetorical concepts that you can use to strengthen your writing, and these are commonplaces (which we've already touched on), something called stasis, deductive reasoning, and inductive reasoning—again: commonplaces, stasis, deductive reasoning, and inductive reasoning. These words and phrases might seem a little odd or awkward, and I'm not expecting you to finish this lecture and go around using these terms on a daily basis, but you might keep a small piece of paper next to your computer or on your writing desk with these terms and the ones we're going to discuss in our next two lectures written down on it. The idea here would be that this is a little "cheat sheet"; it could serve as a reminder to you, when you're writing, to consider these elements. Doing this will probably make whatever you're working on a better piece of writing—at the very least, it will cause you to focus your attention more intently on a particular moment or aspect of your writing—and thus, it will make it better.

What we're going to cover today is by no means an exhaustive survey of the four ideas of commonplace, stasis, inductive reasoning, and deductive reasoning. If you want to grasp the full extent of what ancient and classical rhetoric can offer us on these topics, that would take years of study, and I don't think we have time for that. What I'm providing for you here are basic versions of what scholars of rhetoric would speak of in much greater depth and probably in a much more nuanced, sophisticated way than what I'm going to do here today. But we can cover enough in one lecture to make these terms useful and helpful to you in your own work.

We've already touched on one important and easy-to-use rhetorical notion: the commonplace. Let's explore this a bit more before we move on to the other tools that I think you're going to find useful when you're writing, no matter what the specific situation is.

For our purposes today I think the best way to define a commonplace is to call it a piece of truth that is wrapped up in easily recognizable language. The notion of truth I'm getting at here is not some empirical fact or piece of data—rather, it's some kind of thought or behavior that's familiar and recognizable enough to a certain group of people that they're going to respond positively to it, even if they can't always precisely identify what it is that they find familiar or correct about that commonplace.

An example of a commonplace for most Americans is the notion that we have a right to the pursuit of happiness. It's one of the most widely recognized and accepted ideas from the Declaration of Independence, and I think it's a safe bet to make that the majority of U.S. citizens, no matter what their politics, would respond positively if a writer were to invoke this idea. Those same citizens would (and do), of course, have widely differing opinions about what happiness is and how one might go about pursuing it. Those differing opinions would, of course, require their own commonplaces if a writer wants to go on and forge a connection with the various members of these various audiences.

But the point here is that effective writers must identify an idea, a belief, or an action that the majority of their readers will find both recognizable and acceptable—and what this does is creates a sense of solidarity and good feeling, and once you've done this, the writer can then move on to address other points that might generate disagreement. In other words, it's a way of getting everyone into a similar, comfortable, intellectual space before you start to present a case or idea that may not be so familiar or comfortable to them.

Let's take another example—and this one is a little more specific to my own position. As a university professor, I respond positively to the idea of tenure. For those of you unfamiliar with the workings of academia, tenure means essentially that after a probationary period—and this is usually around six years—in which I have the chance to prove that I'm doing my job well—and this means I'm teaching my classes; I've published research in my field, and I've done my fair share of service to my department, to my university, and to the larger profession—well, after that probationary period, then I'll be granted tenure, which means job security.

People can and have lost their tenure—it does happen, but it's unusual, and in order for this to happen, you would have to essentially check out of doing your job. But to me, tenure is a commonplace that signifies the freedom to pursue research without fear of censure.

If I happen to be a medieval literature scholar (which I am, by the way), and the president of my university happens to hate Chaucer and all other medieval writers (which, by the way, is not at all true, but let's roll with it for the sake of this example), if I have tenure, my president can't fire me or try to redirect my scholarship. He or she can't say: "Work on something more relevant to today's world than Chaucer, or you're going to lose your job." Tenure protects me from that threat.

Again, let me be clear that this is a hypothetical example—my own university president has been very supportive of the Liberal Arts in general and the

English Department in particular. Also, I would say, I can list any number of reasons why it's incredibly important and relevant to today's world to study Chaucer, but we're not going to go into that here.

There are a number of different issues and arguments associated with tenure, but in a general sense, most university professors would recognize what it means, and most would see it in a positive light. Any writer who wanted to address an audience of university professors could use the commonplace of tenure as a way of generating a sense of solidarity; we would all recognize its meaning and agree, more or less, that it's a good thing.

That same writer could then go on to discuss some of those other issues and arguments associated with tenure—several of which might identify its downsides and its drawbacks—but that writer would already have given herself or himself a better chance of keeping and holding the audience's attention by invoking the commonplace as a source of general agreement and good feeling.

My take-away point here is that good writers make an effort to identify and regularly employ commonplaces that are relevant to their readers—whether that's a group of businesspeople working in a particular field, or members of a certain profession like law or medicine, or even an individual age group or particular demographic.

It's not simply a matter of knowing your audience (although, obviously, figuring that out is usually a pretty good first step); rather, what it's about is identifying what ideas or beliefs are so powerful and so widespread among members of that audience that you can be sure they'll take your writing seriously—even if at the end of the day they might end up disagreeing with your ultimate conclusions.

The next concept I want us to look at is called stasis. In classical rhetoric, stasis refers to the general agreement between opposing parties about what the terms of the argument are—in other words, a commonly held definition or understanding of the issue in dispute. The problem, as you might guess, is that very often the parties that are in conflict with one another or won't agree on a common definition or understanding of the argument's terms can't move beyond that initial disagreement.

If I refer to the issue as one thing, but you see it as something else, we're not likely to be able to stage a productive argument about it. We'll certainly disagree with each other—maybe passionately so—but our argument is not going to go anywhere because we'll spend all our time fighting over the terms and the labels we want to use.

You can probably see already how the concept of stasis is related to the notion of the commonplace—both hinge on the need for agreement. Let's go back to my example of the commonplace for most Americans of the right to the pursuit of happiness. I mentioned earlier that while most U.S. citizens would agree that this right is a good thing, they may have very different views on what constitutes happiness and how one should pursue it—and here is where the idea of stasis comes into play.

Imagine you are someone who loves playing the poker game Texas Hold'em, and you especially love playing for money, and you happen to live in Las Vegas, where such gambling—perfectly legal. For you, playing Texas Hold'em for money is the epitome of the pursuit of happiness. Now imagine that you have a spouse, and that your spouse was raised to view card playing as a sin and to view sin as especially egregious if there's money at stake. For your spouse, gambling is the devil's work.

As long as the two of you can't agree on what the terms of the argument are—is card playing for money a source of happiness, or is it a sign of moral turpitude?—then we can say that stasis has not been achieved. Even if you both accept the commonplace that Americans have the right to the pursuit of happiness (and that, since we're in Las Vegas, gambling isn't a legal transgression), you still haven't achieved stasis since you can't agree on whether Texas Hold'em is innocent entertainment or a state of perdition.

So why should stasis matter when it comes to writing? Just as effective writers must make an effort to identify commonplaces that are relevant to their readers, they also have to make an effort to identify the terms of an argument and recognize when those terms have been agreed upon and when they have not.

I'm not suggesting that writers must always strive for stasis or that they must change their terms or viewpoints in order to do this—that is not my point. But it's possible to craft a powerful piece of writing simply by showing readers how and why stasis has not been achieved with regard to a particular issue: to identify the terms that are problematic and to clarify the overall scope and the content of the debate, even if it seems that the debate itself can't be resolved—because certainly we all recognize that some debates can't be brought to a close, and we can all benefit from having a better sense of why the parties involved continue to remain in dispute with each other.

In addition to a lack of stasis, one of the reasons that certain debates are not easily resolved—or ever resolved—is because the writers who address the issue don't make effective use of different forms of reasoning to appeal to their audience. In this final section of the lecture, we're going to cover two types of reasoning—deductive and inductive—and classical rhetoricians like Aristotle viewed the methods by which we move from the knowledge we already have to the knowledge that is yet to be discovered and articulated as being achieved by deductive and inductive reasoning.

Let's start with deductive reasoning—the kind that many people are familiar with from detective stories and murder mysteries. I mean the entire *Law & Order* television franchise depends on writers who understand how to use deductive reasoning, although for entertainment purposes rather than generating knowledge. Deductive reasoning begins with a generally accepted declaration or premise—something that most people take to be true most of the time. The writer then uses that premise to make sense of a specific event, a specific occurrence, or a specific phenomenon.

In most Sherlock Holmes stories, for example, the detective relies on what he knows to be generally true, and these would be things like a certain type of mud can only be found in a certain region of England, and then he uses this knowledge to make sense of individual clues—well then, if that type of mud appears on a man's shoes, we can reasonably deduce that the man, or at least his shoes, were recently in that part of England. To put all this another way—when we reason deductively, we reason from the general in order to make sense of the particular or the specific.

The opening lines of Jane Austen's famous novel *Pride and Prejudice* set up just such an occasion for deductive reasoning by establishing a general premise about the circumstances of wealthy, unmarried men, and as you may recall that opening line is: "It is a truth universally acknowledged that a single man in possession of a good fortune must be in want of a wife."

Indeed, most of the rest of the novel could be read as an attempt to make sense of the actions and the words of particular characters—and a lot of these characters if you've read the book you know they're lots of young men with fortunes and several characters who are young women with the potential to be wives. So we might, then, read the whole rest of the book in light of that opening claim, and so long as the characters act or speak in ways that seem to affirm Austen's foundational premise, everything that happens within the fictional world of the novel makes sense.

Now if you're thinking to yourself, as you very well might be right now, that Austen's opening premise sounds a lot like the concept of the commonplace, which we discussed earlier, I would say that you are thinking absolutely correctly, and you don't have to be a novelist to use this connection to your advantage.

Once you have identified your commonplace and you have framed it as a premise—or if we want to go back and use Austen's words, framed it as "a truth universally acknowledged"—you have given your readers just what they expect—and just what they need—to then interpret any of the descriptions, the claims, or the information you might offer them in the pages to follow.

Even if the material you include doesn't always seem to affirm this opening premise—just like the actions and the words of some of Austen's characters don't always seem to support her claim that all single men with money are all looking for wives—it remains likely that your readers will stick with you. They may even overlook some inconsistencies or discrepancies because they have been primed to accept the deductive process as a useful source of knowledge—and generally speaking, as a reliable way of trying to make sense of the world, or at the very least make sense of the world of the book.

As you might guess, not all instances of reasoning follow the deductive pattern. Sometimes a process is inductive—meaning a writer will examine particular events or subsets of phenomena and use them as the basis for then constructing a premise that would apply to any events or incidents that are similar to that one.

In other words, to reason inductively is to move from particulars to generalizations—you go from specific examples to broader assertions about how something based on this evidence is true or how something works. So, what you're doing here is rather than using preexisting theories to make sense of whatever evidence or clues you have, you would use those clues and those bits of evidence to then construct your theories.

If we were to rewrite *Pride and Prejudice* following an inductive pattern, we would begin not with those famous first lines, but we'd begin by describing the words and actions of each single male character, assessing any differences and oddities of behavior, weighing them against similarities— and, ultimately, identifying the most common traits linking them to each other.

Our descriptions would probably have to then take into account how each single male interacted with female characters who could be potential wives, and we'd want to make it apparent to our readers that, in general, the men with more money seemed to be operating under the assumption—which was sometimes not spoken aloud; sometimes it was openly stated—that getting yourself a spouse would be a good and a necessary thing to do.

Only then—after a comprehensive, descriptive survey—could we help our readers formulate the theory that single men with good fortunes must want wives, and this would be in opposition to the many other possible theories we could construct based on the evidence that we have before us. We could come up with a theory like: All single men with money tend to make poor first impressions. That's absolutely a legitimate conclusion that you could reach after reading Austen.

Or, we could come up with: Rich, young men aren't very good at conveying their true feelings for young women; or: Well-off, single men must really like to attend formal parties and balls. If you have read *Pride and Prejudice*, you might see what I'm getting at. Inductive reasoning opens up lots of potential theories, but it's up to the writer to decide which ones are most important to identify for the reader. All of which, by the way, still leave us unsure about whether Mr. Darcy and Miss Elizabeth Bennet really were suited for each other after all.

My take-away points here are that inductive reasoning can be put to effective use in your writing, and that you should always keep it in mind as an alternative to the deductive process—especially when you're faced with a writing task that compels you to describe a wide range of evidence—and try and make sense of it for your audience. As the ancient and classical rhetorical scholars would remind you, as the writer, you are in charge of determining what commonalities or links in your evidence are most important and most worthy of being presented as truths that should be "universally acknowledged."

In our next two lectures, we'll build on our discussion of the four rhetorical concepts we've covered here—commonplaces, stasis, deductive and inductive reasoning—and we're going to examine another four terms and ideas that you can incorporate into your own writing to make it more persuasive and compelling. These four terms are invention, arrangement, ethos, and pathos. In our next lecture, we're going to focus on invention and arrangement.

Invention and Arrangement
Lecture 16

Kairos was so intriguing and significant for ancient rhetorical figures that the idea was manifested in the form of an actual mythical creature. The surviving depictions of Kairos show a human form in what we'd call, I think, a precarious balancing act—it's trying to grasp new opportunities without losing hold of what he already possesses.

The goal of this lecture is to enlarge the critical frame we've created through our study of commonplaces, stasis, and inductive and deductive reasoning in order to better illustrate and explain two broader areas of ancient classical rhetoric—invention and arrangement. We'll look at how elements of invention and arrangement can help us build stronger arguments, especially in the areas of business and professional writing.

"Invention" is a rhetorical term that refers to the process by which we generate arguments—meaning how we come up with the topics we write about. When business management gurus urge people to "think outside the box," they're really asking for versions of what we call invention. "Arrangement" is a rhetorical term that refers to the way arguments are organized—it's the formulas and the expectations that dictate the way a piece of writing is structured. The classic five-paragraph essay is an example of formula-based arrangement.

I'd like you to do what the ancient Greeks did when they were involved in the invention process and needed to generate ideas and arguments.

I'd like you to do what the ancient Greeks did when they were involved in the invention process and needed to generate ideas and arguments. First, consider the kairos of your situation. Kairos refers to the opportunities that a particular set of circumstances might present to you—and it also refers to the need to time your response so as to make the most of whatever opportunities have presented themselves. In other words, kairos is really about saying—or writing—the right thing in the right way at the right time.

Kairos needs to be part of our writing tool kit insofar as it serves to remind us that each writing situation is unique in some way, and that when we're in the middle of the process of invention, we'll do ourselves a huge favor if we attend closely to each situation's contingencies, demands, and opportunities. Put another way, never assume that one writing moment is the same as another, and always enter into each writing task without a preconceived notion of what argument you'll make or exactly how you'll make it.

Please don't mistake my meaning here—I'm not suggesting that the concept of kairos requires you to change your core beliefs or take a position that undermines your own ethical standards. In fact, one of the benefits of maintaining a flexible stance and an awareness of changing circumstances is that it puts you in a better position to articulate and circulate your beliefs should the opportunity present itself.

The ancient Greeks also offered a tool to help make those "kairotic" moments—analogy. Analogy is simply drawing connections between two things that may not necessarily be associated with each other by a particular audience. If the issue you're writing about doesn't seem to have a kairotic quality to it, you can create that kairos for yourself by constructing an analogy that links your idea with something that's part of the current zeitgeist. The take-away point is two-fold: First, kairos is incredibly powerful; second, good writers can create their own kairos by using analogies to connect their subject to something that stands at the center of everyone's attention. In the process, they can invent new arguments that lead to deeper and more meaningful discussion of the issue at hand, and they can get more people to focus on it.

Kairos is crucial not only for the invention process but also for arrangement—meaning it can inspire you to modify or even radically restructure those received formulas for how things like a business letter or a memo should look, or it can cause you to rethink and revise the terms and the language you might use when you're writing one of these. Moving beyond received models and conventional instructions—when the opportunity, circumstances, and timing seem right—can be a powerful way of setting your writing apart from everyone else's.

So what can you do to not only invent new ideas and arguments but also create new arrangements for them? An important addition to your writing tool kit should be a virtual permission form that states that you are no longer required to begin a piece of writing by crafting the introduction. Don't start at the start—start somewhere else! The reason is if you're crafting an introduction to something that you haven't yet written, you're undercutting the possibility that in the very act of writing, you might discover something new and important to say about your topic.

Instead of following a pattern, pick an aspect of your topic that seems most interesting or challenging and develop that in as much depth as you can. If, in the process of developing that point, you conceive of some new aspect of your topic, go ahead and develop that next—and don't worry about transitions; you can build those back in later. Your goal should be to use the writing process as a means of discovering what elements of a subject deserve the most attention. It's only by letting go of conventional formulas and expectations that writers can imagine new ways of arranging the arguments and the knowledge they've both invented and discovered. ■

Suggested Reading

Clouse, *The Student Writer*.

Crowley and Hawhee, *Ancient Rhetoric for Contemporary Students*.

Exercises

1. Most of the time, we don't recognize kairotic possibilities until after the fact (i.e., if only I had seen that connection between idea A and idea B, or if only I had worded the sentence this way instead of that). Using the benefit of hindsight, go back to a piece of professional writing and revise it to capitalize on that missed opportunity.

2. Rearrange the traditional business memo formula. How would you organize or word it if you didn't have to worry about meeting conventional expectations for how a memo is supposed to look and sound?

Invention and Arrangement
Lecture 16—Transcript

Welcome back. In the previous lecture, we studied four concepts from ancient and classical rhetoric that can readily and effectively enhance the quality of your writing. We learned how identifying and incorporating commonplaces into our work can help us establish a sense of solidarity with readers—and how that solidarity, in turn, can allow us to better explore alternative or opposing points of view.

We also learned about the concept of stasis—when opposing parties agree on the terms of an argument—and how a lack of stasis can forestall an argument's resolution. Recall that I suggested that you don't necessarily have to change your position on an issue in order to achieve stasis, but your writing can be more persuasive if you use your knowledge of the situation to clarify for your readers the problems and the tensions that prevent stasis from occurring. In other words, sometimes the best thing writers can do for their audiences is to explain precisely why a particular argument never seems to move any closer to resolution.

Finally, we looked at the processes of deductive and inductive reasoning—both of which are meant to help us use the knowledge we already possess to discover something new, and they're essentially two sides of the same coin. We saw how deductive reasoning begins with a general premise or preexisting theory and then uses it to explain the meaning of particular events or occurrences, and we learned about inductive reasoning's capacity to use bits of evidence—surveying and comparing them—to then generate a broader explanation about how the world works.

The goal of this lecture is to enlarge the critical frame we've created through our study of commonplaces, stasis, and inductive and deductive reasoning in order to better illustrate and explain two broader areas of ancient classical rhetoric—and here I'm talking about invention and arrangement. In other words, we're going to enlarge what I like to call our "rhetorical toolkit." We'll look at how elements of invention and arrangement can help us build and present stronger arguments, especially in the areas of business and professional writing.

Invention is a rhetorical term that refers to the process by which we generate arguments—meaning how we come up with the topics and questions we write about. When business management gurus urge people to "think outside the box" or consultants advise companies to brainstorm new ideas, they're really asking for versions of what we call invention, even if they don't realize that that's what they're doing.

Arrangement is a rhetorical term that refers to the way arguments are organized—it's pretty much just what it sounds like. Arrangement is the formulas and the expectations that dictate the way a piece of writing is structured or worded. The classic five-paragraph essay or the genre of the formal business letter are all examples of formula-based arrangement—we all know what these pieces of writing are supposed to look like, and we then shape our work to fit those expectations.

Rather than thinking outside the box or brainstorming—I'd like you to do what the ancient Greeks did when they were involved in the invention process and needed to generate ideas and arguments. First, consider the *kairos* of your situation. Kairos, spelled k-a-i-r-o-s, for our purposes today refers to the opportunities that a particular set of circumstances might present to you—and it also refers to the need to time your response so as to make the most of whatever opportunities have presented themselves.

In other words, if you put it simply, kairos is really about saying—or writing—the right thing in the right way at the right time. One more time: Kairos is about saying—or writing—the right thing in the right way at the right time. But first, you have to be able to spot these "kairotic" opportunities in order to really make the most of them.

Anyone involved in the world of finance—the world in which the mantra is always buy low, sell high—knows that kairos can mean the difference between turning a handsome profit and taking a major hit or loss. If the timing is right, the market can make you rich; if the timing is off, not only will you miss out on the opportunity to make gains with your portfolio, but you might then leave yourself vulnerable to a downturn.

Kairos was so intriguing and significant for ancient rhetorical figures that the idea was manifested in the form of an actual mythical creature. The surviving depictions of Kairos show a human form in what we'd call, I think, a precarious balancing act—it's trying to grasp new opportunities without losing hold of what he already possesses. Kairos is also depicted with a rather unique hairstyle. There are long locks above the forehead—clear of the eyes—that seem to imply a need to stay vigilant for something good and to reach for it before the moment passes.

Kairos was also a way for ancient thinkers to acknowledge that the circumstances from which ideas and arguments emerge are not always static or fixed, but rather they're always kind of in flux. Each situation carries with it a unique set of possibilities and limitations—all of which have to be studied, monitored, and to which you constantly have to adjust yourself in order for an argument to be successful. It's really kind of about a super-heightened awareness of a particular situation.

Now you might be thinking—and you would be right if you were thinking this—that there's a certain amount of luck involved here; let's just be honest about that upfront. It's really not often that we discover the perfect paragraph for a particular writing task, and that we then deliver it at the perfect moment to achieve maximum success. President Abraham Lincoln managed to do it with the Gettysburg Address, which is proof enough that kairos is an elusive quality that most of us don't manage to fully capture in our writing processes most of the time.

You might have heard the story that Lincoln composed the speech totally in the moment, on the back of an envelope while riding the train to Gettysburg. Most scholars now believe that this, in fact, is not the case—Lincoln had been working on and crafting the speech for some time in advance of giving it. But still, talk about kairos—in one of our nation's darkest hours, Lincoln managed in the space of just 271 words to invoke the principles on which the United States was founded, address the trauma of the current Civil War, and then provide a vision—a way to move forward. The opening of this speech, with its formality and what you might call a kind of epic-historical tone, seems itself drawn from the world of classical rhetoric and its practices. You probably all know this opening, but let's listen to it and be thinking of the kairos of this moment as you listen:

> Four score and seven years ago our fathers brought forth on this continent a new nation, conceived in liberty, and dedicated to the proposition that all men are created equal.
>
> Now we are engaged in a great civil war, testing whether that nation, or any nation, so conceived and so dedicated, can long endure. We are met on a great battle-field of that war. We have come to dedicate a portion of that field, as a final resting place for those who here gave their lives that that nation might live. It is altogether fitting and proper that we should do this.

He acknowledges the moment in which he finds himself compelled to provide such a wrenching memorial, but instead of a simple honoring or a consecration, he takes this opportunity, he recognizes the kairos—he takes this opportunity to provide his audience with an idea of what could come next, and he emphasizes that this really is a chance, it's an opportunity, to learn from this horrible situation and make the United States something new and better than what it had been before. He then goes on to say:

> But, in a larger sense, we can not dedicate, we can not consecrate, we can not hallow this ground. The brave men, living and dead, who struggled here, have consecrated it, far above our poor power to add or detract. The world will little note, nor long remember what we say here, but it can never forget what they did here. It is for us the living, rather, to be dedicated here to the unfinished work which they who fought here have thus far so nobly advanced. It is rather for us to be here dedicated to the great task remaining before us— that from these honored dead we take increased devotion to that cause for which they gave the last full measure of devotion—that we here highly resolve that these dead shall not have died in vain— that this nation, under God, shall have a new birth of freedom—and that government of the people, by the people, for the people, shall not perish from the earth.

It's a brilliant piece of oration—with images, rhythms, and cadences that have made it one of the most studied pieces of text in the whole American literary tradition. Lincoln's understanding of the kairos of the situation in which he found himself—whether or not he consciously recognized this specific classical concept—it's a wonderful illustration of how kairos should function.

Kairos needs to be part of our writing toolkit insofar as it serves to remind us that each writing situation is unique in some way, however slight, and that when we're in the middle of the process of invention (or if you want to call it brainstorming or outside-the-box thinking, whatever you prefer), we'll do ourselves a huge favor if we attend as closely as possible to each situation's contingencies, demands, and opportunities. Put another way—never assume that one writing moment is the same as another, and always enter into each writing task without a preconceived notion or certainty of what argument you'll make or exactly how you'll make it.

So, the key to coming up with that new idea or argument is to pay careful attention to the circumstances you find yourself in, and always be prepared to adjust your topic or alter your position slightly depending on what new information is coming your way. Just as a good financial advisor warns a client not to get emotionally invested in a particular stock so that he or she fails to recognize that market conditions have really shifted, and that stock that you like so much is really no longer worth owning—so, too, does a good writing advisor warn students not to become so attached to a particular idea or argument that they fail to recognize when its value or its relevancy has dissipated—or, in fact, disappeared entirely.

Please don't mistake my meaning here—I'm not suggesting that the concept of kairos requires you to change your core beliefs or take a position that undermines your own ethical or moral standards; kairos is not at all about that. In fact, one of the benefits of maintaining a flexible stance and an awareness of changing circumstances is that it puts you in a better position to articulate and circulate those beliefs and standards should the opportunity present itself. Lincoln's Gettysburg Address is a prime example. Nothing about the conditions under which the address was written or delivered changed any of Lincoln's core ideas and beliefs about the nation and the war—but those conditions did give him an opportunity to express those ideas and beliefs in a much more powerfully moving way than he ever had before.

One of my colleagues several years ago wrote a book on the subject of 19th-century literary representations of terrorism in American culture, and the timing ended up being such that this book was actually published just in the wake of the 9-11 terror attacks. Absolutely none of the book's research dealt directly with 9-11; nearly all of that work was completed prior to the attacks happening, and my colleague chose not to change or supplement any of his core arguments as a result of 9-11. He believed very strongly in the conclusions he had reached and saw nothing associated with 9-11 that would have changed his core ideas about the role of terrorism in American culture.

But at the same time, my colleague was keenly aware of the kairotic quality of the moment—not because he sought to exploit the timing to sell more books, but because of the country's new and heightened awareness of the issues that he had been working on for so many years, and this allowed him to articulate his research in a more powerful and persuasive way than would otherwise have been possible. The fact that he was able to maintain a flexible stance and an awareness of changing circumstances did not mean he shifted his core arguments; instead, this flexibility and this awareness gave him the opportunity to express those arguments more persuasively and to reach a wider audience.

This is not at all to say that he refused to incorporate aspects of the experience of 9-11 into his discussions of his work. In point of fact, when he was subsequently called on to speak or write about the phenomenon of terrorism on American soil, he made a careful effort to draw connections between the research he had already done and the events that both led up to and then unfolded after the attacks on the Twin Towers and the Pentagon. In other words, he saw a kairotic opportunity for invention—a chance to generate new ideas and questions that didn't exist prior to the attacks.

In the best tradition of ancient and classical thinkers, he didn't view this as an opportunity for personal gain at all—but instead as a chance to bring some new knowledge into being to develop and enhance the discourse that already existed on this subject. So here, kairos helped him as he worked on that first key term we've been dealing with today—invention. It helped him see how and what to write about next.

It's not often that kairotic moments present themselves in such a way as that which my colleague experienced. As the ancient Greeks recognized, timing is elusive, and the windows for inventing new ideas and arguments are not always opened so dramatically or completely. Still, they didn't leave themselves entirely subject to the whims of the god Kairos. Interestingly enough, they also suggested that successful speakers (and, of course, by extension, this means successful writers) had the capacity to create their own kairotic moments—to open up new ways of thinking about an issue or a topic by actually creating a connection to current conditions and circumstances.

They believed that individuals had the power to make their arguments resonate with the major events and questions of their day, even if opportunities didn't readily present themselves at first. In other words, they thought that kairos could be created to help with invention.

They also offered a tool to help make those kairotic moments—and this is one that I suspect you're already familiar with, but I also suspect you don't always make full use of this in your writing—and that tool is analogy. Analogy is simply drawing connections and similarities between two things that may not necessarily be associated with each other by a particular audience. If the issue or topic you're writing about doesn't seem to have a kairotic quality to it, you can, in effect, create that kairos for yourself by constructing an analogy that links your idea with something that's part of the current zeitgeist and truly of the moment.

This all sounds well and good in theory, but how can you put this analogy thing into practice—how can it be used to create kairos? One of my close friends works for a construction company that specializes in commercial real estate—and specifically, warehouses and other large-scale storage buildings. While her company handles most of the big-picture issues—and these are things like acquiring the land, securing building permits, finding tenants—they rely on multiple subcontractors to do a whole lot of the actual construction.

One of my friend's responsibilities was to audit the purchases of the subcontractors—make sure they were buying and using the materials that her company said they had to. At some point, she started to notice that one of the subcontractors was not buying the right kind of fire safety equipment and was not purchasing enough of it to adequately protect structures of the size her company was contracting to build.

So in response to this, she wrote multiple e-mails and memos—to the subcontractor, to her supervisors—and she was trying to alert them to this issue, and she was warning them that any short-term savings are going to be more than offset by potential losses they could face if an accident occurred due to the negligence of the subcontractor. Her bosses ignored her warnings, and they effectively gave the subcontractor tacit permission to keep cutting corners. They just sort of looked the other way. Finally, after sending out four separate memos on the subject, my friend gave up, and she tried a new approach.

What's important here is I should mention that these events were occurring at approximately the same time that the oil company BP was dealing with this huge financial and political fallout from the explosion of the Deepwater Horizon offshore drilling rig—as you'll recall, this explosion cost the lives of 11 crewmen and set off one of the largest oil spills in history.

You might also recall that BP leased this rig from another smaller company, Transocean, which also faced potential liability for the disaster. You might remember that prior to the explosion employees on the rig had actually noted several violations of safety protocols that management hadn't paid any attention to, no matter how many times they had tried to call their attention to these issues.

So, now, back to my friend and her dilemma; instead of sending out a fifth memo—and we can all imagine if the first four memos didn't do any good, why would the fifth—instead of sending out a fifth memo to her supervisors and the contractor, she crafted a press release, and she modeled it after some of the press releases that were issued after the oil rig explosion and spill. We don't have time in this lecture for me to read the full text of her mock press release, but what she did is draw a very clear, very clever—and for her bosses and the subcontractor a totally unnerving—analogy between the BP/ Transocean incident and what she believed would happen if her company continued to ignore the safety protocol violations that were being committed by the subcontractor.

This time, as you might have guessed, her writing efforts were immediately rewarded. The analogy she created with the mock release was so compelling that it was circulated to the highest levels of her company within the span of just one business day. On the morning of the second day, the subcontractor was fired—and even better, my friend received an immediate promotion to Head Compliance Officer. So, it was a win, win, win for everybody in this case.

The take-away point here is two-fold: First, kairos is incredibly powerful— the climate in the aftermath of the oil spill in the Gulf was such that no company could afford to be caught ignoring safety protocols for the sake of profit; second, good writers can create their own kairos by using analogies to connect their particular subject or issue to something that stands—for better or for worse—at the center of everyone's attention. In the process, they can invent new arguments that lead to deeper and more meaningful discussion of the issue at hand, and they can get more people to focus on it.

Kairos is crucial not only for the invention process but also for arrangement— meaning it can inspire you to modify, or even radically restructure, those received formulas and expectations for how such things like a business letter, or a memo, or a press release should look; or, it can cause you to rethink and revise the terms and the language you might use when you're writing one of these. I don't at all mean to suggest that the next time you have to compose an urgent e-mail or memo to your boss you should draw an analogy with a natural disaster or rely on a mock press release. What I do want to suggest here is that moving beyond received models and conventional instructions—when the opportunity, circumstances, and timing seem right— can be a really powerful way of setting your writing apart (in a good way) from everyone else's.

Of course, obviously, there are going to be some risks involved if you're not following standard procedures for composing written work—or for arranging your writing in ways that don't immediately conform to received notions. But it's also true that there are risks in repeating established formulas and following prescribed patterns, and those risks can be considerable as well. How many lost opportunities to stand out from the crowd and catch the attention of readers who might do wonderful things for you and your career? Think about that.

How many missed chances to wow somebody with your writing rather than simply pass inspection? As I demonstrated with the story about my college application essay in the first lecture of this series, my first try at that essay was perfect in terms of subject matter and style. It wasn't offensive in any way. There weren't any typos or grammatical errors. It had a logical progression, but it was ultimately too safe.

Like I said, I don't even remember what that first essay was about—probably something about learning how to be an effective leader—blah, blah, blah, blah, blah—in other words, probably just like the gabillion other essays the poor admissions committee was forced to read. My second essay, while I'm not arguing at all that it was rising to the level of great literature by any stretch of the imagination, but I'm sure that that second essay was definitely more interesting. It was more likely that the admissions officer would remember this one, and that's what I was going for—I didn't want to get lost in the crowd.

So what can you do to not only invent new ideas and arguments but also create new arrangements for them? An important addition to your writing toolkit should be a permission form—and let's make it an imaginary or a virtual one—and this permission form should state that from this moment on, you are no longer required to begin a piece of writing by crafting the opening or introduction. In other words, don't start at the start—start somewhere else.

The reason is if you're crafting an introduction to something that you haven't yet written but perhaps you have outlined or you have thought deeply about it, you're undercutting the possibility that in the very act of writing itself, you might discover (or invent, to use the classical rhetorical term) something new and important to say about your topic, issue, or question.

You might have encountered this strategy someplace else—someone advised you to save the introduction until last because, after all, you'll just end up rewriting it anyway. That's a really good piece of advice, but it's also important to understand that there's a deeper rationale for this than simply trying to save yourself some time and energy. The real drawback to writing the opening first is not the time and energy it's going to cost you when you have to go and revise—but rather the intellectual and creative possibilities that are going to be foreclosed when you lock yourself into that introduction-writing mode.

Taking a top-down approach to writing has the effect of narrowing the field of possible ideas and diminishing the impulse to ask new questions. To be clear—very often, especially with inexperienced writers, narrowing the field is a really necessary thing. It prevents an argument from becoming fragmented, or disconnected, or wondering off in weird directions. But for more experienced writers, fragmentation and disconnection aren't so much of a problem.

So, once you have got your topic in hand and you're fully capable of offering a clear, straightforward analysis and critique, you can easily avoid distracting tangents or underdeveloped points; or, if that's the case for you—or even if it's almost the case for you—well, then, I give you permission—indeed, you have every right and reason—to push back against conventional arrangement models that call for you to start with an introduction and then move methodically from point, to point, to point until you reach your conclusion (and at that point, of course, you're going to summarize what you have just told us).

Instead of following that pattern, instead pick a point or aspect of your topic that seems most interesting or challenging, and develop that in as much depth as you can. If, in the process of developing that point, you encounter or conceive of some new aspect or dimension of your topic, go ahead and develop that next—and don't worry about transitions; you can build those back in later. Your goal should be to use the writing process itself as a means of discovering what elements of an issue or subject deserve the most and best attention. It's only by letting go of conventional formulas and expectations—even if this is only for a short while—that writers can imagine new ways of arranging the arguments and the knowledge they have both invented and discovered.

Along with the commonplace, stasis, and deductive and inductive reasoning, you have seized the opportunity—in the true spirit of kairos—to include the ideas of invention and arrangement in your toolkit of rhetorical terms and concepts. In the next lecture, we're going to expand that toolkit even more by introducing two more concepts—ethos and pathos—that, taken together, will boost the persuasive power of your writing far beyond its current horizons.

Ethos and Pathos
Lecture 17

Some of the most compelling writers we've studied in this course—particularly Benjamin Franklin and Frederick Douglass—were actually students of classical rhetoric.

In our last lecture, we talked about two of four major concepts in classical rhetoric—invention and arrangement. In this lecture, we analyze another two rhetorical concepts—ethos and pathos. These ideas are particularly useful in writing situations where you are attempting to persuade somebody to give you something—like job application letters or grant proposals. Ethos means the perception that readers have of your reliability or character; pathos means inspiring emotion in your readers, especially feelings of sympathy.

There's nothing intrinsically ethically problematic with simple pathos-based appeals, but as a general rule, attempts to persuade are much more successful when they combine pathos and ethos. So how do you establish ethos? Generally speaking, ethos is established through patterns of behavior. Figures in the public eye have established an ethos based on what's widely known about their actions. "That's all fine and good," you might be saying, "but how do I construct an ethos in a piece of writing if the audience doesn't actually know me personally?" In this case, you have to demonstrate expertise, and/or you've got to speak from a position of authority in the writing itself. In order to make your writing have the greatest pathetic appeal, you need to establish your ethos fairly early on.

Attempts to persuade are much more successful when they combine pathos and ethos.

Let's look at an example that models a mix of ethos and pathos. In this case, we're going to return to Frederick Douglass's *Narrative*—a text that's intended, in its broadest terms, to persuade its audience to support the abolition of slavery. In the first part of the quote below, Douglass establishes his ethos—his authority to speak on this subject.

I have no accurate knowledge of my age, never having seen any authentic record containing it. By far the larger part of the slaves know as little of their ages as horses know of theirs, and it is the wish of most masters within my knowledge to keep their slaves thus ignorant. I do not remember to have ever met a slave who could tell of his birthday. They seldom come nearer to it than planting-time, harvest-time, cherry-time, spring-time, or fall-time.

So how does Douglass establish his ethos and his right to speak on the matter of slavery? First and foremost, there's the fact that he was a slave. But here, when it comes to the particular matter of slaves knowing personal information like their birth dates, he establishes himself as someone who has paid close attention to this issue specifically—and thus someone who has a right to comment on it. Douglass establishes ethos by providing specific information. He tells us how slaves reckon or remember their birthdays, and his language here indicates that he has asked numerous slaves if they know their birthdays—he's done research into the matter.

Notice how carefully he qualifies his statements. He acknowledges that there's some outer limit to his knowledge, and this further enhances his ethos—he's cautious, he's reliable, and he does not claim to know things that he can't know. This balance of humility with authority is part of what makes his writing so powerful and also so persuasive. So that's the establishment of ethos—and I think we can agree that Douglass does a pretty good job of this. He then continues on to work some pathos into this passage by saying:

A want of information concerning my own [birth date] was a source of unhappiness to me even during childhood. The white children could tell their ages. I could not tell why I ought to be deprived of the same privilege. I was not allowed to make any inquiries of my master concerning it. He deemed all such inquiries on the part of a slave improper and impertinent, and evidence of a restless spirit. The nearest estimate I can give makes me now between twenty-seven and twenty-eight years of age. I come to this, from hearing my master say, some time during 1835, I was about seventeen years old.

What makes this so pathetically powerful is that Douglass takes a relatively understated tone. He offers a matter-of-fact discussion of slave-holding culture's practice of keeping slaves ignorant of such basic personal information as birth dates. When he does this, he doesn't pile on negative adjectives—he doesn't even really characterize the practice as specifically as he could have. He keeps the tone calm—the lack of this knowledge, he says, is "a source of unhappiness"; it's very understated, "a source of unhappiness." He's confused as to why he can't know this information, and we get a very circumspect description of his master's attitude. So the understatement Douglass uses here allows us to imagine the reality as somewhat more unpleasant, and he does not come across as trying to prey on our sympathies. He presents the facts straightforwardly, and most readers will feel sympathy for his situation—why can't a slave even know his or her own birthday? Of course, he doesn't understand why one group of children could know their birth dates and another group would be ignorant of this information for no other reason than the color of their skin.

In order to really appreciate and recognize this understatedness, we have to remember that Douglass is speaking to an audience of mostly white Northerners. Douglass was strongly aware of the need to introduce them to the nature of slave-holding culture, but he needed to do that as judiciously as possible. The concern here is that his audience might become so emotionally overwhelmed by the description of the horrors of slavery that they would just stop listening. Perhaps even worse than the possibility of overwhelming his audience would be if they listened and thought his story was so incredible that it couldn't possibly be true. Douglass has to take care so that his audience does not disbelieve him, but at the same time, he also recognizes that pathos is a powerful tool for persuading his audience to join the antislavery movement.

While Douglass's example really drives home how the ideas of ethos and pathos work, you don't need to have lived through a horrible situation in order to establish a compelling ethos—nor do you need to recount horrific events in order to get a pathetic response from your audience. So, what you can take away from today's lecture is an understanding of how ethos and pathos can work together—and how it's usually more effective to have more ethos than pathos to create a really compelling piece of writing. An awareness of the elements of classical rhetoric that we've covered in this lecture and the two before it can help you become a better writer, simply by calling your attention back to what we might call the basics of good writing. You may never use the words kairos, ethos, or any of the others, but knowing and understanding them will definitely be a benefit. ■

Suggested Reading

Crowley and Hawhee, *Ancient Rhetoric for Contemporary Students*.

Exercises

1. Draft the first two paragraphs of a fundraising letter for your favorite charitable cause. How will you establish your ethos such that people will feel comfortable enough to donate money at your request?

2. Imagine you are organizing a community blood drive and need to compose a flyer asking people to participate. How would you generate sufficient pathos to convince donors to show up?

Ethos and Pathos
Lecture 17—Transcript

Welcome back. In our last lecture, we talked about two of four major concepts in classical rhetoric—and these concepts were invention and arrangement. As you probably remember, invention is the process of figuring out what you can write about in a given situation or in relation to a particular topic or question.

When you're starting to think about a piece of writing, it may seem silly to actually stop and ask yourself the basic question: What can I say about this topic, issue, or question? Most likely, you have something in mind or you wouldn't be writing anything. But sometimes, calling our attention back to the most basic questions or issues—like: "What can I say about this?" helps us to focus so that we can move forward and produce a really engaging piece of writing.

The other term we talked about was arrangement, and this is pretty much just what it sounds like—it's the process of choosing which things to include in your writing, and which order you want to put them in.

You want to arrange the elements of your writing so that they are the most effective they can be in any given situation. You'll pick and choose which elements to include and the order and style in which you treat them based on how you deal with the issue of invention. Again, arrangement seems like a really basic concept—and one that you maybe don't even have to consciously think of—of course, you're going to arrange your writing!

But you don't just want to throw a jumble of words or ideas on a page and hope that someone can figure out your main point. Okay, I take that back—I have seen some pieces of writing that seem to have followed this model of organization. But you don't want to do that, and again, returning your focus to a very basic question like: "How do I arrange and present this stuff?" can help make it better.

As we've already discussed, these terms and others—like *kairos*—come from the world of classical rhetoric—from the ancient Greek and Roman worlds, where good public speaking and persuasive writing were actually considered art forms. The Greeks and the Romans were almost fanatical in the way they broke things down into steps, the way they gave certain elements of their writings categories or labels that probably wouldn't even occur to us to try and name, and they were famous also for the rigorous and dedicated way they studied and tried to master these concepts.

You're probably asking: "So just what does that have to do with me and writing in the modern world?" As I've already pointed out, some of the most compelling writers we've studied in this course—particularly Benjamin Franklin and Frederick Douglass—were actually students of classical rhetoric.

As you may recall, Douglass in particular treasured his copy of *The Columbian Orator*, which he had managed to purchase when he was 12 years old. Douglass famously said in an interview: "Every opportunity I got, I read this book." *The Columbian Orator* was a foundational text in the schools of early America, and it contained lots of speeches and argumentative pieces that employed the techniques of classical rhetoric. Children were supposed to study and try to imitate the pieces in this text, with the idea that through practice and imitation they could master these concepts.

You'll have to admit, in the case of writers like Franklin and Douglass, this seems to have worked rather well. Their writing is compelling; it's engaging; it's persuasive—it's all the things you want to be in your own writing. So logically, if studying classical rhetoric worked so well for them, surely it can work for us, too.

As I've already mentioned, although you're learning terms like kairos, invention, arrangement, etc., etc.,—and in this lecture, we're going to study two more, ethos and pathos—you never need to actually use those words in your own writing. I find it helpful simply to have a post-it note on my computer that lists these words—that my attention is brought back to them.

It's a reminder that I should pause and consider how anything I'm working on uses these concepts—and whether or not I'm using them effectively.

Again, it's all about being intently mindful or hyperaware of what's going on in your own writing so that you can make it the best it can be.

So as I said, last time we talked about two of four key terms, and those two were invention and arrangement. In this lecture, we're going to focus and analyze another two rhetorical concepts, and these are ethos and pathos. These ideas are particularly useful in writing situations where you are attempting to persuade somebody to give you something—like job application letters or grant proposals.

You'll learn different ways to establish ethos—and this in a nutshell means simply the perception that readers have of your reliability or character. We're also going to look at some methods for inspiring pathos—and pathos really means simply inspiring emotion in your readers, especially feelings of sympathy.

A quick note here—pathos, spelled p-a-t-h-o-s, is sometimes pronounced "pah-thos," but most scholars of rhetoric say "pay-thos." It's a similar case with one of the writers we've been discussing in this course—Henry David Thoreau. Some scholars insist that his name should be pronounced "Thor-oh." Whichever way you decide to say pathos or Thoreau, you'll be pleasing some people, and you'll be irritating others. Just pick whichever you prefer and go with it, and don't worry about it.

So to get back to ethos and pathos—careful use of each of these ideas can greatly increase the chances that your written requests for something will meet with success rather than rejection. As I suggested just a moment ago, ethos is a term that in the most general sense refers to the character and the credibility of the person making an argument—while pathos is a term that in the most general sense refers to the emotional aspects or what we would call the affective qualities of an argument.

When I introduce these two concepts to my students, I begin by asking them if they have seen those late-night TV programs that feature images and narratives or stories about impoverished children in developing countries, and those ads usually then ask viewers to send money to sponsor a child or contribute something to help fight hunger or disease. Most of my students in the class when I ask them about this, they say: "Yea, we've seen these programs." I then ask them to raise their hands if they have actually sent a check or if they have made a donation. A few hands usually go up—and usually it's somewhere in the realm of maybe 2 or 3 people in a class of about 35.

I tell the ones who say that they have sent in money that I admire them for it—they're good people. I tell the other students that I don't judge them negatively since I consider this to be an issue of individual choice, and absolutely everyone has the right to say no without being criticized or condemned for it (and least of all by me).

But I then tell them that I've never written a check in response to one of those pleas from the people on television—but I also say I have written checks for similar groups in response to requests from people that I know. For example, I have some friends who have done volunteer work fighting poverty and disease, like in those places we see on TV. I have some friends who work for Doctors Without Borders. I say to my class that the reason I write checks for people I know is that they have a kind of built-in ethos with me—they have credibility because I know them. I trust them, and I know exactly what kind of work they have been doing.

It's not, let me be clear, it's not that I distrust the people on TV—it's just that they haven't offered the combination of ethos and pathos that I find really persuasive. If you think about it, obviously, the pathos is definitely there. How could images of starving children not arouse feelings of sympathy or make you have a desire to help? But the pathos that's inspired by those images is not effective if I really don't know much about the person or the group that's showing me these images and asking me for my money.

That's why some of these charity organizations get celebrity spokespeople to help them make their pleas—and the idea is something like, if I see actress Charisma Charming make this request, and I like Ms. Charming's movies, and I like what I've learned about her from reading magazine articles, etc., etc,.—then the thinking goes, I'll be more inclined to donate money because she has an established, positive ethos—at least for me.

I'm not at all suggesting here that these organizations are trying to trick me in some way by using celebrity spokespeople. In most instances, almost all of these organizations are really doing fantastic work, and what they're doing by getting celebrities to speak for them is simply employing a strategy from classical rhetoric—whether or not they actually know that that's what they're doing—and they're doing this in order to get me to help them out. There's absolutely nothing wrong with this—and there's a whole lot that's right about it, as long as it's done ethically and responsibly.

But let's take another example. I imagine that almost every one of us has gotten an e-mail from someone claiming to be in charge of a bank account in Nigeria. This e-mail usually begins something like: "Dearest one," and then a hard luck tale follows, and then the writer usually says something like: "If you'll just help me access this account worth 5 million U.S. dollars, I'll give you a cut. So just send me your account number, and then we'll be good to go!"

Other e-mails of this type claim to be from people who have an illness, or they have got a family member who is sick or recently deceased, and they either need help paying for medical bills or else they need—for some reason it's always your bank account number—but they need your bank account number in order to help them access, say, an inheritance.

How would you describe the ethos connected with these e-mails? I tend to think of the word "sketchy" when I think of e-mails like this. I don't know anything about the writer; they don't seem to have any idea who I am; they never use my real name, and I've got no way of verifying their identity or checking on their situation. Now let's consider, what if I got an e-mail from a friend of mine who happens to be in Nigeria, and this friend is there working with an organization like Doctors Without Borders?

If she says that she needs my help with a financial matter, I am much more likely to offer help, and this is because she has established an ethos as someone who is reliable, trustworthy, and working for a noble cause.

What goes wrong with these e-mails from unknown sources, among a whole list of things that are wrong with them, but one thing that goes wrong is that they are heavy on the pathos but light on ethos. There's nothing intrinsically ethically or morally problematic with just simple pathos-based appeals, but—as a general rule—attempts to persuade are much more successful when they combine pathos and ethos, and usually they're successful if they emphasize the ethos instead of the pathos. So let me just say that again: The most successful attempts combine ethos and pathos, and they're usually most successful if the ethos is sort of the dominant element rather than the pathos. You can give me the most pathetic—in the kind of classical rhetorical sense of the word—the most pathetic argument ever, but if I don't trust the ethos, it's not going to get you very far.

So how do you establish ethos? Generally speaking, ethos is established through habits or patterns of behavior. Figures in the public eye—people like celebrities or politicians—they have established an ethos based on what is widely known about their actions, about their words in interviews, publicity about their charity work, their statements about positions on certain issues, etc., etc.—all of this works together to create an ethos. "That's all fine and good," you might be saying, "but how do I construct an ethos in a piece of writing if the audience doesn't actually know me personally?"

In this case, what you have to do is demonstrate knowledge and expertise and/or you have got to speak from a position of authority in the writing itself. In order to make whatever it is, whatever your writing is about, have the greatest pathetic appeal—and again, I'm using "pathetic" here in the classical sense, not the sort of common, everyday way we use it nowadays—you need to establish your ethos fairly early on. If you're trying to figure out how to balance ethos and pathos, less pathos—as I've said before—is usually better than more.

Let's look at an example of an attempt to persuade readers to do something that models a mix of ethos and pathos. In this case, we're going to return to Frederick Douglass's *Narrative*—it's a text that is intended, in its broadest terms, to persuade its audience to support the abolition of slavery. In the first part of the quote I'm about to read to you, Douglass establishes his ethos—his authority to speak on this subject. This is what he says:

> I have no accurate knowledge of my age, never having seen any authentic record containing it. By far the larger part of the slaves know as little of their ages as horses know of theirs, and it is the wish of most masters within my knowledge to keep their slaves thus ignorant. I do not remember to have ever met a slave who could tell of his birthday. They seldom come nearer to it than planting-time, harvest- time, cherry-time, spring-time, or fall-time.

So how does he establish his ethos and his right to speak on the matter of slavery at all? Obviously, first and foremost, there's the fact that he was a slave, and this in and of itself certainly makes him qualified to speak on the subject—but this, of course, is an aspect of ethos beyond anyone's control—it just simply is.

But here, when it comes to the particular matter of slaves knowing personal information like their own ages or their birth dates, he goes ahead and establishes himself as someone who has paid close attention to this issue specifically—and thus, he's someone who has a right to comment on it.

Douglass establishes ethos by providing some specific information. He tells us how slaves reckon or remember their birthdays (and this is usually in terms of seasons), and his language here indicates that he has asked numerous slaves if they know their birthdays—so this means that he has done a little research into the matter. His language also here suggests that while his personal experience absolutely is the key part of the establishment of his authoritative ethos and his right to speak on this topic, what we get from this passage is the sense that he has looked beyond merely his personal experience; he has inquired about slaves and their relationship to their personal information. He says at one point: "It is the wish of most masters within my knowledge," and he also says: "I do not remember to have ever met a slave," so he presents himself as a source of information on slave-holding culture whose authority is based both on firsthand personal experience and on further investigation and inquiry.

Notice there how carefully he qualifies his statements. He does not come out and say: "All masters do this" or "Not a single slave knows his or her birthday." He is quite careful to put bounds or limits around his authority to speak. He acknowledges that there is some sort of outer limit to his knowledge, and this further enhances his ethos. He is cautious. He is reliable, and he does not claim to know things that he can't know. This balance of humility with authority is part of what makes his writing so powerful and also so persuasive.

So that's the establishment of ethos—and I think we can agree that Douglass does a pretty good job of this. He then continues on to work some pathos into this passage by saying:

> A want of information concerning my own [birth date] was a source of unhappiness to me even during childhood. The white children could tell their ages. I could not tell why I ought to be deprived of the same privilege. I was not allowed to make any inquiries of my master concerning it. He deemed all such inquiries on the part of a slave improper and impertinent, and evidence of a restless spirit. The nearest estimate I can give makes me now between twenty-seven and twenty-eight years of age. I come to this, from hearing my master say, some time during 1835, I was about seventeen years old.

What is your first reaction to this portion of the passage? Probably some of you registered feelings of shock, of outrage, of sympathy. But what makes this so pathetically powerful is that Douglass takes what I think we can all agree is a relatively understated tone. He offers a matter-of-fact discussion of slave-holding culture's practice of keeping slaves ignorant of such basic personal information as birth dates and ages. When he does this, he doesn't pile on negative adjectives—and he doesn't even really describe or characterize the practice as directly and specifically as he could have. He could have said: "This was cruel," or he could have said: "My master yelled in anger whenever I asked," but instead, he keeps the tone calm— the lack of this knowledge he says is "a source of unhappiness"—it's very understated, "a source of unhappiness." He is confused as to why he can't know this information, and we get a very circumspect description of his master's attitude. Douglass is simply, as he puts it, "not allowed" to make any inquiries; his master "deemed all such inquiries on the part of a slave improper and impertinent." Again, this really seems like understatement if we think about everything we know about slave-holding culture.

So the understatement Douglass uses here allows us to imagine the reality as somewhat more unpleasant, and he does not come across as trying to prey on our sympathies. He presents the facts straightforwardly, and most readers will feel sympathy for his situation—why can't a slave even know his or her own birthday? Of course, he doesn't understand why one group of children could know their birth dates and another group would be ignorant of this information for no other reason than the color of their skin.

In order to really appreciate and recognize this understatedness, what we have to remember is that Douglass is speaking to an audience of mostly white Northerners who, while interested in the question of abolition, might have had little to no knowledge of actual slave-holding culture. Douglass was really strongly aware of the need to introduce them to the nature of slave-holding culture, but he needed to do that as carefully and as judiciously as possible—and the concern here is that his audience might become so emotionally overwhelmed by the description of the horrors of slavery that they would just stop listening.

Remember those commercials featuring starving children I mentioned at the beginning of this lecture? How many of us have turned the channel when they come on simply because they're so upsetting? The horrors of starving children—just like the horrors of slavery—are really hard to see or to hear about.

For Douglass, perhaps even worse than the possibility of overwhelming his audience so much that they just stopped listening would be if they listened and thought his story was so incredible that it couldn't possibly be true. In other words, Douglass has to take care so that his audience does not disbelieve him—but at the same time, he also recognizes that pathos is a powerful tool for persuading his audience to join the antislavery movement—so what he is doing here is really walking a very, very fine line. He wants to draw them in. He wants to educate them about slavery, but he doesn't want to make them leave the room or turn the channel, as it were, because they're so overwhelmed by that story.

I once heard a Holocaust survivor, Rose Van Thyn, speak of her experiences. The horrors she described were emotionally wrenching for her audience, but I was struck by how while she detailed what happened to her in various concentration camps, there was one about which she said: "And that—I cannot even talk about what happened there," and then she waved her hand as if to brush it away, and she went on with the rest of her story—and make no mistake, the things that she actually did describe were truly horrific.

I'm guessing that certainly Mrs. Van Thyn was not concerned so much with how we, her audience, would react to this moment as much as she was aware that this something that she didn't want to speak about, this something was so horrible she couldn't even tell it to others without causing herself excessive pain—but the fact remains that when she did this, it has a similar effect, intentional or not, to Douglass's restraint that he demonstrates in his own work.

Until her death this year at the age of 88, Mrs. Van Thyn regularly spoke to groups about her experiences in the Holocaust—so, clearly it was important to her that people were aware of what had happened, and that people did not forget.

> And then we came in Auschwitz, in cattle cars. The Hitler's elite, the SS, were waiting for us and they literally beat all the old people out of the cattle cars and they were put in a row. I was put with another hundred women between the ages of 18 and 45, and we were set apart. The other people went by truck to gas chambers, but they didn't know. We didn't know about gas chambers.

It was certainly hard to listen to, and I have no doubt that it was also hard for her to relive these experiences over, and over, and over.

Rose Van Thyn had an amazing ethos, and it was made all the stronger by the things that she did not say, by the moments when she held back, and also by the fact that in the midst of an account of humanity's darkest days, she still found a way to work in some humor and jokes.

I remember her laughing when she related how after the war, she and her husband came to the United States after being sponsored by a family in Shreveport, Louisiana, and this family owned a pipe company. They were allowed to immigrate to the U.S. because this family had guaranteed her husband a job, and when they arrived, they were surprised to discover that the company did not make pipes for smoking, but pipes for plumbing. They had assumed that he'd be working in a pipe factory that would make pipes that people smoked.

> But, like I said, we were very blessed to come to Shreveport [Louisiana] and to America. And we couldn't come to … I told you, that this country made a special one for Holocaust. And Louis was a diamond cutter in Holland, and he went into the pipe business. Oil pipe. We thought, in the papers, it said "pipes," and we thought it was smoking pipes!

By the end of her talk, Mrs. Van Thyn had managed to brilliantly mix ethos and pathos so that the audience regarded her as an authority, absolutely, and her words had considerable weight.

> We bought this house in South Broadmore [Shreveport] and all the neighbors came and they brought coffee and they brought cake, and I was so surprised, I mean … And we're still very good neighbors. Except for one, who were … doesn't like Jews. Too bad! I can't change! And why should I change?

When someone asked her if she missed her homeland, if she ever felt like she wanted to leave the United States and return home to Europe—to the Netherlands, which had originally been her home—she said, I remember this so clearly, she said: "No, because this is the greatest country in the world. It may not be perfect, but if something is wrong, you are allowed to speak up and say something about it."

Now if we can imagine, say, a 17-year-old, born in North Dakota who spends part of his childhood in New York and part of his childhood in Texas—if this hypothetical 17-year-old said something similar, how persuasive would his statement be? I mean, he may be totally sincere, and he may be perfectly correct, but does it have the same effect as Mrs. Van Thyn making the same statement?

You're all thinking I hope: "Of course, not." If Mrs. Van Thyn had opened her talk with a comment about how great the United States is, rather than concluding with it, would it have been as powerful a statement? Not quite. It's because the account of her experiences establish her as an authority on the Holocaust and its aftermath—giving her a compelling ethos—and it's because the events she relates definitely create pathos. It's because of this ethos-pathos combination that her concluding remarks about the United States of America being the greatest country in the world are powerful, compelling, and persuasive.

I'm guessing—and I'm also hoping—that most of us don't have personal situations similar to Frederick Douglass and Rose Van Thyn. While their examples really drive home how the ideas of ethos and pathos work, you don't need to have lived through a horrible situation in order to establish a compelling ethos—nor do you need to recount horrific events in order to get a pathetic response from your audience. Let's take something as simple as a letter to your local city council requesting the installation of a speed bump in your neighborhood. What kind of ethos and pathos do you get from the following letter: "Dear City Council: I'm writing to request the installation of a speed bump on Main Street between First and Second Avenue. Cars drive too fast through this neighborhood, and it's only a matter of time before someone's pet or kid gets hit."

How's the ethos and pathos here? It's a good attempt at getting a pathetic response—certainly the idea of pets or children getting hit by cars draws on the readers' sympathies and emotions. But this falls short, mostly because there's no compelling ethos—in fact, there's not even really an ethos at all. We don't know why this person wants a speed bump, beyond the obviously stated reason—and we don't know if he or she lives in the neighborhood, or how long this person has lived there, or whether or not they know something about traffic engineering. With just a few tweaks, the ethos and thus the letter as a whole can be improved. Consider this rewrite of the letter:

Dear City Council: As a long-time resident of Friendlyville, I'm writing to call your attention to a traffic situation. As you know, the closure of Concord Street and re-routing of traffic along Main has caused an increase in cars traveling down this street. As a 25-year resident of 1234 Main, I have witnessed this increase firsthand, and I have also seen the average speed of cars traveling this street increase.

In the last month alone I have witnessed five near-misses between pets and cars, and one instance in which a child narrowly avoided being hit by a car. I am writing to suggest that the installation of a speed bump on Main between First and Second Avenue would help slow traffic and potentially save lives. Thank you.

What's the difference? The writer tells us where he lives, how long he's had the experience of living on this street. He has got a knowledge of traffic patterns in the area, and he gives a firsthand report of some close encounters between pets, people, and cars. With that authoritative ethos established, his pathetic plea—that the installation of a speed bump could save lives—is much more effective than it otherwise would be.

So, what you can take away from today's lecture is an understanding of how ethos and pathos can work together—and how it's usually more effective to have more ethos than pathos to make a really compelling piece of writing. An awareness of the elements of classical rhetoric that we've covered in this lecture and the two before it can help you become a better writer—simply by calling your attention back to what we might call the basics of good writing. You may never use the words kairos, or ethos, or any of the others, but knowing and understanding them will definitely be a benefit.

In today's lecture, we've spent a considerable amount of time discussing how to establish yourself as an authoritative voice in your writing by focusing on certain concepts. In our next two lectures, we're going to get down to the nuts and bolts of setting yourself up as an authority by focusing on the process of conducting research.

Finding What You Need
Lecture 18

The writer Umberto Eco, whose medieval murder mystery *The Name of the Rose* has become really a classic, tells a story about how he had decided that in *The Name of the Rose*, the poison in the book would be applied to the corners of the pages of a book that was read by medieval monks, and the monks in the story would be poisoned through the act of licking their fingers before they touched the corner of each page to turn it. Without thinking this through too much, he wrote to an acquaintance who specialized in plants, and he asked that friend if he knew of some substance that could poison someone if it was administered in this way—but Eco neglected to say that he wanted to know this as part of research for a novel he was writing! Understandably, this acquaintance replied with something like: "Um, yeah, I don't think I'm going to be able to help you with this."

In this lecture, we move our attention to a more practical concern of writing—the process of conducting research. There are several writing situations in which you might find yourself needing to do research, from a college paper to a magazine article to a letter to the editor. In other words, almost any type of writing can be improved with a little research.

Before you begin, it is most helpful to try and identify what your objective is. Is it to prove a particular position or support a belief that you hold? Is it to educate your audience on a certain topic? Is it to entertain? After identifying your objective—however nebulous it might be at this point—your next action will be to find your hook, or the way into your research. For example, let's say you want to write a murder mystery. If that's all you know—and that's totally fine at the earliest stages—then starting research can seem like a really daunting task, as you could just start looking things up and reading about them and never stop. But maybe you could find a way to give yourself a clearly defined way in—for example, you might start small and decide to look up the articles about every murder that's occurred in your town in the last 20 years. Or you could decide to model yourself after certain mystery writers, in which case you might start by reading the works of those writers to get some inspiration.

In addition to finding a hook, it is imperative that you have some sort of schedule. This can be really general, something as simple as "This week I'm just reading and taking notes; next week I'll start writing"—or it could get really specific, something like "Monday: two hours reading, a half-hour drafting ideas." I promise you will be more productive and focused if you give yourself a schedule and some deadlines.

How do you actually begin to do research? You might start with an Internet search: It's quick and easy. The problem here is also one of the most exciting things about the Internet—that millions of pages of information will be at your fingertips almost immediately. How do you sort through this information? Better yet, how do you decide which information is useful and which is not? That's the tough part, and I'm going to try and give you some tips to make this a little easier.

There's absolutely a time and a place for Internet research; however, relying on the Internet as your sole source of information can be dangerous.

There's absolutely a time and a place for Internet research; however, relying on the Internet as your sole source of information can be dangerous. I have found that the information on Wikipedia is more or less reliable, but this is also a source that can be altered by anyone. It's not rigorously fact-checked, and Wikipedia entries can be slanted depending on the interests of the person writing the entry.

Academic websites are a reliable source both for basic information and to guide you to other reliable sources of more specific information. If a site has an "edu" ending, this would tend to mean that it is affiliated with a university. If you want to research microbes in space, you can bet that you'll find the most reliable information in a scientific journal like *Nature*. Other reliable sources of information are long-established scholarly entities, like the Encyclopedia Britannica or the Oxford English Dictionary. You also absolutely want to stay away from sites that sell research papers on a variety of topics. These are simply tools for helping people plagiarize.

For scholarly writing, I can't stress enough how important it is to actually go to the library. Many electronic resources that would be helpful with a project like this can only be accessed from libraries. There are a lot of databases that can help you with this kind of writing, including many geared toward particular fields. If you're not sure what the most useful databases are for your field of interest, ask a librarian.

Here's something to remember as you're wandering the stacks of your library looking for a particular call number—once you find the book you're looking for, don't just take it off the shelf and walk away; take a moment to stop and look at what books are around the one that you just grabbed. On a related note, when you're conducting research you may find an article or book that you thought was going to be helpful, but it's clear from the first page that it doesn't actually relate directly to your topic. Do not just put it down and forget about it—spend a few minutes perusing the notes and the Works Cited section. Very often when you do this, you might find a reference to another article or book—or a point being made that does relate to what you're working on.

Even in the Internet age, libraries are crucial sources of information.

I talked earlier about the importance of having a research schedule. The activities of researching and writing are necessarily going to overlap, but it's important to have an idea of how long the one and the other will generally last. At a certain point when you're still researching, you may get a really clear idea of how you want to open your piece. Should you not start writing just because you're not into your writing week yet? Of course not. If you feel inspired to write, you should start—while keeping in mind that you may change what you've written, or you may throw it out altogether once you've done a little more research. By the same token, at a certain point you may have to make yourself stop reading and start writing. In our next lecture, we'll talk about putting all your research efforts to work as you start the process of writing. ■

Suggested Reading

Bullock, *The Norton Field Guide to Writing.*

Lynn, *Literature.*

MLA Handbook for Writers of Research Papers.

Oliver, *The Student's Guide to Research Ethics.*

Exercises

1. Pick a text we have discussed previously in this class, and try entering it in a variety of different online search engines—Google, Yahoo, Bing, and so on. Is there a difference in terms of which or what kind of pages come up? Which of these webpages seem reliable as documentary sources for a research project involving this topic? How can you tell?

2. Repeat this exercise, but this time use your local library's database or the MLA catalog. What is different about the sources you discover?

3. Now, go in person and find a scholarly book on one of these topics or pieces we've discussed. Look around to see what other books are nearby. What did you observe?

Finding What You Need
Lecture 18—Transcript

Welcome back. In our last few lectures, we discussed how understanding the elements of classical rhetoric can help make you a better reader and writer. By this point in the course, you have also come to understand different genres or categories of writing. You have learned how to unpack or engage poems, short stories, drama, essays, and autobiography, and you have explored the issues of voice or tone, and you have learned how important it is to understand and respect your audience.

In this lecture and the next one, we're going to move our attention to some more practical concerns of writing—specifically, the process of conducting research and then putting that research to use in a piece of writing. So put simply, today we're going to talk about how to find stuff, and in the next lecture we're going to focus on what to do with all that stuff once you have found it.

There are several writing situations in which you might find yourself needing to do some research, and these can range from the most obvious and classic example—like the college research paper—to a magazine article, or a short story, or a letter to the editor of a paper. In other words, almost any type of writing can be improved with a little research.

Although the specific example I'm going to use today comes from the academic world, the steps I'm going to outline apply just as easily to an article for a magazine that you're researching, or a report for work, or even a story or novel that is set in a time and place about which you maybe need to learn a little more. The key things for all of these types of writing are knowing your objective, knowing where to look, narrowing your focus, finding a hook, and then figuring out how much time you have for research and when you need to start writing—and you need a plan to get you through all of these steps.

As I just indicated, there are several steps that can help with the process of research—and before you begin, it is most helpful to try and identify what your objective is. Is it to prove a particular position or support a belief that you hold? Is it to educate your audience on a certain topic? Is it to entertain?

I find that it also helps to write out what I think my objective is, and I have to keep in mind that as I research and find more information, my objective might change a little bit. Although the objective may change somewhat as you research, having some goal in mind can help you avoid wasting valuable time as you're doing this work.

I'm sure you can imagine how discouraging it is to spend several hours researching a subject related to your main topic, only to discover that when it comes time to write the thing up, you really don't need that extra research in order to make your point. Then you think: "But I did all this work! Let me show you what I did!" and the end result could be that you end up muddying your main point rather than clarifying it.

After identifying your objective—however nebulous it might be at this point—your next and perhaps most important action will be to find your hook or the way in to your research. For example, let's say you want to write a murder mystery. If that's all you know—and that's totally fine at the earliest stages—then starting research can seem like a really daunting task, as you could just start looking things up and reading about them and never stop.

But maybe you could find a way to narrow your research and give yourself a clearly defined way in. For example, you might start small and decide: "I'm going to go to the library or my local newspaper's archives, and I'm going to look up the articles about every murder that's occurred in my area in the last 20 years." Or you could decide: "I want to write a mystery like Agatha Christie or Ellis Peters—in which case, you might start by reading the works of those writers very carefully in order to get some inspiration.

Maybe after starting with this as your way in, you decide you want to narrow your focus to let's say poison—so then you start reading about different poisons, eventually narrowing your specific focus to let's say arsenic or something similar. But obviously, in a case like this you do need to be a little careful. The writer Umberto Eco, whose medieval murder mystery

The Name of the Rose has become really a classic, tells a story about how he had decided that in *The Name of the Rose* the poison in the book would be applied to the corners of the pages of a book that was read by medieval monks, and the monks in the story would be poisoned through the act of licking their fingers before they touched the corner of each page to turn it.

Without thinking this through too much, he wrote to an acquaintance who specialized in plants, and he asked that friend if he knew of some substance that could poison someone if it was administered in this way—but Eco neglected to say that he wanted to know this as part of research for a novel he was writing! Understandably, this acquaintance replied with something like: "Um, yea, I don't think I'm going to be able to help you with this."

Sometimes in a case like this, you have to do research in order to know what it is that you want to research. This sounds a little silly, but at the early stage of researching, before you have a topic really narrowed and limited to something that is workable for the length of your assignment, it's ideal to read as much as you can on anything related to your general topic. Or, as I tell my students, you might reread a particular text or poem you enjoyed and try to figure out why you enjoyed it. Or was there something in the text that you found puzzling, that grabbed your attention? That might be the way to focus your energies in terms of research and provide you with a place to start.

Here's an example of finding a hook from my own graduate school days. I was trying to write a research paper on Sir Thomas Malory's version of the Arthurian legend, and I was totally lost. I decided to focus on the quest for the Holy Grail, so I read that section of the book over and over, and then I went and I read Malory's source for that story—and something caught my attention. At a key moment in the story, King Arthur orders his nephew Gawain to do something. Gawain obeys the order. He fails at the task, and then he's told that he shouldn't even have tried. "I know that," he says in response, "but I could not disobey my lord"—and in this case when he says "lord" he means his uncle, the king.

That's what he says in the French, but in Malory's version one word has been altered—"I could not disobey my uncle," Gawain says. He doesn't say "lord"—he says "uncle." I was intrigued by the shift in emphasis. Why did Malory want to call attention to the family relationship rather than the ruler-subject one? With this as my hook, as a way to focus my research, I discovered all sorts of changes in Malory's version of the Grail Quest, and a lot of these changes related to the matter of families. With this as a focus, researching got a whole lot easier.

Or here's a semi-fictional example from that recent best-seller *The Girl Who Kicked the Hornet's Nest* by the late Stieg Larsson. At one point in this thriller, a minor character who is a magazine reporter wants to do an article on why rents and appliances cost so much in Sweden. Where to start? He notices that two companies that sell toilets sell almost the identical toilet for dramatically different prices.

"Okay," he thinks, "here's a hook. Let's start with toilets." I mean, everybody needs toilets after all, right? So, good place to start. He researches where and how they're made—all the way in Indonesia he discovers—and then he investigates the conditions in which the workers produce them. This leads him to discover some appalling facts about labor laws—or actually, specifically the lack of labor laws—and he discovers some other things about human trafficking and kickbacks—and finally discovers that a powerful man on the board of directors of his own magazine is, in fact, an evil opportunist, and all of this starts from toilets.

This is a classic example of how your research project can change once you get started, and here you have to be careful—but come on, if you're trying to write a compelling investigative piece, human trafficking is going to get your work more attention and potentially more Pulitzer Prizes than an article on the inflated prices of toilets—although since, as I noted before, everyone needs toilets, that piece, too, would probably find an interested audience, to be sure.

In addition to finding a hook or a way in to your research project, it is imperative—and I cannot stress this enough—it is imperative that you have some sort of schedule. This can be really general, something as simple as: "This week I'm just reading and taking notes; next week I'll start writing"— or it could get really specific, something like: "Monday: two hours reading, a half-hour drafting ideas or points for an article or essay; Tuesday: four hours reading"—or if you have identified some key articles or books that you think will be central to your research, you can identify by which day you hope to have read through each of these. If you're working on something like an article or short story that you're composing for your own pleasure or satisfaction, you may be thinking: "Well, I don't need a schedule.

I don't really have an external deadline—it will be done when I finish it." That's okay, but I promise you, you will be more productive and focused if you try to give yourself a schedule and some deadlines. You may not meet those deadlines, and the planned schedule may go totally wonky at some point because of life getting in the way, but at least having a schedule will help you focus and move forward.

So let's look at a rather classic example of the kind of writing that demands research and explore the process by which you might try to complete it. Whenever I teach a course called The Arthurian Tradition—and this is a class that focuses on literature that tells the story of King Arthur; it covers works written in the Middle Ages up to the present day—I always finish the course with a research assignment, and it's usually something like: "Use at least seven secondary sources, and then make an argumentative claim that you support with both direct textual evidence from a primary source, and that you also support with secondary evidence you've discovered in your research."

Given an assignment like that, where would you begin? The assignment, as I've given it, is deliberately broadly described, and it's really non-specific because when I teach this class, I really want to hear what my students have found most interesting in the course, and I want to give them the freedom to explore a theme or an idea that most appeals to them. As you can probably guess though, some students are totally at a loss when it comes to finding the hook or the way in to start the research. So what happens next is I usually have a conversation with the student, and I try to find out what he or she found most interesting, or intriguing, or puzzling in the class.

Sometimes it's a single text that we read in this Arthurian Literature course, and it's a single text that's stayed with them, and the student might say something like: "I'm interested in how important the role of magic is in Arthurian literature." The student could then start researching King Arthur and magic as a means to narrowing the topic still further. In other words, what he finds in this initial research period might then help him to zero in on something particular about magic and King Arthur. Who wields magic? For what ends? In what text is magic most important? These could all be questions that the student asks and looks into as he is doing his research.

That is all well and good, but how do you actually begin to do that? You might start with an Internet search. It's quick; it's easy—you don't even have to get out of your chair to do it, and in some cases literally millions of pages of information will be at your fingertips almost immediately.

So you might ask: "What's the problem here?" The problem is also one of the most exciting things about the Internet, and that is that literally millions of pages of information will be at your fingertips almost immediately. How do you sort through this information? Better yet, how do you decide which information is useful and which is not—which information comes from a responsible scholar who has done some thorough research, and which comes from someone who has a crazy theory and it's all built out of wild conjecture? That's the tough part, and I'm going to try and give you some tips to make this a little easier.

There is absolutely a time and a place for Internet research, and I will admit right up front that I use the Internet all the time for all kinds of research. At the same time, however, relying on the Internet as your sole source of information can be dangerous. Remember, anyone can post anything they want on the Internet, and there is really no way to fact check what you find unless you, guess what, do a whole lot more research—and not just on the Internet.

For example, last week I did a Google search for King Arthur. The first page to come up is one for a company called King Arthur Flour. They make very fine flour for all your baking needs—including Queen Guinevere cake flour, Sir Lancelot high-gluten flour, etc., etc.—but that is not going to help anyone trying to do a research paper on King Arthur. The next page that comes up after King Arthur Flour is the Wikipedia page for King Arthur.

Nine times out of 10, I have found that the information on Wikipedia is more or less reliable, but this is also a source that can be altered by anyone. It's not rigorously fact-checked in terms of the way that the academic world would think rigorous fact checking should be done, and Wikipedia entries can be slanted—depending on the interests of the person writing the entry.

You might look here certainly for an overview of information, but I'll tell you right now, if you are writing a college-level paper or an article for a magazine, citing Wikipedia as a source will not earn you any points with your professors or your editors. After the Wikipedia site, there's a website dedicated to the movie *King Arthur*, which starred Clive Owen, along with some images of him as King Arthur, and these are lovely to look at but they're not going to help you with your research paper.

Next comes the Britannia source for info on King Arthur. As an academic source, this is pretty reliable, but it doesn't do much to give you a handle on whatever specific topic you want to research—except it can serve as a really basic starting point.

Obviously, your research is going to turn up a few other sites—one of these is the website of Arthuriana, the premier scholarly journal on all things Arthurian. Full disclosure here—I have recently become the Editor-in-Chief of this journal, and I think it's very, very important and does very good work providing the world with the latest solid research on all things Arthurian. The website of Arthuriana has links to pages with resources on teaching. It has got a list of key texts for anyone interested in the Arthurian tradition, and you can also subscribe to the electronic version of the journal, and that gives you access to the latest scholarly research on the legend of King Arthur.

Obviously, as an academic website, this is a reliable source both for basic information and to guide you to other reliable sources of more specific information. But in my Google search, this site was immediately followed by the website of a guy who thinks he's the reincarnation of Arthur, and then that was followed by a site that publishes Arthurian fan-fiction. Fan fiction is when people rewrite stories or imagine new episodes of a well-known, long-established story. If you are trying to write a scholarly essay on Arthur, obviously those sites aren't going to help you any.

So what are some clues that sources online might be reliable and might point you in the right direction? One clue would be if a site has an edu ending—this would tend to mean that the website and its author are affiliated with a university, where people make a living studying these kinds of things.

But you do have to be careful that you're dealing with an official site edited by a scholar—and not a student at the same university simply posting his or her thoughts on the topic. The same criteria apply for print sources that have an online component. If you want to research microbes in space you can bet that you'll find the most reliable information in a scientific journal like *Nature*. Fairly reliable information—although, perhaps, not as scientifically detailed—you might find on the website for the New York Times, and if you find an article on microbes in space in the *National Enquirer*, well, obviously, you're probably going to want to stay far, far away from that.

You also absolutely want to stay away from those sites that claim to be able to sell you research papers on a variety of topics. These are simply thinly disguised tools—or I would say in many cases they're not even disguised at all—for helping people plagiarize. The quality of the papers on these sites is not very good; it's a total waste of time and money. Other reliable sources of information would be long-established scholarly entities—like the Encyclopedia Britannica or the Oxford English Dictionary, things like that.

Let's go back to our hypothetical example of the research paper on Arthurian literature. So the web, obviously, is just a starting point. For this kind of writing, I can't stress enough how important it is to actually get into the library. Many electronic resources that would be helpful with a project like this can only be accessed from libraries. There are a lot of different databases out there that can help you with this kind of writing, and there are many databases geared toward particular fields.

For example, for a paper like this, I'd tell my students to do a search for their topic in the MLA—or Modern Language Association—database, or else the Arts and Humanities Citation Index, or there are some full-text databases like Project Muse and JSTOR. Nearly every field of interest has specialized databases for reliable information in that field. In my field, literature, the MLA Database is the gold standard, and there are several other good ones as well.

You should find out what the most useful databases are for your field of interest, and if you're not sure, ask a librarian. Databases come and go; they change; they get updated, but these are not entities with minds or self-awareness. Librarians make it their business to keep up with the changes, to be able to listen to what you're working on and help you find the sources that will best help you at that moment.

In this age of amazing computer technology, the human factor often gets overlooked. But remember, librarians have experience. They know the idiosyncrasies of this or that database, and they're there to help you. So please, ask them for help—as they can certainly, at the very least, guide you to the database that's going to be of most help to you, and they're going to help you get there much more quickly than you could find it on your own.

So once you have got a range of books and articles, you're going to want to get your hands on as many of them as possible. Sometimes this is really easy. You check to see if your local library has one of the books on your list. The library's catalog says it does, and off you go to pull it off the shelf. Here is something to remember as you're wandering the stacks of your library looking for a particular call number: Once you find the book you're looking for, don't just take it off the shelf and walk away. You really should take a moment to stop and look at what books are around the one that you just grabbed.

Very often what you'll find is that there are other books in this same area that are related to your topic—and some of them may, in fact, have not come up in your initial database search for a variety of reasons. I learned this lesson when I was in graduate school, and I was working on my dissertation. Once, while I was in the library to get a book, I noticed that there was this series of monographs on the shelf that were directly related to my main topic. They were just one shelf above the book that I was actually looking for. So while I was there, I grabbed those books as well as the one I had originally come in search of. I checked them out, and I found these unexpected monographs to be really helpful. A few months later, sometime after I'd returned them, I realized that I wanted to look at one of them again.

I knew what the title was so I went back to my library, and I did a search in the catalog to find the location of the book so I could check it out again. When I searched for the title, it didn't come up. So I tried the next approach; I searched for the editor's name, and luckily I remembered this name as well. No luck. I then tried a key word search. No dice. Finally, what saved me is that I remembered the book that I had been looking for before when initially I had accidentally stumbled across these texts—so I did a search for that book, the one that I had originally looked for. I got the location, went back to the general area, and then I looked at the shelves around nearby until I found the book that I had wanted. So this is a good lesson: Some things aren't always easily found or accessible when you do database searches, and you really should take the time to look around you.

On a related note, when you're conducting research you may get a hold of an article or book that you thought was going to be helpful, but it's clear from the first page or so it doesn't actually relate directly to your topic. Do not just put it down and forget about it. Before you set aside an article or a book and you decide that it's really not going to be helpful for your research project, you really should spend a few minutes perusing the notes and the "Works Cited" section. Very often when you do this, you might find a reference to another article or book—or a point being made that does relate to what you're working on. In fact, in several instances I have found the notes and the bibliography of a book or an article to be more helpful than the content of that article itself.

Now that we've covered some basics of research, let's go back to our specific example of the research paper on Arthurian literature—and again, the techniques I'm discussing here are easily translated to research for other kinds of writing—it's not just for the scholarly essay. But by using this one specific example, I hope you can see how this approach can work in practice.

Let's examine some possible topics for this paper. How about: "The Figure of King Arthur in Literature"? Obviously, this is way too broad for a paper like this; you could write a book, or 5, or 12 on this topic alone, so we've got to narrow that—so let's try again. How about: "The Figure of King Arthur in Medieval Literature"? That is more specific, but once you start researching, you'll probably, again, realize that this could fill an entire book or more.

So we need to get a little more specific. What if we went with: "The Characterization of King Arthur in Sir Thomas Malory's *Morte Darthur*"? This is closer to what we're looking for; it focuses on just one text and just one character. But Malory's text is over 700 pages long in paperback, so this topic is probably still too big for a college-level research paper. If we were dealing with a shorter text—something like the medieval text *Sir Gawain and the Green Knight*—then an analysis of the character of King Arthur in just that one text might work, but in this case it doesn't.

It's possible that you can go too far toward the opposite end of the spectrum, and you can have topics that are far too narrow. For example, you could think: "Alright, I'll focus in on a key scene, and I'll do a topic like: "The Importance of the Moment When Arthur Pulls the Sword from the Stone in Malory's Text." This is possibly workable, but you may run out of things to say well before the end.

A more satisfactory topic might be something like: "The Significance of the Shift in Arthur's Character Once He Has Founded the Order of the Round Table." This topic has as its main focus a particular moment in Malory's text, but then it also leaves you free to discuss moments both before and after it. In other words, it's focused, but it can be expanded. It's flexible while still having a great deal of specificity, and you can adequately address it in sort of the length that you might expect a college-level research paper to be.

At the beginning of this lecture I talked about the importance of having some kind of research schedule—of setting yourself some deadlines to help motivate you as you move through the process of writing. So how long do you think you should give yourself to work on a project like this?

First of all, as you can imagine, everyone works at a different pace. Some people read quickly. Some people have great retention when they read. Others need to go back and reread some things a few times to really get the gist of what is important or key in terms of your topic or goal. But for an assignment like this, I would estimate that most people, depending on how many hours per day they can devote to it and how familiar they are with the topic to start with, I am estimating that this paper could get done in about two weeks—one week to do research, take notes, start to brainstorm the structure of the paper, and then maybe another week to take everything you have read and make use of it in your argument.

Now to be sure, these two activities—researching and writing—are necessarily going to overlap, but it's important to have an idea of how long the one and the other will generally last. At a certain point when you're still researching, you may get a really clear idea of how you want to open your essay, or short story, or magazine article. Should you not start writing just because you're not into your writing week yet? Of course not. If you feel inspired to write, you should start—while keeping in mind that you may change what you have written, or you might throw it out altogether once you have done a little more research, or you may come across a quote that you want to use as one of your supporting points that would occur midway through the paper. By all means, go ahead—write it down, and do some drafting of the way you're going to use this point in your argument.

By the same token, at a certain point you may have to make yourself stop reading and start writing. When you're researching you may feel that you just can't write yet—there's so much more you could read, and it's important to remember that that's always going to be true. There is always something else you can read. There's always more research you can do. But at some point you're going to have to put down the book, and you're going to have to put the pen to the paper—or your fingers to the keyboard, as the case may be.

When you start writing in earnest, you're going to need to be able to have all that research you spent so much time collecting easily accessible so that you can use all that stuff that you looked up online, that you tracked down at the library, that you found through perusing footnotes—and you read, and reread, and reread. In our next lecture, we'll talk about putting all your research efforts to work as you start the process of writing.

Using What You Find
Lecture 19

In order to cite properly, you need to be able to find the quote you have in mind. It does you absolutely no good—trust me on this one, no good—if you think: "I remember that being in the middle of some book that had a brown cover," and then you spend precious time searching for it.

Now that you've mastered some of the basics of finding information, you need to start figuring out how to keep track of it. Everybody works and thinks differently, so it may be a matter of doing this a few times before you figure out which style of information storing and sorting works for you.

The most important and useful advice I can give you is simply to start early. In exchange for your audience's time and interest, you have an obligation to know what you're talking about. This means you need to read up on your topic and absorb the information. Then you'll need to review a lot of your research materials so that you have an understanding of other points of view on your topic. Next, you need to be able to articulate your own position in respect to those other points of view. Finally, you have to make a convincing case as to why your particular focus or argumentative position is important.

If you're in the early stages of your project and not quite sure what approach you want to take to a particular topic, you might start with reading through the material you've collected and using tabs to identify pages that contain material you find interesting and relevant to your topic. After you've gone through an initial reading of your material, it's time to take more detailed notes. The way I tend to work is by taking notes on a particular text, either in longhand or on the computer. When I do this, I try to sum up a scholar's general argument and then note particularly interesting points individually—making sure to identify on which page they appear.

When I've worked my way through taking notes on a text, I either print the typed notes or staple my handwritten notes together. This way, when it comes time to start the drafting process, I can read through my notes to remind myself what's important about a book rather than having to reread it. I am always careful to write down my own questions or counterarguments as they come to me, so that I don't forget a flash of insight.

Another variation on this note-taking approach is the note card version—many of us probably learned some form of this in high school. It's just what it sounds like: You write a quote or an important argumentative point on each note card. In the top corner of the card, you should also designate who the author is, which text the idea or quote comes from, and which page number you found it on. The benefit of this approach is that it's a little more flexible, because you can shuffle the cards to further organize your research by subpoints.

> **One of the trickiest things is to make your voice heard while using the work of other experts as a means of support.**

When you're organizing your research into an article, one of the trickiest things is to make your voice heard while using the work of other experts as a means of support. You want to make your research support your idea, but you need to give proper accreditation where it's due. The best way to generate an original argument for a research project is after doing your research, decide what your particular stance is on a topic, and then try and articulate your position. Generate a rough outline indicating where supporting points could be helped by the use of secondary sources. When you're doing this, you absolutely need to identify critics who have expressed opinions that disagree with your own. Sometimes an opposing view or counterargument can help you prove your own point; you can even use a counterargument as a way of structuring your own argument.

One of the major dangers when writing a research paper is the issue of plagiarism, which you need to avoid at all costs. In a nutshell, plagiarism is using the words or ideas of others without giving proper credit where credit is due. There is obvious, outright plagiarism, and then there is accidental plagiarism, which is what you have to guard against most vigilantly. Let's say you've read lots and lots of books and articles on your subject; you've taken lots and lots of notes; and you've become an authority on the topic. This is great because it means that you've internalized much of what you've been reading. The danger is that your original thoughts on a particular topic may somehow get mixed up with what other scholars have to say. As you're reading over your notes or note cards, you might forget whether they contain what a scholar said about your topic or your own reaction to what you were reading.

This is why I tend to note direct quotes by putting quotation marks around sentences or phrases I find important—or if I'm paraphrasing, I might write something like: "Professor Eminence spends two pages discussing the history of Malory scholarship, focusing particularly on where early 20th-century scholars went wrong." Now when it comes to my research, I might be in full agreement with Professor Eminence's thinking about how early 20th-century scholars were wrong in a particular area, and I can say that—but I also need to cite Professor Eminence as having made this argument first.

Even if I arrive at a conclusion or position on my own, independent of another scholar, once I start doing research and discover that other scholars have already observed this point, I need to make sure that I give them credit. Actually, when you discover that what you thought was an original insight on your part is, in fact, a point that someone else has already made, you should be encouraged that you seem to be thinking like the experts. ∎

Suggested Reading

Bullock, *The Norton Field Guide to Writing.*

Lynn, *Literature.*

MLA Handbook for Writers of Research Papers.

Oliver, *The Student's Guide to Research Ethics.*

1. For each passage below, even though you don't know the research sources, can you identify where the citation fails and what the red flags are?

   Many Malory scholars now disagree with Eugène Vinaver's argument that Malory composed eight separate tales; several, in fact, argue that Malory's text is the "most comprehensive before the modern period" and others have gone so far as to suggest that it is "the first novel." In any event, we can agree with Dorsey Armstrong that Malory's *Morte d'Arthur* is something "new and original" (33).

   People have always told stories. Back in the Middle Ages, people wrote some of the most popular stories ever to be told. Medieval people liked stories about knights, combat, and ladies in distress. Today, people tend to like the same kinds of stories, but with a modern twist.

   Studies have shown that when light-rail moves into a neighborhood, property values go down. Neighborhoods with light-rail stations are noisier, more prone to crime, and more likely to incur instances of vandalism. It is estimated that if a light-rail station were to be built in this neighborhood, all property values would drop by at least ten percent.

2. Correct the citation format in the examples below so that it conforms to MLA style. Now correct it so that it conforms to APA style. Repeat for Chicago style. Notice the similarities and differences.

   Jane Austen's *Pride and Prejudice*; quote from page 1 (published by Penguin Books in London, 2002): "It is a truth universally acknowledged that a single man in possession of a good fortune, must be in want of a wife."

   Dorsey Armstrong's *Gender and the Chivalric Community in Malory's Morte d'Arthur* (published in 2003 by University Press of Florida, in Gainesville) quote from page 1: "The particular construction of gender in Malory's text is critical to any attempt to engage with its narrative project."

Ryan Schneider's *The Public Intellectualism of Ralph Waldo Emerson and W. E. B. Du Bois: Emotional Dimensions of Race and Reform* (published by Palgrave Macmillan, New York, 2010), quote from page 137: "Despite the epic-heroic, sacrificial connotations of their rhetoric, Du Bois and Stewart refuse the argument that violence is a morally just and ethically viable means of bringing about the kinds of radical changes in the social order necessary to ensure reciprocal relations across the color line."

Using What You Find
Lecture 19—Transcript

Welcome back. In our last lecture, we discussed how to get started on a research project. As a model, I gave you the research assignment that I typically assign my undergraduate Arthurian Literature course, but the strategies that we walked through last time are easily applicable to a magazine article, a short story, or some kind of presentation—whether it's in public or at the office. We talked last time about how to find a hook or a way in to your research in order to get yourself started.

We also discussed the pros and cons of using the Internet, the powerful search tools available in libraries, and the importance of paying attention to what is around a particular book once you locate it on a library shelf. Finally, we discussed the importance of having some kind of schedule. While a research and writing schedule will often change as you go along, it's important to have some kind of idea when you're going to do what—at least as a guideline, at the very least.

Now that you have mastered some of the basics of finding information, you need to start figuring out how to keep track of it. Everybody works and thinks differently—so it may be a matter of doing this a few times before you figure out which style of information storing and sorting fits with your personality and your research style.

The most important, and helpful, and useful advice I can give you when it comes to researching actually has nothing to do with the means by which you're going to organize all the volumes of data you accumulate—rather, the most important piece of advice I can give you is, simply, start early. In exchange for your audience's time and interest, you have an obligation to know what you're talking about, so you actually have to really know your subject. No matter what your task or what you're writing, starting early is still important.

This means you need to read up on your topic. You need to absorb the information—then, you'll need to reread and review a lot of your research materials so that you have an understanding of what other points of view on your particular topic are. Then, after you've done that, you need to be able to articulate your own position in respect to those other points of view, and then you have to make a convincing case as to why your particular focus, or your argumentative position, or your arrangement of information is important or useful—or answers a particular question.

If you start researching at the very last minute, then pretty often the materials you're reading become texts that you aren't really engaging—rather, what you often end up doing is trolling through them quickly looking for quotes or citations that you can then make fit into whatever you have decided your argument is going to be. This is what happens if you begin a research paper two days before it's due; on day one, you end up reading things and jotting down quotes that you think you can use in your paper—and in day two, you sort of mash that all together into something that resembles a research essay. Let me just say, I have read plenty of these in my time as a college professor, and the haste always shows.

On the other hand, this two-day intensive approach could be a good way to establish a working outline or a rough draft of your paper, but by no means should it be the way that you produce your final essay, or final version of your article, or your short story, or whatever it is that you're working on.

Consider the following two paragraphs that I've lifted from research papers on roughly the same topic. This is the topic we discussed in our last lecture. As you'll remember, we examined several possible thesis statements in an attempt to find one that would work well for a research paper. What we finally came up with as a guiding idea for our research was "The Significance of the Shift in King Arthur's Character Once He Has Founded the Order of the Round Table."

Here's the opening from one of these sample papers:

> When Malory's novel begins, King Arthur isn't even born yet, but we know that he is supposedly destined to be a great king. He doesn't start out that way, but eventually, as everyone knows, he pulls the sword from the stone and takes the throne. In order to stay on the throne he has to fight a lot of wars, but once he gets married

and founds the Round Table, he stops being active and pretty much disappears from the story, as a lot of people have pointed out.

So what does this paragraph do well, and where does it fall short? We get a pretty clear idea of what the author is going to be writing about, and what the author is focusing on is how King Arthur's character is one way before he founds the Order of the Round Table, and then it seems to change afterward. How does this writer use research to convince you of his position? You may have noticed that aside from a comment like "everyone knows" or something like "as a lot of people have pointed out," we don't get any indication that the writer has done any research at all.

These statements are vague, and while they might be true, the lack of any indication of specific research to support them weakens the argument as a whole. Also, with the first sentence this writer has set himself at a disadvantage in that he refers to Sir Thomas Malory's text as a "novel," and I see my undergraduates do this all the time. They refer to any piece of writing as a novel. The *Morte Darthur*, the text that is under discussion here, predates the Modern period and the rise of the novel, so it's not proper to refer to it in this way. This might seem like a minor detail at first, but it actually is really important.

Would you expect most people to know this fact? Absolutely not. But would you expect someone who has done research on Malory's text to know this? Absolutely. Certainly, the audience for this paper—in this case, the college professor, which is me—would know this. So what it tells me from the very first words is that this person obviously didn't do any kind of substantial research, so the writer starts off at a disadvantage in terms of earning my respectful attention—or a good grade—because the writer demonstrates that he just hasn't done his homework.

Now let's consider a different version of this same opening:

> Arthurian scholar Alistair Eminent was arguably the first to state that the character of King Arthur in Sir Thomas Malory's *Morte Darthur* starts off as naïve and ill-prepared when he assumes the throne (Malory's *Morte*, p. 95). Other scholars such as Arabella

Distinguished have described King Arthur's actions late in the text as "inadequate" and even "embarrassing" ("The Character of the King," p. 187). Between these two stages however, there is a period when King Arthur acquits himself admirably in his role as ruler. The major shift in Arthur's character comes not when he assumes the throne, as James Oxford and others have suggested (*Sword from the Stone*, p. 12), but rather, it occurs at the moment when he creates the Order of the Round Table. This paper will explore the events that lead up to the founding of the Round Table—and Arthur's active role in this—and then examine the striking contrast in the king's character later in the text when his knights have essentially become the major players in Malory's narrative.

Which paper do you think is going to wind up being the more impressive of the two? I hope that most of you right now are thinking: "Well, paper two, of course!" Why is this? From the opening lines, this writer establishes herself as an authority—she makes it clear that she has read significant scholarship on her topic, and she is able to cite specific critics and texts to support some of the key points she is making here. Not only does she cite scholars and texts, but at times she also quotes directly from them, and she does what any responsible researcher should do—she then gives the title of the work cited and the page or pages on which the quoted material can be found.

The style of citation as I've given it to you here—obviously, it comes across a little bit awkwardly when I'm trying to read the passage aloud and then let you know where a citation falls in that passage—but this style is something called MLA citation. You might remember that MLA stands for Modern Language Association; they're considered one of the major authorities when it comes to the research and writing of an essay like this one.

In the last lecture, you'll recall I mentioned the MLA Bibliography as a great resource for doing research in the Humanities. In fact, at Purdue University, where I teach, all students taking Introduction to the Major—which is English 301—are required to have on hand at all times the MLA Handbook.

There are lots of other guidebooks that can help you when you're working on a research project—the Chicago Manual of Style, the APA Guide—and there are many, many others—many of which are geared toward one specific kind of publication, or writing, or another. You absolutely should check and see what the standard is in whatever discipline or market in which you're writing so that you can give your teacher, or your editor, or your boss a piece of writing that conforms to basic rules of style that are considered proper for the area in which you're working.

You might be thinking: "This person has obviously done a lot of research. How did she not only manage to take in all this info, but also then organize it in such a way that it flows so nicely throughout her opening paragraph?" Because in order to cite properly, you need to be able to find the quote you have in mind. It does you absolutely no good—trust me on this one—no good if you think: "I remember that being in the middle of some book that had a brown cover," and then you spend precious time searching for it. I have been there, and while I am thumbing through every book that I own with a brownish cover—for over an hour, as it turns out—I was mentally cursing myself for not taking better notes.

So how do you make sure that doesn't happen to you? Again, leaving yourself enough time is really key here. If you're in the early stages of your project and not quite sure what particular approach you want to take to a particular topic, you might start with reading through the material you have collected and using tabs or sticky notes to identify pages that contain material you find interesting, and that you consider relevant to your topic.

As I've said before, when you're doing this it's worthwhile to pay attention to footnotes and the "Works Cited" sections in your research material. Maybe a particular article you have photocopied from a journal doesn't have anything germane to your subject, but the footnotes may direct you to other texts that do—so don't overlook this often-overlooked section of a piece of research when you're conducting your own.

After you have gone through an initial reading of your material, it's time to take more detailed notes, and there are a couple of ways to do this. The way I tend to work is by taking notes on a particular text, either in longhand or on the computer. When I do this, I try to sum up a scholar's general argument and then note particularly interesting points individually—making sure to identify on which page they appear.

When I've worked my way through taking notes on a text, I either print the typed notes or I staple my handwritten notes all together—so when it comes time to start the drafting process, I can read through my notes to remind myself what is important about a particular article or book rather than having to reread the whole text. When I'm taking notes on a particular text, I am always careful to really carefully write down my own questions or counter-arguments as they come to me, so that I don't forget a flash of insight. Let's say, for example, if I'm reading an article on something like "Gender and Malory's Text," I might write something in my notes like: "My question: This author keeps talking about the female character of Guinevere, but I think that maybe the character of Morgan le Fay, Arthur's half-sister, is more interesting when it comes to gender."

Another variation on this note-taking approach would be what I call the note card version—and many of us probably learned some form of this in high school. It's pretty much just what it sounds like—you have got a stack of 3x5 note cards, and each single card gets a quote or the note of an important argumentative point from a particular author. In the top corner of the card you should also designate who the author is, the text this idea or quote comes from, and then the page number on which you found it.

The benefit of this approach is that it's a little more flexible than direct note-taking onto sheets of paper that you staple together. You can shuffle the cards so that, let's say, you decide you want to further organize your research by sub-points. In other words, let's imagine you want to group together what all the scholars you have read had to say about, maybe, how Merlin helps King Arthur rule—and then you also want to group together what some scholars say about the moment of the founding of the Round Table. You can do this pretty easily by drawing out the individual note cards and then regrouping or restacking them. As long as you have identified on every single card from what text or author each point or quote is coming, then it's going to be no trouble to arrange, rearrange, and then put them back in order.

I actually had a friend who took this kind of organization to new heights. He got some colored stickers, and he assigned each secondary source a particular color. The colors for the sources went in the lower right-hand corner of each card. Across the top, he also had colored stickers, but the stickers on top corresponded to particular themes or points—so, for example, he might assign every quote that had something to do with knighthood a green sticker, every quote that had something to do with gender a blue sticker; warfare got a red sticker. Some cards had three different colors of stickers because it was a quote or a point that related to all of these. If he was looking for basic info, he didn't even need to read the cards themselves before he sorted them into piles that he thought were relevant for his research.

If you're thinking that this sticker-system thing might turn into way too much work or it might become a procrastination technique, you are, of course, right—but some people need this kind of organization to really get their paper into shape. There is something to be said for the act of reading and rereading your notes—eventually, some of what you're reading over, and over, and over again sticks, and gradually you become an authority on your topic.

When you're organizing your research into an article or a presentation, one of the trickiest things is to make your voice and your argument heard while using the work of other people, other scholars, or experts as a means of support. You want to make your research support your idea, but you need to give proper accreditation where it's due. This is pretty easy if your goal is simply to gather the most important or latest information on something and present it to someone else. It's a little trickier if you're trying to make an original argument, if you are trying to claim a new idea, but you need to use the work of others as a foundation on which you build your own research.

The best way to generate an original argument for a research project is after doing your research, decide what your particular stance is on a topic, and then try and articulate your claim or position—and do a really rough overview or outline indicating where supporting points could be helped by the use of secondary sources. When you're doing this, you absolutely need to identify critics or scholars who have expressed opinions that disagree with your own.

One trap that I often find students falling into is when they come across a piece of scholarship that has a point of view that is counter or in opposition to what they want to argue, they just ignore it—they leave it out entirely, and they never mention it. For example, if we go back to our example of the Arthurian research paper, you might imagine that in their research, these two hypothetical students come across a scholarly article that argues that the key moment of transformation in the character of King Arthur is not when he founds the Round Table, but rather it's when his mentor and his advisor Merlin disappears from the text. "Hmm," the students might think, "this person doesn't agree with the point I'm trying to make. I'm not going to use this resource because I'm afraid I might get into trouble, as I really want to make the opposite or different argument." That is exactly the wrong thing to do. First, for a responsible researcher this constitutes a lie of omission. When you're conducting research for whatever kind of writing, you need to clearly articulate the scope of the argument you're trying to make, and you also have to establish what other people have said about it—and not just the other people who happen to agree with you.

Probably right now you can all think of any number of political ads that do just this—that have these lies of omission. They pick and choose facts and details. They omit context or important counter-arguments, and I will tell you right now that if we held political ads to the standards of ethical research and reporting, almost all of them would get an "F."

The other thing is sometimes an opposing view or counter-argument can help you prove your own point. Our hypothetical students might write something like: "Although Professor Eminence has argued persuasively for the disappearance of Merlin as the key moment in the transformation of Arthur's character, I will demonstrate that, in fact, it is the founding of the Round Table that is the most important single event in King Arthur's reign."

The other thing that is nice is that this can provide you with a workable structure. Essentially, you could write with this in mind: "Here's Professor Eminence's first point. Here's why I think it's wrong, and here's what I think is really the key point—for reasons x, y, and z. Now I'll go on to the next point, which might explain how someone might think it's right, and now let me show you why that next point that someone else believes, let me show you why it's wrong." So you can use counter-argument as a way of structuring your own argument.

One of the major concerns and dangers when doing a research paper is the issue of plagiarism, and you need to avoid this at all costs. In a nutshell, plagiarism is using the words or ideas of others without giving proper credit where credit is due.

There is obvious, outright plagiarism, which is usually easy to recognize— and that is if someone were, say, to buy a term paper online or download it off the Internet and then try and pass it off as his or her own writing. This is usually pretty easy to spot, especially as a college professor. I mean if suddenly your student is writing about moments in the poem "Beowulf" that we never discussed in class, or the student is using vocabulary that just doesn't sound like him or her, it tends to make your audience—and in this case that would be me, the professor—a little suspicious.

I highly doubt that anyone who is listening to this course would ever consider doing such a thing, but all of us who do research can be prone to accidental plagiarism, and this is what you have to guard against most vigilantly.

Here's how this can happen: Let's say you have taken lots and lots of notes; you have read lots and lots of books and articles on your subject, and you have become a kind of authority on the topic. This is great because it means that you have internalized and processed much of what you have been reading. The danger for some people is that your original thoughts on a particular topic somehow get blended in or mixed up with what other scholars have to say. As you're reading over those notes or the note cards, you might forget—was I writing down what this scholar said about Beowulf, or Malory, or Ralph Waldo Emerson, or are these my words, my reaction to what I was reading?

This is why you have to be so incredibly careful when you're taking notes on a particular text, and that is why I always distinguish when something is my thought. I gave you an example of that earlier when I said here's my idea, and you can just write it out. You can say something like:"Professor Eminence says x, but I'm thinking z is the more important question"—and right there you have gone ahead and you have said this is what the expert thinks, this is what I think, and the two ideas are distinct from each other.

This is why I tend to note down direct quotes by putting quote marks around sentences or phrases I find important—or if I'm paraphrasing, I might write something like: "Professor Eminence spends two pages discussing the history of Malory scholarship, focusing particularly on where early 20th-century scholars went wrong." Now when it comes to my research, I might be in full agreement with Professor Eminence's thinking about how early 20th-century scholars were wrong in a particular area, and I can say that—but I also need to cite Professor Eminence as having made this argument first.

Even if I arrive at a conclusion or position on my own, independent of another scholar, once I start doing research and I discover that other scholars have already observed this point, I need to make sure that I give credit where it's due. Actually, far from being discouraged when you discover that what you thought was an original insight on your part has, in fact, already been a point that someone else has made, you should be encouraged that you seem to be thinking like the experts.

Let's look at a paragraph that involves some subtle plagiarism that is most likely unintentional and talk about where the student goes wrong. Here's the passage I want you to think about:

> While the moment when Arthur pulls the sword from the stone is arguably the "flip of the switch" that changes the community of Malory's text forever, the moment when King Arthur establishes the Order of the Round Table is actually much more important. Here is where he transfers power to knightly agents—he will be imminent in their deeds while he himself remains safely at home.

What are the issues with this paragraph? The ideas are certainly ones that the student could have come up with herself, the idea of pulling the sword from the stone as being like flipping a light switch—as well as the idea that the character of King Arthur is somehow present in the actions of his knights, even if the king himself is safe at home.

But at the same time, while the student may have come up with the idea independently, the phrasing sounds really distinct and somewhat, I would say, even unique. It really sounds as if she heard or read the phrases "flip of the switch" and "imminent in their deeds" in some of her research, and it sounds as if she internalized them and then reproduced them here. As I said, this may be completely unintentional. You might actually recall some recent news stories about highly respected historians and public intellectuals getting caught up in the same issue.

Doris Kearns Goodwin was one of these. It was discovered that her book *The Fitzgeralds and the Kennedys* had lots of unattributed passages, and in particular these were drawn from the work of a writer named Lynne McTaggart. In a *Time Magazine* piece, Goodwin acknowledged that she had accidentally plagiarized McTaggart's work, and she noted that although she had frequently cited McTaggart's work throughout her book—her footnotes were full of McTaggart—she had, as she herself said, "failed to provide quotation marks for phrases that I had taken verbatim, having assumed that these phrases, drawn from my notes, were my words, not hers. The larger question is to understand how citation mistakes can happen."

This should be a lesson to all of us who conduct research—we have to be very, very careful. In the example I gave you of the student who used the phrases "flip of the switch" and "imminent in their deeds"—well, that student should recheck her notes very carefully and, if necessary, provide proper attribution if it's needed.

What are the key points to take away from today's lecture? Without question, it should be clear to you that when you're working on a project that involves research, one of the most important things to do is give yourself enough time. You're going to need time to read, to reread, to rethink, and maybe even change your topic as your research sends you in new and hopefully interesting directions.

Along the lines of the time issue, you should also try to set yourself some deadlines. Even if you end up not making those deadlines, having them will help give your research activity structure. You also need to have some sort of system in place for taking notes, and you have to have an idea as to how you're going to organize all those notes. Every idea, or phrase, or direct quote must be properly attributed to the scholar who made it first. As I always say to my students: "When in doubt, cite." If it's too much citation or we don't really need it, you can always take it out later—but trying to remember a source after you have made use of it in your writing is a mistake that can cost you hours of your precious time.

Speaking of time, in our next lecture we're going to talk about getting started with writing first drafts. In some ways, this can be the hardest part of writing anything. Sometimes, if you have given yourself enough time, it can be really hard to get started because you think: "Oh, I have plenty of time, so I'll just do the laundry first"—or you can have a looming deadline and out of fear and panic put off starting until the very last second because the task seems so overwhelming. Next time I'll give you some strategies for getting started so that you can avoid trying to write beautiful prose at 3 AM before a 9 AM deadline—or so that you don't end up cleaning out every closet in the house as a way to avoid sitting down at your desk, picking up the pen, or setting your fingers to the keys.

Getting Started—Writing First Drafts
Lecture 20

> I cannot tell you how often I see students who hand in a paper that begins a little wobbly, but by the end, they've expressed some wonderfully original insight that they didn't have when they started. This phenomenon is called "writing your way to an argument," and while this is wonderful, what would be ideal is if this happened in the first draft of a paper or an article or a letter, and that the writer then had time to go back and revise—keeping that insight they achieved at the end as the guiding force that now drives the paper forward.

Sometimes the hardest part of producing a polished piece of writing is simply the act of getting started. The blank screen on the computer or the blank sheet of paper in front of you can seem particularly daunting if you have several ideas and you're unsure where to start—or even worse, if you know you need to compose something but feel as if you have no ideas. Let's look at some techniques that can make starting a piece of writing seem a little less formidable than might at first seem to be the case.

Let's say you are writing a letter to apply for a job. First, you might do some free-writing or brainstorming—for example, you might make a list of the specific qualifications that the job requires, and then you might make another list of your own qualifications. Lists like these can help you figure out how to organize your letter. Maybe you're currently a gardener, but you want to apply for a job as an editorial assistant. Should you mention your current job as a gardener first, or should you maybe mention before that the fact that you were an English major in college and that you wrote for your college's newspaper?

Obviously, while you certainly should discuss your current job, you don't want that to be the first thing you mention in a letter like this. You might want to do a little research—research about the company to which you're applying. Maybe you'll discover that you and the CEO are from the same small town in the Midwest or that you went to the same college. As long as you can manage it without seeming forced, it might be helpful to include these details in your letter—so instead of writing, "When I was in college I wrote for my school's newspaper," you might write, "During my junior year at St. Excellence College, I was a reporter for the *St. Excellence Daily*, the campus paper."

What if you are feeling blocked even about beginning the brainstorming stage? I'll give you a few strategies that have worked for me and for friends and colleagues of mine. One thing that works against us as we attempt to get started with a process of writing is the desire to produce a really good piece of prose. Sometimes in order to get to the good writing, you have to slog through some garbage. In other words, one way to get to a point where you produce something decent is to give yourself permission to write poorly. Giving yourself this permission can really be liberating: It allows you to type ideas or points in no particular order, with poor grammar, bad spelling, and incomplete sentences. The key here is to simply get whatever ideas you have out of your head and onto the screen.

Finding a writing partner or a writing support group is a great way to get yourself motivated.

After a break—it's extremely important to take a break and come back to your writing with fresh eyes—you can come back and take a look at what you've written, and then you can start to think about how the pieces that you've put on the page could be rearranged into something that resembles a coherent argument. Another thing to realize is that very often the process of writing itself can help you figure out what it is you're trying to say.

Finding a writing partner or a writing support group is a great way to get yourself motivated. If you know that you have a deadline when you actually have to hand something to someone else, who will in turn be passing something he or she has written to you for your comments, you can usually manage to get some words down on the page.

Serving as a reader for someone else's work can also make you a better writer. As you edit a friend's writing—as you're looking for the thesis, as you're circling supporting points that aren't satisfactorily fleshed out— you're also learning more about writing in a way that you can apply to your

317

own work, and you can apply it almost immediately. As I've suggested several times before, if you want to improve your writing, read as much as you can—the more you read and write, the better you'll become at both. ■

Suggested Reading

Bullock, *The Norton Field Guide to Writing.*

The Chicago Manual of Style.

Clouse, *The Student Writer.*

Griffith, *Writing Essays about Literature.*

Lanham, *Revising Prose.*

———, *Style.*

MLA Handbook for Writers of Research Papers.

O'Connor, *Words Fail Me.*

Strunk and White, *The Elements of Style.*

Trimble, *Writing with Style.*

Tufte, *Artful Sentences.*

Exercises

1. Imagine that you have just been asked to write a paper—the main argument is up to you—on an often-anthologized story (such as William Faulkner's "A Rose for Emily" or James Baldwin's "Sonny's Blues" or some other short story that you have read relatively recently). Set yourself a strict limit of 15 minutes and allow yourself the ability to "brainstorm" or "free-write" anything that comes to mind and that interests you about this text.

2. Set your free-writing aside for at least an hour—preferably a day. After that time, come back to it and see if you can find at least two thesis statements that look like they could be promising as you set out to write a five- to seven-page paper on the story you've selected.

Getting Started—Writing First Drafts
Lecture 20—Transcript

Welcome back. In our last two lectures, we discussed the process of conducting and using research. Whether you're writing a magazine article, or a short story, an essay for class, or a presentation for work, there are very few types of writing that wouldn't benefit from a little research. So in Lecture 18, we discussed how to go about acquiring information—and in Lecture 19, we discussed how to use that information once you have found it, paying particular attention to things like issues of concern that pop up—like proper attribution and avoiding plagiarism.

But sometimes the hardest part of producing a polished piece of writing is, in fact, simply the act of getting started. The blank screen on the computer or the blank sheet of paper in front of you can seem particularly daunting if you have several ideas and you're unsure where to start—or even worse, if you know you need to compose something and you feel as if you have no ideas, let alone how to begin organizing them into a persuasive piece of text. This lecture will help introduce some techniques that can make starting a piece of writing seem a little less formidable than might at first seem to be the case.

Today we'll talk about how to get your pen moving or your fingers clicking across the keyboard. I've found that once I get started, as long as I have a clear idea in my head about what I want to say and how I want to say it, the writing process is easier, and it even becomes fun once I get past the initial hurdle and I'm a couple of paragraphs in.

But that's me—you might be totally different. You might be the kind of person who gets going but runs out of steam partway through. So the first thing to do, and arguably the most important thing, is to try and get a sense of what kind of person and what kind of writer you are. Take a moment—try to think about how you might describe yourself. Do you prefer organization? Do you have a label-maker that you use regularly? Do you work better with materials strewn around so that they're within easy reach, or do you like things put neatly away so you can find them again?

As I've said repeatedly—and as you're probably getting really tired of hearing me say—No matter what kind of writer you are, it's important that you give yourself time whenever you're starting a new writing project; that means whenever possible don't begin something the night before it needs to be handed in or mailed off. To produce a really polished piece of writing, you might give yourself three days. Set aside one day for brainstorming or pre-writing; one for drafting the letter, or the short essay, or whatever other document it is that you need to produce; and then one day for revising. If you don't have three days—and despite the best of intentions, all of us at one point or another find ourselves trying to write something the night before the deadline—in that case, if you don't have three days, try to at least give yourself three breaks. Maybe take a short break after brainstorming; then, give yourself an hour off after writing the first draft, and then give yourself at least another hour—if not a whole night—between the initial composition and the revision process. We'll talk more about revision in a later lecture, but I can't stress enough how important it is to try to look at your writing with fresh eyes at some point in the process, and that means even if you just set the first draft aside, go out for a walk, and then pick it up again. That little time away from it can help you to see your writing in a more objective and critical light; it helps to give you enough distance from it so that you can make it the best it can be.

Let's take an example from earlier in the course. Let's say you have been given an assignment to write an argumentative essay about the short story "The Yellow Wallpaper" by Charlotte Perkins Gilman, and we discussed that in a few lectures earlier in this course. We focused particularly on it in Lecture 5, where we talked about fiction, and finding your voice, and having respect for your audience. As you may remember, this story is told in the first person. It's as if we're reading the main character's diary, and what the diary chronicles is her descent into insanity. It's a decline that seems to be triggered and sped up in part by this hideous yellow wallpaper in the narrator's bedroom. Let's say the assignment is wide open. You have to write on "The Yellow Wallpaper," but you have no idea where to begin.

First, you'll need to do some brainstorming, and you have to try and find out what really intrigues you about this text. Again, you need to find a hook or a way in. So take a moment, and given what you know about "The Yellow

Wallpaper," you might make a quick list, and it might look something like this, and these are just some ideas I jotted down quickly. You might write on a piece of paper:

1. Narrative style interesting—story is told in the first person by an unreliable narrator.

2. Clues at certain moments contribute to major impact at the end—narrator grows more and more obsessed with yellow wallpaper.

3. Increasingly ominous tone—narrator at first describes room as a former nursery, but details make it sound more like some type of prison—bed is bolted to the floor, bars on the windows, rings attached to the walls.

4. Problematic conclusion—we shift from reading her words on the page to reading her thoughts—problem with consistency.

5. Issue of gender—much of the plot seems to hinge on the fact that doctor has prescribed strict rest for narrator, but the treatment, specifically geared toward a woman, seems to be making things worse rather than better.

So, there you have a list of five interesting things—some of these overlap—and now you have to find a way to craft an argument based on the list of things you have found compelling or interesting about the text. So what interests you the most? It might be the unreliable narrator and the way that Charlotte Perkins Gilman makes a mistake, asking us essentially to ignore the fact that she moves near the end from giving us the narrator's written thoughts to giving us her actual thoughts. But it might be that although this is a story about insanity, it's really a story about gender and the different ways that gender can cause doctors to treat their patients. Just a little bit of research into Charlotte Perkins Gilman's life reveals that this does, indeed, seem to be one of the things that interested her and encouraged her or inspired her to write this story.

Any biographical information on Charlotte Perkins Gilman contains the fact that after suffering from post-partum depression, her doctor ordered her to undergo a rest cure, which is very much like the one described in this story. She was forbidden to write or to really take care of her child, and it's a situation that she later said drove her right to the brink of insanity.

She stated on numerous occasions that the only way she pulled herself out of this state was to do the opposite of what her doctor had ordered—most importantly, she started writing again. This experience convinced her that medicine at the time—with its emphasis on the idea that women had delicate constitutions—actually contributed to making them subservient to men, contributed to preserving the status quo of gender inequality at the time.

So after doing this little bit of research, you may have some idea that this is a topic to which you can do some justice. Your main focus is manageable—it's a single short story—but there looks to be a fair amount in the way of secondary sources that you could use to help you with your research. So to guide you as you start writing, you might choose something like this as your main idea or thesis: "Although on the surface Charlotte Perkins Gilman's short story 'The Yellow Wallpaper' is about one woman's decline into insanity, closer analysis reveals that it is really a critique of gender relations in the late 19th and early 20th centuries."

So, what next? Your next step would be to find some key pieces of evidence supporting your point, and here you want to make use both of what we call primary and secondary sources, and I've mentioned these terms before. The primary source is the original piece of writing, the short story itself, and the secondary sources would be books and/or articles about Charlotte Perkins Gilman and about this particular short story.

First, you might reread the story carefully, noting any instances of what seem to be references to the matter of gender. You might highlight the passage where the narrator mentions that she and her husband have retreated to the country to help her "get well," or the moment where she says there's a nurse who is responsible for caring for her young child, and that the journal she's keeping is written on the sly—more than once the narrator makes references to the fact that she needs to keep her writing hidden, as she is not supposed to be writing a word.

With this as your base, you might turn to any secondary sources you have found. Here, you might copy onto your note cards or into your note file what other critics have said on this topic, especially how they analyze certain scenes in the story, and you might certainly look at biographical data—evidence of relevant events in the author's life and, indeed, her own comments on the story itself; she made several. From here, you have a decent argumentative framework that you can fill in with your own argument about the topic.

This same process can work in a variety of other situations, like if you are writing a letter applying for a job. First, you might do some free-writing or brainstorming—for example, you might make a list of the specific qualifications that the job requires, and then you might make another list of your own qualifications.

A list like this can help you figure out how to organize your letter. Maybe you're currently a gardener, but you want to apply for a job as an editorial assistant. Should you mention your current job as a gardener first, or maybe should you mention before that the fact that you were an English major in college, and that you wrote for your college's newspaper?

Obviously, while you certainly should discuss your current job, and there's no reason to hide it, you don't want that to be the first thing you mention in a letter like this because you're not applying for a job as a gardener. As with "The Yellow Wallpaper" example, you might want to do a little research— research about the company to which you're applying. Maybe you'll discover that you and the CEO are from the same small town in the Midwest or that you went to the same college.

As long as you can manage it without seeming awkward or forced, it might be helpful to include these details in your letter—so instead of writing: "When I was in college I wrote for my school's newspaper," you might write: "During my junior year at St. Excellence College, I was a reporter for the *St. Excellence Daily*, the campus paper."

Right about now you may be saying: "Okay, that's all well and good, but I am feeling blocked about even beginning the brainstorming stage." So

I'll give you a few strategies that have worked for me and for friends and colleagues of mine—and in doing this, I'm probably going to reveal far too much about what will appear to be my own neuroses, but I hope you won't mind indulging me just for a moment or so.

One thing that works against all of us as we attempt to get started with a process of writing is the desire to produce a really good piece of prose. On the surface this might seem totally contradictory—wanting to do something well actually makes it harder to do it—but when confronted with a challenge that seems particularly daunting, the desire to do well can make it seem totally impossible.

Sometimes in order to get to the good writing, you have to slog through some garbage. In other words, one way to get to a point where you produce something decent, something good, is to give yourself permission to write poorly. Giving yourself this permission can really be liberating. It allows you to scribble or type ideas or points in no particular order, with poor grammar, bad spelling, incomplete sentences. The key here is to simply get whatever ideas you have out of your head and onto the paper.

One thing that can help you get started with this deliberately bad writing is to set a time limit on yourself. Let's say you have the whole day to write an essay or letter. In some ways, this can actually hinder you from getting started because you think: "Well, I have all day. I'll empty the dishwasher first, or I'll do the laundry," and then pretty soon you're organizing all your closets; you have cleaned out the refrigerator; you have alphabetized and arranged all your books according to the Dewey Decimal System, and you're using a label-maker, and you're labeling things like timer or microwave—things that don't need labels.

So this is where leaving yourself enough time ahead of due dates can work in your best interest. If you start three days before something is due, on the first day it might help you if you actually set a limit and say, for example: "Today I am only allowed to write for one hour, and then I have to stop."

Setting these kinds of boundaries can actually motivate you to start. The task has a definite ending time, so it might be nice to get it out of the way. Then, you sit down at your desk or at the computer, and you can write on the topic in any way you like. You would be amazed at how productive you can be if you have told yourself: "I only have an hour" or "I get to stop as soon as I've done my hour."

You may think this next part is a little nuts, but I took this approach to extreme lengths when I was working on my Ph.D. dissertation. What helped me initially was that I had a really supportive, understanding professor as my major professor and director of my dissertation. I had finished my coursework. I had passed my written and my oral exams, and then I was supposed to start writing my dissertation, and I was utterly paralyzed. I took up knitting, which conveniently took up some time when I should have been researching or writing, and my apartment was spotless.

After about a month of this, my dissertation director called me, and he said that I needed to bring him 8 to 10 pages of something the following Friday. "This something," he said on my answering machine, "would most likely be terrible," and he actually said this. I should have saved the message— it's a great message—but anyway: "This is probably going to be awful, and that's fine—we have to start somewhere," and probably somewhere in the terribleness of the 8 to 10 pages I brought him he'd find a good idea that we could start working with.

So I showed up at his office at 9 AM on Friday. I handed him my eight and a half pages of what I was sure was the worst garbage ever written on the legend of King Arthur in the Middle Ages, and it was pretty bad—maybe not the worse, but it came close. But my director was right—and giving myself permission to write poorly quickly became liberating as I figured out a way to keep my momentum up. So, after we talked about it, my professor was able to help me pick out what was useful or interesting in that chunk of bad writing, and then I could keep going.

The strategy that I then used was to tell myself that I needed to write a certain number of hours per day, at least five days a week, and I tried to figure that in a typical 8-hour workday, maybe about 4 of those are actual, serious work, so I decided to start small, and I set myself what seemed at first to be this really manageable, paltry goal of just 20 hours a week—but those were 20 real hours. So when I sat down at my desk every day—and here's where the crazy comes in—when I sat down at my desk, I noted the time on a small note card. I then read; I wrote; I reread; I edited until there was some sort of interruption—let's say, the phone rang or I wanted to get myself something to drink. When that interruption happened, I immediately noted the time on the note card, and then I added up the minutes that I had worked so far.

So if I started working at 8 AM, and the phone rang at 8:06, I had done 6 minutes out of the 240 that were my goal for that day. What I discovered pretty quickly is that this approach made me want to start sooner because I told myself that once I had done my 240 minutes, I was free to do whatever else I wanted or whatever else I needed. I could prepare for the classes I was teaching that semester. I could go to the gym. I could knit for awhile, whatever. Pretty soon it became a game. More often than not, when I reached the four-hour mark, I was in the middle of an interesting idea or I was writing down what I thought was a particularly good insight, and I didn't want to stop.

So what did I do with those extra minutes that I was working? I told myself: "If I work some more minutes now, I can work fewer tomorrow," and then I began thinking: "What if I do eight solid hours of dissertation work today— why, I could take all of tomorrow off!" Then, on weekends, even though I technically had given myself permission not to do any work, I figured I could get a little work done, and then I could count that time toward the next week's total. You can see what's happening here—pretty soon I was in a steady rhythm, and I was playing mind games with myself and imagining that I could get so much work done that I could take a whole month off, and then the next thing I knew the dissertation was done.

I still find this approach useful today when I have a chunk of substantial writing and research to do if I'm working on an article or a book chapter. I set myself a goal of a certain number of minutes per day or hours per week, and I try to meet that—and even if I don't quite make it, it's still an excellent motivator that helps me to be more productive. My husband says he always knows whenever I'm working on a writing project because he finds little slips of paper all over the house that have times and numbers of minutes written on them.

326

Part of what makes this approach particularly useful is something I like to call the scattershot approach. In other words, you throw all your ideas out of your head and onto the page—with little or no concern for order, spelling, grammar, all that important stuff—and you leave the unholy mess there, and then you return to it after some time away.

After a break—and remember, we've talked at considerable length about how important it is to take a break and come back to your writing with what I like to call fresh eyes—after some time away, you can come back and take a look at what you have written, and then you can start to think about how the pieces that you have put on the page could be rearranged into something that you hope resembles a coherent argument. Another thing to realize is that very often the process of writing itself can help you figure out what it is you're trying to say.

I cannot tell you how often I see students who hand in a paper that begins a little wobbly, but by the end they have expressed some wonderfully original insight that they didn't have when they started.

This phenomenon is called "writing your way to an argument," and while this is wonderful, what would be ideal is if this happened in the first draft of a paper, or an article, or a letter, and that the writer then had time to go back and revise—keeping that insight they achieved at the end as the guiding force that now drives the paper forward. On these papers I inevitably end up writing something in the margins like: "As a first-draft, this is an A; as a final draft, more like a B-." You need to give yourself time to play with your argument because often that is how you discover what it is that is really important about what you're trying to say.

Even if you have moved past the initial writer's block, starting your article, or short essay, or short story, or letter can still be really difficult. If you find yourself just totally paralyzed because you're struggling to figure out where to start with your writing, my advice—and I've mentioned this before—my advice is always: Don't begin at the beginning. I had a good friend in graduate school, and she and I regularly exchanged pieces of our writing. Every week, usually on Thursdays, we'd give each other 10 pages or so, and then we met the next day, on Friday afternoon, to comment on and critique each other's work and have a talk about it.

Without exception, the first two pages of everything my friend wrote were somewhat awkward. The language was clunky. It was kind of stilted—but then by page 3 it was as if a completely different person was writing. By page 3, her argument was humming along; her style had improved appreciably—and by the end, she usually had produced an excellent piece of writing that was articulate, witty, and original—and ultimately, that's the kind of writing we all want to produce.

What she and I both learned from this experience is that sometimes you leave the first for last. Skip the introduction, and get right to the meat of the argument. When you have made the claims that you want to make and you have summed up everything in a satisfying conclusion, then you can return and you can write an introduction that will probably be much smoother and more pleasing to read than the one that you have struggled to write for so long that you tore your hair out over, and you have done all this work, all this sweating, expended all this effort before you have even gotten to the meat of your argument. So, it can really actually detract from your overall argument if you spend too much time on the introduction and it's just not coming.

By the way, finding a writing partner or a writing support group is a great way to get yourself motivated. If you know that you have a deadline when you actually have to hand something to someone else, who will in turn be passing something he or she has written to you for your comments, most people usually manage to get some words down on the page.

Serving as a reader for someone else's work can also make you a better writer. As you edit a friend's writing or a colleague's writing, as you're looking for the thesis, as you're circling supporting points that really aren't fully or satisfactorily fleshed out or supported, you're also learning more about writing in a way that you can apply to your own work, and you can apply it almost immediately. As I've suggested several times before, if you want to improve your writing, read as much as you can—the more you read and write, the better you'll get at both.

For some people, getting to the meat of the argument is the most important thing, but for others, composing an effective piece of writing comes much more easily if you get the "bones," if you want to call them that, the bones of the piece down first. Some people work better with an outline—even if it's just tentative and you have told yourself: "Okay, this may change." But some people if they at least have an outline as a guide, it can help them as they move through their argument. When I say "outline," this could be anything from the sort of classic Roman numeral followed by capital letter type of outline that a lot of us learned how to create when we were in school, or it could just simply be a quick jotting down of main point, supporting points, evidence, and conclusion.

At the other end of the scattershot approach that works for me, at the other end of the spectrum, there are those few people who move clearly and logically straight through whatever the writing piece is with no need for substantial tweaking and editing. My roommate my freshman year of college was this way, and this was back in the days before computers were common, and occasionally I would type up her handwritten papers for her, as she didn't type and I did.

Her papers were clearly structured; they were methodically organized; they moved logically from point to point, and her writing never showed signs of difficulty or struggle, and I was insanely jealous of this fact every time I typed her papers up—because it felt like I had to work a whole lot harder to produce something. My husband, who is also a college professor, he writes this way as well. He spends what feels like to me like a really long time working on just an introductory paragraph or the discussion of a key quote that supports a claim he's trying to make.

At the end of an hour of work, he may have produced one paragraph while I've generated four pages with my scattershot approach, but his careful attentiveness and his precision means that he almost never has to go back and do any substantial editing or rewriting, while my approach means that I always do. When he reaches the end of a paragraph of an article or a chapter, he's pretty much finished—except for maybe some very minor revising.

When I reach the concluding point of what I want to say, when I reach that final paragraph, it means that the serious work of editing and restructuring is still before me. He and I simply work differently, although we both manage to be quite productive—and here again, it's just a matter of figuring out what kind of writing temperament you have and then using an approach that works best for you.

But what to do if you're just totally blocked and you can't figure out how to move forward? This may sound like contradictory advice, but I've found that it works—get away from the computer or the desk, and do something physical. Studies have found that physical activity doesn't just help your body—it helps your brain. So, in the middle of a paper or a short story, when you're stuck on a particular point, get out of the house and go for a walk or a run, or put your notebook in your pocket and go for a short walk—and I bet you 15 minutes in, an idea will come to you that has something to do with your project, and you'll have your notebook right there so you can be ready to jot it down.

The husband and wife writers Michael Chabon and Ayelet Waldman talk about how when they're stuck with their own writing, they go on what they like to call "plot walks" together. The late science-fiction writer, Isaac Asimov, said that whenever he was totally stuck, he'd go to the movies. He said it had to be a movie that would engage his consciousness without asking his subconscious to do too much work—in other words, something like an action movie or a romantic comedy.

A bleak documentary or a foreign film with subtitles was not going to work for him. He said that, without fail, this strategy allowed his subconscious to do some work on the problem he was encountering in his writing, and that when he left the theater, 9 times out of 10 he'd hit on a way to move forward. Obviously, the danger here is that you could spend a lot of time going to movies, and then you could claim that you're working, but if you use this strategy judiciously, it really can help.

I hope that you have found some of my strategies for overcoming writer's block helpful, and I hope you don't think I'm completely neurotic, although I wouldn't blame you—I mean, seriously, counting your minutes does sound a little extreme. But as I said, once I started doing this and it became a kind of game, my dissertation moved very quickly to completion. Your task is to find out what makes writing possible for you.

Now that we've discussed how to get an early draft down on paper, we're going to turn our attention in our next lecture to editing that draft and making it as strong, and persuasive, and compelling as it can be.

> Because [the editing] stage is so crucial and can make the difference between a piece of writing that's okay and one that's actually great, I have reminded you over, and over, and over again to give yourself the opportunity to put a piece of writing aside—even if it's just for an hour—and then come back and look at it with fresh eyes.

Many people find writing an essay, letter, or other piece of text such a draining process that when they reach the end, they just want to get the thing out of their sight—so they hand it in immediately. If they've waited until the last minute to work on this assignment, then often there is really no choice. This is a major error. While getting the darn thing written certainly feels like the biggest part of the writing process, editing is arguably just as important—and in some cases, it's more important than the actual writing itself.

When it comes to editing, there are two basic models at opposite ends of the spectrum: There's the line-by-line approach, and then there's the holistic approach. A line-by-line approach is just what it sounds like: You start with the first line of the piece—you read through it and each successive line as carefully as possible, revising the phrasing, the word choice, and so on.

The holistic approach is about stepping back from the work and taking a macroscopic view. This approach allows you to ask questions about the piece: What is it trying to say? How does it say it? You can then change or rearrange chunks of the paper—and then you gradually work down to the level of word choice and punctuation. Most people tend to use a combination of these approaches. In this lecture, we explore how to best use elements from each editing style on a piece of text with serious macro-level problems.

Let's consider the classic example of the five-paragraph essay. The idea with a five-paragraph essay is that you have an introductory paragraph, then you have three paragraphs of supporting evidence, and then you've got a concluding paragraph that sums up your argument. Quotes can often work in the interest of supporting your points—they function as concrete evidence that work to prove what you're trying to say. But all too often, I see students including quotes as if they're just trying to fill up space, with very little commentary or discussion of the quote. You cannot simply find a quote that works to support your main claim, plug it into the paper, and leave it to your reader to figure out how it fits. A good rule of thumb is that if you are including a quote of three lines, you should spend at least an equal number of lines explaining why that quote is important.

When you're taking the holistic approach, the first thing you should do after reading through the essay is to try and state in a sentence what the main argument of the essay is. A good way to check for this in your own writing is to try and underline your main claim—and ideally, your main claim should be stated somewhere near the end of the first paragraph (unless it's a very long paper). Your reader should be able to tell almost immediately what the main point is.

Your reader should be able to tell almost immediately what the main point is.

The key for a paper to be strong and organized is for the writer to make every supporting point connect back explicitly to this main claim. So our next step in trying to determine how well or poorly an essay connects back to that claim would be to write an outline of the paper as it stands. This doesn't have to be in formal outline style; for me, the easiest thing to do is just write a sentence or a couple of phrases for each paragraph. In this way, we quickly identify the basic structure of the paper—and if you look at it closely, you can see where it might fall apart.

After you've identified some flaws in the broad outline of the paper, you can try and revise the outline to make the paper stronger. Once you've dealt with the larger sweep of the paper, you can start to focus in on some of the details. As you rewrite, you want to make sure that it's absolutely clear how each point works to support the main claim. You want to make sure that the quotes you've selected actually do the work that you want them to do. Are there other quotes that might help you make your point a little bit better or a little more clearly? You might want to replace them now. As you rewrite, you'll also want to check for awkward phrasing and out-and-out errors. In our next lecture, we'll get down to the business of rewriting an essay from start to finish. ∎

Suggested Reading

Bullock, *The Norton Field Guide to Writing.*

The Chicago Manual of Style.

Clouse, *The Student Writer.*

Griffith, *Writing Essays about Literature.*

Harmon and Holman, *A Handbook to Literature.*

Lanham, *Revising Prose.*

———, *Style.*

Lynn, *Literature.*

MLA Handbook for Writers of Research Papers.

O'Connor, *Woe Is I.*

———, *Words Fail Me.*

Strunk and White, *The Elements of Style.*

Trimble, *Writing with Style.*

Tufte, *Artful Sentences.*

Exercise

1. Below is a short essay. Using the techniques described in the lecture, work through the essay, identifying (1) what its main claim is, (2) how it is structured, (3) whether the supporting points work or not, and (4) which issues of phrasing, punctuation, and so on, if left unattended, will detract from the major claim of the piece.

Beowulf is one of the greatest works of English literature. It was written in a language called Old English that looks very little like Modern English. Because of this, you need to take a special course on Old English just to be able to read it in the original language. It is worth the effort, however, because it is a great poem that is not so great if you only read it in translation. In *Beowulf*, the hero, named "Beowulf" fights three different monsters—Grendel, Grendel's mother, and a dragon. All of these fights are important, only one of them is really important in terms of defining Beowulf's identity.

The first fight Beowulf undertakes is against a monster named Grendel who has been attacking the mead hall of King Hrothgar of the Danes for twelve winters. Beowulf hears of this trouble and journeys across the sea to offer Hrothgar his assistance. He seems to do this because he likes a challenge, and he wants to establish his reputation as a great warrior. After he defeats Grendel, he has to fight her mother, who lives at the bottom of a lake. This fight is a little more difficult for Beowulf because he has to fight her underwater, but he still wins. Finally, after he has been king of his people for 50 years, he has to fight a dragon. There is a big debate as to whether or not Beowulf does the right thing because in the end he dies and leaves his people without a king, they are sure to be attacked by the Swedes once he has died.

Some quotes from the poem show how important Beowulf's identity is, and they also show that reputation is really important in this society. When he arrives at Hrothgar's court, he says that "I had a fixed purpose when I put to sea/As I sat in the boat with my band of men,/I meant to perform to the uttermost/what your people wanted or perish in the attempt,/in the fiend's clutches. /And I shall fulfill that purpose,/prove myself with a proud deed/or meet my death here in the mead-hall." (632-638) When he's fighting Grendel the narrator tells us that "Hygelac's kinsman kept thinking about his name and fame: he never lost heart" (1529-1530). At the end, when Beowulf fights the dragon, he makes a formal boast "I risked my life/ often when I was young. Now I am old,/but as king of the people I shall pursue this fight/for the glory of winning, if the evil one will only/ abandon his earth-fort/ and face me in the open." (2510-2515) Indeed, the final lines of the poem, eulogizing Beowulf, note that "it was said that of all the kings upon the earth /

he was the most gracious and fair-minded / kindest to his people and keenest to win fame." (3182–3184).

If we consider all this evidence together, it seems clear that his first fight, with Grendel, is the most important. It establishes Beowulf's reputation and sets the scene so that he can win other battles, including the one with the dragon. The fact that his people seem to think that it is positive that he sets out to "win fame" shows that according to the values of this society he is doing what he is supposed to. And he couldn't do that if hadn't fought Grendel.

Editing—Finding What's Wrong
Lecture 21—Transcript

Welcome back. In our last lecture we discussed how to get started writing first drafts. We talked about the importance of figuring out what kind of writing personality you have. Do you need to perfect the introduction before you can start to work on the rest of your essay, or do you need to start in the middle—with the meat of your argument—and then tidy up the beginning and the ending later? Or are you like me—I'm someone who works best with the scattershot approach—throwing everything I think might be interesting or relevant to my topic up on the page and then editing, rewriting, deleting, adding to, rearranging until finally I've got a presentable piece of writing?

We also talked last time about how daunting it can be to get started, and I gave you some tricks that have worked for me and for friends of mine to get past the initial writer's block. The thing that I've found works best is to set a goal of a certain number of hours or a certain number of pages per day and give myself permission to stop after I've reached that point.

Very often, when you know that there's a boundary around what you need to accomplish—something like: "I need to get three pages written," or "I need to work for 90 minutes"—then it's easier to get started, because the sooner you start, the sooner you will be done and you're able to go salsa dancing, or out for a run, or to a movie, or you can sit on the couch and watch Law & Order.

In our last lecture, I probably also revealed that I'm a little nuts and kind of obsessive compulsive when it comes to writing schedules, but I'm sure many of you out there right now understand—you do what it takes to get the job done.

Once I found the approach that worked for me, my progress on this huge writing project was steady and mostly satisfying. The day after I handed in my thesis, I woke up; I poured myself a cup of coffee; I sat down at the computer; I noted the time on a slip of paper, and then suddenly I realized that I had nothing I needed to do. But what's important is that I was ready—I was in a kind of writing habit, and getting into that kind of habit can also really help your productivity.

Many people find that writing an essay, or letter, or other piece of text is such a challenging and draining process that when they reach the end, they're relieved, and they just want to get the thing out of their sight—so they hand it in or they mail it off almost immediately. If they have waited until the last minute to work on this assignment, then often there is really no choice—regularly have students come into class five minutes late on the day a paper is due.

They may have stayed up all night finishing it, or they may have gotten up early to write the concluding paragraph, but what they put into my hands is assuredly hot off the printer—and almost as assuredly it has not been edited. This is a major error—and it's one that we've all been guilty of making yours truly included—but it very often means the difference between an "A" and a "B," or a persuasive letter that gets read and makes someone stop and think as opposed to one that simply gets filed or put into the recycle bin.

One more time, I'm going to emphasize how important it is to give yourself plenty of time. I know it's not always possible—sometimes you will have to write something that is both first and final draft at 4 AM, and you have to hope that you do a good enough job to get by. It happens to all of us. Your goal should be to try and have this happen only very rarely—and the more you practice, the better those occasional 4 AM pieces of writing are going to be.

While getting the darn thing written certainly feels like the biggest part of any portion of the writing process, editing is arguably just as important—and in some cases, it's more important than the actual writing itself. Because this stage is so crucial and can make the difference between a piece of writing that's okay and one that's actually great, I have reminded you over, and over, and over again to give yourself the opportunity to put a piece of writing aside—even if it's just for an hour—and then come back and look at it with fresh eyes.

338

When it comes to editing, there are two basic models at extreme opposite ends of the spectrum—there's the line-by-line approach, and then there's the holistic approach. A line-by-line approach is just what it sounds like: You start with the first line of the piece; you read through it and each successive line as carefully as possible, and you make revisions in the moment—so you fix the phrasing, the word choice, etc., sentence by sentence.

The holistic approach is about stepping back from the work and taking what we call a macroscopic rather than microscopic view, and you can ask them questions about the piece: What is it trying to say? How does it say it? This approach, then, would start with sort of moving, or changing, or rearranging larger chunks of the paper—and then you'd gradually work down to the level of word choice and punctuation.

Most people tend to use a combination of these approaches. In this lecture, we're going to explore how to best use elements from each editing style to identify serious and not so serious problems with a piece of writing—and then how to get ready to polish it to perfection.

For today, let's consider the classic example of the five-paragraph essay, and for this exercise I've gone back to Charlotte Perkins Gilman's "The Yellow Wallpaper"—and we've talked about it quite a bit in this course, so you probably have some idea about the plot, about how the text works, the kind of narrator we're dealing with—even if you haven't read this story yourself.

But just as a quick reminder—it's a short story told in the first person, as if we're reading the main character's journal. We gather from the opening entries of the journal that the woman who is writing down these words is experiencing some sort of nervous breakdown. She's been ordered to rest, and she finds herself spending the summer at a large estate where she's ordered to do essentially nothing. Under the strain of not being allowed to perform even enjoyable tasks, she gradually goes insane—hallucinating all kinds of strange things, especially in relationship to the ugly yellow wallpaper in her room.

Let's imagine that a teacher has assigned you the task of writing a five-paragraph essay on "The Yellow Wallpaper." This structure, the five-paragraph structure, is sort of the classic example of academic and argumentative writing—and while it's certainly not the ideal form for every writing task you might have, if we study it today I think it works well to demonstrate how the editing process can work. The idea with a five-paragraph essay would be that you have an introductory paragraph; then, you have three paragraphs of supporting evidence, and then you have got a concluding paragraph that sums up your argument.

I'm going to give you a really short example of a five-paragraph essay so we can work with this form a little bit. As I'm reading this, you might want to think to yourself: "Can I identify what the main goal of this piece of writing is? What are the points that support it? Where do I get confused or lost?"

I should note also that reading aloud is another one of the best ways to check your writing for errors. Very often when you read something aloud, this helps you to spot a mistake that your eye might just skip over if you're reading silently to yourself. As you listen, you may notice that when I'm reading passages from this five-paragraph essay, I'm making some mistakes—particularly in terms of grammar maybe or sentence structure—and what I'm doing here is reading the piece exactly as the student originally wrote it, errors and all, so that's maybe why it will sound a little awkward here and there.

So, here's the first paragraph:

> "The Yellow Wallpaper" is a story by Charlotte Perkins Gilman about how a woman goes crazy. We read the story as if we are reading her journal, and this is how we learn that she is going mad. The readers can see that she is losing her grip on reality because she describes things that can only be hallucinations. But Charlotte's story isn't really about going crazy, it's about how women in her day were considered inferior to men.

That's paragraph one, in which the author is trying to introduce us to his subject and his argumentative position concerning it. From there, he moves on to paragraph two, which should contain his first piece of supporting evidence, and here is paragraph two:

The story starts with us reading the narrator's journal, and we learn that she's living in a house out in the country. From her journal we learn she's having some sort of nervous breakdown. She writes: "If a physician of high standing, and one's own husband, assures friends and relatives that there is really nothing the matter with one but temporary nervous depression—a slight hysterical tendency— what is one to do? My brother is also a physician, and also of high standing, and he says the same thing. So I take phosphates or phosphites—whichever it is—and tonics, and air, and exercise, and journeys, and I'm absolutely forbidden to 'work' until I am well again." So, from this passage we learn the main character's basic situation.

That's the second paragraph—our writer here gives us a rather long quote that tells us something about the plot of the story, but really not much more. As I'm reading this, I'm already starting to wonder does the writer have a clear progression of his paper, or is he simply going to describe the narrative from the beginning to the end. When you're writing something like this, plot summary is certainly necessary to a certain extent, but you always need to be sure that your plot summary or your quotes are working in the interest of a larger argument. What this paragraph should be doing is making clear the first point that works in support of the author's argument as he laid it out in the introduction. Can you even remember what that point is now? Let's see if you can recall it—if not, you're not alone, and we'll talk about why that is in a moment. The paragraph following this one I just read to you should elaborate the second supporting point. Here is the writer's third paragraph:

Charlotte's story really gets interesting when she describes the bedroom where the narrator is staying. Her description starts off very positively—it's a 'big airy room, with windows that look all ways and air and sunshine galore'—but then the description gets more ominous. The narrator tells us that the ripped wallpaper is incredibly ugly: 'The color is repellent, almost revolting: a smoldering unclean yellow, strangely faded by the slow-turning sunlight. It is a dull yet lurid orange in some places, a sickly sulphur tint in others. No wonder the children hated it! I should hate it myself if I had to live in this room long.' It becomes clear as we as readers continue to read that this bedroom of the narrator is not really a playroom or nursery—but more like a prison. Charlotte is suggesting that her husband has put her in prison.

That's paragraph three, and again, it's a paragraph with a long quote in it. Quotes can often work in the interest of supporting your points—they function as concrete evidence that work to prove what you're trying to say. But all too often, I see students including quotes as if they're just trying to fill up space, and then there is very little commentary or discussion of the quote. You cannot simply find a quote that works to support your main claim, plug it into the paper, and then just leave it there as if your reader is going to figure out how it fits. Remember the example I gave you of the prosecutor in the Law & Order episode just pointing to the murder weapon and not explaining how it connects? If you're going to use a quote, it's the same thing. You must discuss it! A good rule of thumb is that if you are including a quote of three lines, you should spend at least an equal number of lines explaining why that quote is important.

This third paragraph also concludes with a statement about how the room in the story seems to be something other than what it is. The student writer is on to something here, but he doesn't really develop this point fully. Why is it important that we understand that there is some mystery about the room and its hideous wallpaper—and what's more important, how does that connect back to the writer's main claim—and can we remember what it is? The main claim was that this story is really about gender issues.

With every supporting point you make in a piece of writing like this, you need to be sure that you explicitly connect it back to your main claim. Another mistake is that this student writer immediately seems to conflate or confuse Charlotte Perkins Gilman, the author of the story, with the narrator who is the main character of the story. Although it's clear that Gilman drew on her own experiences to write this text, this is fiction—it's not autobiography. So instead of saying: "Charlotte is suggesting that her husband has put her in prison," it would be better to say something like: "Gilman seems to suggest that the narrator's husband has put her in prison." You'll notice also that it's more correct to use the author's last name—Gilman—rather than to call her "Charlotte," as if she happens to be the writer's good friend.

Let's move on to the fourth paragraph of the essay:

> As we reach the end of Charlotte's story, we see that the narrator has gone insane. She tells us in her journal that she sees a woman behind the pattern of the wallpaper who is trying to get out. She writes "sometimes I think there are a great many women behind, and sometimes only one, and she crawls around fast, and her crawling shakes it all over. ... And she is all the time trying to climb through. But nobody could climb through that pattern—it strangles so. ..." She goes on to say that she now believes the woman has escaped, and she can see her outside, "creeping about." The writing at the end of the story gets more and more disjointed as the narrator jumps from idea to idea and continues describing the yellow wallpaper in greater and more horrific detail. She clearly has become totally insane.

That's paragraph four—again, the writer gives us a quote; it's a good instinct. The quote helps support a point, but what is the point exactly? The paragraph seems to be offering evidence that the narrator has gone insane, but if we think back to the opening of the paper, the intro paragraph seemed to be trying to suggest that this story is really not about insanity; instead, it's about gender. Has the writer forgotten what his main claim was? At this point, the answer seems to be "yes," and if this writer is planning on turning the paper in as it is, then you can be pretty sure the grade isn't going to be very good—a first draft that is also a final draft almost never is.

So if this is a five-paragraph essay, we've got one paragraph to go. Let's see if the writer is going to try and save it. Here's what he wrote:

> In conclusion, we can see that although the insanity is the most obvious issue in Charlotte Perkins Gilman's 'The Yellow Wallpaper,' the more important issue is that of gender inequality. The narrator goes mad because she has been ordered to rest and not exert herself, even in activities that she likes. These decisions are made by men—her husband and her brother—and by the end of the story, we can see that the idea of the woman trapped behind the wallpaper functions as a metaphor for the narrator's own life.

What do we make of this conclusion? You can tell that the writer has obviously suddenly remembered that he was supposed to be writing about gender, not insanity. In the space of a few sentences, he makes some claims—that it's men who have decreed the narrator rest, that the woman that the narrator sees in the wallpaper in some way symbolizes herself—and these claims are the start of a really good argument. Unfortunately, it's too little too late, and while this paper does have some good parts, it does not hang together as a coherent, persuasive whole.

If this were a first draft, I would say this is great—the introduction understands that it's an introduction; the conclusion tries to conclude things; and in between you have the start of what is an argument that uses individual points, but as a final draft—really not so great. It wanders. The quotes don't necessarily advance the argument as it is stated in the introduction, and there is an imbalance between plot summary and argument—way too much plot summary, not enough explanation or analysis of the quotes to make it rise to the level of an argument that is going to persuade someone.

So, if we consider the range of editing approaches we discussed briefly at the beginning of this lecture, we should try to figure out which approach is going to be most helpful in turning what is a rather mediocre attempt into a compelling piece of writing. In this case, do you think it makes more sense to edit line by line or more holistically? I'm guessing with an example like this, most of you would say the holistic approach. It's kind of hard for us to do this if you don't have the written paper in front of you, but we're going to try and work through it so that you can at least get some sense of how you might go about starting the editing process.

The holistic approach—when you're taking this approach, the first thing you should do after reading through the essay is to try and state in a sentence or phrase what the main goal or argument of this essay is. A good way to check for this in your own writing is to try and underline your main claim—and ideally, your main claim should be stated somewhere near the end of the first paragraph.

If it's a longer piece of writing, the first paragraph might be introductory, while the second states the main lines of your argument. But no matter what, the reader should be able to figure out by the second paragraph what it is you're really trying to say. If you can't figure out what to underline, then you know you have a problem, and you need to find a way to rephrase your main point or thesis. So in a nutshell—whether you're writing a magazine article, or a letter, or a report for work, your reader should be able to tell almost immediately what the main point is.

You would be surprised how many people try to write without having clearly articulated what their main idea is, even in their own minds. I've seen a letter to the editor of our local paper begin by stating something like: "Government is becoming too intrusive in people's lives." After this statement, there was a list of excessive restrictions on the rights of local citizens. Then, the letter ended by condemning the recent city council decision not to allow people living within city limits to raise chickens. Only with the final sentence was the main point of the letter clear. As it stood, the letter came across as a rant by a person with a whole lot of upset feelings—but no clear idea for organizing them in a fashion that would make an impact.

We've already established that the main idea in this essay is pretty clear— the writer says in the first paragraph that insanity is an important element of "The Yellow Wallpaper," but gender is actually more important. The key for this paper to be strong and organized is for the writer to make every supporting point connect back explicitly to this main claim. So, our next step in trying to determine how well or poorly this essay connects back to that claim would be to try and write up an outline of the paper as it stands now. Again, this doesn't have to be formal outline style—you don't have to do Roman numeral 1, capital A, all that nonsense—but you can do that if that's what you're used to and that's what you like. For me, I find the easiest thing to do is just take a blank sheet of paper and write a sentence or a couple of phrases for each paragraph.

Given how the essay stands now, my outline on a page might look something like:

> Paragraph one: Intro, "Yellow Wallpaper" seems to be about insanity, really about men treating women as inferiors.

Paragraph two: Plot summary—we learn narrator is in country house for a nervous condition; there's a quote about how her husband and brother both agree this is what she needs. Story is told through her journal entries.

Paragraph three: Description of the ugly yellow wallpaper and how her bedroom seems like a prison—writer suggests that narrator's husband has put her in prison.

Paragraph four: Narrator has gone completely insane; believes she can see a woman behind the pattern of the wallpaper.

Paragraph five: Conclusion—argues that preceding examples show how this story is about men dominating women because husband and brother have prescribed this regimen, and woman in the wallpaper symbolizes the narrator's confinement.

So very quickly, then, we've identified the basic structure of the paper—and if you look at it a little bit closer, you can see where it might fall apart. Again, it's always a good idea to try and sum up in one or two sentences what each supporting point is and then how it supports the main idea. Again, when you're doing this, you want to make sure that each supporting point connects back to your main claim as clearly and emphatically as possible. Never assume that just because you see how the quote you have selected makes a connection, your readers are going to get it as well.

I know it has been several minutes since you heard me read the intro paragraph aloud, but you're probably remembering there were some awkward stylistic moments; it didn't flow very well; there were some typos or misused words. We're just going to file that information away. We're not going to worry about finer details here—we're trying to fix the overall structure of the paper. We've already established that the introductory paragraph does a pretty good job of stating the main claim—the story is about insanity, and this writer thinks Charlotte Perkins Gilman really is mostly concerned with gender. That's a decent argumentative claim, but as it stands, the intro paragraph could be more specific. What three points, exactly, support this argumentative claim? In the intro paragraph, at least give us a hint. So we'll come back to the intro paragraph.

Let's review our outline and look at paragraph two; it included some plot summary and a quote about how the narrator's husband and brother said this is what she needed. Here is a prime opportunity for the writer to make an explicit connection. The quote shows how male figures join together to make a female figure do something she would rather not; however, the writer never points this out explicitly. We can infer this if we read the quote carefully, and we can connect the dots on our own, but the writer ends the paragraph by telling us that now we know the "basic situation"—and like I've said before, it seems as if the writer has already forgotten what his own main claim was.

As we've noted in our outline, paragraph three gives us a quote describing the yellow wallpaper. This is obviously critically important—the story, after all, is called "The Yellow Wallpaper." The writer of this essay also makes the statement that the narrator's husband has essentially put her in prison. But if you look at the quote, it's really about how ugly the wallpaper is, and it's not about prison.

The writer does mention here that the narrator's description of the room makes it sound ominous, like a prison, but he doesn't show any evidence of that. So what we can figure out is that paragraph three seems to be trying to make use of two possible pieces of evidence—and these would be (1) the prison-like quality of the room, and (2) the extreme ugliness of the ripped wallpaper—but because they're put together when maybe they should be separated into their own paragraphs, each of the points isn't made as clearly and effectively as it might be.

As our outline shows, paragraph four describes how the narrator seems to have gone completely insane—because she believes she can see a woman behind the pattern of the wallpaper. Again, the author of this essay seems to have forgotten that his main claim is really about gender inequality. He just seems to be giving us plot summary. Paragraph five, the conclusion, is clearly an attempt on the part of the author of this essay to bring us back to the main point of the introduction—and he is sort of retroactively suggesting that what the writer has just described proves that "The Yellow Wallpaper" is about gender inequality.

So, now we've identified some flaws in the broad outline of the paper. Let's try and revise the outline—and again, we're just going to do this in the general, broadest sense we can so that we can think about how we can move on and make the paper stronger. As I've said before, in general, the first paragraph seems to be okay, although it needs some fine-tuning—but the major point of the essay is clear.

But now that we've been thinking and reading on this topic for awhile, we need to come up with three paragraphs that each support that main claim about gender inequality, and if you're trying to do this on a sheet of paper you might scribble something like:

> Paragraph two: The role and description of men in the story. Paragraph three: The description of the narrator's bedroom as a prison. Paragraph four: The yellow wallpaper itself and the image of the woman trapped behind it that the narrator imagines. Paragraph five: Conclusion—recap of main points, restatement of main claim.

So here you see we've separated the two claims that were together in paragraph three, the two points, and we've given them each their own paragraph. So now that we've dealt with the larger sweep of the paper, we can start to focus in on some of the details. As we rewrite, we want to make sure that it's absolutely clear how each point works to support the main claim. You want to make sure that the quotes you have selected actually do the work that you want them to do. Are there other quotes that might help you make your point a little bit better or a little more clearly? You might want to replace them now. As you rewrite, you'll also want to check for awkward phrasing and out and out errors.

In our next lecture, we'll get down to the business of rewriting this essay from start to finish, and then we'll practice the editing and rewriting process on a very different type of writing—a job letter. What we'll discover is how easily these editing and writing tools can translate from one type of prose to another.

Rewriting—Fixing What's Wrong
Lecture 22

Very often, the problems that occur in the later sections of a paper or in portions of a letter arise from the fact that the writer has not really articulated a clear main position.

In the first step of the editing process, we've identified what some of the issues are, and we've thought about some ways to improve the problem areas of an essay. Now it's time to put our thoughts into action and start rewriting. As I've said before, step one is always make sure that you are working with a clearly articulated main claim. If your main claim is clear and you keep it foremost in your mind, then often the supporting points simply fall into place, and the structure is logical from the outset. If you're not sure of what exactly it is you're trying to argue, then the paper or letter or article can wander.

You may be thinking—and you may be rightly thinking—that the editing and rewriting process is really easy to describe and demonstrate when we're dealing with an academic essay. The essay is a form that's trying to make an argument, so it's relatively easy to spot weaknesses. But what about other types of writing?

Let's consider something that's not an essay. How about a letter to your mayor, asking her to get behind renaming something in honor of John and Jane Smith—a couple that has been very active in charitable activities in your community? Let's consider a first draft of this letter and then see how we could maybe make it better.

Dear Peggy,

I absolutely idolize John and Jane Smith, I cut out every newspaper article I read about them. They are always giving money to good causes and helping people live better lives. I've never heard of them asking for recognition for all the good things they do. I just think they deserve to have some recognition after everything they've done for people in our community, and in other communities, and for the arts, and for cancer research and special education needs. I think we should name something after them, even if it's just a rock in the Community Park. Please help me honor John and Jane Smith.

Sincerely,

Rita Neighbor

What does this letter have going for it? It's definitely sincere and heartfelt, but the writer is so eager to get this recognition for John and Jane Smith that she doesn't seem to have taken much time in the writing of the letter— the words come out kind of breathlessly; they're sort of tumbling over one another, as if she was just writing every thought the moment it came into her head.

How would we start to edit this and make it stronger? Let's start from a holistic perspective. The first thing that strikes me is that the letter writer starts out by talking about herself. That's all very nice, Rita Neighbor, but the goal of this letter is not to let people know what Rita Neighbor thinks about John and Jane Smith but rather to get recognition for them. Rita Neighbor's longtime interest in their philanthropy can certainly be used to support her desired objective, but she needs to make John and Jane Smith the main focus from the beginning of the letter, and she needs to move herself to a secondary position.

We can also zoom in on John and Jane Smith's accomplishments—as of now, they're listed kind of haphazardly. These accomplishments are all very important, but they should each get their own moment within the letter. Finally, we might need some indication that other people besides Rita Neighbor think this is a good idea.

On a finer level of detail, a few things leap out. First, when you're writing a letter to the mayor, even if she has been your best friend since kindergarten, you probably want to address her as "Mayor Friendly" rather than "Peggy." There are also some grammatical and mechanical errors: The first sentence is a run-on due to a comma splice, and there are some moments where the tone is far too casual. Examples include "I've" instead of "I have" and "they've" instead of "they have."

After identifying and editing in terms of some of the major issues, we can rewrite the letter so that it's more powerful and more effective. Here's the revised version:

Dear Mayor Friendly:

As I'm sure you are well aware, local residents John and Jane Smith have changed our community and many others through their generous acts of philanthropy. I have followed their charity work for many years and been consistently impressed with how they have given large sums of money to causes as diverse as the arts, cancer research, and special education. I and many others in our neighborhood would like to honor the Smiths by renaming Neighborhood Park, John and Jane Smith Park.

Although it is a small, token act of recognition, we hope that it would be meaningful to the Smiths since it is their neighbors who wish to honor them. Those of us interested in making this happen would be grateful if you could tell us how to go about setting the wheels for this in motion.

Sincerely,

Rita Neighbor

What's different? This letter is no longer about Rita Neighbor's long, individual idolization of the Smiths, but it's about the Smiths themselves. Her longtime interest in their activities, however, is still useful—as she can cite the different areas in which the Smiths have made significant charitable contributions. Her writing tone is a little more formal, and she also takes care to indicate that she is not alone in this request. Finally, she asks the mayor for information on the steps necessary to make the renaming of a park possible—she indicates that she is willing to take an active role to accomplish whatever needs to be done.

So what is the most important thing to take away from this lecture? State a main idea that is as clear and specific as possible. If you keep this main idea firmly in your mind as you write, and then you explicitly connect supporting points back to it, chances are you'll find that your writing flows much more naturally. The structure of your writing will be easier to figure out, and your audience will be better able to follow you.

Never assume your audience understands the point you're trying to make.

A related point is make sure that you never assume your audience understands the point you're trying to make. For example, if you find a quote from a text that you think helps make your point, you cannot simply insert it into your essay. Always spell things out—signpost, in other words, so that your audience doesn't have to work too hard to follow whatever it is you're trying to say. You now have the basic tools to assess what needs to be edited in a piece of writing, and you have some guidelines for how to go about making those changes. ■

Suggested Reading

Bullock, *The Norton Field Guide to Writing*.

The Chicago Manual of Style.

Clouse, *The Student Writer*.

Griffith, *Writing Essays about Literature*.

Harmon and Holman, *A Handbook to Literature*.

Lanham, *Revising Prose*.

———, *Style*.

Lynn, *Literature*.

MLA Handbook for Writers of Research Papers.

O'Connor, *Woe Is I*.

———, *Words Fail Me*.

Strunk and White, *The Elements of Style.*

Trimble, *Writing with Style.*

Tufte, *Artful Sentences.*

1. Take the edited version of the sample essay from Lecture 21 (below) and, using the skills we've practiced in that lecture and this one, rewrite the entire essay so that it is clear, coherent, well supported, and free from errors of punctuation and mechanics.

While on the surface "The Yellow Wallpaper" seems to be about one woman's descent into insanity, closer analysis reveals that the story is really a comment on the gender inequality of Gilman's day, as the depictions of male characters, the description of the narrator's bedroom, and the symbolism of the yellow wallpaper make plain.

From these and other similar comments the narrator makes throughout the story, it's clear that she feels helpless in the face of the male authority of her husband and brother. She seems not to have a say in her own recovery—for example, she's unsure exactly what kind of medicines and tonics she's taking—and she uses negative words like "forbidden," which suggest that she is being ordered to do things—or not to do them—against her will.

In addition to the description of how the men in the narrator's life seem to have taken away the narrator's free will, the description of the bedroom functions to cast an ominous and forbidding aura over the narrator's situation. Her description of the bedroom starts off very positively—it's a "big airy room, with windows that look all ways and air and sunshine galore"—but then the description gets more ominous. She comments that it must have been a nursery at one time because of the bars on the windows, and then perhaps a gymnasium because there are rings mounted on the wall. Other details in her description—the bed is nailed to the floor, and the bedposts look as if they have been "gnawed on"—all combine to produce the image of imprisonment. The images conjured up by this description of the room point clearly toward a comment on gender inequality, especially because the narrator says her husband insisted that she take this room for her own.

By far, however, the most compelling piece of evidence that this is a story about gender issues and not simply insanity is made clear through the yellow wallpaper of the story's title. It is ripped in places—clearly deliberately torn—and the narrator tells us that "the color is repellent, almost revolting: a smoldering unclean yellow, strangely faded by the slow-turning sunlight. It is a dull yet lurid orange in some places, a sickly sulphur tint in others. No wonder the children hated it! I should hate it myself if I had to live in this room long." As the story progresses, the hideous wallpaper preys upon the mind of the narrator, who has been forced by her husband to spend long hours in a room that she detests. Eventually, the narrator hallucinates what is arguably a metaphor for her own situation. She tells us that she sees a woman behind the pattern of the wallpaper and says: "Sometimes I think there are a great many women behind, and sometimes only one, and she crawls around fast, and her crawling shakes it all over..... And she is all the time trying to climb through. But nobody could climb through that pattern—it strangles so...." The word "strangles" in this passage, along with the description of the woman as being behind the pattern and trying to get out, all suggest that there is something about the quality of being a woman, rather than being insane, that is at stake in Gilman's story. The story concludes with the narrator imagining that she and the woman in the wallpaper are the same person, and just like the woman behind the pattern, the narrator chillingly "creeps" around her room in an act so obviously insane that her husband faints at the sight of it.

Taken individually, the depiction of men, the description of the bedroom that sounds more like a 19th-century lunatic asylum than a nursery, and the narrator's obsessive hallucinations involving the yellow wallpaper could all be considered important elements in a story about one woman's descent into insanity. When we consider them altogether, however, it becomes clear that the narrator's madness is a direct result of issues of gender inequality: Her husband dictates her rest cure and then assigns her a room that's more prison than anything else. Once in that room, the narrator's feelings of imprisonment, the feeling that her situation is literally killing her, manifest themselves in her hallucination of the woman in the wallpaper, who stands as a symbol for the narrator herself. "The Yellow Wallpaper" uses the idea of madness or insanity to demonstrate the dangers of sexual inequality in American society of the time.

Rewriting—Fixing What's Wrong
Lecture 22—Transcript

Welcome back. In our last lecture, we discussed the process of editing our writing, and we talked about the two major approaches—a holistic approach that considers the essay as a whole and then works down to the level of the sentence or the phrase, and we talked about line-by-line editing, which is just what it sounds like—reading each line carefully in order to correct and strengthen the essay.

As practice, we started the editing process by examining an example of a five-paragraph essay on Charlotte Perkins Gilman's short story "The Yellow Wallpaper." After a quick read through in which we analyzed the essay, we identified its main claim and paid some attention to whether or not the supporting points helped to prove that main claim. We then crafted an outline of the essay in its present form, and this allowed us to see some weaknesses almost immediately. For example, we noted that the main claim that the essay made was pretty clearly stated—and this main claim was that "The Yellow Wallpaper" appears to be about the narrator's decline into insanity, but what our writer really wants to argue is that it's actually about gender inequality.

Fair enough—but as we worked our way through the essay, we noted that the writer seemed to lose sight of his thesis statement as he worked through it, and he only really remembered it in the final paragraph.

Although the three supporting paragraphs in the middle of the essay each had direct quotes that could be used in support of the main claim, the writer neglected to explicitly explain and analyze those quotes with an eye toward shoring up the main claim of the paper—instead, the quotes were more or less left to stand on their own, and the reader had to infer how they worked in support of the thesis statement.

There were also some awkward phrases, some typos, and some incorrect punctuation. In the first step of the editing process, we've identified what some of the issues are, and we've thought about some ways to improve the problem areas of the essay. Now it's time to put our thoughts into action and start rewriting.

One more time—you're going to get so tired of hearing me say this, but step one is always make sure that you are working with a clearly articulated main claim, or thesis, or argumentative position. Very often, the problems that occur in the later sections of a paper or in portions of a letter arise from the fact that the writer has not really articulated a clear main position.

If your main claim is clear and you keep it foremost in your mind, then very often the supporting points simply fall into place, and the structure is logical from the outset. If you're not sure of what exactly it is you're trying to argue, then the paper, or the letter, or the article can wander—but be assured, in early drafting such wandering can be a good thing, and it can be hugely productive.

For example, you might discover on page 5 of a paper that you thought was about the lack of authority of King Hrothgar in the medieval poem *Beowulf,* that what you're really interested in is how the character of Beowulf himself uses the example of Hrothgar as a guide to what not to do once he becomes king. So, suddenly, on page 5, your main focus shifts, and the rest of the paper ends up being about Beowulf, not Hrothgar. That's all fine, but what it does is make for a split-personality paper—and that is one that lacks coherence.

This is why editing is so important—once you have realized this, you can go back, edit, and rewrite the paper so that you're still able to use much of that same evidence about King Hrothgar, but now you're recasting it as being in support of a main claim about the character of Beowulf. Ultimately, it's not too much of a change, but it's a change that has to happen if the paper is going to make sense.

So while wandering can be useful in the drafting stage, it is not something that your audience will necessarily appreciate. A compelling piece of writing is going to engage your audience from the beginning; it's going to guide them through a claim that is clearly articulated from the outset. You don't want your audience to have to stop, to think, to return to your main claim, and try to figure out on their own how some of these disjointed pieces all fit together.

Let's go back to our example of an attempt at a five-paragraph essay, and let's pay careful attention to the thesis. Here is the introductory paragraph as it stands now. It says essentially:" 'The Yellow Wallpaper' is a story by Charlotte Perkins Gilman about how a woman goes crazy." So here's how that paragraph reads:

> "The Yellow Wallpaper" is a story by Charlotte Perkins Gilman about how a woman goes crazy. We read the story as if we are reading her journal, and this is how we learn that she is going mad. The readers can see that she is losing her grip on reality because she describes things that can only be hallucinations. But Charlotte's story isn't really about going crazy—it's about how women in her day were considered inferior to men.

Again, as I've said before, the thesis statement is actually pretty clear here—we could underline it if we wanted to without any real problem—but while it's certainly an argument, the question should be: Is it specific enough to guide the writer through the rest of the paper? I would say that the intro paragraph could definitely benefit from a little more detail.

If you'll recall from our editing exercises in the last lecture, we decided that we would try and identify three points that work to support a main claim about gender inequality in this story. Those three points were the way the male characters in the story are depicted, the way the bedroom in which the narrator spends most of her time is described, and then the third point would be something to do with the image of the wallpaper, behind the pattern of which the narrator thinks she can see a woman who is trying to escape.

So what we should do now is try and put those details into the thesis statement, and while we're at it, we're going to go ahead and correct another error—which is the use of the author's first name, Charlotte, rather than her last, as would be much more appropriate in a formal essay like this one. So now, the thesis statement in the intro paragraph might read something like this:

While on the surface "The Yellow Wallpaper" seems to be about one woman's descent into insanity, closer analysis reveals that the story is really a comment on the gender inequality of Gilman's day, as the depictions of male characters, the description of the narrator's bedroom, and the symbolism of the yellow wallpaper make plain.

This thesis statement is much more polished and more specific than it was before, and it clearly signposts where this paper is going—paragraph two should deal with the depiction of men, paragraph three with the description of the bedroom, and paragraph four should deal with the wallpaper itself. So let's see if the paper goes on to do that. Here's paragraph two:

> The story starts with us reading the narrator's journal, and we learn that she's living in a house out in the country. From her journal we learn she's having some sort of nervous breakdown. She writes: "If a physician of high standing, and one's own husband, assures friends and relatives that there is really nothing the matter with one but temporary nervous depression—a slight hysterical tendency—what is one to do? My brother is also a physician, and also of high standing, and he says the same thing. So I take phosphates or phosphites—whichever it is—and tonics, and air, and exercise, and journeys, and am absolutely forbidden to "work" until I am well again." So from this passage we learn the main character's basic situation.

If we remember that this paragraph is supposed to be making the point that the depiction of men in the story is intended to comment on gender inequality, well, the quote itself is just fine—it makes clear that the narrator has had her situation defined and diagnosed by both her husband and her brother, and it's pretty clear that she also feels helpless. She says: "what is one to do?" She feels helpless in the face of their masculine authority, but unfortunately, as it stands now, the writer of the essay leaves that up to us to figure out—offering only the comment that now we know what the narrator's "basic situation" is.

This is a classic example of an imbalance of quotes or plot summary in relationship to argument. What we need is more analysis after the quote. So if we delete the last sentence and substitute some analysis that connects back to the main claim, we've got a much more workable second paragraph—something like this:

> From these and other similar comments the narrator makes throughout the story, it's clear that she feels helpless in the face of the male authority of her husband and brother.
>
> She seems not to have a say in her own recovery—for example, she's unsure exactly what kind of medicines and tonics she's taking—and she uses negative words like "forbidden," which suggest that she is being ordered to do things—or not to do them—against her will.

This is much better—and, in fact, the writer could even devote another several lines to describing evidence for the portrayal of men as domineering tyrants, but for the purposes of our short essay today, this revision works, as it offers comment on the evidence, and it connects back explicitly to the main claim.

So, one more time, let's think back to the thesis statement, and because we made that thesis statement so specific, we know exactly what the next paragraph should be about—it should discuss the description of the narrator's bedroom and how that contributes to the main claim about gender inequality. Here's what the paragraph says:

> Charlotte's story really gets interesting when she describes the bedroom where the narrator is staying. Her description starts off very positively—it's a 'big airy room, with windows that look all ways and air and sunshine galore'—but then the description gets more ominous. The narrator tells us that the ripped wallpaper is incredibly ugly: 'The color is repellent, almost revolting: a smoldering unclean yellow, strangely faded by the slow-turning sunlight. It is a dull yet lurid orange in some places, a sickly sulphur tint in others. No wonder the children hated it! I should hate it myself if I had to live in this room long.' It becomes clear as we, as readers, continue to read that this bedroom of the narrator is not

really a playroom or nursery, but more like a prison. Charlotte is suggesting that her husband has put her in prison.

There are some positives and negatives in this paragraph. The first part of the paragraph sets us up to anticipate a move from positive to negative adjectives that describe the narrator's bedroom, and it sets us up for this pretty nicely, but then it only goes there in paraphrase—it would be much more effective if we saw a couple more direct quotes.

Then, when it does move to the negative, it shifts to the yellow wallpaper itself, which—as, arguably, the main element of the story—really should get its own paragraph. Then, the comment at the end—that it seems clear that the narrator's husband has essentially put her in prison—well, this would work well if it was expanded just a little bit—but as it is now, in general it does okay in that it does sort of point us back to the main claim.

Before we rewrite this paragraph, let's go ahead and let's consider the next paragraph, the fourth. So we're going to sort of revise paragraphs three and four together. As it stands now, the fourth paragraph says:

> As we reach the end of Charlotte's story, we see that the narrator has gone insane. She tells us in her journal that she sees a woman behind the pattern of the wallpaper who is trying to get out. She writes: "Sometimes I think there are a great many women behind, and sometimes only one, and she crawls around fast, and her crawling shakes it all over. ... And she is all the time trying to climb through. But nobody could climb through that pattern— it strangles so. ..." She goes on to say that she now believes the woman has escaped, and she can see her outside, "creeping about." The writing at the end of the story gets more and more disjointed as the narrator jumps from idea to idea and continues describing the yellow wallpaper in greater and greater horrific detail. She clearly has become totally insane.

As we discussed last time, the writer at this point seems to have forgotten his main claim about gender and instead is focusing on trying to show us that the narrator has become insane—and this is a point that really doesn't need any proving—in fact, it's sort of the main plot of the story itself. So, essentially, this paragraph has a quote that could be used to make an argument, but it's only being used here in the interest of plot summary.

So let's try and rewrite those two paragraphs so that they match up with our new thesis statement. Here's a shot at improving paragraph three, which we decided should be about the narrator's bedroom:

> In addition to the description of how the men in the narrator's life seem to have taken away the narrator's free will, the description of the bedroom functions to cast an ominous and forbidding aura over the narrator's situation. Her description of the bedroom starts off very positively—it's a "big airy room, with windows that look all ways and air and sunshine galore"—but then the description gets more ominous. She comments that it must have been a nursery at one time because of the bars on the windows, and then perhaps a gymnasium because there are rings mounted on the wall. Other details in her description—the bed is nailed to the floor, and the bedposts look as if they have been "gnawed on"—all combine to produce the image of imprisonment. The images conjured up by this description of the room point clearly toward a comment on gender inequality, especially because the narrator says her husband insisted that she take this room for her own.

This paragraph is much better in the way it explains the quote and then adds further details about the description of the room, and it also gives us a great opportunity to transition into that fourth paragraph, which is supposed to be about the yellow wallpaper itself. Here, what we can do is take parts of paragraphs three and four from the original essay, and we can revise and recombine them to make a persuasive point.

So here's our new paragraph four:

> By far, however, the most compelling piece of evidence that this is a story about gender issues and not simply insanity is made clear through the yellow wallpaper of the story's title. It is ripped in places—clearly deliberately torn—and the narrator tells us that

"The color is repellent, almost revolting: a smoldering unclean yellow, strangely faded by the slow-turning sunlight.

It is a dull yet lurid orange in some places, a sickly sulphur tint in others. No wonder the children hated it! I should hate it myself if I had to live in this room long." As the story progresses, the hideous wallpaper preys upon the mind of the narrator, who has been forced by her husband to spend long hours in a room that she detests. Eventually, the narrator hallucinates what is arguably a metaphor for her own situation. She tells us that she sees a woman behind the pattern of the wallpaper and says: "Sometimes I think there are a great many women behind, and sometimes only one, and she crawls around fast, and her crawling shakes it all over. ... And she is all the time trying to climb through. But nobody could climb through that pattern—it strangles so. ..." The word "strangles" in this passage, along with the description of the woman as being behind the pattern and trying to get out, all suggest that there is something about the quality of being a woman, rather than being insane, that is at stake in Gilman's story. The story concludes with the narrator imagining that she and the woman in the wallpaper are the same person, and just like the woman behind the pattern, the narrator chillingly "creeps" around her room in an act so obviously insane that her husband faints at the sight of it.

Again, this paragraph is stronger because it has a single focus—the yellow wallpaper. It has direct quotes, and it has sufficient explanation so we can see how this connects back to the main claim and how it connects back to that intro paragraph that set us up to be in this place at this time. You always want to finish strong—you want to reiterate the main points of your introductory paragraph without simply restating them. Here's how the fifth and final paragraph reads as it stands right now:

In conclusion, we can see that although the insanity is the most obvious issue in Charlotte Perkins Gilman's "The Yellow Wallpaper," the more important issue is that of gender inequality. The narrator goes mad because she has been ordered to rest and not exert herself, even in activities that she likes. These decisions are made by men—her husband and her brother—and by the end of the story, we can see that the idea of the woman trapped behind the wallpaper functions as a metaphor for the narrator's own life.

There's some good stuff here—we're reminded what the thesis was, and the writer also reminds us of the depiction of the male characters and how that would seem to contribute to the idea of gender inequality.

But the other two points—about the bedroom and the wallpaper itself—they don't really get full treatment. While I obviously think that a certain amount of what we might call "signposting" is really helpful in getting your reader to follow your argument more easily, starting the concluding paragraph with "In conclusion" is really too predictable and cliché.

So let's try and rewrite that final paragraph so that it has a smoother transition from the one before it, so that it sums up all the evidence and it restates the main claim without simply repeating the intro paragraph verbatim. Why don't we try this as a concluding paragraph?

"Taken individually, the depiction of men, the description of the bedroom that sounds more like a 19th-century lunatic asylum than a nursery, and the narrator's obsessive hallucinations involving the yellow wallpaper could all be considered important elements in a story about one woman's descent into insanity. When we consider them all together, however, it becomes clear that the narrator's madness is a direct result of issues of gender inequality: Her husband dictates her rest cure and then assigns her a room that's more prison than anything else. Once in that room, the narrator's feelings of imprisonment, the feeling that her situation is literally killing her, manifest themselves in her hallucination of the woman in the wallpaper, who stands as a symbol for the narrator herself. 'The Yellow Wallpaper' uses the idea of madness or insanity to demonstrate the dangers of sexual inequality in American society of the time."

This conclusion reminds us of the three main points of the paper. It restates them in terms that are somewhat different from that of the introduction, and it sums up the main idea quite nicely. Is this essay perfect? No—certainly not. Is it better now that it has been edited and rewritten? Absolutely!

You might be thinking—and you might be rightly thinking—that the editing and rewriting process is really easy to describe and demonstrate when we're dealing with an academic essay—that is a form that is trying to make an argument, so it's relatively easy to spot weaknesses. You can ask: "Where does the argument fall apart? Where does it fail to persuade? But what about other types of writing? I believe that anything can be made better with some editing and some rewriting.

So let's consider something that's not an essay. How about something that's a letter to your local mayor asking her to get behind renaming a local park in honor of John and Jane Smith—a couple who have been very active in charitable activities in your community? Let's consider a first draft of this letter and then see how we could maybe make it better. Here's the letter:

> Dear Peggy: I absolutely idolize John and Jane Smith, I cut out every newspaper article I read about them. They are always giving money to good causes and helping people live better lives. I've never heard of them asking for recognition for all the good things they do. I just think they deserve to have some recognition after everything they've done for people in our community, and in other communities, and for the arts, and for cancer research and special education needs. I think we should name something after them, even if it's just a rock in the Community Park. Please help me honor John and Jane Smith. Sincerely, Rita Neighbor.

What does this letter have going for it? It's definitely sincere and heartfelt, but the writer is so eager to get this recognition for John and Jane Smith that she doesn't seem to have taken much time in the writing of the letter— the words come out kind of breathlessly; they're sort of tumbling over one another, as if she was just writing every thought the moment it came into her head.

How would we start to edit this and make it stronger? Let's start from a holistic perspective. What are your first impressions? The first thing that strikes me is that the letter writer, Ms. Rita Neighbor, starts out talking about herself. She says, if you remember: "I absolutely idolize John and Jane Smith, I cut out every newspaper article."

That's all very nice, Rita Neighbor, but the goal of this letter is not to let people know what Rita Neighbor thinks about John and Jane Smith—but rather to get recognition for them. Rita Neighbor's longtime interest in their philanthropy can certainly be used to support her desired objective, but she needs to make John and Jane Smith the main focus from the beginning of the letter, and she needs to move herself to a secondary position.

Speaking holistically, we can also zoom in on John and Jane Smith's accomplishments—as of now, they're listed kind of haphazardly and in no particular order. These accomplishments are all very important, but they should each get their own "moment" within the letter, so to speak. Finally, we might need some indication that other people besides Rita Neighbor think this is a good idea.

On a finer level of detail, a few things leap out. First, when you're writing a letter to the mayor, even if she has been your best friend since kindergarten, you probably want to address her as "Mayor Friendly" rather than "Peggy." There are also some grammatical and mechanical errors: The first sentence is a run-on due to a comma splice—that's probably harder for you to hear than if you were looking at it on the page, but trust me, comma splice there—and there are some moments where the tone is far too casual. There is an "I've" instead of "I have" and "they've" instead of "they have."

So now that we've identified and edited in terms of some of the major issues, let's try rewriting the letter so that it's more powerful and more effective. Here's the revised version:

> Dear Mayor Friendly: As I'm sure you are well aware, local residents John and Jane Smith have changed our community and many others through their generous acts of philanthropy. I have followed their charity work for many years and been consistently impressed with how they have given large sums of money to causes as diverse as the arts, cancer research, and special education. I and many others in our neighborhood would like to honor the Smiths by renaming Neighborhood Park, John and Jane Smith Park.

Although it is a small, token act of recognition, we hope that it would be meaningful to the Smiths since it is their neighbors who wish to honor them. Those of us interested in making this happen would be grateful if you could tell us how to go about setting the wheels for this in motion. Sincerely, Rita Neighbor.

What's different? This letter is no longer about Rita Neighbor's long, individual idolization of the Smiths, but it's about the Smiths themselves. Her long interest in their activities, however, is still useful—as she can cite the different areas in which the Smiths have made significant charitable contributions.

Her writing tone is a little more formal, and she also takes care to indicate that she is not alone in this request. Finally, she asks the mayor for information on the steps necessary to make the renaming of a park possible. She doesn't just make a request and dump it in the mayor's lap—she indicates that she is willing to take an active role to accomplish whatever needs to be done.

So what is the most important thing to take away from today's lecture? I think that number one: It is to state a main idea, or claim, or a thesis that is as clear and as specific as possible. If you keep this main idea clearly articulated and detailed, and you keep it firmly in your mind as you write, and then you explicitly connect supporting points back to it, chances are you'll find that your writing flows much more naturally, and the structure of your writing will be easier to figure out, and your audience is going to be better able to follow you.

A related point is to make sure that when you're writing, you never assume that your audience understands the point you're trying to make. For example, if you find a quote from a text that you think helps make your point, you cannot simply insert it into your essay and then not bother to explain it. Always spell things out—signpost, in other words, so that your audience doesn't have to work too hard to follow whatever it is you're trying to say.

So, after this lecture and the one before it, you now have the basic tools to assess what needs to be edited or changed in a piece of writing, and now you have some guidelines for how to go about actually making those changes.

One of the things that we mentioned briefly in our last example about the letter but we didn't have a chance to talk about at any great length is the very finest level of detail in terms of editing and rewriting, and this would be grammatical and mechanical mistakes—a misspelled word, a comma when it should be a semicolon, using "I" when you should say "me," and vice versa. Although these details might seem minor, they are crucially important to producing a persuasive piece of writing—and next time we'll devote an entire lecture to a discussion of 10 common errors and how to avoid them.

Avoiding Common Errors in Grammar and Usage
Lecture 23

A famous story tells how Winston Churchill was reading through proofs of a piece he had written, and he noticed that his editor had rewritten his sentences so that there was no preposition at the end. In the margins, Churchill wrote back, "This is a situation up with which [I] shall not put."

In the last lectures, we discussed the revision process, one of the most important—but also most overlooked—stages of producing an effectively written piece. Many of the strategies we discussed are also useful tools for avoiding the common errors in grammar and punctuation that are the topic of this lecture. For example, we talked about how important it is to set aside a piece of writing and then return to it with fresh eyes, allowing you to better spot places that need revision. Even better is to ask for someone else to look it over for you. One of the easiest and quickest ways to spot errors and awkward moments is simply to read your piece out loud. Reading aloud forces you to slow down, and your eyes are less likely to skip over a typo.

One of the easiest and quickest ways to spot errors and awkward moments is simply to read your piece out loud.

Let's look at 10 of the most common errors that I have seen in my experience teaching college-level writing. The common error that I find the most distressing is the incorrect use of "I" when it should be "me" and vice versa. Which of the following two sentences is correct: "It was such a wonderful time for Michelle and I" or "It was such a wonderful time for Michelle and me"? The answer is the second sentence. The reason is that the compound object "Michelle and me" is the object of the preposition "for"—and because of this, the first-person pronoun has to be in the objective case. An easy way to check for the correctness of our first example would be to take "Michelle and me" and make it singular. Now we have "It was such a wonderful time for I" or "It was such a wonderful time for me." For most

of us, we don't even need to know the rule—our ear tells us that the secon
sentence is correct.

The second common error is that of subject-pronoun agreement. Which o
these sentences is correct: "If a person has a complaint, he or she shoul
contact the Human Resources Department" or "If a person has a complain
they should contact the Human Resources Department"? Sentence two i
simpler and more economical—but, in fact, it is incorrect. The reason is tha
"person" is singular, but "they" is plural; in other words, they don't agree
That sentence could easily be corrected by simply turning "person" int
"people"—"If people have complaints, they should contact ... ."

By using a sentence like "If a person has a complaint, he or she shoul
contact ... ," not only do you manage to have your pronouns agree—person
he, and she are all singular—but you also avoid the pitfall of using gender
exclusive language, our third common error. When I was in high school,
was taught that when you were trying to get your pronouns to agree, it wa
all right to use "he" to stand in for the universal subject—thus, "If a perso
has a complaint, he should contact ... ." This didn't seem quite fair to me
and by the time I got to college, the grammar police seemed to agree. A
this point, it was suggested that subject-pronoun agreement be achieved b
composing sentences like "If a person has a complaint, he or she shoul
contact ... ." This solution also seemed somewhat unsatisfactory, as did th
more streamlined: "If a person has a complaint (s)he should contact ... ."

Today, I think the smartest thing to do is try and follow the rules abou
subject-pronoun agreement and gender-inclusive language as closely a
possible. The easiest way to do this is to use a plural construction throughout
"If people have complaints, they should contact ... ." Or if you're reall
committed to using the singular form, the word "one" works nicely: "If on
has a complaint, one should contact ... ."

Another common error that I see all too frequently is the misuse o
apostrophes. Students tend to add apostrophes where they are not needed o
omit them altogether. The construction that trips most people up is the tiny
word "its" in its various forms. The problem here is that apostrophes can be
used to show possession and are also used in contractions. When you turn "i

is" into "it's," that is when you use an apostrophe; if you are merely stating that something belongs to "it," there is no apostrophe. There is one easy rule to remember: Possessive nouns always use an apostrophe, but possessive pronouns never do.

Number five on our list of errors is the misused comma. This is a major issue when it comes to writing properly structured sentences. In many of the papers I've graded, commas seem to have been sprinkled randomly throughout. Commas should be used to separate ideas in a sentence, to separate multiple adjectives describing the same thing, and to prevent confusion when the meaning of a sentence would otherwise be unclear.

The sixth of our top 10 common grammar and punctuation errors is misplaced or dangling modifiers. A dangling modifier can be a word or a phrase that is referring to a word or idea that is not clearly present in the sentence. See if you can figure out what is wrong with this sentence: "After being lost for years, John Smith discovered the crown jewels hidden behind a staircase." Most of us can probably figure out what that sentence is trying to say—that a guy named John Smith found the crown jewels, which had been lost for some time. The way it is written, however, the phrase "after being lost for years" is misplaced—the sentence reads as if John Smith, and not the jewels, had been lost.

Number seven on my list is the rampant use of the word "ironically" when the speaker or writer really just means "coincidentally." Newscasters in particular seem to be in love with "ironically," and they consistently use it when they shouldn't. Let's take this example, which was uttered by a sportscaster on the late-night news not too long ago: "The team will play its next game in Toronto—which, ironically, is where their coach began his career 25 years ago." Is it ironic that the coach is going back to the place where his professional career began? In fact, it's coincidental. Here's an example of the correct usage of irony: "Ironically, the fire station burned down."

Number eight on our list of common errors is misspelled words. Granted, with modern word-processing programs, a lot of these errors get caught on the computer screen, but some words may slip through. For example, I have had students misspell the proper names of authors and characters that they are writing about. If you do this in any context, it's going to cause you to lose credibility in the eyes of your audience. Take a look at the list below of 50 commonly misspelled words.

Fifty Commonly Misspelled Words

Have a friend test you on these frequently misspelled words.

1. acceptable	18. gauge	35. medieval
2. accidentally	19. guarantee	36. memento
3. accommodate	20. harass	37. millennium
4. argument	21. height	38. minuscule
5. believe	22. hierarchy	39. mischievous
6. calendar	23. immediate	40. occasion
7. category	24. independent	41. occurrence
8. committed	25. indispensable	42. pastime
9. conscience	26. inoculate	43. receive
10. conscientious	27. jewelry	44. referred
11. consensus	28. judgment	45. reference
12. definite	29. leisure	46. schedule
13. discipline	30. liaison	47. separate
14. embarrass	31. library	48. supersede
15. exhilarate	32. license	49. vacuum
16. fiery	33. maintenance	50. weird
17. foreign	34. maneuver	

Another common error in usage has to do with the problem of words that sound like other words. Most frequently, I see this error in the phrases "could have," "should have," and "would have"—as in "I could have gone to the park, but I had a lot of work to do." The problem comes from the penchant of English speakers to contract words in order to speak more quickly: "I could've gone to the park." The contracted form sounds an awful lot like "could of," and people frequently write these forms unthinkingly.

The final common grammar and usage mistake is the frequent misspelling of the various forms of "there" and "your." "They're going to put their stuff over there." Although when spoken it sounds as if the same word is used three different times, in fact three different spellings are required. "They're" is really a contracted form of "They are." "Their," as in "their stuff," indicates possession. The spelling differentiation helps to keep this meaning distinct from the final form, in which "there" indicates a location. These are easy mistakes to make—and again, this is why it's always a good idea to set your writing aside for awhile and then come back to it with fresh eyes. ■

Suggested Reading

The Chicago Manual of Style.

Clouse, *The Student Writer.*

Gordon, *The Deluxe Transitive Vampire.*

Griffith, *Writing Essays about Literature.*

Lanham, *Style.*

O'Connor, *Woe Is I.*

———, *Words Fail Me.*

Strunk and White, *The Elements of Style.*

Trimble, *Writing with Style.*

Truss, *Eats, Shoots and Leaves.*

Tufte, *Artful Sentences.*

Exercise

1. Identify the errors in the sentences below and then rewrite them so that they are correct.

   They're dog is tired, he's been playing in the backyard all day.

   To who did her give the present?

She brought plenty of food for us to eat: salad's, muffins, and hamburgers

Its hard when someone breaks there promise.

Your not being very nice to him.

Avoiding Common Errors in Grammar and Usage
Lecture 23—Transcript

Welcome back. In our last lecture, we wrapped up our discussion of the revision process, one of the most important—but also most overlooked—stages of producing an effectively written piece. Many of the strategies discussed in Lectures 21 and 22 are also useful tools for avoiding the common errors in grammar and punctuation that we're going to discuss today.

For example, in our last lecture we talked about how important it is to set aside a piece of writing—even if it's just for an hour or so—and then return to it with fresh eyes, allowing you to better spot places that need revision. Even better is to ask for someone else to look it over for you—whether it is a business letter, a resume, or a magazine article. Having someone with some distance from the piece can help you identify moments that are perhaps confusing or unclear. If your friendly reader has trouble understanding a point you've made or how your argument is moving, then you can be sure that the intended audience of the writing is most likely going to have some trouble with that as well.

Of course, one of the easiest and quickest ways to spot errors, awkward moments, confusing turns of phrase, and typos is simply to read your piece out loud. Reading aloud forces you to slow down, and your eye is less likely to skip over a typo like a misspelling or even a missing word—those are things that can happen when you're reading your own work silently to yourself.

Today we're going to start to focus on some more specific, common errors—for which every good, conscientious writer should check when doing a final revision. This is a topic, I think, that we could probably spend several hours on, but in the interests of time I'd like to limit myself today to 10 of the most common errors that I have seen in my experience teaching college-level writing over the past decade or so. I've selected these errors because I see them crop up again, and again, and again—and what I would love, more than anything in the world, is to never see them again.

The errors I'm going to discuss in the next few moments are issues to which writers should be attentive no matter the audience, and I'd like to begin with the common error that I, personally, find the most distressing—and that is the incorrect use of "I" when it should be "me," and vice versa. So let me start by asking you to consider which of the following two sentences is correct: "It was such a wonderful time for Michelle and I" or "It was such a wonderful time for Michelle and me."

Which one uses the first-person pronoun correctly? The answer is the second sentence: "It was such a wonderful time for Michelle and me." If we can stray into the world of grammar rules for a moment, the reason that the second sentence is correct is because the compound object "Michelle and me" is the object of the preposition "for"—and because of this, the first-person pronoun has to be in what we call the objective case. Here, you need to remain aware of the difference between what we call the subject and the object form of a pronoun. For example, "I" is the subject form— "me" is the object; "he" is the subject—"him" is the object"; "she" is the subject—"her" is the object; "we" is the subject—and "us" is the object. You get the idea, I think.

Here are another two sentences: "She loves her" or "Her loves she." I'm sure your ear can tell you right away that the first sentence is correct—"She" is the subject of the sentence, so the pronoun is in the subject case; "her" is the object of the verb "loves," so it is in the object case. While it's useful to know the rule—and I think it's a good idea to invest in a comprehensive grammar book that you can consult when you're writing and you get stuck or you're unsure—it's also possible to use your ear in most cases to figure out the correct usage.

For example, an easier way to check for the correctness of our first example would be to take "Michelle and me" and make it singular. So, here are those two sentences again: "It was such a wonderful time for I" or "It was such a wonderful time for me." For most of us, we don't even need to know the rule—our ear tells us that the second sentence is correct; once you know that, you're fine—the rule doesn't change when just "me" becomes "Michelle and me."

Now let's invert this sentence and see what happens. Which is correct: "Me and Michelle had a great time" or "Michelle and I had a great time"? In this example, we have a compound subject, and so the pronoun would be in the subject case—and that's "I." Again, you can check this by ear simply by making the subject singular: "Me had a great time" or "I had a great time."

The first sounds a little like caveman dialogue in a bad "B" movie; the second one sounds so right that any native speaker of English wouldn't even have to think twice. But let's take a slightly trickier example. Which one is correct: "just between you and me" or "just between you and I"? Here, you can't simply do an ear check, and in this case, knowing the rule is what will save you—"between," just like the word "for" in that first example, is a preposition, and prepositions need to be followed by pronouns that are in the object case. So the correct answer is "just between you and me."

I think that what has happened is that many people mistakenly believe that the use of "I" is somehow more formal—so they use it in an attempt to sound educated and sophisticated. The misuse of "I" when it should be "me" has become so common that I have heard CEOs, university presidents, and heads of state use it incorrectly—and for a time, actually the grammar check on a popular e-mail software program was miscorrecting "me" to "I." Just because its misuse is widespread, however, does not mean that there are not plenty of people who do understand how it should be used, and any number of those people might be potential employers to whom you send a cover letter and resume, or teachers to whom you submit an essay.

I personally know of a few instances when a candidate was actually removed from consideration for a position simply because this misuse appeared in the cover letter when the candidate applied for the particular position—so I can't stress enough how important it is to get this correct.

The second common error I want to address also relates to pronouns, and it's something called subject-pronoun agreement. To illustrate this issue, let's examine another two sentences. Here is the first one: "If a person has a complaint, he or she should contact the Human Resources Department." Here is sentence two: "If a person has a complaint, they should contact the

Human Resources Department." Sentence two sounds simpler, and it's more economical—but, in fact, that is the sentence that is incorrect.

The reason is that "person" is singular, but "they" is plural; in other words, they don't agree. That sentence could easily be corrected by simply turning "person" into "people"—"If people have complaints, they should contact the Human Resources Department." "People" and "they" are both plural—and thus, they agree.

By using a sentence like "If a person has a complaint, he or she should contact the Human Resources Department" not only do you manage to have your pronouns agree—person, he, and she are all singular—but you also avoid the pitfall of using what we call gender-exclusive language, and that's the third common error of which you should be aware.

When I was in school, I was taught that when you were trying to get your pronouns to agree, it was all right to use "he" to stand in for the universal subject—thus, the sentence "If a person has a complaint, he should contact the Human Resources Department" would be considered correct, as it's understood here that in this sentence "he" is referring to all people, not just men—the masculine here was working in the same way that "mankind" is understood to refer to all humanity.

As a female myself, this didn't seem quite fair to me when I learned it as a high school student, and by the time I got to college, the grammar police, whoever they are, seemed to agree—and thus, it was suggested that subject-pronoun agreement be achieved by composing sentences like "If a person has a complaint, he or she should contact the Human Resources Department."

This solution also seemed somewhat unsatisfactory, as did the more streamlined: "If a person has a complaint (s)he [with the "s" in parentheses before "he"] should contact the Human Resources Department." I was obviously not the only one who found this solution somewhat awkward and unwieldy, and I have been told by some of my recent college students that their high school teachers have instructed them to use the plural pronoun "they" even if it is paired with a singular subject like "person." The idea here would be to try not to offend anyone, and it works—except for the fact that it really offends anyone who cares about proper grammar.

Today, I think the smartest thing to do is try and follow the rules about subject-pronoun agreement and gender-inclusive language as closely as possible. The easiest way to do this is to use a plural construction throughout—"If people have complaints, they should contact the Human Resources Department"—or if you're really committed to using the singular form, the word "one" works nicely: "If one has a complaint, one should contact the Human Resources Department." You may be wondering right about now why I don't suggest using "you": "If you have a complaint, you should contact etc., etc." Because this is a rather informal lecture, it's technically okay for me to use "you" throughout as I address you, my audience.

There is a difference, however, between the spoken and the written word—and in formal writing, like in an essay, "you" is generally not considered proper form; in a cover letter to a business, however, it makes perfect sense to say something like: "Please contact me if you have questions or require additional information. I look forward to hearing from you soon."

Another common error that I see all too frequently is the misuse of apostrophes. This seems to be the most common punctuation error these days, and it is the top of my list of mechanical errors that personally drive me crazy.

Very frequently, students add apostrophes where they are not needed, or they omit them altogether. The construction that trips most people up is the tiny word "its" in its various forms. The problem here is that apostrophes can be used to show possession—that something belongs to someone—and they are also used when we contract two words and combine them, as when we take "can not" and make "can't." So let's take an easy example: "That is my aunt's house." Where does the apostrophe go? A lot of you are probably thinking: "Oh, okay, that's easy enough. The apostrophe goes between the 't' and the 's' in the word 'aunt'—so you have 'aunt's,' and you're indicating that this is your aunt's house—it belongs to her." But what if you have three aunts who all live together? The same sentence "That is my aunts' house" still works, but you need to move the apostrophe to after the "s" to show that this house belongs to your multiple aunts.

But if we can return to "its" for a moment, the problem is that there is one rule for how to write this when you are indicating possession, and there is another rule when it's a contraction of "it is." When you turn "it is" into "it's" that is when you use an apostrophe; if you are merely stating that something belongs to "it," there is no apostrophe.

So consider the following sentence: "The snake shed its skin." Where does the apostrophe go? Nowhere. How about this sentence: "It's interesting to watch a snake shed its skin." There needs to be an apostrophe in the first "It's," but not the second. The first "It's" is a contraction of "It is," while the second one merely indicates possession.

The desire to place apostrophes where they are not needed has turned into some kind of disease, and every day I see apostrophes misused on business signs, in letters, in e-mails, etc., etc. For example, if you are sending out letters and want the return address to indicate that the letter comes from the Armstrong family, how should you write "the Armstrongs"? All too often, I see return addresses, or even address signs on houses, that will add an apostrophe—so Armstrongs becomes "Armstrong's" with an apostrophe between the "g" and the "s."

This is incorrect—you are not indicating possession of anything or even a contraction; no apostrophe is needed. One could argue that signs on houses are claiming ownership or possession—and if that is the case and you're saying that this is the Armstrongs' house, then really the apostrophe should go after the final "s." So one more time: In that case, an apostrophe is okay, but only if it comes after the final "s"—so you spell out Armstrongs and tack an apostrophe on the end because this shows that the house is the home of all the Armstrongs and not just one Armstrong. Recently, I was in a copy shop, and this business had a sign on display saying that they could do "resume's, poster's, and other document's," and each word had an apostrophe before that final "s." Every single apostrophe was unnecessary, and it did not make me feel inclined to trust them with any of my copying needs.

Adding to this feeling was another small sign they had near the cash register, which said, and I quote: "At our store, our customers needs come first." There was no apostrophe in the sentence. Think about it for a second—should there be, and where should it go? The answer is "yes, there needs to be an apostrophe," and it needs to come after the final "s" of "customers" since the management is discussing how they would deal with the needs of the customers—the apostrophe is needed to show possession.

I could talk about misused apostrophes all day, but suffice it to say this is an area in your writing that will always need close attention, and I would suggest—again—reference to a good book on grammar and punctuation just to make sure you haven't made any mistakes. One easy rule to remember is: Possessive nouns always use an apostrophe, but possessive pronouns never do.

Almost as problematic as misused apostrophes is the number five on our list of errors—and this is the misused comma. This is a major issue when it comes to writing elegantly and properly structured sentences. In many of the papers I've graded in recent years, commas seem to have simply been sprinkled randomly throughout—as if the student said to him or herself: "Well, I probably need some commas, so I'll just stick a few in here and there."

Commas are most frequently used to separate ideas in a sentence, to separate multiple adjectives describing the same thing, and they can help prevent confusion when the meaning of a sentence would otherwise be unclear. Let's start with that last issue, which has become something of a sensation with the publication of Lynne Truss's humorous take on grammar and punctuation entitled *Eats, Shoots & Leaves*, and I highly recommend this book. The meaning of the following sentence should be clear: "The giant panda eats shoots and leaves." Punctuated thusly, the sentence is telling us about the diet of a particular animal—pandas consume bamboo shoots and leaves.

But if we sprinkle in some commas and we get "The giant panda eats, shoots, and leaves"—with commas where I paused—"The giant panda eats, shoots, and leaves" well, we then have a sentence describing how a single large animal consumed some food, fired a gun, and then departed. While this certainly might be a more interesting sentence than the first one, we can be sure that the misuse of commas here has obscured what the writer originally intended to say.

Commas are also commonly misused in such a way as to produce what is called a run-on sentence or a comma splice. This is an easy mistake to make when you have two closely related ideas that you're trying to talk about. Let's take this sentence: "I was tired, but I kept working until the project was done." Then, let's take a sentence with the same idea but phrased this way: "I was tired, I kept working until the project was done." Both use commas, but one is a proper sentence, and one is a run-on or a comma splice. Which one is correct? The first one is. The use of the coordinating conjunction "and" or "but" makes this work. When you remove the "and" or the "but," you have two totally independent clauses—and properly speaking, these should be separated by a semicolon or a period because they can stand alone.

As you might guess, I could continue to discuss commas and their abuse for the rest of this lecture, but I'd like to move on to the sixth of our top 10 common grammar and punctuation errors, and this involves something called misplaced or dangling modifiers. A dangling modifier can be a word or a phrase that is describing or referring to another word or an idea that is not clearly present in the sentence.

That definition is a little confusing—so, again, it's best to illustrate with some examples. See if you can figure out what is wrong with this sentence: "After being lost for years, John Smith discovered the crown jewels hidden behind a staircase." Most of us can probably figure out what that sentence is trying to say—and what it is trying to say is that a guy named John Smith found the crown jewels, which had been lost for some time. The way it is written right now, however, the phrase "after being lost for years" is misplaced—the sentence reads as if John Smith, and not the jewels, had been lost, although probably anyone could figure out what the original intent was. So think about that, and then consider this sentence: "Polished smooth by thousands of years of wave action, Jane Doe picked up the speckled rock." Again, the first part of the sentence, which should modify "the speckled rock," dangles—it sounds as if Jane Doe is the one who has been rolling around in the sea for thousands of years the way the sentence is written now.

Number seven on my list is the rampant use of the word "ironically" when the speaker or writer really just means "coincidentally." Newscasters in particular seem to be in love with "ironically," and they consistently use it when they shouldn't. I have noticed that this is a practice that seems to have encouraged the misuse of the word by the general population.

Let's take this example, which was uttered by a sportscaster on the late-night news not too long ago: "The team will play its next game in Toronto—which, ironically, is where their coach began his career 25 years ago." Is it ironic that the coach is going back to the place where his professional career began? If the definition of irony is using a word to mean the opposite of its dictionary meaning, then how on earth could this event be "ironic"? In fact, it's coincidental.

Also, ironic has been used incorrectly to describe situations that are simply not good, and the blame for this has to be laid, at least in part, at the feet of singer Alanis Morissette—who, in her hit song "Ironic," taught a whole generation of young people that ironic happenings included "a black fly in your chardonnay," or "rain on your wedding day," or meeting "the man of your dreams and then his beautiful wife." None of these situations are desirable or pleasant, but there is nothing ironic about them—they are simply unfortunate. Now here's an example of the correct usage of irony: "Ironically, the fire station burned down." That is ironic. It is also coincidental maybe, but definitely it fits our definition of ironic.

Number eight on our list of common errors is misspelled words. Now granted, with modern word processing programs, a lot of these errors get caught while they're still fresh on the computer screen, but some words may slip through. For example, I have had students misspell the proper names of authors and characters in essays they are writing, and that shows they just aren't paying close attention.

If you do this in any context—from a short story or an article you have submitted for publication, to an essay, to a letter—it's going to cause you to lose credibility in the eyes of your audience. Take a moment and see if you can spell these common words—how about "independent," "occurrence," "accommodate," "acknowledgment," "commitment"? These are some of the most common ones I see. If you had difficulty or a moment when you were unsure how you might spell those words, you might want to refer to our guidebook that has a list of 50 commonly misspelled words.

Another very common error in usage has to do with the problem of words that sound like other words. Most frequently, I see this error in the phrases "could have," "should have," and "would have"—as in "I could have gone to the park, but I had a lot of work to do," or "I should have gone to the gym, but I had a lot of work to do," or "I would have done my work, but *Raiders of the Lost Ark* was on TV." As I've said these words just now, there's no problem understanding what the sentences mean and how the words in them should be spelled.

The problem comes from the penchant of English speakers to contract or combine words in order to speak more quickly: "I could've gone to the park" or "I should've gone to the gym." The contracted forms—spelled, for example, "should've"—sound an awful lot like "should of," with the word "of" in place of the "ve," and people very frequently will write these forms unthinkingly. In other words, they will write "could of" when they really mean "could have." For an astute reader, this kind of mistake is going to leap off the page, so you really need to be careful about it.

Like the previous example, the final common grammar and usage mistake I want to discuss today also has to do with the frequent misspelling of words that sound alike, and in this case I'm talking about the various forms of "there" and "your." Listen to the following sentence and try to supply the proper spelling for each form of the word "there": "They're going to put their stuff over there." Although it sounds like the same word is used three different times, in fact three different spellings are required.

First, "They're going to put" is really "They are going to put," and so the proper spelling in that case would be "T-h-e-y-'-r-e," as this is a contracted form of "They are." The second "their," as in "their stuff," indicates possession, and it needs to be spelled "t-h-e-i-r." The spelling differentiation helps to keep this meaning distinct from the final form, in which "there," spelled "t-h-e-r-e," indicates a location, a place. Similar mistakes happen with "your" and "you're"—"y-o-u-r" and "y-o-u-'-r-e"; the first indicates possession—things that belong to you—and the second is a contracted form meaning "you are."

So in the following sentence, which form goes where? "You're doing lots of good things with your money." The first "You're" indicates action—something "you are" doing, and so it is a contracted form, and it requires the spelling "Y-o-u-'-r-e." The second usage indicates possession, money that belongs to you, and so it is simply "y-o-u-r." As anyone who has ever spent anytime online reading blogs or postings in response to a news article, anyone who has done this knows the confusion and misuse of the various forms of "your" and "there" is rampant, and very often it is obviously due to laziness instead of ignorance. It's an easy mistake to make if you're up late, writing, and you're not entirely focused on details—and again, this is why it's always a good idea to set your writing aside for awhile and then come back to it with fresh eyes—and even better, get someone else to read through it for you.

Now I've come to the end of the 10 most common errors of grammar and usage, and some of you may be wondering about two features of grammar that are not on my list. These two grammatical issues are the rules against splitting an infinitive and ending the sentence with a preposition. I'll explain the logic behind the rules as well as my logic for not finding them worthy of being in the top 10, and then you can decide how you feel about it.

Let's start with split infinitives. An infinitive is simply the "to" form of a verb—so in English, "to love," "to run," "to walk," "to have," "to give," "to do." When the first self-appointed grammarians began trying to make rules for English several centuries ago, most of them—because they were educated Englishmen of a certain class—looked to the language of Latin for guidance as to how they should go about doing this. They're the ones who gave us the split infinitive rule.

Their logic was this: Infinitive forms, the "to" form, in Latin and the language developed from it can't be split—they are all one word. So, *amare* means "to love"; *audire* means "to hear"; *scribere* means "to write." The thinking here was that because Latin infinitives can't be split and Latin was considered the perfect language, then we shouldn't split English infinitives either. The problem, of course, is that it's perfectly possible to split English infinitives—and until these grammarians decreed otherwise, there really wasn't a good reason not to do this. Today, people tend to fall pretty vociferously on either side of this debate, and I fall into the camp of those who think splitting infinitives is usually alright. Perhaps it's just the *Star Trek* fan in me, but I feel quite strongly that the phrase "to boldly go where no one has gone before" sounds a whole lot better than "to go boldly where no man has gone before" or "boldly to go where no man has gone before."

Still, as I've said repeatedly, the most important thing is to know you audience—so while in principle I'm fine with the split infinitives, I correct any I find in my own writing if I think it's going to be an issue for my reader Always err on the side of caution, and follow the rules—occasionally you can break them, but I think it's a good idea to at first demonstrate that you know what the rules are.

> The same people who policed infinitives are also the ones who gave us the rule for not ending a sentence with a preposition. Prepositions are words that link other words in a sentence and indicate location. Common prepositions include to, for, of, by with, from, and a whole host of others. The logic for forbidding the placement of prepositions at the end of a sentence is found in their name—"preposition" seems to suggest that this word has to come before something else and it can't stand alone. As a rule, I would suggest—if you can—rewrite or revise a sentence so the preposition doesn't come alone at the end, as a lot of readers will feel that this is a rule that you have to follow, but sometimes what you have to go through in order to do this is just plain silly.

A famous story tells how Winston Churchill was reading through proofs of a piece he had written, and he noticed that his editor had rewritten his sentences so that there was no preposition at the end. In the margins, Churchill wrote back: "This is a situation up with which [I] shall not put." Which sounds better: "This is something I won't put up with" or "This is something up with which I shall not put"? Most of us will say the first sentence sounds better, even if the second might be technically correct.

We're totally out of time, and we've barely scratched the surface when it comes to matters of grammar and punctuation. Still, today's lecture has identified 10 common errors and given you the means to check for them in your own writing. When it comes to our "bonus" errors—infinitives and prepositions—I'm going to leave it up to you to decide which side you're going to take.

Over the last 23 lectures, we've explored multiple issues surrounding how to be a good reader and writer. In our final lecture, we're going to conclude this course with some examples of beautiful, compelling, intelligent writing— and we're going to discuss what makes these pieces so engaging.

The Power of Words
Lecture 24

If I had to give you one piece of advice for becoming a more engaged reader and a more effective writer, it is simply to read and to write as much as you can.

I began this course with an example of appallingly bad writing. What I would like to do in this final lecture is discuss an example of wonderful writing, in the hope that it inspires you to keep up the practice of writing and reading long after this course is over. I've chosen the American classic *Walden*, by Henry David Thoreau—a text that is in some respects both essay and autobiography. Here are the opening lines:

> When I wrote the following pages, or rather the bulk of them, I lived alone, in the woods, a mile from any neighbor, in a house which I had built myself, on the shore of Walden Pond, in Concord, Massachusetts, and earned my living by the labor of my hands only. I lived there two years and two months. At present I am a sojourner in civilized life again.

Thoreau is not often given credit for the beauty of his prose, probably because most readers are drawn to his work by the ideas he expresses rather than the manner in which he expresses them. The Thoreau most people know and understand is primarily a thinker and an activist. His status as a writer is something of a secondary concern, if it is a concern at all.

But the opening paragraph of *Walden* is among the most carefully crafted pieces of writing in all of American literature. It's not only a lucid summary of the book's content,

The opening paragraph of *Walden* is among the most carefully crafted pieces of writing in all of American literature.

but it's also a really elegant reflection of its overall structure. In other words, you can find in these few lines a microcosm of the most intriguing and most important ideas that *Walden*, as a whole, has to offer, and it's also a model of the form that those offerings take.

Moreover, the passage provides a kind of guide for how to read *Walden* insofar as it establishes the terms of the relationship between narrator and reader, and it also mirrors the relationship between Thoreau and the social world from which he partially and temporarily withdrew during those two years and two months on the shores of Walden Pond.

Let's start by looking at that sense of partial and temporary withdrawal—because for many scholars it's the most important thematic dimension of *Walden*. While many people think of Thoreau as withdrawing from the world because he wanted to get away from its burdens and preoccupations, it's also true that his larger purpose in getting away was to better understand those burdens and the preoccupations that go along with them by giving himself a new relationship to them, one that involved less participation and more observation. His purpose was not to leave his home environment, but rather to give himself a chance to view and experience it from a position that was slightly off-center. We can think of Thoreau as wanting to hold his life in Concord at arm's length.

We can see this in the content and the structure of those opening lines. Each detail builds on the next to tell us something more about how he removed himself from his previous life. These details are held together like links in a chain—each phrase is discrete but connected to all of the others by a series of commas to form a single complete sentence, which creates a sense of distance and a sense of connection all at the same time. The very structure of that sentence compels us to recognize the narrator's desire—and Thoreau's desire—to maintain a link to the world while, as I said, holding it at arm's length.

The remove is not permanent though. Just as the conclusion of *Walden* advises readers to break away from their own social worlds so they can learn something new about them, so too does the opening paragraph emphasize the need to eventually lessen that distance and ultimately reengage with the social world.

Finally, this structural pattern of the opening lines—carefully marking out a series of steps that take one away from that which is known and familiar, and then eventually acknowledging the need to turn back around again and look at the familiar with new eyes—is itself a guide for how to read *Walden*.

Each chapter, and all the chapters taken together, follows a similar pattern: a deliberate movement outward and away from the status quo, away from that which is recognizable and easily comprehended—followed, eventually, by a return to the same territory where we started. Yet because of the removal and displacement we've experienced, we're now sojourners with a different feel for the ground we've walked before. Thoreau's piece is a masterful example of engaging an audience—he conveys to his audience his main argument not just in the content of his words, but in the style with which he executes his argument.

If you really want to be an astute, engaged reader and writer, then my best piece of advice would be: Be promiscuous—read everything you can; write whenever you can. You can make yourself a beautiful space in which to write. Write with a pen or a pencil, on the computer, on the back of an envelope. Read everything you can—editorials, short stories, histories, biographies, novels, poems, plays. The world around us is filled with words; take in as many as you can, and then give us some back. ∎

Suggested Reading

Lunsford and Ruszkiewicz, *Everything's an Argument*.

McLaughlin and Coleman, *Everyday Theory*.

Roberts, *Writing about Literature*.

Strunk and White, *The Elements of Style*.

Tufte, *Artful Sentences*.

1. Take an issue about which you feel strongly, and draft an opening paragraph of an argumentative essay. Paying attention to all the issues we've discussed in this course—concerns about audience, tone, style, establishing an ethos, using powerful language, and so on—make sure that your main claim is clear and specific and that you point toward the direction your argument will go.

2. Now write the concluding paragraph to an essay on this same topic. Remember that a strong conclusion recapitulates the main points of your argument without simply restating what you wrote in your introduction.

The Power of Words
Lecture 24—Transcript

Welcome back, and congratulations! You've made it to the final lecture in our course on engaging with and writing about anything. Along the way we discussed the different styles of writing—from poetry, to prose, to drama and beyond—and we talked about the specific expectations that we bring to both reading and writing about these kinds of texts.

We've explored the basics of making an argument, seen how the principles of classical rhetoric can be applied to writing today in useful and productive ways, and we learned the basics of conducting research responsibly. We've also discussed strategies for overcoming the dreaded writer's block, and we've gone step by step through the process of editing and rewriting an essay. We examined 10 common grammatical and mechanical errors, learned why they're both so common and so wrong, and we discussed key ways to avoid them.

You have taken away lots of information I'm sure from all of these lectures, but if I had to give you one piece of advice for becoming a more engaged reader and a more effective writer, it is simply to read and to write as much as you can. All right, maybe that's two things if you want to get really technical about it—but really, reading and writing go hand in hand, and when you think of them as a symbiotic process, you'll find that your own writing and reading skills improve dramatically.

When I began this lecture series, I started with an example of appallingly bad writing. You may recall that this passage was from the annual Bulwer-Lytton contest, and it was written so that it was deliberately bad—so bad, in fact, that it won a prize for badness. What I would like to do today in this final lecture is leave you with some examples of wonderful writing, in the hope that they inspire you to keep up the practice of writing and reading long after this course is over.

I've chosen three selections that I think are particularly fine examples of the genres to which they belong, and I'd like to start with the opening of the American classic, *Walden*, by Henry David Thoreau—a text that is in some respects both essay and autobiography, and that we talked about a little bit earlier in the course. Here are the opening lines:

> When I wrote the following pages, or rather the bulk of them, I lived alone, in the woods, a mile from any neighbor, in a house which I had built myself, on the shore of Walden Pond, in Concord, Massachusetts, and earned my living by the labor of my hands only. I lived there two years and two months. At present I am a sojourner in civilized life again.

Thoreau is not often given credit for the beauty or the lyricism of his prose, probably because most readers are drawn to his work by the ideas he expresses rather than the manner by which or in which he expresses them. The Thoreau most people know and understand is primarily a thinker and an activist. His status as a writer is something of a secondary concern, if it is a concern at all.

But this passage—the opening paragraph of his most famous work, *Walden*— is among the most carefully crafted pieces of writing you'll find in all of American literature. It's not only a lucid summary of the book's content, but it's also a really elegant reflection of its overall structure. In other words, you can find in these few lines a microcosm of the most intriguing and most important ideas that *Walden*, as a whole, has to offer, and it's also a model of the form that those offerings take. If you studied this one part long enough, you would be able to get a view of the whole of *Walden*, in other words.

Moreover, the passage provides a kind of guide for how to read *Walden* insofar as it establishes the terms of the relationship between narrator and reader, and it also mirrors the relationship between Thoreau and the social world from which he partially and temporarily withdrew during those two years and two months on the shores of Walden Pond.

Let's start by looking at that sense of partial and temporary withdrawal— because for many scholars it's the most important thematic dimension of *Walden*. While many people think of Thoreau as withdrawing from the world because he wanted to get away from its burdens and preoccupations, it's also true that his larger purpose in getting away—just partially and temporarily—

was to better understand those burdens and the preoccupations that go along with them by giving himself a new relationship to them, one that involves less participation and more observation.

But his goal was never to suspend his participation in his previous life entirely—it was never to break away completely from the social world and the physical environment of Concord. Indeed, aside from his college years in Cambridge, some trips to Maine and Cape Cod, and a few lecture tours that took him to various other parts of New England, Thoreau spent most of his life—just as he wrote in most of his pages—within a 10-mile radius of Concord and Walden Pond.

His purpose was not to leave his home environment, but rather to give himself a chance to view and experience it from a position that was slightly— and temporarily—what we might call "off-center." We can think of Thoreau as wanting to hold his life in Concord at arm's length—not breaking away from his hometown, but methodically distancing himself from it while still remaining in relatively close proximity.

We can see this in the content and the structure of those opening lines. Each detail builds on the next to tell us something more about how he removed himself from his previous life yet how these details are held together like links in a chain—how each phrase is discrete, but it's connected; it's bound to all of the others by a series of commas to form a single complete sentence— so it creates a sense of distance, and it creates a sense of connection all at the same time.

The very structure of that sentence compels us to recognize the narrator's desire—and Thoreau's desire—to maintain a link to the world while, as I said, holding it at arm's length. Listen to the opening sentence again, and pay attention to the pauses that indicate there's a comma, a pause, a sub-clause:

> When I wrote the following pages, or rather the bulk of them, I lived alone, in the woods, a mile from any neighbor, in a house which I had built myself, on the shore of Walden Pond, in Concord, Massachusetts, and earned my living by the labor of my hands only.

The sentence leads you on, but it also holds you back at the same time—deferring your arrival at the conclusion.

The remove is not permanent though. Just as the conclusion of *Walden* advises readers to break away from their own social worlds so they can learn something new about them—and then return back so they can report what they have learned—so, too, does the opening paragraph emphasize the need to eventually lessen that distance and ultimately reengage with the social world. Consider again those last two lines: "I lived there two years and two months. At present I am a sojourner in civilized life again."

Finally, this structural pattern of the opening lines—carefully marking out a series of steps that take one away from that which is known and familiar—and then, eventually, an acknowledgment of the need to turn back around again and look at the familiar with new eyes—it is itself a guide for how to read *Walden*.

Each chapter—and all the chapters taken together—follow a similar pattern: a deliberate movement outward and away from the status quo, away from that which is recognizable and easily comprehended—followed, eventually, by a return to the same territory where we started. Yet because of the removal and displacement we've experienced, we're now sojourners with a different feel for the ground we've walked before.

Thoreau's piece is a masterful example of engaging an audience, drawing them along, but simultaneously holding them at arm's length. He conveys to his audience his main argument not just in the content of his words, but in the style with which he executes his argument. Another writer who plays with audience expectations is William Shakespeare, perhaps the greatest writer of the English language to ever hold a pen.

Even if you have never studied drama or poetry in any sort of formal way, everyone is probably at least familiar with the idea of who Shakespeare was, and that he was a creative genius. You're also probably familiar with some of the most common clichés in love poetry—namely, when a poet describes his beloved, he compares her to all sorts of beautiful flowers, or jewels, or fruits, things like that.

We've all heard someone with red lips being described as having "ruby lips" or "having cheeks the color of ripe apples," "eyes like two limpid pools of blue water," etc., etc. During Shakespeare's day this style of writing and describing the beloved was so common that there's actually a name for it—the blazon, which is a word that signifies this is a poem describing a woman's beauty using poetic devices.

In Shakespeare's sonnet number 130, the poet plays with this idea, and he cleverly turns it on its head and still manages to compliment his beloved. Shakespeare wrote a series of sonnets that follow a progression, and we could spend days just talking about this, but what I do think is important here today is that we know that the sonnet is a stylized form—in other words, there's a pattern or a rhyme scheme that the author has to work with, but in this case, as you'll see, the constraints of the form allow Shakespeare to really show his skill.

As many of you know, the Shakespearean sonnet is 14 lines long, and it has a rhyme pattern of ababcdcdefefgg, and it's proper and common to speak of the Shakespearean sonnet as being broken down into three quatrains and one couplet. The main idea of the sonnet—or what scholars call a "conceit"—is used throughout the poem, but there is a shift in emphasis from quatrain to quatrain, and the move to the final rhyming couplet is called "the turn"— where the whole poem is given new meaning by what those final two lines say. Here is the poem I want you to consider, and the first time through I'm going to read it in its entirety:

> My mistress's eyes are nothing like the sun;
> Coral is far more red than her lips' red;
> If snow be white, why then her breasts are dun,
> If hairs be wires, black wires grow on her head.
> I have seen roses damasked red and white,
> But no such roses see I in her cheeks;
> And in some perfumes is there more delight
> Than in the breath that from my mistress reeks.
> I love to hear her speak, yet well I know,
> That music hath a far more pleasing sound;
> I grant I never saw a goddess go;

My mistress, when she walks, treads on the ground.
And yet, by heaven, I think my love as rare
As any she, belied with false compare.

In this poem, Shakespeare begins with a series of images that are truly startling and unexpected considering the time in which he composed this poem—hey, he says, my beloved doesn't have lips as red as coral; she doesn't have eyes that shine like the sun, and her hair is kind of wiry, and her complexion is not perfect. As readers at this point, we're startled into surprise at the juxtaposition of the word "mistress," someone who is beloved, in combination with these negative assessments of her appearance. A mistress is the woman that you love—and usually, as they say, you would expect a man to find his beloved beautiful.

In the second quatrain, Shakespeare shifts the emphasis a bit, and he makes it specifically about what he sees and thinks—the word "I" is used here several times. He says, for example:

I have seen roses damasked red and white
But no such roses see I in her cheeks;
And in some perfumes is there more delight
Than in the breath that from my mistress reeks.

In each of these two lines he starts with something beautiful or pleasant—roses or perfume—and then when he makes the comparison to the mistress the poem moves to negative words—describing her breath as "reeking," for example.

In the third quatrain, he shifts his voice to start to suggest that he loves his mistress, despite all these poetic shortcomings:

I love to hear her speak, yet well I know,
That music hath a far more pleasing sound;
I grant I never saw a goddess go;
My mistress, when she walks, treads on the ground.

This sets us up just a little bit for what comes with the final turn of the poem to the rhyming couplet:

> And yet, by heaven, I think my love as rare
> As any she, belied with false compare.

In other words, he loves his mistress, and she is a real woman. What he is saying seems to be: All these poetic devices and elaborate comparisons of women with jewels, with the natural world, with music, with perfume—it doesn't mean anything if the love is not real. His love, he assures us, is real. It's not just that he's saying that his mistress lacks these poetic attributes—but more than that, he's actually saying that all real women do as well, and the poems that others compose that make use of this exaggerated, overblown comparison of a beloved's appearance to rubies, and oceans, and flowers—he's saying that those poems are insincere. So, Shakespeare manages to critique and satirize this poetic form even as he demonstrates that he is the best at it.

This sonnet and the others in his sonnet sequence yield even greater treasures and pleasures the more you read and reread them, and I hope if you have never read Shakespeare before—or if you have and it has just been some time since you read through his sonnet sequence—I hope that you take a look at his writing to appreciate how masterful it is—how he holds onto a single idea throughout a sonnet while making it part of a larger whole, of a sequence—and how within a single sonnet, he moves to differently nuanced treatments of that main idea as he goes from quatrain to quatrain, with a final surprise or a "ta da" at the end.

So far, we've talked about an example of great writing from the genre of the essay and from the genre of poetry. As our final example of great writing in today's lecture, I want to share a piece of writing from a specific subgenre of non-fiction writing, and that's the obituary.

On more than one occasion in this course, I've asked you either to think about or attempt to write an obituary. This can be a very useful exercise, as obituaries demand a certain approach, and the expectation is that they will contain certain kinds of information—how old was the person who died, what members of his or her family survive, where is the memorial service, what were the important accomplishments of his or her life, etc., etc. Obituary writing can be some of the most basic, uninspiring writing you'll ever read, but as my friend and colleague Porter Shreve's first novel *The Obituary Writer* proves, it can also be some of the most interesting.

So I want to close our examples of fine writing today with an obituary that moves far beyond the level of interesting and I think actually rises to the level of magnificence. All the important details are included. The heading tells us when and at what age a man named Bill Millin died—but instead of a catalogue of a life, we get a truly moving story that brings a lump to the throat because it is so beautifully written, and it's true. Here is how the obituary of Bill Millin, which appeared in *The Economist* on August 26th, 2010, begins:

> Any reasonable observer might have thought Bill Millin was unarmed as he jumped off the landing ramp at Sword Beach, in Normandy, on June 6th 1944. Unlike his colleagues, the pale 21-year-old held no rifle in his hands. Of course, in full Highland rig as he was, he had his trusty *skean dhu*, his little dirk, tucked in his right sock. But that was soon under three feet of water as he waded ashore, a weary soldier still smelling his own vomit from a night in a close boat on a choppy sea, and whose kilt in the freezing water was floating prettily around him like a ballerina's skirt. But Mr. Millin was not unarmed; far from it. He held his pipes, high over his head at first to keep them from the wet (for while whisky was said to be good for the bag, salt water wasn't), then cradled in his arms to play. And bagpipes, by long tradition, counted as instruments of war.

What this obituary writer has done has taken the most fascinating, compelling moment of this man's life (and he did live to be 88), and the obituary writer starts there. For anyone who remembers what it was like to live through World War II and hear stories of the Normandy landing—and even for those of us too young to remember, but who are old enough to know someone who did, or even for those of us who have just studied this event in school—the place and time where the obituary begins grabs your attention and commands that it stay right where it is. Notice it doesn't read like a summary. We don't get: "Bill Millen was present at the Normandy invasion on Sword Beach, where he famously played his bagpipes." That statement is no match for the vivid description of the cold water, his kilt floating like a ballerina's skirt, the smell of vomit left over from seasickness, and the image of Millen holding the bagpipes over his head so that they didn't get wet.

For many of us, we're hooked by the fact that in the age of modern warfare a bagpiper dressed in full regalia from an earlier time was even there amidst the mortars and the gunfire. The words of this obituary create an image stunning in its contrast and its anachronism—and even better, if you read the obituary in the magazine, it's accompanied by an actual photo of Millin as he prepared to go ashore, the bagpipes held over his head. Still, the writing is so good we don't even need the photo—the writer has given us an indelible image to hold in our minds.

As the obituary continues, it's so fascinating that it's hard to believe that this is real life and not a novel. The writer tells us how during basic training this lower-class, blue-collar guy, Bill Millen, became friends with the aristocratic Lord Lovat, a noble Scotsman with a castle or two who would be leading the 1st Special Service Brigade. Lord Lovat also seems, in the best tradition of British eccentricity, to be slightly off his rocker, and it was his idea that pipes would lead the invasion when the Allied forces waded ashore. The writer, after having given us this information, continues the obituary—picking up the action once they were onshore, when Lord Lovat says:

> "Give us a tune, piper." Mr. Millin thought him a mad bastard. The man beside him, on the point of jumping off, had taken a bullet in the face and gone under. But there was Lovat, strolling through fire quite calmly in his aristocratic way, allegedly wearing a monogrammed white pullover under his jacket and carrying an ancient Winchester rifle, so Mr. Millin struck up "Hielan' Laddie." Lovat approved it with a thumbs-up, and then he asked for "The Road to the Isles." Mr. Millin inquired, half-joking, whether he should walk up and down in the traditional way of pipers. "Oh, yes. That would be lovely."

At this moment, as you're reading, you really can't help but smile at the aristocratic leader who is strolling casually through gunfire with an antique weapon and who is more concerned with which song the piper is going to play next it seems. The obituary writer has us firmly in his or her pocket (and I wish I knew who it was, but all writing in *The Economist* is anonymous, but it's also some of the best writing you'll ever read in your life). I would highly encourage you to check out *The Economist*—particularly its book reviews and obituaries, which have some of the most moving, interesting writing I've ever come across. So at this point in the obituary, now that we really can't stop reading, the writer deftly moves from the humorous to the serious. After Lord Lovat's suggestion that Millin walk while he piped, the writer tells us this:

> Three times therefore he walked up and down at the edge of the sea. He remembered the sand shaking under his feet from mortar fire and the dead bodies rolling in the surf, against his legs. For the rest of the day, whenever required, he played. He piped the advancing troops along the raised road by the Caen canal, seeing the flashes from the rifle of a sniper about 100 yards ahead. … He took them across two bridges, one (later renamed the Pegasus Bridge) ringing and banging as shrapnel hit the metal sides. … All the way, he learned later, German snipers had had him in their sights but, out of pity for this madman, had not fired.

Here, the obituary writer reminds us of the high cost of war, of the human loss and suffering—although this man survived, so many did not. I don't think the image of a piper—dressed in his kilt, walking and playing while dead bodies wash against his legs—is one anyone of us is going to forget anytime soon. The detail about the German snipers not firing—it's a tiny bit of fair play in what was otherwise such a horrific experience for so many; this little detail gives one a kind of hope for humanity, even at what is arguably the moment of its darkest expression.

The obituary concludes with a few details about Millin's life after the war (surely, although this is the most interesting part of his life, we do want to know what he did afterward), and then the obituary writer ties things together with a perfect touch that seems as if it was scripted in a movie.

Although Millin survived the war, he tells us that alas, the pipes did not, taking a direct hit at some point after the initial successful invasion. Then, the writer finishes the obituary with this—and here, when he starts out, he's talking about the pipes:

> The last tune they had piped on D-Day was "The Nut-Brown Maiden," played for a small red-haired French girl who, with her folks cowering behind her, had asked him for music as he passed their farm. He gave the pipes later to the museum at the Pegasus Bridge, which he often revisited, and sometimes piped across, during his long and quiet post-war career as a mental nurse at Dawlish in Devon. On one such visit, in full Highland rig with his pipes in his arms, he was approached by a smartly dressed woman of a certain age, with faded red hair, who planted a joyous kiss of remembrance on his cheek.

That last detail, about a little red-haired girl grown into a woman who never forgot the kindness of the gift of music in the middle of war, brings a lump to the throat and a tear to the eye, and it's yet another indelible image that this masterful writer creates, and that those of us lucky to hear or read this piece will not soon forget.

This is great writing, and I might never have seen it if my father had not given me a gift subscription to *The Economist* a few years ago. I'm an English professor, and matters of economics (unless it's medieval economics) are usually not high on my list of things that I'd like to pay attention to or read about. I still remember the day I read that obituary—it moved me so much that I immediately went to my computer and using the Internet tried to find out more about Millin, about the wonderfully eccentric Lord Lovat, about the tradition of Scottish bagpiping, about the relationship between Scots and English, about other landings on that day at Normandy. In other words, really good writing can inspire you to read more, to learn more, to engage more with your world.

If you really want to be an astute, engaged reader and writer, then my best piece of advice would be: Be promiscuous—read everything you can; write whenever you can. You can make yourself a beautiful space in which to write with a special desk, a lamp, paper, a special pen, but sometimes while this approach can be a way of claiming "I am a writer—this is what I do," it can also be intimidating and prevent you from getting started. Write with a pen or a pencil, on the computer, on the back of an envelope. Read everything you can—editorials, short stories, histories, biographies, novels, poems, plays. The world around us is filled with words; take in as many as you can, and then give us some back.

Bibliography

Barnet, Sylvan, and William E. Cain. *A Short Guide to Writing about Literature*. New York: Longman, 2008. Particularly useful for its sample student essays and step-by-step guides to "unpacking" a text.

Bullock, Richard. *The Norton Field Guide to Writing*. New York: W. W. Norton and Company, 2009. A user-friendly guidebook that allows students to explore the writing process in brief and in depth.

Carpenter, Scott. *Reading Lessons: An Introduction to Theory*. Upper Saddle River, NJ: Prentice-Hall, 2000. An introduction to the reading and writing process with emphasis on theoretical/critical approaches.

The Chicago Manual of Style. 16th ed. Chicago: University of Chicago Press, 2010. The style guide for writing and publishing, especially in the academic world.

Clouse, Barbara Fine. *The Student Writer*. 5th ed. New York: McGraw-Hill, 1999. Geared toward students who are just taking the first steps in becoming writers.

Crowley, Sharon, and Debra Hawhee. *Ancient Rhetoric for Contemporary Students*. 2nd ed. Boston: Allyn and Bacon, 1999. Demonstrates how the application of classical rhetorical strategies can be useful in the modern student's quest to improve his or her writing.

DiYanni, Robert. *Literature: Approaches to Fiction, Poetry, and Drama*. New York: McGraw Hill, 2006. Introduces students to basic approaches to writing about these three different literary genres.

Freedman, Diane P., and Olivia Frey, eds. *Autobiographical Writing across the Disciplines*. Durham, NC: Duke University Press, 2003. Uses examples of some of the best autobiographical writing in a variety of circumstances to help you learn to make use of autobiography in your own writing.

Gardner, Janet. *Writing about Literature*. New York: Bedford St. Martin's, 2008. Geared for college students; provides strategies for engaging with and writing about literature.

Gordon, Karen Elizabeth. *The Deluxe Transitive Vampire: A Handbook of Grammar for the Innocent, the Eager and the Doomed.* New York: Pantheon, 1993. A grammar and punctuation guide whose examples include a memorable cast of gargoyles, monsters, and other exotic creatures.

Griffith, Kelley. *Writing Essays about Literature: A Guide and Style Sheet.* Boston: Wadsworth, 2010. Full of practical, useful advice and examples both of essays about literature and of writing intended to generate the student essay.

Guerin, Wilfred, Earle Labor, Lee Morgan, Jeanne Reesman, and John Willingham. *A Handbook of Critical Approaches to Literature*. New York: Oxford University Press, 2010. An excellent introduction to major trends in critical approaches to literature, including gender/feminist, Marxist, postcolonial, and formalist.

Harmon, William, and Hugh Holman. *A Handbook to Literature*. Upper Saddle River, NJ: Prentice Hall, 2008. A handy reference book with more than 2,000 definitions of key literary and linguistic terms and concepts.

Kennedy, X. J., and Dana Gioia. *Literature: An Introduction to Fiction, Poetry, Drama, and Writing.* 11th ed. New York: Longman, 2009. An excellent introduction to engaging with and writing about various genres of literature.

Lanham, Richard A. *Revising Prose*. 5th ed. New York: Longman, 2006. A step-by-step guide to improving your prose writing.

———. *Style: An Anti-Textbook*. Philadelphia: Paul Dry Books, 2007. A witty and at times ruthless examination of offenses against style and how not to make them.

Lunsford, Andrea, and John J. Ruszkiewicz. *Everything's an Argument.* New York: Bedford St. Martin's, 2009. Introduces students to the idea that everything—from ads to vehicles to clothing—can be read as an argument.

Lynn, Steven. *Literature: Reading and Writing with Critical Strategies.* Shows you how to use critical approaches to improve your writing. New York: Pearson Longman, 2004.

McLaughlin, Becky, and Bob Coleman. *Everyday Theory: A Contemporary Reader.* New York: Pearson Longman, 2005. For those who wish to become more serious students of approaches to argumentation and writing.

MLA Handbook for Writers of Research Papers. 7th ed. New York: Modern Language Association, 2009. The standard reference book in most undergraduate English programs in the United States.

O'Connor, Patricia T. *Woe Is I: The Grammarphobe's Guide to Better English in Plain English.* 3rd ed. New York: Riverhead Trade, 2010. A clear and humorous guide to recognizing and avoiding common grammar, punctuation, and style issues.

————. *Words Fail Me: What Everyone Who Writes Should Know about Writing.* New York: Mariner Books, 2000. An excellent reference tool for beginning writers who want to know how to most effectively craft an argument to reach a particular audience.

Oliver, Paul. *The Student's Guide to Research Ethics.* Maidenhead, UK: Open University Press, 2003. A guide to avoiding common errors in research, with particular emphasis on ethical concerns about plagiarism and original argumentation.

Ramage, John D., John C. Bean, and June Johnson. *Writing Arguments, Concise Edition: A Rhetoric with Readings.* 5th ed. New York: Longman, 2009. A good basic introduction to rhetorical approaches to writing.

Bibliography

Roberts, Edgar V. *Writing about Literature.* Upper Saddle River, NJ: Prentice Hall, 2009. A guide with clear, concrete examples for composing essays about various types of literature.

Smith, Sidonie, and Julia Watson. *Getting a Life: Everyday Uses of Autobiography.* Minneapolis: University of Minnesota Press, 1996. A guide to using autobiography appropriately in your writing.

Strunk, William, and E. B. White. *The Elements of Style.* New York: Longman, 2008. The classic handbook for writers in a new 50th anniversary edition.

Trimble, John. *Writing with Style: Conversations on the Art of Writing.* Upper Saddle River, NJ: Prentice Hall, 2000. Clever and witty; helps students generate ideas and then perfect them in written form.

Truss, Lynne. *Eats, Shoots and Leaves: The Zero Tolerance Approach to Punctuation.* New York: Gotham, 2006. A humorous guide to common punctuation errors and how to avoid them.

Tufte, Virginia. *Artful Sentences: Syntax as Style.* Cheshire, CT: Graphics Press, 2006. How to move beyond the utilitarian to the artful in the composition of essays.

Credits

Notes

Notes